EDVARD MUNCH
Symbols & Images

EDVARD MUNCH
Symbols & Images

Introduction by
ROBERT ROSENBLUM

Essays by
ARNE EGGUM

REINHOLD HELLER

TRYGVE NERGAARD

RAGNA STANG

BENTE TORJUSEN

GERD WOLL

National Gallery of Art, Washington   1978

Copyright © 1978 Trustees of the National Gallery of Art, Washington

Cover: *Anxiety* (detail), 1894, Munch-Museet, Oslo
Frontispiece: *Madonna*, hand-colored lithograph, 1895-1898?
the Art Institute of Chicago, Print and Drawing Fund Purchase

This publication was produced by the Editors Office
National Gallery of Art, Washington
Printed by Eastern Press, Inc., New Haven, Connecticut
The type is Baskerville, set by Composition Systems Inc., Arlington, Virginia
The text and cover papers are Warren Lustro Offset Enamel Dull

Designed by Frances P. Smyth

Library of Congress Cataloging in Publication Data
Munch, Edvard, 1863-1944.
Edvard Munch : symbols & images.
1. Munch, Edvard, 1863-1944. 2. Symbolism in art.
3. Art—Themes, motives. I. United States. National
Gallery of Art.
N7073.M8A4 1978b 760'.092'4 78-22070

Exhibition dates at the National Gallery of Art
November 11, 1978—February 19, 1979

TABLE OF CONTENTS

Self-portrait with Skeleton Arm, 1895. G/L 192-54. Munch-Museet, Oslo (cat. no. 120)

PREFACE

With *Edvard Munch: Symbols and Images*, the National Gallery of Art has mounted the most comprehensive exhibition of Munch's art ever held in the United States. The greatness of Munch's achievements and the significance of his contributions to the traditions of modern art have been, we believe, underappreciated in America. Surprisingly, very few paintings by Munch exist in public collections in the United States. Munch's reputation achieved international stature during his lifetime; however, in this country many still associate him with a few singular, haunting images. It is the purpose of this exhibition to provide viewers an opportunity to experience the full range of Munch's genius, both in painting and also in graphic work, in which he was one of the virtuosos of his age. In so doing, we hope to provide the viewer insights into the emergence of expressionism in northern Europe, and allow him to explore the relationships that recent scholarship has shown to exist between expressionism and the stylistic imperatives of impressionism and the School of Paris.

Many of the works of art in this exhibition have never before been allowed to leave Norway, where over ninety percent of Munch's art remains. It has been only because of the generosity of the great Norwegian repositories and private collectors that this exhibition was made possible.

To undertake the complex series of negotiations which culminated in the final selection of the objects, a Norwegian working committee was formed. The committee, headed by Alf Bøe, director of the Munch Museum in Oslo, includes Knut Berg, director of the Norwegian National Gallery, and Jan Askeland, director of Bergen's Billedgalleri. Arne Eggum, chief curator of the Munch Museum served as the exhibition's scholarly coordinator and contributed to the catalogue. The National Gallery is deeply indebted to them for their efforts on behalf of this exhibition. We would also like to express our gratitude to Anne Høegh Brand who served as the National Gallery's exhibition coordinator in Nor-

way. The hospitality and cooperation of all the Norwegian officials and colleagues shown to all of us who traveled to Norway on various occasions to work on this exhibition have been extraordinary.

Warm thanks are due also to Trygve Nergaard, Bente Torjusen and Gerd Woll for their essays on Munch's life and work for the catalogue and to Robert Rosenblum for his introduction. We were fortunate that the late Ragna Stang contributed an essay before her recent untimely death. We are also indebted to Reinhold Heller for his contribution to the catalogue and the educational labels for the exhibition, and to Paula Smiley for her editing of the catalogue. Andrew Robison and Gaillard Ravenel of the Gallery staff have made valuable contributions to the exhibition over the long period of its gestation, and we are indebted to Earl A. Powell, III, of the National Gallery staff who served as overall coordinator of the exhibition.

A very special note of thanks must be extended to Lionel Epstein, who has been instrumental in making this exhibition possible. Mr. Epstein went to Norway for the Gallery on repeated occasions and has not only been exceedingly generous with loans from his and Mrs. Epstein's own collection, but also has consented to serve as guest curator for the master print section of the show.

The exhibition has been supported in part by a generous grant from the Mobil Oil Corporation and by a Federal indemnity from the Federal Council on the Arts and the Humanities.

It is finally to all the lenders of these beautiful and evocative images that we are most deeply indebted. They share in the important task of preserving Edvard Munch's great visual contribution for the world to enjoy; we can all rejoice in the unprecedented opportunity they have granted to us to see so much of that contribution assembled in one place.

J. Carter Brown
Director

Patrons of the Exhibition

Their Royal Highnesses
Crown Prince Harald and Crown Princess Sonja
of Norway

Lenders to the Exhibition

Dr. and Mrs. David Abrahamsen, New York
Mrs. Heddy Astrup, Oslo
The Art Museum of the Ateneumin, Helsinki
Museum of Fine Arts, Boston
The Art Institute of Chicago
Mr. and Mrs. Lionel C. Epstein
Fogg Art Museum, Harvard University, Cambridge, Massachusetts
Göteborgs Konstmuseum, Sweden
The Solomon R. Guggenheim Museum, New York
Klaus-Bernt Hegewisch, Hamburg
Kunsthaus, Zürich
Rasmus Meyers Samlinger, Bergen
The Museum of Modern Art, New York
Munch-Museet, Oslo
Nasjonalgalleriet, Oslo
City Museum of Oslo
Mr. and Mrs. Alan Press
The Gift of Rolf Stenersen to the City of Oslo
Mr. and Mrs. Philip Straus
Vassar College Art Gallery, Poughkeepsie

fig. 1 Edvard Munch, *Rue Lafayette,* 1891, Nasjonalgalleriet, Oslo

fig. 2 Gustave Caillebotte, *A Balcony, Boulevard Haussmann,* 1880, Private Collection, Paris

INTRODUCTION

Edvard Munch: Some Changing Contexts

Robert Rosenblum

EVEN THE MOST PARIS-CENTERED INTERPRETATIONS of the history of postimpressionist art have been obliged to consider the grand and disturbing presence of the strange Norwegian master Edvard Munch. His haunting images of life, love, and death, his capturing of a near-hysterical collision between private feelings and a hostile, oppressive environment—such achievements have annexed him to the great traditions of modern art and stamped his work indelibly upon the awareness of anyone concerned with a new language of form and feeling appropriate to our age of anxiety. Already in the 1890s, when Freud was publishing his first papers on hysteria, Munch's work was as well known in both Paris and Berlin as were the dramas of his compatriot Ibsen; and by 1912, his fame not only extended across the Atlantic, where he was given his first American show in New York, but he was virtually canonized in Cologne, at the Sonderbund exhibition by being shown on equal terms (a room to himself) with the Holy Trinity of modern painting's founding fathers: Cézanne, Gauguin, and van Gogh. It was clear in the early twentieth century that Munch was a pioneer of modern painting and of modern emotional experience.

But any artist of Munch's vast international stature demands constant reexamination. What do we think about him today in the late twentieth century? What questions are helping us to learn more about him? One general answer has to do with a recent historical about-face, that is, an effort to look at Munch not only as an artist who created in the 1890s an utterly new tradition relevant to our century alone, but also as an heir to existing nineteenth-century traditions. We are becoming more curious about his sources, about his roots in the art and experience of the last century, just as in historical retrospect, other postimpressionist fathers of modern art—Cézanne, van Gogh, Seurat, Gauguin—are disclosing more clearly their deep connections with the nineteenth as well as the twentieth century.

For example, we may have to rethink the whole issue of Munch's borrowings from French painting of an earlier generation. What did he see in Paris on his first visit of 1885 and then, during his sojourn of 1889-1891, which could help trigger off his new interpretations of figures in space, so alarming that they can still unbalance us in mind and body? With recent research, we are now learning one answer to this question: the art of Gustave Caillebotte. For here, in the 1870s, was a Parisian master whose paintings already defined, in relatively objective terms borrowed from the convergent and divergent perspectives of photographic schemata, the axial structures of swiftly receding avenues, bridges, balconies that we know so well from Munch's nightmare scenes of modern Olso. In at least one case, the *Rue Lafayette* of 1891, Munch painted, as Kirk Varnedoe has shown,[1] what is virtually a reprise of a vertiginous balcony view by Caillebotte (figs. 1, 2). And given such clues, it becomes easier to understand how decisive for Munch was this new pictorial image of modern, Haussmannized Paris, in which regimented city boulevards, stretching infinitely from near to far, tilt up and down at angles of breathtaking velocity; in which large foreground figures abruptly clash with glimpses of tiny pedestrians at a distant crossing; in which anonymous faces suddenly loom past us as in a phantom promenade. Looking at Munch's successive interpretations of Oslo's main thoroughfare, Karl Johansgate—first on a spring day in 1891 and then, in the following year, during an evening walk (cat. no. 28)—makes us realize how he used the human and spatial premises of Parisian urban images of the 1870s as the foundation for his rapid shift from the external to the internal world of the modern city-dweller. The funneling perspective lines of an urban axis suddenly move, as they threaten to do in Caillebotte's paintings, from reason to feeling, from the measurement of city spaces to a suicidal plunge; and the anonymous pedestrians constantly encountered singly, in pairs, or in crowds in the city streets are swiftly transformed into the immediate terror of a confrontation with skull-like, menacing faces in the foreground or the potential terror of an encounter with tiny, shadowy figures lurking in the remote distance. Pressing further Caillebotte's images of the new rectilinear facts of Paris city-planning and the new human facts of crowds of strolling, middle-class strangers, Munch turned these urban truths of the late nineteenth century into a private nightmare that accelerated dizzyingly in *The Scream* (1893; cat. no. 29) and *Anxiety* (1894; cat. no. 34). To be sure, this rush from the brink of objectivity to the depths of private fear had to be the product of Munch's personal turmoil and, as such, inaugurates a new world of modern psychological responses to the city, from the feverish pitch of swarming crowds and agitated spaces in Kirchner's Berlin scenes to the paralyzing strangeness of distant cast shadows and irrationally inverted perspective systems in de Chirico's dreamlike resurrection of Italian Renaissance city spaces. Yet it should not be forgotten that Munch's art, in turn, looks backward to Parisian urban painting of the 1870s, where that tension between the individual and the modern city was first defined.

Munch's art looks backward, too, to many other areas of nineteenth-century pictorial and emotional experience, especially as explored in the romantic art of Northern European nations.[2] As we have come to think more and more in terms of the themes and images of nineteenth-century art rather than in terms of its purely formal language, we have discovered that Munch often appears to be a late and melancholy heir to motifs first charged with feeling by the romantics. Figures alone by a window or sea-coast; bleak, uninhabited landscapes remote from the life of the city; probing, head-on confrontations with other souls or with the self as seen in mirrored or symbolic form; magical, glowing orbs of sun and moon that seem, like deities, to give strange life to the natural landscape below—such vehicles of private expression are as abundant in German and Scandinavian romantic painting as they are in Munch.

Already in the 1880s, when Munch's art still remained within the confines of a mid-century genre realism, such themes are apparent. Often prefiguring the acute tension in the 1890s between the city-dweller and an alien social organism, many of these works isolate a single figure within a confining envi-

ronment. In an early painting of 1884, the potentially cheerful genre image of a girl seated at the edge of her bed facing the morning light (cat. no. 24), already posits that silent, meditative dialogue between an interior and exterior world that restates a familiar polarity extracted from the romantics' subjective reinterpretation of Dutch seventeenth-century genre painting. By 1889, this image of a single figure in grave contemplation of something beyond can become, as in Munch's painting of his sister Inger seated on a rocky coast (cat. no. 25), a virtual reprise of one of Friedrich's most persistent motifs. This direction reached a climax in 1890, in *Night in St. Cloud* (cat. no. 26), where Munch resurrects the intense pathos potential to the romantic window view, in which a figure (or sometimes only the actual spectator of the work of art) confronts an unspecified vista of endless, imaginative dimensions. In the case of Munch's painting, the sitter—now identified as Munch mourning his father—is almost dissolved into a ghostly, top-hatted shadow as he immerses himself, head on hand, in the silent contemplation of a moonlit suburban view of which we can only make out a distant riverboat on the Seine. Like the fragment of a boat seen beyond the mullions in Friedrich's archetypal statement of this romantic theme, his *Woman at the Window* (fig. 3), a mundane, Seine-side fact helps to transform the sitter's mood into one of intense longing and confinement, just as the contrast between the palpability of the curtain at the left and the impalpability of the deep-blue shadows that absorb the rest of this domestic interior becomes a metaphor, still within empirical terms, of a duality between an objective and subjective world. We recall Munch's manifestolike entry in his 1889 St. Cloud diary, stating that "no more interiors should be painted, no people reading and women knitting. They should be living people who breathe, feel, suffer, and love. People shall understand the holy quality about them and bare their heads before them as if in church." *Night in St. Cloud* is just on the brink of this realization, pushing, as so much romantic genre painting had done, the limits of a prosaic realism to a pitch of such emotional intensity that everything takes on an aura of almost sanctified mystery, with even commonplace objects becoming symbols of something solemn and uncommonly important.

How quickly Munch was to arrive at this "holy quality" can be seen in *Melancholy, The Yellow Boat* (c. 1891; cat. no. 27), in which the traditional romantic motifs found in *Night in St. Cloud*—a contemplative figure, a distant boat—are reduced to almost an iconic extreme. In the lower right foreground, strangely enlarged and unexpectedly cropped by

Munch's grand, overriding ambition in the 1890s was, in fact, the creation of a quasi-religious series of paintings that he was to call "The Frieze of Life," a pictorial equivalent of a philosophical commentary on modern man and his fate, presented with a symbolic starkness that was to usurp the role of earlier religious imagery. In this, too, he followed in the footsteps of those romantic masters—Friedrich, Runge, Blake—who tried most ardently to fill through the private intensity of their art the enormous void left by the eighteenth-century demise of collective, public religious faith and symbolism. It is worth noting that the typical structural means of these artists to achieve a kind of modern icon—heraldic compositions commonly based on patterns of elementary symmetry—are resurrected by Munch in the 1890s as well as by his Swiss contemporary Ferdinand Hodler. Thus, in both *Eye in Eye* (cat. no. 35) and *Dance of Life* (cat. no. 47), all is pruned to a rudimentary symbolic and formal truth. Horizon lines and verticals are baldly emphasized, figures tend to be disposed in frontal, profile, or dorsal postures around central axes—pictorial means, that is, which tend to immobilize the image as a universal, primitive emblem that would pinpoint for all time the mysterious core of man and his place in nature. Even such a quasi-medieval device as Munch's symbolic borders surrounding a centralized, almost holy image (as in some of the print versions of his modern interpretation of a *Madonna* [cat. no. 216]) has romantic precedents in an ambitious cosmic fantasy like Runge's *Tageszeiten (Times of Day)* (fig. 4), where sanctified images of nature and Christianity, organized on axes of vertical symmetry, are surrounded by borders of burgeoning flowers and putti, the innocent, pre-Darwinian and pre-Freudian counterpart to Munch's spermatic hieroglyphs that would establish, in marginal decorations, the elementary truths of psychology and biology.

Although Munch's candid disclosure in his work that men and women are the helpless pawns of emotional and sexual forces deep below the level of consciousness appears to be the first artistic harbinger of the Freudian thought of the twentieth century, his attitudes, as recently defined by Peter W. Guenther in an excellent essay,[3] are no less indebted to prevailing nineteenth-century views of the conflict of the sexes. Like his friend the Swedish playwright (and painter) Strindberg and like so many of his artist-contemporaries, from Toorop and Delville to Beardsley and von Stuck, Munch was obsessed with the concept of the *femme fatale,* whom he reincarnated in multiple guises: a modern Eve, a blood-sucking vampire, a flamelike bacchante, an archetypal murderess (usually identified as Char-

fig. 3 Caspar David Friedrich, *Woman at the Window,* c. 1818, Staatliche Museen, Berlin

the frame, is a brooding, modern reinterpretation of the conventional Melancholia figure, head on hand; and in the background, attained by the pulsating contours of the coastline, is a remote tableau of a couple, polarized in stark white and black, who, headed toward a yellow boat, stand on a pier. The Northern maritime commonplaces of figures, rocks, coasts, piers, boats are here recreated in a passionate but eternally fixed statement of such timeless themes as sexual jealousy, desperate isolation, intense longing for inaccessible experiences—themes expressed here with such potency that, as in the work of Friedrich, the conventional category of genre painting is elevated by means of a grave new language that speaks of the human condition in a tone better suited to a shrine than to a bourgeois interior. Moreover, the frequent polarity in romantic art between extremes of foreground and background (the spatial expression of a poignant near-and-far duality between the individual and a vast world beyond) is here oppressively restated in terms of modern anxieties.

fig. 4   Philipp Otto Runge, *Morning,* 1803, Kunsthalle, Hamburg

fig. 5   Holman Hunt, *The Awakening Conscience,* 1853, Coll. Colin Anderson

lotte Corday), a demonic temptress disguised as a consoling Madonna. But here, too, Munch's imagery looks backward, especially to Victorian sources, for this strange polarization of female sexuality in two symbolic extremes, virgin and harlot, angel and demon. It is perhaps no surprise to discover Munch's attraction to the Pre-Raphaelite interpretation of this motif as embodied in Rossetti's own *femme fatale* image of the 1860s[4]—a sultry, full-jawed woman with gorgeous auburn locks whose flowing contours, in Munch's more abstract vocabulary, can be transformed into organic linear fantasies that turn the whiplash patterns of art nouveau into sperm, flame, smoke, wind currents, entrapping webs or tentacles. But it is worth mentioning too that, as has been recently suggested,[5] the most famous Victorian image of troubled sexuality, Holman Hunt's *Awakening Conscience* of 1853 (fig. 5)

(in which an adulterous woman, arms crossed, face aghast, rises in moral revelation and anguish from her lover's lap) may be the ultimate source (via Félicien Rops) for Munch's no less famous image of psychosexual turmoil, *Puberty* (cat. no. 38). Again, Munch may turn his nineteenth-century antecedents inside out, transforming external physical descriptions to internal psychic ones and translating their messages into a symbolic language that almost visualizes the concept of the id; but once more, he is emerging more clearly as an artist deeply rooted in nineteenth-century experience.

   We need, as well, to locate Munch more firmly within the context of his compatriots. Munch's reputation as the *one* Norwegian or even Scandinavian artist worth looking at should make us at least question the degree to which this old prejudice is justified. In the later twentieth century, a more United Nations view of European nineteenth-century art is fortunately gaining popularity (Paris, for example, has recently held exhibitions of Russian, Polish, and

fig. 6   Anders Zorn, *Midsummer Dance*, 1897, Nationalmuseum, Stockholm

fig. 7   Christian Købke, *Entrance to Castle*, 1834, Ny Carlsberg Glyptotek, Copenhagen

fig. 8   Peder Krøyer, *A Summer Evening on Skaeyen Beach*, 1899, Hirschsprung Collection, Copenhagen

German nineteenth-century painting), and it is high time we were better informed about all of Scandinavian art both before and during Munch's long career. For example, to see pictures of the bacchic Scandinavian midsummer night dances painted by the Swede, Anders Zorn, in the 1890s (fig. 6) is not to reduce the originality of Munch's own *Dance of Life,* but rather to understand better how a great artist could metamorphose an ethnic Scandinavian genre scene into a universal statement about the grim biological destiny of men and women. To see how the Dane Christian Købke painted, in the 1830s, the charming genre theme of children gazing quietly over the railing of a bridge (fig. 7) is to realize more fully how Munch turned this innocent early nineteenth-century subject into an ominous cluster of provincial girls before their ghostly, bone-white country houses (cat. no. 49), creating an image that

can rival, for bleakness and fearful portent, the best of Ingmar Bergman. To see how another Danish painter, Peter Krøyer, a contemporary of Munch's, interpreted the Scandinavian theme of a couple standing on a shore and facing a distant ship and a midsummer night sun (reflected, like Munch's, in a vertical strip across the waters) (fig. 8) is again to have a more accurate measure of the degree to which Munch both shared and transcended the community of Scandinavian pictorial experience.

We need, then, to see far more Scandinavian art of the nineteenth century. Christian Krohg, for one, is

fig. 9   Halfdan Egedius, *Dance in the Grange*, 1895, Nasjonalgalleriet, Oslo

always named in monographs on Munch, but seldom, if ever, illustrated in them, nor are such other mid-century Norwegian realists as Harriet Backer, Adolf Tidemand, or Erik Herenskiold. And to locate more precisely Munch's achievement as a landscape master who, as in *Starry Night* (cat. no. 62), can often rival van Gogh, we need to learn more about earlier Norwegian painters who evolved from the great romantic landscape tradition of Friedrich—Johan Christian Dahl, Thomas Fearnley, August Cappelen, Hans Gude—painters who recorded the same sublime Nordic scenery as Munch, even occasionally including, as he was to do, one or two awestricken figures who stand, their backs to the spectator enrapt in overwhelming vistas of fjords, birches, and infinitely winding coastlines. And we should like to know more, too, about Munch's relationship to the art of his Scandinavian contemporaries of a comparably symbolist persuasion. There is, for one, the short-lived Norwegian painter, Halfdan Egedius, whose images of midsummer folk dances (fig. 9) and landscapes belong to the at once paralyzing and passionate domain of Munch, as well as the Danish painter, Jens Willumsen, who like his exact contemporary, Munch, painted strange images of human anxiety before the primal forces of nature. And there is the better-known Norwegian sculptor, Gustav Vigeland, who was part of Munch's circle of friends in Berlin in the 1890s and whose Wagnerian achievements in stone—megalomaniac profusions of nude figures enacting, in an abstract universe, the gloomy cyclical dramas of the conflict of the sexes and the ultimate destiny of man—may cast further light on Munch's own Nietzschean role as artist-philosopher. And Munch might well be considered, too, in the context of those strange late nineteenth-century Swedish artists Carl Hill and Ernst Josephson who, like him, could reveal directly through their art the painful pressures of their own psychic imbalance.

If we are becoming more inquisitive, then, about Munch's relations with Scandinavian art (as we should also be about van Gogh's and Ensor's with nineteenth-century Dutch and Belgian art), so too are we now more curious about Munch's imposing position within the broader international patterns of late nineteenth-century art. To be sure, the recent enthusiastic revival of interest in symbolist art, resurrecting artists from, among other countries, Russia, Finland, Italy, Scotland, Poland, has made many of these pan-European connections—like the ubiquitous *femme fatale* motif or the importance of Pre-Raphaelite sources—quite clear;[6] but others are only beginning to emerge. For every time we expand our knowledge of Munch's European contemporaries, we also learn more about Munch. Thus, in the admirable recent exhibition, *Els Quatre Gats; Art in Barcelona around 1900,*[7] many paintings by little-known Spanish masters of the 1890s provided shocks of recognition in their treatment of themes we might have thought belonged to the biographical traumas of Munch alone. For example, Ramón Casas's *Anxiety* (c. 1891) (fig. 10) offers a counterpart to Munch's contemporary renderings of the claustrophobic sickroom atmosphere he knew so well from his family history; and Santiago Rusiñol's *Morphine Addict* (1894) (fig. 11) closely approaches in its grim social commentary and startling bedroom candor Munch's own *Day After,* an equally truthful account of the effects of, in this case, alcohol upon a young girl.[8] Even across the Pyrenees artists of Munch's generation were preoccupied in the 1890s with the same gloomy themes of personal tragedy and social evil.

Munch's vision, to be sure, could go far deeper than the documentation of such dark contemporary facts as tuberculosis, venereal disease, drug addiction; and as is amply demonstrated in his obsessive variations on the theme of embracing lovers (cat. nos. 43, 55) he could move from a contemporary urban environment that evokes a specific time and place in the modern world to a timeless, spaceless realm of universal symbols. Again, Munch's quest for a distilled, elementary form and image that could speak for all of human experience is best understood within the framework of late nineteenth-century art. The romantics had already created a foundation for this ambitious search for frozen emblems of a cosmic truth; and even the great realist master Jean-François Millet may have provided clues for Munch through his genius for

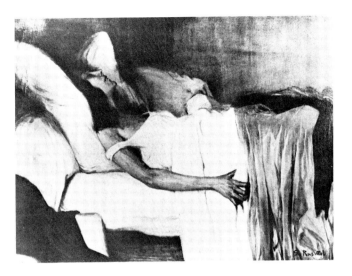

fig. 11   Santiago Rusiñol, *The Morphine Addict*, 1894, Cau Ferrat, Sitges

fig. 10   Ramón Casas, *Anxiety*, c. 1891, Instituto Amatller, Barcelona

transforming the most ordinary field workers into symbolic pairs, Adams and Eves who, like the stark duos of male and female in Munch's work, evoke by their immutable symmetries and polarities the richest range of human archetypes. But Munch's pursuit of grave and simplified landscape and figural compositions, which approach patterns of lucid parallels and perpendiculars, profile and frontal postures, belongs more generally to the idealist world of artists like Puvis de Chavannes and Hans von Marées, who similarly tried to resurrect an image of timeless truth that could take on the quasi-religious cast of mural painting in an earlier, more sacred civilization than ours.

That Munch participated fully in this tradition is amply evident in the achievement of the murals for the Aula (Great Hall) of the University of Oslo (1909-1911), whose archaizing mood and even specific figural imagery in the *History* and *Alma Mater* allegories often seem a grand and final variation on the world-renowned wall paintings Puvis de Chavannes executed for nineteenth-century museums, universities, and libraries.[9] But in the 1890s, before he became an official, award-winning

national hero, Munch translated Puvis' public statements into a more urgent private language that could introduce into the grand solemnity of archaic mural harmonies subversive elements of mystery and unrest, as if, in Freudian terms, the id of the nineteenth century were finally exposed. Arcadia began to be haunted by consuming sexual passions, by death, jealousy, anxiety; the Garden of Eden was seen after, not before, the Fall. In this, Munch's personal dialogue with the public mural art of the nineteenth century parallels that of Gauguin and Hodler in the same decade, attempting as they all did to create a valid universal statement that stemmed more from private, subjective experience than from untroubled communal myths inherited from earlier centuries.

Munch's connections with Gauguin's art, especially in his adaptation of strong, pulsating contours and flat, unmodulated colors that could evoke both mysterious, primal emotions and timeless symbols, have often been commented on; but further analogies need to be explored. Of these, one of the most provocative concerns what may well be a major source for Munch's *Scream* (cat. no. 29). From the late 1880s on, as Wayne Andersen has shown,[10] Gauguin was again and again drawn to a macabre object displayed at the Trocadéro (the new ethnographic museum of Paris) and probably at the 1889 World's Fair as well: a Peruvian mummy, its legs and body bound together, its hand raised to its head (fig. 12). This chilling relic of death and fear, transported from a primitive world to a modern one, was constantly recreated in the figural postures of Gau-

fig. 12   Peruvian Mummy, Musée de l'Homme, Paris

The Scream, 1893, Nasjonalgalleriet, Oslo (cat. no. 29)

guin's anguished women. Was it no less potent a stimulus for Munch, who could easily have known both the original in Paris as well as its reinterpretations by Gauguin? There seems to be far more than coincidence between Munch's *Scream* and the Peruvian mummy. The panic-stricken compression of the arms against the body, the hands desperately cupped around the face, the skull-like baldness and hollowness of the heads with their gaping orifices, the very sexlessness of this anguished core of a being (which in both cases transcends male or female gender)—such analogies suggest that Munch, no less than Gauguin, depended heavily on this image of primal terror as an almost psychoanalytic means of plummeting to the depths of the anxiety to be found in, as Munch was later to call it, "modern psychic life."

Munch probably used this mummy as a kind of "objective correlative" in his search for images of elemental fear and passion that could cut almost literally to the bone, just as he also used skeletons, masks, and shadows as metaphors of the deeply disturbing emotional states that underlay the smug facades of late nineteenth-century middle-class society. In this, too, he is joined by many of his contemporaries, and most conspicuously by James Ensor, who was born just three years before Munch and also lived to be an octogenarian. Like Munch, the Belgian master began within the stifling confines of a realist genre style and then sought out equivalents in observed experience that could help him crack the armor of a provincial society and uncover the inferno of emotions that seethed beneath it. Again, masks, skulls, and skeletons provided metaphorical keys for these corrosive unveilings of both the generalized menace of urban crowds—the Brussels or Ostend equivalent of Munch's Oslo streets—and the phantoms of death and animal brutality that lurked behind individual countenances. The tension between the temporal and the timeless, the factual and the symbolic, the falsehoods of society and the truths of emotions could be expressed by Ensor, as by Munch, through these ugly and morbid reminders of authentic feelings and ultimate human destinies. And like Ensor, Hodler, and many other artists of his symbolist generation, Munch seems to have achieved a complete statement of his art before 1900, after which he was often obliged to repeat, decade after decade and at times with diminishing intensity, the great images that were molten at the moment of their late nineteenth-century origins.

In lengthening retrospect, then, Munch's art seems to stand Janus-faced at the end of the last century, offering, on the one hand, a series of astounding formal and psychological prophecies that can thrust us quickly ahead to the twentieth-century world of German expressionism or even to Picasso's symbolist modes from the pessimistic ambiance of *La Vie* of 1903 to the female life and sexual cycle explored in the *Girl Before a Mirror* of 1932;[11] and on the other, a compelling and ambitious synthesis of both public and private goals that haunted nineteenth-century artists from the romantics on. That Munch's forms, images, and emotions can deeply echo the concerns of so many different generations of nineteenth- and twentieth-century artists and spectators is not only a testimony to his genius and to his central position in the history of modern art, but also a promise that his work will reveal yet other, unexplored facets to the future.

NOTES

1. See Kirk Varnedoe and Thomas P. Lee, *Gustave Caillebotte; A Retrospective Exhibition* (Houston, Museum of Fine Arts, 1976-1977), 149-150.

2. For a fuller elaboration of Munch's art as the heir to German romanticism, see my *Modern Painting and the Northern Romantic Tradition: Friedrich to Rothko* (New York, 1975), chapter IV.

3. In his exhibition catalogue, *Edvard Munch* (University of Houston, The Sarah Campbell Blaffer Gallery, 1976), especially pp. 33ff. This important catalogue also offers a particularly useful bibliography.

4. Munch's borrowings from Rosetti were first elaborated in Edith Hoffmann, "Some Sources for Munch's Symbolism," *Apollo, 81* (February 1965): 87-93.

5. Erika Klüsener, "Das erwachende Bewusststein; zur Ikonographie der Malerei des 19. Jahrhunderts," *Das Münster, 20,* no. 31 (1975): 145-153. The general relationship between Hunt and Munch was first pointed out in Werner Hofmann, *Das irdische Paradies* (Munich, 1960), 328f.

6. The most important and international of these manifestations was the exhibition, *Le Symbolisme en Europe*, Brussels, Musées Royaux des Beaux-Arts, 1976.

7. Princeton University Art Museum and Hirshhorn Museum and Sculpture Garden, 1978.

8. The connection between Munch's and Rusiñol's paintings was first pointed out in Anthony Blunt and Phoebe Pool, *Picasso: The Formative Years* (London, 1962), figs. 44-45.

9. For a close study of particular borrowings from Puvis de Chavannes, see Ida Landau Sherman, "Edvard Munch: The Alma Mater Mural," unpublished M.A. thesis, Georgia State University, Atlanta, 1973.

10. See "Gauguin and a Peruvian Mummy," *Burlington Magazine, 109* (April 1967): 238-242; and Andersen's elaborations on this influence in *Gauguin's Paradise Lost* (New York, 1971), 89-90 and passim.

11. By a curious historical coincidence, Munch's last version of the important motif of the three stages of woman was painted in 1932 (Munch Museum, OKK M375), the same year as Picasso's *Girl Before a Mirror*, which it parallels closely in its vision of the unity of female sexual evolution with the biological rhythms of nature.

Self-Portrait, 1886.
Oil on canvas,
33 x 24.5 cm.
Nasjonalgalleriet, Oslo (cat. no. 3)

Munch's Self-Portraits
Arne Eggum

My art has been a confession   Edvard Munch

MUNCH'S SELF-PORTRAITS DO NOT CONSTITUTE A uniform, easily definable group of motifs. He used the self-portrait for different purposes at different times. Thus to distinguish the strict self-portrait from other genres may pose problems. *The Flower of Pain* (cat. no. 6), for example, has been analyzed as both an allegory about the artist and as a self-portrait. On the other hand, it is typical of Munch to place himself in his own compositions as is evident in the deathroom scenes. Later expressionist compositions, such as *Death of Marat* (cat. no. 53), are especially difficult to analyze adequately because Munch intended to communicate important statements about human existence by depicting strictly private and bitter experiences. There are a great number of pictures in which Munch showed himself next to a model. These are often both studies from life and self-revealing documents, since in later years he often entered into close relationships with his models.

If we focus only on the strict self-portraits, they have at least one pronounced common characteristic. In each picture the artist seems to pose the question: Who am I? To Munch, the self-portrait was a mirror to reflect fundamental problems regarding our own existence. The great majority of them have a very personal stamp, and most of them were never exhibited by Munch himself. The self-portraits that he did exhibit seem rather to have the character of artist's portraits which tell about Munch's changing objectives for his art.

In the following pages I will be concerned mainly with his most important early pictures, not so much to supply a detailed characterization as to take up certain problems which perhaps have not been sufficiently illuminated.

From the 1880s, we have only three small self-portraits, one at present in the Munch Museum (cat. no. 1), another in the Oslo City Museum (cat. no. 2), and the third in the National Gallery in Oslo (cat. no. 3). The wrong dating of the one in the Munch Museum and especially the one in the City Museum has led to highly imaginative theories. The incorrect dating was originally perpetrated by Jens Thiis, when, in the catalogue for the retrospective Munch exhibition in Oslo in 1927, he erroneously dated the City Museum's version 1880 and that of the Munch Museum, also misleadingly, 1882. All those who have since written systematically about the self-portraits have used these dates and have overlooked the fact that Thiis later corrected them in the footnotes to his Munch biography of 1933.[1]

In 1933 Thiis dated the version in the Munch Museum 1881, because the picture was painted before the Munch family moved from Fossveien 7. This information was probably based on conversations with the artist's sister Inger Munch, and there is every reason to believe that what she said is correct, since the picture had a prominent place in the family's home and later in her home. Since the family didn't move from Fossveien 7 until February 1882, it cannot be ruled out that the picture might have been entirely or partly painted in January of that year. In his Munch biography Thiis repeated several times that the version that was later to hang in the Munch Museum was the first picture made of the artist, but he did not touch at all upon the date of the much larger version in the City Museum.

This characterized the small self-portrait in the Munch Museum as being ascetic and severe. It is a characterization which covers the most essential aspects. Munch depicted himself in a three-quarter pose, from the shoulders up, with an expression of sober evaluation. He was obviously much more interested in showing the construction of the cranium and tiny details than in providing a psychological characterization of himself.

In the autumn of 1881 Munch entered the School

Self-Portrait with Cigarette, 1894/95. Oil on canvas, 110.5 x 85.5 cm. Nasjonalgalleriet, Oslo (cat. no. 4)

Self-Portrait with Lyre, 1897/98. Pencil, india ink, watercolor and gouache, 68.5 x 52.5 cm. OKK T 2460. Munch-Museet, Oslo (cat. no. 5)

Self-Portrait/Salome Paraphrase, c. 1898. Watercolor, india ink, and pencil, 46 x 32.6 cm. OKK T 369. Munch-Museet, Oslo (cat. no. 7)

*Self-Portrait with
Brushes,* 1904/05. Oil
on canvas, 197 x 91.5
cm. OKK M 751.
Munch-Museet, Olso
(cat. no. 10)

Self-Portrait/Inner Tumult, c. 1919. Oil on canvas, 151 x 130 cm. OKK M 76. Munch-Museet, Oslo (cat. no. 16)

Self-Portrait 1882/83. Oil on plate, 25.5 x 18.4 cm. City Museum of Oslo (cat. no. 2)

Self-Portrait 1881/82. Oil on plate, 25.5 x 18.4 cm. OKK M 1049. Munch-Museet, Oslo (cat. no. 1)

of Drawing in Christiania. His unique talents soon led to his skipping all the elementary courses and being placed in the class for modeling, his instructor being the sculptor Julius Middelthun. This artist adhered to a conservative, classical tradition, which cultivated the cool surface of the marble and its clean and pure forms. Even though the self-portrait was at least partly painted in his childhood home, it is reasonable to regard this first self-portrait as a piece of work done under the supervision of Julius Middelthun. This explains the smooth, hard surface of the self-portrait, as well as the wealth of details.

Based on Jens Thiis's arguments, we ought to put a later date on the version in the Oslo City Museum. The larger format as well as the technique and the general impression call for dating it subsequent to the autumn of 1882, when Munch came under the influence of Christian Krohg. At this time Munch, with a few younger colleagues, rented a studio at Pultosten on top of the building owned by *Morgenbladet* in Christiania. Christian Krohg also rented a studio in that building, and he guided and

corrected the younger artists without making them feel that they were his pupils. On the back of a portrait of Singdahlsen, Munch wrote: "Painted by Christian Krohg and Edvard Munch—83." This portrait is relatively neatly organized, with a wealth of detail, but there are short, corrective strokes added in just those places where the interest in detail spoiled the general characteristics of the picture. Such details were the shaping of the ear, the nose, the hair, and mustache. The corrective strokes were probably made by Krohg. Thus, Munch was in this case corrected in line with principles completely contrary to those upheld by Julius Middelthun. From a technical viewpoint, the self-portrait in the City Museum was painted in the same way as the portrait of Singdahlsen (fig. 1), with the same type of corrective strokes, no matter whether added by Munch or by Krohg. In this self-portrait, too, we can see that all unessential details, such as the ears, the wings of the nose, and the hairline, have been blurred so as not to detract from what is important. The great interest in the construction of the cranium in his first self-portrait has here changed into an equally strong interest in the incidental—in

fig. 1 *Portrait of A. Singdahlsen,* 1883, OKK M 1054, Munch-Museet, Oslo

how the skin is marked by the problems and joys of the day, but with a predilection for the "naturalistic" details, such as bags under the eyes, green shadows, and so on.

In line with the above,[2] it is therefore reasonable to look upon the self-portrait in the City Museum as the work of an apprentice in the style of Christian Krohg, painted in the winter of 1882-1883 and not as previously accepted in 1880.[3]

Self-Portrait, 1886 in the National Gallery is, as I see it, a portrait of the creator of *The Sick Child* (cat. no. 42). It is the portrait of an artist who *knows* that he has come into a domain that is wholly his own. Technically speaking, it is in its way just as interesting as *The Sick Child.* The face was modeled with a spatula in the same way that a sculptor works with a clay model. To highlight the most expressive parts of the face, Munch scraped away the paint around it all the way down to the canvas. The structure and color of the canvas play a part in the general impression of the picture. Munch made the background around the head look blurred and utilized a tech-

nique involving washing the areas with a diluent. From a coloristic viewpoint the picture is concentrated and extremely expressive through the play of subdued red and green hues. The green in the eyes and the red in his lips and around his right eye have been extremely well placed from a coloristic point of view. Thus Munch, in his own portrait, stressed the sickliness that he created in *The Sick Child,* but the sickliness in the portrait borders on artistic oversensitivity. In this painting Munch laid himself bare in a way that seems to imply an artistic program. When he painted this self-portrait, he still had impressions of the Louvre and of Rembrandt in his retina.[4] There is reason to believe that the negative reception accorded *The Sick Child* made Munch fail to pursue this expressive aspect of his talent during the following years.[5]

Self-Portrait Under the Mask of a Woman (cat. no. 8) has at various times been dated to each year from 1892 to 1895. It is evident that theories about what the picture expresses and what main trends of the time it represents depend on how we date it. None of the proposed dates has been buttressed by any facts or reasons, except the one by Ingrid Langaard,[6] who is in favor of c. 1893, since Munch looks younger than in the portraits from 1895. All authors who have treated the painting, however, see in it a reflection of the Berlin bohemian group and the concept of women held by the group's leading characters, August Strindberg and Stanislaw Przybyszewski.

An analysis of the picture reveals some unsureness in the method of painting, too much attention to detail, and indicates that Munch didn't know just what he wanted. It appears as if Munch wished to give his face the character of a mask and that he experimented by scraping in the paint representing the color of the skin. Still, it is difficult to differentiate precisely between what was done by Munch and what was caused by subsequent wear and tear of the picture. The woman's mask above his head was painted freely and elegantly, without revealing any understanding of the synthetic form language he was familiar with. From a purely psychological viewpoint, too, the picture may be said to be unclear. I don't believe Munch would have expressed himself with such great uncertainty in this form language after 1892.[7] In 1892, for example, Munch completed *Melancholy, Yellow Boat* (cat. no. 27), now in the National Gallery, *Evening on Karl Johan Street* (cat. no. 28) in Rasmus Meyers's collection, and *At the Roulette,* now in the Munch Museum.

The portrait which in regard to color is most similar to *Self-Portrait Under the Mask of a Woman* is the one of Jacob Brattland (fig. 2). It has the same

Self-Portrait under Mask of a Woman, 1891/92. Oil on canvas, 69 x 43.5 cm. OKK M 229. Munch-Museet, Oslo (cat. no. 8)

fig. 2 *Portrait of Jacob Brattland*, c. 1891, OKK M 229, Munch-Museet, Oslo

ornamental character and tries in the same way to let the "soulful" quality find expression "through" a mask. Munch must have felt satisfied with the portrait of Brattland, since he exhibited it frequently between 1892 and 1894. We do not know just when the portrait of Brattland was painted; there are equally good reasons for dating it either 1891 or 1892.[8]

A third piece of circumstantial evidence for dating the self-portrait 1892 or earlier is the fact that there is no trace of a mustache on it. When Munch went to Berlin in November 1892 he was interviewed and drawn with a mustache by Christian Krohg (fig. 3). All the photographs we know about taken between 1892 and 1895 show Munch with some kind of mustache. We also know from a drawing in a sketchbook dated November 29, 1891, that

Munch was not sporting a mustache at that time. Most probably the mustache was grown in the summer of 1892.

Everything considered, the most probable date for the picture is the winter of 1891-1892. Thus, it was painted before Munch came into contact with the milieu in Berlin and does not exemplify with any immediacy the view of woman held by Strindberg and Przybyszewski. The picture does, on the other hand, show some connection with Munch's literary diaries, in which he depicted himself as an artist who feels hunted, threatened, and attracted to a woman whom he called Mrs. Heiberg. *Self-Portrait Under the Mask of a Woman* is also a reflection of the synthetist form language Munch found in Paris and Brussels to serve new purposes in his art. His main intention could have been to communicate the haunted soul of a symbolist artist by using mask forms.

In 1895 Munch completed two self-portraits that

fig. 3 *Edvard Munch*, drawing by Christian Krogh, 1892, OKK B 2480 (F), Munch-Museet, Oslo

are major works in his artistic production. They are the oil painting *Self-Portrait with Cigarette* (cat. no. 4) and the lithograph *Self-Portrait with Skeleton Arm* (cat. no. 120). In the painting he positioned himself in a room filled with bluish smoke, explained by the cigarette he holds in his right hand. A strong light, as if from a projector, illuminates him from below. The light emphasizes the hand with the cigarette and the face. The hand was painted with great sensitivity, appearing at the same time strong and delicate. The face expresses something of the same duality. It is as if the artist looks into himself, concerned only with what happens behind the retina, still having a firm basis in reality. The hand is holding a cigarette and not a brush. This indicates that he as an artist now evaluated the thought and the idea as being more important than the execution. The portrait may thus be regarded as an artist's portrait showing an inspired painter who is living in his own universe.

When Munch painted this portrait he had completed the most important of the "Life Frieze" motifs, thought by many to be spontaneous expressions of a sick mind. The press had pictured Munch as being hypersensitive and nervous, and his

popular image was that of being decadent. His art was looked upon as anarchistic in the sense that it violated prevailing rules and norms. To many, Munch was a problem child; others worshiped him as a genius. When Munch depicted himself in an oil portrait, the notions that people had about the artist were applied to the portrait.

At a meeting of the Students' Association in Christiania on September 5, 1895, a debate followed a lecture by the young lyricist Sigbjørn Obstfelder. A student, Johan Scharffenberg, who was later to become a professor of psychiatry, stood up and stated his opinion that the artist was insane and that Munch's self-portrait indicated that the artist was not a normal person.[9] Munch was present in the auditorium, and subsequent notes by him seem to indicate that he was hurt by that public statement.[10] Munch's insanity was also implied by those who spoke on his behalf; they pointed to the fact that other artists who were suffering from hereditary insanity had been able to create first-rate art. On closer inspection the self-portrait reveals an artist who seems haunted by dreadful psychic experiences.

That same year Munch created his most significant lithographic self-portrait, *Self-Portrait with Skeleton Arm*. The picture is in the form of a sepulchral tablet. At the top, in a border, it says in block letters: "Edvard Munch. 1895." At the bottom of the picture this border is repeated in the form of the hand of a skeleton. The same kind of illumination is used here as in the oil painting; only the head is illuminated on the black surface of the sepulchral tablet. The self-portrait may thus basically be looked upon as a memento mori.

Technically speaking, the portrait exemplifies how brilliantly Munch mastered the combination of lithographic india ink and crayon on stone. The deep, black background is due to the india ink, and with the lithographic crayon he has created the fine details of the head. The scraping tool was used whenever he wanted to diminish a contrast that had become too marked. It is this technical base that makes it possible for him to preserve the naturalistic picture of the person in his lithographic portraits in spite of new stylistic criteria.

This lithograph has become *the* picture of the symbolist painter Edvard Munch. It is also the most sensitive portrait that he created. By simply letting one eye stare straight ahead and making the left eye look downward and inward, he managed to express a balance in the way the subject's soul is revealed. The stress placed on the head also strengthens the impression of receptivity.

A number of photographs from the first half of

the 1890s provide an impression of the artist as a refined aristocrat. With this lithograph Munch reverted to the *Self-Portrait Under the Mask of a Woman,* but concentrated and simplified the motif. While the head was placed a bit to the right in the oil painting, it is in dead center in the lithograph. An unresolved play with collar and shirt against the dark suit was carried over into the lithograph, where the entire head serves as a contrast to the black background of the sepulchral tablet. The fateful woman's mask was replaced by a symbolism which unambiguously stands for death.

It is an unsolved problem in the literature on Munch what the skeleton's hand actually means. Ingrid Langaard saw a connection with an earlier portrait of Stanislaw Przybyszewski, in which his head is floating above human bones, as in Munch's self-portrait.[11] She is of the opinion that Munch depicted Przybyszewski as the author of *Totenmesse* (Requiem Mass), in which the main conflict is the battle between Sex and Brain. Her interpretation is also buttressed by Przybyszewski's own statements in his reminiscences, *Erinnerungen an das literarischen Berlin,* in which he pointed out that Munch was greatly influenced in his art by just this book.[12] The main character in Przybyszewski's *Totenmesse* faced the tragic choice in which, if the brain won out—and that was the only possibility for an artist if he wanted to create art—then it would mean death. Strindberg, in his *Inferno,* interpreted Munch's self-portrait the same way; referring to the lithograph, he wrote that Munch faced the choice between the greatest fame and sexual joy.[13] The framework for this interpretation was the same: the world view that is expressed in Przybyszewski's novel *Totenmesse.*

There is another portrait of Przybyszewski which serves either to comment on or be commented on by Munch's lithograph and the 1895 painting. In Przybyszewski's novel *Overboard,* published in 1896, a portrait of him (fig. 4) by the Polish artist Anna Constenoble is reproduced.[14] Przybyszewski is here, as Munch appears in his *Self-Portrait With Cigarette,* pictured full face from the hips up, standing in a smoky room with a cigarette in his hand. The most important difference between the two portraits is that Munch's hand points upward, the traditional gesture to call attention to spiritual values, while Przybyszewski's hand points downward toward material values. Aside from the cigarette, Munch's hand is bare, while Przybyszewski wears a heavy gold wedding ring on his middle finger. In the upper left corner of the Przybyszewski portrait the name "Stanislaw Przybyszewski" appears in block letters in the same spot that "Edvard Munch" appears in block letters in the lithograph. The picture

fig. 4 *Stanislaw Przybyszewski,* painting by Anna Constenoble, OKK B 2442 (F), Munch-Museet, Oslo

of Przybyszewski is also dated 1895. *Overboard* is a *roman à clef,* in which "Munch" arrives in Berlin with his fiancée "Dagny Juell," loses out to "Przybyszewski" and takes his own life in a jealous fit. Munch's painting *Jealousy* (cat. no. 39) was done in 1895, and it shows Przybyszewski turning green from jealousy while looking at the couple in the background picking apples from the Tree of Knowledge. There was indeed a strange mental dialogue among Munch, Przybyszewski, and Strindberg during the middle of the 1890s. Munch's self-portraits from 1895 may be most simply "explained" in the context of the milieu that these three men and Dagny Juell, who married Stanislaw Przybyszewski in 1893, created in Berlin.

The debate in Christiania that surrounded Munch's *Self-Portrait With Cigarette,* having to do with insanity, how sickly it is to love one's own sickness, and the artist's morbid world of ideas, provided no motivation for Munch to paint additional self-portraits. Instead he continued, as is shown in

fig. 5 *Bathing Boys,* 1904, OKK M 901, Munch-Museet, Oslo

The Flower of Pain, 1898. India ink, wash, watercolor and chalk, 50 x 43 cm. OKK T 2451. Munch-Museet, Oslo (cat. no. 6)

Death in the Sickroom (cat. no. 41), to "enter into" his own world of images. The border between self-portrait and allegory is no more than a hairline in pictures such as *The Flower of Pain* (cat. no. 6) or *Self-Portrait with Lyre* (cat. no. 5) and in the paintings *Metabolism* (cat. no. 46) and *Dance of Life* (cat. no. 47). Munch appears in a group portrait in the two motifs from the Kristiania Bohème that have come down to us as etchings. But these pictures, too, are primarily pictures of ideas that refer to memories of certain situations.

In regard to *Self-Portrait/Inferno* (cat. no. 9), the likeness is so pronounced that the picture must primarily be classified as a self-portrait. The picture is a commentary on and a counterpart to the *Self-Portrait With Cigarette.* As in *With Cigarette* the artist is enveloped by an unreal atmosphere, illuminated by a garish light from below. *Inferno* is as warm as *With Cigarette* is cold. The body here appears in the nude,

light yellow in contrast to the dark face. A suffocating shadow is indicated with red paint on the neck, and behind the artist a threatening dark shadow grows forth. Munch rests one hand on his hip, while the other arm hangs straight down, and he is shown from below the waist up. The picture is revealing and harsh and a bit unpleasant.

An unbroken tradition dating back to 1945 holds that the picture was made in 1895. This tradition came into being after Munch's death and was based merely on intuition. In my view, the picture does not bear the stamp of having been painted in the 1890s, as far as motif and colors are concerned.

The earliest time the *Self-Portrait/Inferno* can be proven to have existed is January 1906. At that time the picture was photographed in Commeter's art salon in Hamburg and was registered in his list of Munch's collection of paintings as number 21.[15]

In 1911 we find another trace of the picture. Erik Kruskopf has made it seem probable that the picture was exhibited in Helsinki in 1911 under the title *Self-Portrait* and was offered for sale for 1,500 kroner.[16] This low price for a picture by Munch and the very fact that the picture was offered for sale, make it improbable that the picture had been painted in the 1890s.

The next trace of the picture is in a listing of 1911, in which the picture is called *Inferno,* and the picture was finally exhibited in Tannhäuser, Munich, in 1912.[17] Just like the exhibit in Helsinki, this one also consisted in the main of more recent works.

A close analysis of the colors used and the brushstrokes also makes it probable that a later date is the correct one. The use of washes of diluted colors in the background shows similarities with other pictures by Munch painted between 1902 and 1905,

Self-Portrait/Inferno, 1904/05.
Oil on canvas,
81.5 x 65.5 cm. OKK M 591.
Munch-Museet, Oslo (cat. no. 9)

such as parts of *Youth on the Beach* in the "Linde Frieze." The rough strokes with which the face was painted also point to this particular period.

In regard to a later work by Munch, *Men Bathing* (cat. no. 54), painted in Warnemünde in 1907, I have shown that Munch, while being a vitalist in daylight, also painted the night or dark side of things, grotesque erotic passion, in a series of pictures entitled "From the Green Room."[18] The *Self-Portrait/Inferno* is a similar pendant to the monumental *Bathing Boys* (fig. 5), painted in Ås- gårdstrand in 1904. A close examination shows that Munch's yellow body and brown face in *Inferno* was

painted with the same palette as were the figures in *Bathing Boys*. Munch, the "symbolist painter," was hardly sunburned in 1895. It was not until now, with the dawn of vitalism, that Munch worshiped the sun. In *Inferno* Munch showed himself with short hair and just a hint of mustache. This is the way we also see him in a photograph of him nude and in the same pose in which we see him in *Inferno*, but flooded in sunlight. If we compare this photograph with the painting *Bathing Boys*, we will see that Munch's body is practically identical with the boy in the front of the painting. A structural analysis of *Bathing Boys* reveals that the picture has the same

fig. 6   *Sphinx*, 1927, OKK M 801, Munch-Museet, Oslo

compositional construction as *Death in the Sickroom* (cat. no. 41). Munch made himself the figure in the foreground, assuming the same position that Inger does in *Death in the Sickroom*. A detail such as the penis was not painted in; in that area the canvas was not touched.

In *Bathing Boys* Munch discovered an entirely new method of depicting himself in his own paintings. The symbolist pictures of the 1890s were closed memory images without any direct contact with external reality. In *Bathing Boys* the artist moved into the sunlight and laid himself bare in an entirely new way. Since many of the background figures form couples who overtly act in a homosexual manner, the idea behind the picture is hard to grasp. Its great size—it measures 194 by 294 centimeters—and its homosexual motif make it quite a unique work in modern pictorial art. It ought to be mentioned here that there is no reason to believe that Munch was bisexual or homosexual. We may obtain a basis for an interpretation by also taking account of two other motifs: *The Flower of Pain* (cat. no. 6) from 1898 and

Sphinx (fig. 6) from about 1927. *The Flower of Pain* is a personification of an artist who is sacrificing himself. Pål Hougen regards this motif as a masculine counterpart to *Madonna* (cat. no. 37).[19] *Sphinx* is another allegorical self-portrait that was used as a frontal figure in Munch's later monumental *The Human Mountain*. Munch here pictured himself with a pair of female breasts.

The *Self-Portrait/Inferno* may also be regarded in conjunction with the *On the Operating Table* (fig. 7), in which Munch showed himself lying on the operating table during an operation for the purpose of removing a bullet from his left hand. This picture, which became the direct point of departure for another portrait of ideas, *Death of Marat* (cat no. 53), for the first time shows Munch completely nude. This aspect of the motif is repeated in *Inferno*. Johan Langaard's 1947 book about the self-portraits is mainly based on photographs, without his having inspected the primary material.[20] Since the book has been widely circulated, many wrong dates have been difficult to eradicate. For example, the following strict portraits in Langaard's book were said to have been painted in the period 1900-1905: *With Hat and Overcoat* (no. 12), *Indoors with Overcoat* (no. 13), *With Bandaged Hand* (no. 14), and *Full-Length Portrait with Light Overcoat* (no. 15). In a catalogue for the exhibition of self-portraits in the Munch Museum in 1963, Langaard indicated that all these portraits had been made around 1915.[21] In the same catalogue the picture *With a Bowler Hat* (no. 16) was dated c. 1913. All these dates were changed following thorough comparisons with other paintings for which we have definite dates, and so far have not been seriously disputed.[22]

One conclusion is that Munch painted few strict self-portraits before 1904, and that it is after that time that Munch may be likened to Rembrandt in his production of self-portraits. It may be quite natural that Munch, with his newly awakened interest in the nature around him, also took an interest in his own appearance. But it may be even more important that the self-portrait provided Munch with a medium through which he could ever confront himself.

Munch's profound interest in self-portraits after 1904 was paralleled by an intensive use of photographs. We know of photographs which he used as aids for the most important self-portraits that he painted during the next several years. He took most of the photographs himself with a simple camera. To Munch, the self-portrait was no longer primarily a psychological portrait based on a lengthy and intense study of himself in a mirror. He provided himself with a certain freedom and distance in his

fig. 7   *On the Operating Table,*
1902/1903, OKK M 22,
Munch-Museet, Oslo

painting by the fact that the portrayal was based on a
photograph. During Christmas 1904 he painted his
full-length portrait in yellow and blue, standing with
brushes in his hand (cat. no. 10). The picture was
painted at the home of Dr. Linde in Lübeck, but
Munch used a photograph (fig. 8) he had taken
during a visit to the home of Count Kessler in
Weimar. Munch depicted himself as the "Court
Painter." The great contrast between yellow and
blue, which once signified death, stands here for the
power and the vitality of the artist as a portrait
painter.[23]

As I have previously shown in the "Linde Frieze,"
it was not until 1904 that Munch again turned to the
full-length portrait as an art form and as a possible
source of income. The self-portrait with brushes
must also be viewed as being related to his wish to
master this art form. In that year, 1904, and not as
usually assumed in 1901, he also painted the
portraits of his friends Archinard and Schlittgen.[24]
In the *Self-Portrait With Brushes* (cat. no. 10), Munch
depicted himself at the height of his power, with the
brushes ready for cutting and slashing. No longer
was he the spiritually troubled painter of *The Sick
Child,* no longer the inspired poet of the 1890s, but
an artist who thought he could rely on his brushes.

The next significant portrait by Munch shows him
sitting in front of a bottle of wine in the restaurant of
the Artists' Society in Weimar (cat. no. 11). In one of

fig. 8   Munch in Weimar, photograph, 1906, OKK B 1854 (F),
Munch-Museet, Oslo

Self-Portrait in Weimar, 1906. Oil on canvas, 110.5 x 120.5 cm. OKK M 543. Munch-Museet, Oslo (cat. no. 11)

the photographs (fig. 9) that he must have used as a basis for his picture, he sits in his hotel room in a very relaxed manner, with all the lines leading down to the slack-looking hands. The picture was taken with an automatic timer. What was to become the main feature of his enormous production of self-portraits, namely loneliness, was clearly expressed for the first time in this painting.

Self-Portrait in Weimar tells us more convincingly than words can that Munch felt he had entered a blind alley as far as his art was concerned. Taking

over Munch's role in France, the fauves had gained attention as young revolutionaries with their use of strong colors, and the young Brücke artists in Dresden wanted to put his name on their banner. But Munch could not reach a decision either to join the young German group of artists or to prepare a major exhibition in Paris. He could have obtained a studio in the capital of the grand duchy of Saxe-Weimar and become a "court painter," but he couldn't make up his mind about this either.

No important self-portrait came from Munch's

fig. 9 Munch in a Hotel
Room, photograph, 1906,
OKK B 2491 (F),
Munch-Museet, Oslo

hand the following year, except for his manic work
on the motif *Death of Marat.* This picture is not a real
self-portrait but a new group of motifs, which
should be dealt with separately. The interesting
thing is that the borderline between self-portraits
and pictures of ideas, in which Munch created new
motifs, became ever narrower. The basis for his new
compositions was no longer memories of the past
but reactions to his own present situation.

We have mentioned above how he inserted his
own body into *Bathing Boys,* painted in 1905. Two
years later he took a number of photographs of
himself and his models in the nude on the beach at
Warnemünde; this was at the time he was working
on *Men Bathing* (cat. no. 54). Some of the photographs show how he demonstrated poses for the
models as if he were a theatrical director. The picture's later alteration into a triptych is cryptically
commented on by a photograph taken outside his
home at Am Strom 53 (fig. 10). On the left we see a
picture of healthy children—*Children in Warnemünde.* The artist stands at the center at the height of
his powers, transilluminated by an unfinished repetition of *The Sick Child,* and to the right of the artist

fig. 10   Am Strom 53, Warnemünde, photograph, 1907, OKK
B 1863 (F), Munch-Museet, Oslo

Self-Portrait with Cigarette, 1908/09. Lithograph, 56 x 45.5 cm. OKK G/1 277-30, Sch. 282. Munch-Museet, Oslo (cat. no. 12)

Self-Portrait in Bergen, 1916. Oil on canvas, 89.5 x 60 cm. OKK M 263. Munch-Museet, Oslo (cat. no. 15)

there is a picture of old age—*Old Man, Warnemünde.* Munch always thought of new ways to confront himself in his loneliness.

In the *Self-Portrait at the Clinic,* painted at the end of his stay at Dr. Jacobson's clinic in Copenhagen, 1908-1909, he depicted himself as a serious, thoughtful man. The picture is a pendant to the *Self-Portrait in Weimar.* He points with his right hand, as Przybyszewski did in the portrait of him in *Overboard,* at that which is earthy and material. As a man and as an artist, Munch had made a crucial decision: to preserve his health he had decided to stop drinking and smoking and to cut his social contacts to a minimum. He recorded the fact of his last cigarette with the lithograph *Self-Portrait With Cigarette* (cat. no. 12), of 1909, a conscious counterpart to the *Self-Portrait With Cigarette* from 1895.

In making the *Self-Portrait at the Clinic* he also used photographs, but the most important aspect of this picture is the powerful use of the coarse brush technique that he developed in Warnemünde. It was just this brush technique that was further developed in *The Sun,* in its final form as the background picture in the Aula of Oslo University.

It doesn't serve our purpose to try to give a comprehensive analysis of the more than one hundred portraits, paintings, graphic works, and drawings, that Munch created during his last years. In his portraits Munch seemed to be following himself, sometimes in a suspicious manner, sometimes lingeringly, and at other times in a biting, ironic way, as for instance in the series "The Bedroom," [25] in which the artist commented on his own situation in life by linking these current experiences to his earlier life. Such is also the case with *The Wedding of the Bohemian,* where an accidental occurrence was the point of departure for filling the canvas with a group of persons, all of whom had played a role in other dramatic events in his life.

Throughout his whole life Munch created self-portraits that are among the outstanding works of his career. In *Self-Portrait in Bergen* (cat. no. 15), there is an expression of human despair that has

Self-Portrait/Night Wanderer 1920s. Oil on canvas
89.5 x 67.5 cm. OKK M 589. Munch-Museet, Oslo (cat. no. 18)

no counterpart in his art. In *Self-Portrait/The Night Wanderer* (cat. no. 18) he revealed aspects of his life that most people hide: the restlessness induced by loneliness. In other pictures he followed himself with an eagle eye into and out of sickbeds, and ruthlessly, almost contemptuously, he unveiled the situation in which an old man finds himself, in sparkling, colorful watercolors. In some of them it may be said that the fear of death was made very tangible.

During his last years Munch devoted all his pow-ers to two main works, the two masterpieces of his old age. In the *Self-Portrait between the Clock and the Bed* (cat. no. 22) he waxed ruthlessly ironic about his old age and showed himself flanked by two symbols of death: the clock and the bed. He is a lonely figure, backlighted against the pictures hanging on the wall, the ones that represented his life.

And he painted *Self-Portrait by the Window* (cat. no. 20) also merciless in its psychological exploration. It seems as if the proximity of death made the tension in the self-portraits especially more intense. Among

Self-Portrait/By the Window, c. 1940
Oil on canvas
84 x 107.5 cm. OKK M 446
Munch-Museet, Oslo (cat. no. 20)

Self-Portrait between the Clock and the Bed, 1940/42
Oil on canvas
149.5 x 120.5 cm. OKK M 23
Munch-Museet, Oslo (cat. no. 22)

Munch's last self-portraits it is probably *By the Window* which makes the most immediate and the strongest impression: its unusually brutal coloring creates a frightening effect. Ice-cold loneliness but also masculine power and strength are evident in the dark, red face against the frozen, snowy landscape outside the window. Even the warmer elements in the picture seem to be radiating frost. His stance is unyielding and stiff, the corners of his mouth are pulled down, the eyes sharp and strong—defiant against the chill of death that awaits him and which already has clothed nature in a white shroud.

Translated from the Norwegian by Erik J. Friis

NOTES

1. Jens Thiis, *Edvard Munch og hans samtid* (Oslo, 1933), 51, 57.

2. Similar arguments supporting the same conclusion I formulated in the explanatory text to the paintings in the catalogue for the Munch exhibition in Japan 1970/1971, *Edvard Munch* (Kyoto: National Museum of Modern Art, 1971).

3. In *The Portrait Art of Edvard Munch* (Bloomington: Indiana University, 1965) Reinhold Heller makes the acute observation that in the self-portrait in the City Museum, Munch looks four or five years older than in a photograph taken when Munch was sixteen years old in 1879. But instead of questioning the traditional dating, Heller explained this by referring to the wish of an insecure youth who wanted to look older than he really was.

4. Rembrandt's later self-portraits, in particular, must have been of decisive importance to Munch. The works of Albert Besnard and Eugène Carrière could also have led Munch in the same direction. About the influence of impressionism in general see the chapter "The Sick Child" in my essay "Sickness and Death."

5. There is a drawing, RES A 220, of the same self-portrait. Of almost identical size as the painting, the drawing is more detailed and thus probably a sketch for the painting. This is the only full-size sketch on paper with an identical motif to the painting in question. Perhaps his experiences with *The Sick Child* (when overpainted the original composition was lost) made Munch want a 'copy' of the motif enabling him to be more free to experiment with the expressive possibilities in the painting. (Reprod. in Ragna Stang, *Edvard Munch. Mennesket og Kunstneren*, Oslo, 1977.)

6. Ingrid Langaard, *Edvard Munch. Modningsår. En studie i tidlig ekspresjonisme og symbolisme* (Oslo, 1960), 230f. Reinhold Heller, *The Portrait Art*, p. 109, note 126, believes wrongly that the photograph of the painting in Ingrid Langaard's book is from a prerestoration state. The portrait has not been significantly restored since the photograph was taken. Heller compares this self-portrait with Munch's painting *Vision (The Swan)*, OKK M 114, 1892. I disagree with his conclusion that the painting is a self-portrait and with his interpretation of it as showing the transition of Munch's role from being hunted "as a duck" by the critics, referring to the tale of H. C. Andersen "The Wild Duck," to swimming as a swan in the avant-garde milieu in Christiania. There is no factual evidence to be found in Munch's many literary notes on this motif supporting this theory.

7. There is no trace of the painting being exhibited during Munch's lifetime.

8. It could not have been painted before 1891, as the painter Brattland arrived in Christiania for the first time this year. The portrait was first exhibited at the Munch exhibition in Tostrup-gaarden Sept.-Oct. 1892.

9. Protokoll, Det Norske Studentersamfunn, Christiania 1895.

10. *Edvard Munch, Katalog, Tegninger, skisser og studier.* Utstilling i Munch-museet 14. februar - 29. april 1973, s. 3.

11. Ingrid Langaard, *Edvard Munch*, 238ff. Ingrid Langaard sees a convincing likeness between Munch's lithograph and the woodcut by Felix Valloton from the same year. It can be added that Dostoevski was the favorite author of Munch.

12. Stanislaw Przybyszewski, *Erinnerungen an das literarischen Berlin* (Munich, 1965), 222.

13. See also Reinhold Heller, *The Portrait Art*, 40 where the following conversation between Strindberg and Munch in Inferno is recorded:
In the atelier of the Dane, . . . we regard a portrait of Popoffsky. . . . It is solely the head, cut off by a cloud, and underneath is a death's bone such as one sees on tombstones. The clipped off head makes us shiver. . . .
"How did you get the idea for this decapitation?"
"Hard to say, but a disastrous fate rested on this fine spirit: he possessed signs of definite genius and sought the greatest fame, without wishing to pay the price for it. Life permits but one choice: either the laurel wreath or sensual joy."

14. Stanislaw Przybyszewski, *Overboard* (Copenhagen, 1896).

15. The photograph and a transcript of the list is in the Munch Museum document archive.

16. Erik Kruskopf, *Edvard Munch och Finland*, OKK Munch-museets skrifter nr. 4 (Oslo, 1968).

17. Catalogue in the Munch Museum document archive.

18. Arne Eggum, "The Green Room," in *Edvard Munch 1863-1944*, Liljevachs & Kulturhuset, Stockholm, 25. mars - 15. mai 1977, Catalogue (Stockholm, 1977).

19. Pål Hougen, "Kunstneren som stedfortreder," in *Højdpunkter i norsk konst. Årsbok för Svenska statens konstsamlingar* (Stockholm, 1968), 123ff. Similar thoughts are presented by Gøsta Svenaeus in *Edvard Munch. Im männlichen Gehirn* (Lund, 1973), 200ff.

20. Johan H. Langaard, *Edvard Munchs selvportretter. Samlet av Ragnvald Væring* (Oslo, 1947).

21. *Selvportretter*, Munch-museet 1963-64, Katalog (Oslo, 1963).

22. As a student I assisted Langaard and Revold in the preparation of this exhibition.

23. Otto Benesch, *Edvard Munch, Mit 89 Abbildungen* (Cologne, 1960), 31-32, notes that Munch with his long dark coat and the brushes which "appear to be on the edge of a darkly bound volume . . . a Bible" has "the typical attitude of the Protestant divine as he appears before his flock."

24. Arne Eggum, "Linde-frisen," unpublished manuscript in the Munch Museum, 1972. A revised version will be published in German in the spring of 1979.

25. Arne Eggum, "The Bedroom," in *Edvard Munch 1863-1944*, Liljevachs & Kulturhuset 25. mars - 15. mai 1977, Catalogue (Stockholm, 1977).

Morning, Girl at the Bedside

Major Paintings
Commentaries by Arne Eggum

Morning, Girl at the Bedside 1884
(cat. no. 24)
Oil on canvas
96.5 x 103.5 cm
Rasmus Meyers Samlinger

The picture was painted at Modum Blåfargeverk, where Munch's distant relative, the painter Frits Thaulow, conducted an "open-air academy." Like Christian Krohg in the studios at the Pultosten in Christiania, Frits Thaulow here met with younger painters, with whom he shared his more extensive experience. Besides Krohg, Thaulow was at this time Norway's most influential painter, as well as the most well informed in the French art scene. *Morning* shows a seated girl, half-dressed and rustic, in typical Krohg style. But the French-inspired *teint* and the superior rendering of the light in the picture make *Morning* an independent work compared to Christian Krohg's art. The innovative idiom is articulated in the light falling through the window to the left. The light creates the effect of immaterializing the forms of the decanter and the glass, before it is captured in the figure of the girl on the edge of the bed. In the formulation of the girl, Munch used the light more to dissolve the forms than to define them. The painting, which was exhibited for the first time at the Autumn Exhibition in 1884, met with an extremely negative review. The execution and motif were found to be in bad taste. In 1883 Munch had exhibited a head study in the style of Hans Heyerdahl at the Industrial Exhibition, and during the same year he painted *Early Morning,* in Christian Krohg's style. This picture shows a girl preparing to light an oven. *Morning* from 1884 is the last of Munch's paintings that essentially can be described as apprentice works. In 1889 the Norwegian jury selected the picture for participation in the World Fair in Paris. Munch himself had wished to be represented by a more personal work.

Inger on the Beach 1889 (cat. no. 25)
Oil on canvas
126.4 x 161.7 cm
Rasmus Meyers Samlinger

The scene is from Åsgårdstrand, where Munch rented a house for the first time this summer. His sister Inger is sitting on some rocks not far from the house Munch later bought in 1898. With this picture, painted between nine and eleven o'clock at night, Munch captured the light summer night over the fjord by Åsgårdstrand. This motif was to be a recurring theme in his art. The picture of Inger on the beach was exhibited for the first time at the Autumn Exhibition in 1889 under the title *Evening,* and was met by a review as negative as the one given to *Sick Child* only three years earlier. It is apparent from Munch's diaries that during his visit to Paris in 1885 he was already influenced by the art of Puvis de Chavannes. But it was not until *Inger on the Beach* that he let himself be inspired to paint a canvas with homogeneous pale surfaces shimmering with color and with a musical mood. The slumped, seated female figure is, in itself, quite lacking in expression; the quality of soul we read into her is caused by the essential quality of the landscape around her, which becomes an image of her mood.

Inger on the Beach

Night in St. Cloud   1890 (cat. no. 26)
Oil on canvas
64 x 54 cm
Nasjonalgalleriet, Oslo

The setting is Munch's room in St. Cloud, outside
Paris, with its view over the Seine. He stayed there in
the winter of 1890 to escape the plague in the city. As
a model for the slumped figure by the window,
Munch used the Danish amateur poet Emanuel
Goldstein. The picture is traditionally conceived of
as an expression of the artist's own mood, caused by
the news of his father's death. In the otherwise
empty room, the window frame's shadow falls like a

Night in St. Cloud

double cross across the floor and gives immediate associations of death. The picture has a strongly reflective and melancholy character, which is partially caused by the tension between the life outside and the silence inside. The seated figure's thoughts seem to lie far away in time and space, but they are present as pictures of recollection, and their mood marks his immediate surroundings. In several of the

sketches contained in Munch's illustrated literary diary which I have dated 1888/1890, he developed a pictorial idiom that shows the artist slumped and reflective. The reality outside stands as a contrast to his inner world. *Night in St. Cloud* is the first Munch picture where death is presented as a mentally vacated space. He repeated the motif in two additional paintings and in an etching.

Melancholy, Yellow Boat   1891/92
(cat. no. 27)
Oil on canvas
65.5 x 96 cm
Nasjonalgalleriet, Oslo

The picture was painted in Åsgårdstrand in 1891 or 1892. According to tradition, it is supposed to represent the jealous Jappe Nilssen. In the background on the wharf, Oda Krohg is standing with Christian Krohg. They are to be rowed out to a small island where they can make love. Seen as such, the motif carries implications of jealousy, which is the title under which Munch exhibited the picture. The painting was one of the first where Munch clearly let himself be inspired by the most recent tendencies in French synthesist painting. The painting is also an articulation of Munch's distinctive character. Unlike the French, he did not construct but found a landscape where he could see in terms of the new criteria of style. In this picture, we see the large wavy lines, the large surfaces, and the yellow boat which repeats the horizon in the background in a precise and subtle fashion. At the Autumn Exhibition in 1891, Munch exhibited a version of the motif now in a private collection in Oslo. The National Gallery version was either the basis for the numerous sketches he executed to illustrate Goldstein's *Alruner* during the winter of 1891/1892 or it was a result of this work. Both versions were shown at the Munch exhibition in the Equitable Palace in Berlin in 1892/1893. There are altogether five painted versions and two woodcuts of this motif.

Evening on Karl Johan Street   1892
(cat. no. 28)
Oil on canvas
84.5 x 121 cm
Rasmus Meyers Samlinger

The action takes place on Karl Johan Street with the Parliament in the background. The first drafts of the motif are in the illustrated diary, which I have dated 1888/1890. The text in the diary shows that the basic experience behind the picture is Munch's restless search after "Mrs. Heiberg," the woman who was his first unsatisfying love. The lonely figure to the right is traditionally read as an image of the artist himself. The text also explains why the intensely illuminated yellow windows have such a strong pictorial function. When Munch himself was overwhelmed by anxiety, he stared up at these windows to have something to fix his eyes on other than the stream of people moving by. The picture was first exhibited at Munch's one-man show in the Tostrup building in 1892, and the reviews characterized it as insane. Ingrid Langaard has seen in the motif a reflection of the mass psychology of the middle class that brushed aside Munch's art. For me, the rich associations of the masks also call up a pall of death and disaster. Besides reflecting the Pont Aven school's criteria of style, the picture also gives us a sense that Ensor's art must have been of great significance to Munch. *Evening on Karl Johan Street* can also be seen as Munch's answer to Ensor's *The Entry of Christ into Brussels in 1889*, 1888. In a lithograph that Munch made of *Evening on Karl Johan Street*, probably in 1895, there is a border with masks under the main motif. This shows further associations with Ensor's mask art. The lithograph, known in only one edition, was not discovered until a couple of years ago in a private collection in Bergen.

The Scream   1893 (cat. no. 29)
Oil on cardboard
91 x 73.5 cm
Nasjonalgalleriet, Oslo
Gift of Olaf Schou

The Scream is known as Edvard Munch's most central work of art, and it is considered to be a powerful expression of the anxiety-ridden existence of modern man. The painting achieves its strong impact partially by the intensive use of the rhythmic wavy lines and contrasting straight band, so characteristic of art nouveau. The road with the railing, which shoots diagonally toward the left, creates a powerful slant of perspective into the pictorial space, while the soft, curved forms of the landscape give a sense of a precipice in the picture. The strange foreground figure is rendered as a concrete form, even as it personifies a general experience of anguish. Munch described the basic experience behind the picture as follows:

I walked one evening on a road -on the one side was the town and the fjord below me. I was tired and ill -I stood looking out across the fjord -the sun was setting- the clouds were colored red -like blood- I felt as though a scream went through nature -I thought I heard a scream. -I painted this picture -painted the clouds like real blood. The colors were screaming-

The author Przybyszewski puts the picture in the context of symbolist theories of color:

For the new trend, the sound brings about color. A sound can magically conjure up an entire life in an infinite perspective. A color can become a concert, and a visual impression can arouse terrifying orgies from the psyche.

In Munch's handwriting in the upper red area of the painting is written:

Can only have been painted by a madman.

Munch painted the picture in several versions, and he also did it as a lithograph.

The Storm   1893 (cat. no. 30)
Oil on canvas
91.7 x 130.8 cm
The Museum of Modern Art, New York
Gift of Mr. and Mrs. Irgens Larsen and Purchase, 1974

The motif is taken from Åsgårdstrand with the Kiøsterud building in the background, well known from many of Munch's pictures. According to Jens Thiis, the motif was inspired by the experience of a strong storm there. The storm is, however, depicted more as a psychic than a physical reality. The nervous, sophisticated brushstrokes, the somber colors, and the agitated nature are brought into harmony, rendering the impression of anxiety and turbulent psychological conflicts. *The Storm* is also a reflection of Munch's interest in the landscapes of Arnold Böcklin. As in the painting *Evening on Karl Johan Street,* the illuminated windows function as an important pictorial element. The eye is drawn toward them; in a strange way, they radiate psychic life. Munch emphasized controlling the effects rendered by the illuminated windows. He has scraped out the paint around the yellow areas to achieve the maximum effect. It is as though the house becomes a living organism with yellow eyes, which creates contact with the surroundings. In front of the house, a group of women stands huddled together, all with their hands up against their heads like the foreground figure in the painting *The Scream.* Isolated from the group, closer to the center, stands a lonely woman, also with her hands against her head. Like the foreground figure in *The Scream,* she represents anxiety and violent spiritual conflicts. The mood and charged atmosphere indicate that the object of the anxiety is an erotic urge. In the summer months Åsgårdstrand was visited by a great number of women, since most of the summer guests consisted of families whose men worked during the week in Christiania. By now, Munch had formulated an aesthetic which dictated that in his most important motifs, he should represent pictures of recollection as well as the artist's psychological reactions to them. He also made a small woodcut of this motif.

The Voice   1893 (cat. no. 31)
Oil on canvas
87.6 x 107.9 cm
Museum of Fine Arts, Boston
Ernest Wadsworth Longfellow Fund

The motif is probably taken from the beautiful Borre forest, with the famous Viking graves, not far from Åsgårdstrand. Here, in 1889, Munch is supposed to have painted a picture of his friend, Miss Drefsen, and something of this motif may have been preserved in *The Voice* from 1893. Przybyszewski described the pictures as a puberty motif, and this interpretation is supported by Munch's own literary notes. According to these, the painting represents Munch's first childhood romance. He had to stand on a mound to be able to look into the eyes of the taller girl. The suggestive, erotic mood in the picture is created by the interplay between the vertical pine trunks, which repeat the form of the woman, and the shaft of moonlight. As a sign of awakening eroticism, the shaft of moonlight is placed as a phallic symbol on the fjord. The picture was originally called *Summer Night Mood.* It is not known whether Munch approved of the later title. However, the title is a suitable one, since it helps us see its lyrical-auditory quality. If we use Munch's texts as point of departure, we stand as a viewer in front of the woman just as Munch once stood in front of her as a child. But simultaneously, the picture expresses a tension between the couple in the boat and the woman in the foreground. As in other motifs of Munch, for instance *Melancholy, Yellow Boat,* the main character stands alone in contrast to the two who are together in the boat. The woman, depicted in severely closed form, with her hands behind her back, was used by Munch in a series of depictions of women and portraits at this time. The formula is often interpreted as a picture of a woman who is offering herself and holding back at the same time. Besides another painted version, the motif is repeated in a woodcut and an etching.

Starry Night   1893 (cat. no. 32)
Oil on canvas
135 x 140 cm
Private Norwegian Collection

With certain modifications, *Starry Night* is one of the few pure landscapes in Munch's art from the 1890s. We recognize the place as Åsgårdstrand, and the linden tree is the same one that appears in a series of motifs. A wary mood, filled with premonitions, is communicated through the blue velvet night sky illuminated by the golden red stars. The tendency to synthesize large surfaces and sweeping lines has been given a monumental articulation in *Starry Night*. Munch expressed himself by means of a very sophisticated use of line. The soft, undulating line of the beach continues subtly in the contour of the group of trees. The white fence, which shoots diagonally into the picture space, seems to increase the feeling of space without defining it in a precise way. The basic observation of nature is an element of Munch's independent style in relation to contemporary French avant-garde art. Munch depicted a place he saw and was familiar with. At the Berlin Secession of 1902, Munch exhibited the motif as the first picture in the group "The Seed of Love." The vaguely erotic charge of the picture is in keeping with this, as is the motif, since the shadow on the fence suggests a tryst. In the lithograph *Attraction I*, for instance, the shadow from the couple is captured on the same fence. Munch made two other versions of the same motif, these also without the couple in the foreground, but with the shadow preserved on the fence.

Vampire   1894 (cat. no. 33)
Oil on canvas
100 x 110 cm
Private Collection

The motif was first exhibited under the title *Love and Pain*, while the title *Vampire* was inspired by Stanislaw Przybyszewski. Munch adopted the title until, as a reaction to accusations of being too literary, he asserted that the motif merely represented a woman kissing a man on the neck. In *Vampire*, the woman is completely domineering. She actively bends down and sinks her lips into his neck, while he is in a collapsed attitude, passively seeking comfort. Her red hair is cascading down around him, and she dominates the picture space by constituting a diagonal in it. He is positioned passively, parallel to the picture plane. Munch gave the motif a unified monumentality by merging both figures into one pyramid form. A threatening shadow, which repeats their mutual form, rises behind the couple. Active love is a dimension that the woman is fulfilling, while the man is characterized by pain in the relationship. Using Munch's literary notes as the source, this scene has to illustrate one of the many instances when Munch, in the mid-1880s, visited prostitutes with the purpose of satisfying his needs, but without ever having intercourse. The woman has features resembling the whores who are depicted in the painting *Rose and Amelie*. Munch also executed a great number of additional painted versions of *Vampire* as well as a lithograph and a woodcut which he often used together to make a combination print.

Starry Night

Vampire

Anxiety

Eye in Eye

Anxiety   1894 (cat. no. 34)
Oil on canvas
94 x 73 cm   OKK M 515
Munch-Museet, Oslo

The painting can be analyzed as a synthesis of two earlier angst motifs, *Evening on Karl Johan Street* and *The Scream* or *Despair*. The landscapes in *The Scream* and *Anxiety* both depict the inner part of the Christiania fjord, and the figures in *Anxiety* for the most part are taken from the Karl Johan picture. But the bearded man on the left in *Anxiety*, who resembles Stanislaw Przybyszewski, was not depicted in *Evening on Karl Johan Street*. *Anxiety* may have been executed in Berlin, where Munch painted portraits of Przybyszewski. Furthermore, Munch may have had reasons for depicting Przybyszewski in *Anxiety*, if it is true that only after reading Przybyszewski's novel *Requiem Mass* did Munch find the final articulation for the pictorial motif of *The Scream*. The woman, possibly "Mrs. Heiberg," who was Munch's first love, is depicted with a bonnet-shaped or halo-shaped hat, while the man in a top hat—"Mr. Heiberg" (?)—is just about unchanged from the Karl Johan picture. His features are preserved in the lithograph and woodcut of the same motif. In the graphic versions, however, Przybyszewski is no longer depicted, and the man in the top hat stands among three women with bonnet-shaped hats. In Munch's literary notes, he constantly sees "Mrs. Heiberg" in the women passing by. Among French critics in the nineties, the title was considered superfluous. They felt that anxiety characterized so many of Munch's most important pictures that the title should not be reserved for only one of them.

Eye in Eye   1894 (cat. no. 35)
Oil on canvas
136 x 110 cm   OKK M 502
Munch-Museet, Oslo

Like *Red and White*, the painting belonged to the group "The Seed of Love" of the "Life Frieze" at the Berlin Secession in 1902. There is no reliable information as to whether the picture was exhibited earlier. The powerful impasto strokes, especially in the woman's hair, were probably caused by overpainting, done before 1903. The painting has a pronounced childlike quality, an *art naïvisme* that corresponds well with the elements of puberty shown. Munch may have gotten the title from Ola Hansson's book *Sensitiva Amorosa*, where a similar event is described by the same title in a similar setting. The consciously naive manner of painting fits in well with the simple symbolism. The man is deadly white and weak willed under the influence of the vigorous woman. She is painted in the same color as the tree and given a similar robust quality. Behind and above her stands a very simple house. It is as though Munch wanted to imitate a child's way of painting. Seen in this way, the house symbolizes a home or a marriage into which the woman wants to draw the man. In the struggle of the sexes, she is safe and he apprehensive. The purely naive features in the story and in the execution are not repeated in the two lithographic versions of the motif, where the landscape is also a completely different one. The painting *Eye in Eye* can also be seen as an Adam and Eve motif; the couple is placed beneath a tree directly below a branch that is cut off. Munch later executed a series of variations on the Adam and Eve theme, but no direct repetitions.

Red and White   1894 (cat. no. 36)
Oil on canvas
93 x 129 cm   OKK M 460
Munch-Museet, Oslo

From photographs, we realize that the picture was strongly overpainted by 1903. As it is today, the painting represents a woman in white and a woman in red. If we study the painting more closely, we glimpse, underneath the overpaint, a dark-haired woman in profile to the right of the woman in red. It is not known when this third woman was over-painted. The picture must earlier have had a composition similar to the etching *Woman in Three Stages.*

It is customary to regard *Woman in Three Stages* as an image of the three ages of woman, but the picture can also be seen as an analysis of the woman as woman. Seen as such, the motif represents the same woman in various aspects, to the perpetual wonder of the man. In *Red and White,* Munch probably used the woman from the painting *The Voice* as a point of departure for the figure of the woman in red, while we find the woman in white for the first time in *The Lonely Ones* from 1891/1892, now lost. The color symbolism can probably be explained simply as the blood-filled red contrasting with the innocent purity of white. There is also a lithograph of *The Woman,* but it refers back to another painted version in Rasmus Meyers's collection.

Madonna   1894/95 (cat. no. 37)
Oil on canvas
136 x 110 cm   OKK M 68
Munch-Museet, Oslo

The first time *Madonna* was exhibited, it was probably furnished with a frame with painted or carved spermatozoa and embryos, as can be seen on the lithograph of the same title. The frame was later removed and has been lost. Munch must have executed several versions of the motif simultaneously and called the motifs alternately *Loving Woman* and *Madonna*. The pseudo-sacred *Madonna* has been given widely different interpretations by various critics. Some emphasize the purely orgiastic element in the motif; others see the mysteries of birth. Still others, especially Munch himself, emphasize the aspect of death. In "The Tree of Knowledge of Good and Evil," an album in which Munch collected some of his most important motifs, he accompanied *Madonna* with the following text:

The pause when the entire world halted in its orbit. Your face embodies all the world's beauty. Your lips, crimson red like the coming fruit, glide apart as in pain. The smile of a corpse. Now life and death join hands. The chain is joined that ties the thousands of past generations to the thousands of generations to come.

Munch executed the motif in a series of painted versions and repeated it in a lithograph. There exists a closely related etched motif, which perhaps refers back to a now lost version.

Puberty 1894/95 (cat. no. 38)
Oil on canvas
151.5 x 110 cm
Nasjonalgalleriet, Oslo

Munch stated that he had executed exactly the same motif in the mid-1880s, and that this earlier version had been lost in a studio fire. He emphasized that he did not imitate the etching of Félicien Rops, *Le Plus Bel Amour de Don Juan* from 1886, which superficially has the same motif. Munch was, furthermore, supposed to have used a model when he painted the motif in Berlin. The obtrusive, naturalistic details in the upper part of the girl's body reflect decisive intentions in Munch's art in the 1880s. On the other hand, the articulation points toward a direct observation of the model. The threatening shadow that rises over the girl can be seen as a phallic form which alludes to the girl's experience of changes in her own body. But the shadow can also be seen as a shadow of death. The coupling of death and sexuality is not unusual in Munch's art. The motif itself is almost frozen into the picture by the severe contrast between the horizontal line of the bed and girl placed in the middle of the picture. Besides this version, an earlier as well as a much later painted version are in the Munch Museum. The motif was also done as a lithograph and as an etching.

Jealousy 1895 (cat. no. 39)
Oil on canvas
67 x 100 cm
Rasmus Meyers Samlinger

The painting, which was exhibited in Berlin in 1895, is traditionally conceived as a representation of the triangle among Przybyszewski, Dagny Juell, and Munch. In Przybyszewski's *roman à clef, Overboard,* published early in 1896, Munch is described as a jealous rival who kills himself after his fiancée (Dagny) is definitely won over by Przybyszewski. This novel may be Przybyszewski's answer to Munch's picture *Jealousy.* It is constructed on three levels. To the right, we see Przybyszewski's head. He stares straight ahead, wan and pale, and in his mind's eye, he sees the Adam and Eve motif in the mid-level. To the left, in the third level, stands a blood flower, Munch's usual symbol of art. Jealousy was a prominent trait in many of Przybyszewski's novels, and especially clearly articulated in *The Vigil* from 1895. On the cover of *The Vigil,* Przybyszewski used one of Munch's drawings of *Madonna.* In light of this, it is reasonable to see the picture as a literary portrait of Przybyszewski, where he masochistically, as in reality, used his wife as a living model for his writing. This may have been the reason why he freely let her choose other sexual partners, even after they were married. Even if the picture can be analyzed as a literary portrait, this interpretation is too limited, since Munch actually created an image of the nature of jealousy, giving universal traits to this human feeling. Munch repeated the composition shortly afterward in a couple of lithographs and returned to the motif much later in a series of derived versions.

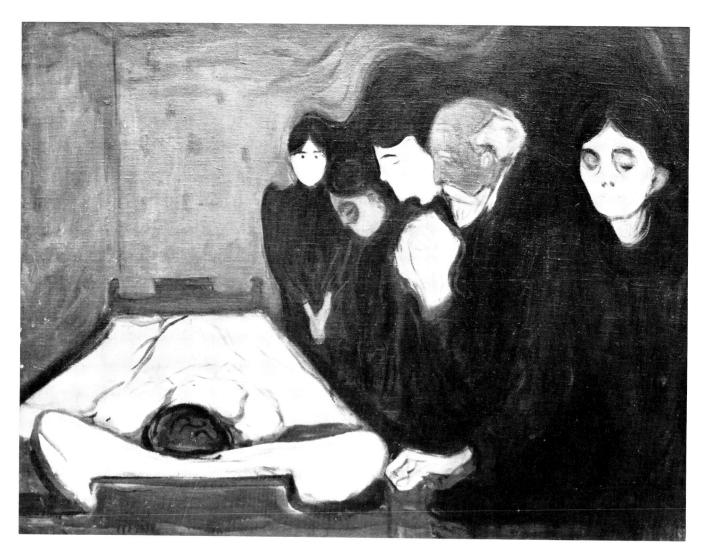

By the Deathbed, Fever   1895 (cat. no. 40)
Oil on canvas
90 x 125 cm
Rasmus Meyers Samlinger

Death in the Sickroom   1895 (cat. no. 41)
Oil on canvas
150 x 167.5 cm
Nasjonalgalleriet, Oslo
Gift of Olaf Schou

By the Deathbed is a subject that goes back to the memory of his sister Sophie's death. She is lying in the bed with folded hands, and to the right stands her family, except Edvard Munch. We do not see the dying one, but through the eyes of the artist we see what she sees and dimly sense what she senses. The identification with the dying one here borders on the pathological. By using simple pictorial effects, Munch is forcing us, as an audience, to participate in his sister's death. There exists a series of studies and sketches of the motif, and he also executed a lithographic version. In a monumental version from about 1915, he repeated the pictorial structure, but it is possible that he here presented himself as the sick one in the bed.

Munch took up the motif in Berlin in 1893, probably with the clear purpose of painting pictures of formative childhood experiences. In the naked picture space, we see Munch and his family present at the death of his sister Sophie. She is sitting in a chair, with her back turned toward the viewer, but not visible to us. In this way, Munch depicted death as an absence or an emotional void that lives on in the survivors as a feeling of privation. A deathlike silence is conveyed by simple and synthesizing artistic means. Munch used simple, suggestive color contrasts; the actors have masked faces, and the action takes place on a sloping stage floor. The picture presents an image of recollection; the family is

portrayed at the age they were when Munch painted the picture, and not at the age they were when the experience took place. In terms of style, the painting is one of the pictures that marks Munch's unique position within the synthetist and symbolist movements with most simplicity and immediacy. The picture can be analyzed from a series of prototypes which range from Degas' and van Gogh's interiors to Gauguin's and Ensor's masked figures. Contemporary critics in the 1890s suggested that Maeterlinck's plays must have been Munch's source of in-

spiration. After Munch had completed the first drafts of *Death in the Sickroom*, he got an offer to illustrate one of Maeterlinck's plays. In the same way as Munch, though in a somewhat more cerebral fashion, Maeterlinck also depicted death as a psychic presence among the survivors. Besides the large versions in the Munch Museum and in the National Gallery, the Munch Museum also has a series of studies and sketches of the motif, which was also repeated in a lithograph.

The Sick Child   1896 (cat. no. 42)
Oil on canvas
121.5 x 118.5 cm
Göteborgs Kunstmuseum, Sweden

This is the earliest painted version based on Munch's first significant work, which was exhibited under the title *Study* in 1886. Even though Munch used a model for the girl with the red hair, and his aunt as the model for the woman in a collapsed attitude, the motif deals on the deepest level with the two dead who were closest to him, his mother and his sister Sophie. The portrayal is one of the best known in Munch's group of motifs. He repeated it as a painting a number of times and executed a lithograph as well as two different etched versions.

Kiss 1897 (cat. no. 43)
Oil on canvas
99.5 x 81 cm   OKK M 59
Munch-Museet, Oslo

In this painting, the fused couple has exactly the same form as in the woodcut. Munch here solved the tensions present in the meeting between man and woman by allowing the two faces to merge into one another in a closed form. Only the man's right ear appears as a differentiated facial part. The unifying form that Munch finally chose for the couple is an erect phallus, and the form is monumentally placed in the middle of the picture. The contrast between the outdoors and the inside is preserved as in the earlier painted versions, and we see indications of people moving about in the sunlight outside. Besides the famous woodcut, there are also several painted versions and an etching.

Inheritance   1898 (cat. no. 44)
Oil on canvas
141 x 120 cm   OKK M 11
Munch-Museet, Oslo

In 1903, the painting was exhibited for the first time at *Le Salon des Indépendents* in Paris. It had its own room at the exhibition and caused both great amusement and indignation. The picture apparently exceeded the limit of what was considered a permissible expression of the hideous. That the title *Inheritance* actually alludes to hereditary syphilis is supported by the fact that Munch himself called the picture *The Syphilitic Child*. The greenish pale child lies in its mother's lap in a pose similar to that of the woman in *Madonna*. The approaching, inevitable death is symbolized by the autumn leaves that form the pattern on the woman's skirt. Munch again employed one of his formulas to create psychic tension. The blood-red face of the woman emphasizes the green features of the doomed child. In a purely thematic way, with this painting Munch harked back to traditional representations of the Madonna with the Christ Child, and this must be a partial reason for the violent reaction. The painting can also be seen as a representation of Munch's own inherited nervous disposition and physical weaknesses. Besides a lithographic version, Munch also painted another version.

Melancholy   1899 (cat. no. 45)
Oil on canvas
110 x 126 cm   OKK M 12
Munch-Museet, Oslo

The picture was probably painted in Hammer's Boarding House, where Munch lived near his family without actually living together with them. The taciturn woman portrayed is, according to tradition, supposed to be Munch's sister, Laura, who was schizophrenic. By placing the woman in a corner of the room, confined between the landscape outside the window and the reflection of the outside on the wall behind her, Munch completely isolated Laura from reality. The bluish landscape outside, inaccessible to her, is in contrast to the flower in a pot on the table in front of her. The flower is the symbol of art for Munch, and it sucks its nourishment from blood. Seen this way, it is plausible that Munch painted the tablecloth as though it were coagulated blood. The melancholy woman seems to have established some sort of contact with the flower but not with the reality outside. Munch later executed several graphic versions of the motif and also a painted version.

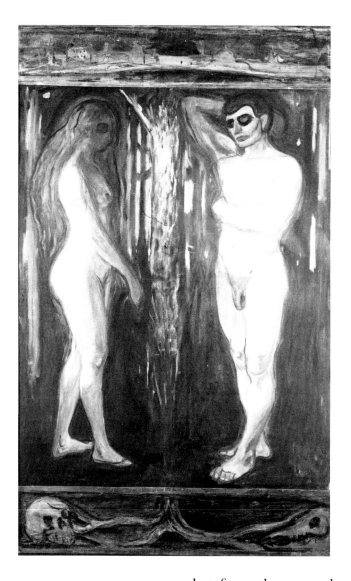

Metabolism 1899 (cat. no. 46)
Oil on canvas
172 x 143 cm   OKK M 419
Munch-Museet, Oslo

In its original form, the picture had another icono-graphic content. Up from the roots in the frame grew a small bush or large flower with a small em-bryo inside. The woman's hand pointed toward the embryo and almost touched it. The leaves of the bush or flower formed a modest cover over the man's penis. A photograph from 1903 shows how centrally the motif was placed in the "Life Frieze," and we see that the upper part of the frame which depicts Christiania, was not yet completed. In his pamphlet *The Life Frieze*, Munch later expressed that he found the picture as necessary for the frieze as a buckle for a belt, even though it deviated some-what from the general content. The picture was probably overpainted in connection with Munch's plans for a monumental execution of the "Life Frieze" motifs. A tree trunk between the man and the woman was added, which covers the bush or flower with the embryo. In this way, he joined the picture to the other monumental "Life Frieze" motifs, without respect for the picture as a historical document. The naked red-haired woman bears a clear resemblance to Tulla Larsen, Munch's fiancée from the turn of the century, and it is reasonable to think of the motif as a comment on their relation-ship. She wanted to get married and have children, but he hesitated. The picture was originally a part of an eschatology of metabolism, but this aspect is almost gone in the final version. The frame around the picture was probably removed by Munch him-self when he overpainted the picture in 1918 and was not put back again until a later exhibition in the Munch Museum.

Ashes   1894 (cat. no. 47)
Oil and tempera on canvas
120.5 x 141 cm
Nasjonalgalleriet, Oslo

A man with an ash-gray face, holding one hand to his head, is huddled on a beach. In sharp contrast stands a sensuous woman; the front of her dress is open, revealing a striking red undergarment. The man seems to be turning away from her. The tension between the two is echoed in the landscape elements. The columnlike shape of the woman is repeated in the tree trunks, while the broken-down figure of the man becomes a part of the shoreline. On close examination it becomes clear that the log has partly turned to ashes, and the man is staring into the smoke which rises from the log, spreading throughout the air like psychic waves.

The tension in the situation is both existential and sexual. An interpretation which corresponds with Munch's other "Life Frieze" motifs is that the man in the picture has failed to curb his desire for the woman, even though his love for her is dead. In the final revision of his "Life Frieze" in 1902, Munch hung this painting in a central position, using it to introduce a group of paintings about the flowering and passing of love. He called it *After the Fall*, meaning that the period of love in Paradise had ended.

The 1896 lithographic version, in which the log is reduced to a pile of ashes, supports this interpretation. In "The Tree of Knowledge" Munch wrote a brief commentary on the motif: "I felt our love lying on the ground like a heap of ashes."

Train Smoke   1900 (cat. no. 48)
Oil on canvas
84 x 109 cm   OKK M 1092
Munch-Museet, Oslo

The picture shows the view from Munch's rooms at Hammer's Boarding House in Ljan, overlooking the Oslo fjord, with islands, sailboats, and heavy gray rain clouds. The middle ground is filled with smoke from a train on its way toward Christiania. Twisted pine trees form ornamental figures in the foreground and correlate rhythmically with the train smoke and the spruce trees in the background. The sea and the sky are painted in the same grayish violet. In depicting the clouds, Munch returned to a technique with which he had experimented in the first version of *The Sick Child* from 1886. He let part of the color run in a controlled way in the sky to form a pattern, probably to indicate the onset of

rainy weather. In *Train Smoke* there is, furthermore, a built-in contrast between the ornamental elements in the foreground and the naturalistic character of the background. Munch later painted another version of the motif.

The Red Vine   1900 (cat. no. 50)
Oil on canvas
119.5 x 121 cm   OKK M 503
Munch-Museet, Oslo

The picture shows a tendency toward the use of stronger color which characterized Munch's art at the turn of the century. At the Berlin Secession in 1902, Munch included the painting in the group of angst pictures, so it must be included among the original "Life Frieze" motifs. The man in the foreground has features resembling Stanislaw Przybys-

zewski, while the house in the background must be the Kiøsterud building, which we recognize from so many of Munch's motifs from Åsgårdstrand. The red ivy appears to be not merely organically but also biologically alive. It grows up around the house like beings in a macabre dance. In contrast to the ivy, the house itself gives the impression of being an empty, blown shell. The windows have the same function as those in *Evening on Karl Johan Street* and *The Storm*, in that they are also "eyes" that draw our eyes toward them. It is as though the house contains a tragedy that the man in the foreground has in his mind's eye. The bare tree trunk with its cut-off stump to the left of the house suggests images of death. The picture has been interpreted as a version of *Jealousy*. Munch again used this pictorial structure in the paintings *The Murderer* from 1910 and *The Murderer in the Avenue* from 1919.

Girls on the Pier   1900 (cat. no. 49)
Oil on canvas
136 x 125.5 cm
Nasjonalgalleriet, Oslo
Gift of Olaf Schou

The picture is among Munch's most harmonious and lyrical motifs. Its original title was *Summer Night,* and we see, indeed, the sun shining over the houses to the left. On the bridge that leads out to the steamship pier at Åsgårdstrand, some girls stand staring down into the water where the tree is reflected. The tree and the shadow can be seen as a phallic symbol, and this explains the girls' sensations. It is again a matter of a puberty motif, crystallized in the fine erotic charge of the summer night. The delicate, French-inspired coloring of the picture is livened up by the yellow full moon and the white, green, and red dresses of the girls. From this popular motif, Munch executed a series of painted versions, and he made several prints—among others, one which is a combination lithograph and woodcut.

Winter Night   1901 (cat. no. 51)
Oil on canvas
115.5 x 110.5 cm
Nasjonalgalleriet, Oslo

The picture was painted in Ljan, outside Christi-ania, with the fjord as a background. At the turn of the century, Munch painted a series of winter land-scapes on a monumental scale and with distinctive musical qualities. A formal, rhythmic main element lies in the interplay between the pointed, jagged forms of the spruce trees and the joined tops of the pine trees in the foreground. The use of the large organic forms and the large surfaces and shadows renders a feeling of space and gives the picture its distinctive art nouveau quality. The basis for this is a desire to decorate, which possibly reflects Munch's wish to execute monumental room decorations.

Summer Night in Åsgårdstrand   1904
(cat. no. 52)
Oil on canvas
99 x 103.5 cm
Private Collection

Death of Marat   1905/08 (cat. no. 53)
Oil on canvas
150 x 199.5 cm   OKK M 351
Munch-Museet, Oslo

The motif is again the group of trees outside the Kiøsterud building in Åsgårdstrand. The bold manner of painting, the forceful formulation of space, and the vitality with which the picture is painted show that this is not a repetition of the mood in the pictures from the 1890s but a testing of new artistic means on an old, known motif. It is in pictures like this one that Munch sought a more powerful expression in his art. Around 1905, Munch developed a more intensely articulated coloring, and his themes ran parallel to and, in part, anticipated, those of the fauves.

While breaking off his unhappy engagement to Tulla Larsen in 1902, Munch happened to shoot himself in the hand with a small revolver. As a consequence, he later developed a hatred toward this woman, and he believed, as time went by, that all his nervous afflictions were caused by her. In the picture, Munch depicted himself as a sacrificed Christ lying on a bed which projects into the picture at an angle. The woman is standing full face, rigid as a statue. The picture expresses a hatred, as well as an insurmountable desire, for a contact that cannot be fulfilled. All the pictorial elements can be explained by Munch's own literary fragments. The blood on

the bed is from the shot in the hand. On the table stands the fruit that Tulla Larsen was in the process of serving before the tension between them was released, and on the table lies one of her impressive hats. Munch later said that he had been painting still lifes with fruits as capably as Cézanne, the only difference being that he, at the same time, portrayed a murderess with her victim. Munch did indeed entitle the first version of the motif *Still Life*. The painting was probably started in 1905, but the powerfully painted sections, especially in the table to the left, must have been executed in 1907, when Munch was in Warnemünde and developed this distinctive,

fauve-inspired technique. The strong emotional charge of the picture makes it seem probable that Munch was experimenting precisely with this technique while working on *Death of Marat*. Besides a series of painted editions and versions of the same motif, Munch also executed a lithograph. He built up several picture series around the motif, for example, "The Green Room," "The Tale of Suffering 1902-09" and "The City of Free Love." In several novel fragments which go back to the relationship between Tulla Larsen and himself, he also commented on the event.

Men Bathing   1907 (cat. no. 54)
Oil on canvas
206 x 227 cm
The Art Museum of the Ateneum,
Antell Collection, Helsinki

Men Bathing was painted during the summer of 1907 at the summer resort Warnemünde, not far from Rostock on the Baltic. Here Munch set up his canvases on the beach and, himself in the nude, painted naked men in dazzling sunlight. Munch documented the work with a series of photographs, probably taken with a self-timing camera. The photographs show how he, like a stage manager in a theater, demonstrated the poses to his models with his own body. The painting was probably intended for either Das Grossherzogliche Schlossmuseum in Weimar, where precisely such bathing motifs were collected, or for Ernst Thiel's art collection in Stockholm. Even without any formal commission, such intentions would explain why Munch used a monumental format. Later on, Munch added two side panels with bathing boys and bathing old men, and finally tentatively added two more sections, with younger boys and older men. By converting the motif to a triptych or a five-paneled version, respectively, Munch emphasized the quasi-sacred element in the motif. In 1908 he tried to exhibit the center panel at Commeter's in Hamburg, but the gallery did not dare show the painting for fear of being reported to the police. Technically, the picture means a further development in the manner of painting seen in *Amor and Psyche* and others. The powerful manner in which the picture is painted conveys an added element of vitality. The motif—the men who come toward us after swimming, naked and in full daylight—must be interpreted as a hymn to manhood. When Munch painted the picture, he was desperately seeking health and strength, in order not to collapse under the pressure of frayed nerves and a completely uncontrolled consumption of alcohol.

Amor and Psyche   1907 (cat. no. 55)
Oil on canvas
119.5 x 99 cm   OKK M 48
Munch-Museet, Oslo

Amor and Psyche was painted in Warnemünde in 1907, while Munch was under intense psychic strain and was experimenting to find new directions in his art. It was natural for Munch now to define his unique character in relation to French fauvism, as well as to the young German Die Brücke group. He expressed himself in a vital and aggressive way on the canvas by means of nearly meter-long horizontal or vertical brushstrokes. The theme—the woman who betrays the man—is a leitmotif in Munch's art.

Amor and Psyche is, however, far more lyrical than the version of *Death of Marat* executed in the same style. The theme is taken from that passage in Apuleius' story where Psyche leaves Amor after having betrayed him on the advice of evil sisters. It is the sunlight that separates the two. Her statuesque figure stands bathed in light, while he forms a shadow in the back-lit scene. The biographical background for this theme is the same as for *Death of Marat*, namely, the breaking off of his engagement with Tulla Larsen in 1902. In the deepest sense, the theme is a variation of *The Lonely Ones* and depicts two human beings who perhaps want to but cannot find their way to one another. In the 1920s, Munch again took up the theme in connection with his monumental "Life Frieze" studies.

Springtime Work in the Skerries   1910
(cat. no. 56)
Oil on canvas
93 x 117 cm   OKK M 411
Munch-Museet, Oslo

The motif is taken from the archipelago outside Kragerø, and it portrays two people who are cultivating a small piece of land. They are seen as a barely separate part of a meager but friendly nature. In the picture Munch used the same artistic means that he developed in Warnemünde, but without any particular trace of the nervousness that characterizes the works from there. He had returned from an eight-month stay at Dr. Jacobson's clinic in Copenhagen and was seeking lonely places along the coast where he could develop a new positive approach to his art. Munch also executed a somewhat dryer statement of the picture, from a coloristic point of view, as well as an etching.

Galloping Horse   1910/12 (cat. no. 57)
Oil on canvas
148 x 120 cm   OKK M 541
Munch-Museet, Oslo

The picture was painted in Kragerø, and the model was a white horse which Munch owned. Munch was at this time mainly occupied with studies for the decoration of the University Aula, and through this work, he developed a new free and bold handling of the brush. The main motif is the dynamic nature of the horse. It bursts forth through the snow, sweeps the minor figures to the side, and races with tremendous force out toward the spectator. The illusion of movement is achieved by means of exaggerated foreshortening, and the impression that the horse cannot be stopped is strengthened by means of the head thrown to one side. The horse is like an unrestrainable monster of brute strength that can barely be controlled by the man on the sled. With reference to Plato's well-known image of the soul, the motif can be interpreted as a self-portrait where the artist lets his own vitality dominate the controlling elements. Italian futurism, as well as film, cultivated similar effects of movement. Munch later executed the motif in a large etching.

The Yellow Log   1912 (cat. no. 58)
Oil on canvas
130 x 159 cm   OKK M 393
Munch-Museet, Oslo

Parallel to the studies for the decorations of the University Aula in Oslo, Munch developed a landscape style of monumental character, with motifs from the archipelago and forests outside Kragerø. A group of such pictures, painted in the winter of 1912, all have cut-down logs as the main subject. In one picture, a lumberjack stands by the cut log. It is otherwise the full-grown, cultivated forest that interests Munch, especially when it bears the mark of human activity. *The Yellow Log* is an example of how Munch varied the use of exaggerated perspective to achieve new goals in his art. If we follow the movement of the weather-beaten log into the picture space, the eye is drawn in to a tree in the far background. By this means, Munch managed to transmit visual dynamics into the forest itself. In the picture, the artist betrays the intention of wresting large constructive forces from nature. Death becomes identical with harvesting as a condition for the continued interaction of life and work.

Winter Landscape   1915 (cat. no. 59)
Oil on canvas
145 x 177 cm
Mrs. Heddy Astrup

During the period 1909-1915 Munch created a series of monumental pictures of scenes from the surroundings of "Scrubben" (the wolf), the property which he rented at Kragerø. He was not interested in the idyllic Kragerø summer landscape but concentrated on the seasons when nature appeared unapproachable and rejecting, but also proud and forceful. In these winter scenes Munch utilized pure white in a bold way. the open blue water, stones, and bushes that were not covered by snow were refreshing spots of color. Paintings like this were especially responsible for creating the "Munch complex" among contemporary Norwegian painters. Although many tried, only he could, with quick and sure strokes, distribute the colors exactly where they had to be to depict a faithful reflection of nature.

The Model by a Wicker Chair   1919/21
(cat. no. 60)
Oil on canvas
122.5 x 100 cm   OKK M 499
Munch-Museet, Oslo

The picture belongs to a group of motifs that depicts the artist and one of his models. The pictures were probably not exhibited during Munch's lifetime be-cause of their private character. In this group of motifs, Munch as an older man analyzed himself in his life together with one of his models. It may be an imagined or a real life together. Munch developed here a new form of picture space, with people in an interior. The rooms are crowded with objects, but they successively open up toward new rooms. Fur-thermore, the interiors burst with colors and clearly contrast with Munch's earlier preference for closed, bare rooms. In the new spatial articulations, there

are, psychologically speaking, unlimited possibilities of escaping, either by preoccupation with the objects or by letting the eyes drift out through the available openings. In these pictures, Munch commented on surrealism as a stylistic movement. In *The Model by a Wicker Chair,* the artist himself is not depicted. The model is posing alone, nude in front of the chair, with bowed head and an arched back, and with her arms hanging down by her side, in a slack attitude. There is something natural and trustworthy in the figure of the woman, while she simultaneously is strangely distant and inaccessible. The powerful use of color makes this picture a rare pearl from these late years.

The Wave   1921 (cat. no. 61)
Oil on canvas
100 x 120 cm   OKK M 558
Munch-Museet, Oslo

We overlook the beach on Munch's property, Nedre Ramme at Hvitsten, which he bought in 1911. It was here that he painted *Alma Mater* for the University Aula, while *History* and *Sun* depict nature at Kragerø. Most of the motifs that Munch painted in Hvitsten are bathing themes with groups of men or women on the cliffs of his property. It was only rarely that Munch painted pure landscapes like *The Wave* from this place. The first version of *The Wave* was painted in 1919, and the version in the Munch Museum is a later repetition. It is typical of the versions of the motifs from Hvitsten that they are far more fluid in their articulation than the originals, which are most often painted out-of-doors and generally with paint taken directly from the tube. From the point of view of color, the subsequent versions are often more exciting than the originals. The motif is taken from a small beach, but it gives the impression of depicting a long coastline. This is evidence of Munch's urge to give monumental dimensions and an eternal quality to his immediate surroundings.

Starry Night   1922/1924 (cat. no. 62)
Oil on canvas
120.5 x 100 cm   OKK M 32
Munch-Museet, Oslo

During a short period from 1922 to 1924, Munch painted a group of winter night pictures in predominantly blue tones, showing the view from his house at Ekely outside Christiania. Most of the pictures are characterized by peace, harmony, and stability. The foreground is usually occupied by tall human shadows. In a couple of the pictures, the human beings are placed together with the shadows. In this way, Munch conveyed an irrational and dreamlike impression. In some instances, the shadow cannot be explained by any given lighting. In *Starry Night,* the shadows are, however, explained by the fact that an intense light from indoors falls out across the snow in the mid-ground. Over the town in the background lies a yellow sea of light which meets the blue of the sky in a violet stripe. In terms of lighting, there is also something happening throughout the entire depth of the picture. During the time that Munch was painting these winter night pictures from Ekely, he must have worked on the illustrations to Henrik Ibsen's play *John Gabriel Borkman.* It may be argued that the shadows in *Starry Night,* among other things, "belong to" *John Gabriel Borkman,* and that the scene is the final one of the play, right before he goes out into the snow to die. The picture may at the same time be seen as a landscape portrait in which the artist is present through his own shadow.

Translated from the Norwegian by Solfrid Johansen

Model Undressing, c. 1925, OKK T 2464, Munch-Museet, Oslo

The Aging Munch: New Creative Power

Ragna Stang

THE YOUNG GENIUS EDVARD MUNCH seemed predestined to die at an early age. He was himself convinced that this would happen. In the 1880s and 1890s, he repeatedly used the death motif with almost monomaniacal interest. When he was thirty-two years old, in one of his earliest lithographs, he put a skeleton arm under his self-portrait in which his pale features stand out with visionary strength against the velvety black background (cat. no. 120). He added name and year in a matter-of-fact way, as though the self-portrait was supposed to be his own epitaph or a memento mori. A series of writings by the young Munch clearly shows that he envisioned that death would soon overtake him. But his fate was to take a different turn. This foremost painter of death and melancholy was to become, in Norwegian art, the interpreter of the powers of life itself, from the time he was at the peak of his creative powers until he died in the occupied Norway of 1944, at the age of eighty.

The young Munch lived a restless and tumultuous existence. He roamed about the continent and held numerous exhibitions. He lived in shabby hotels and run-down boarding houses, which were for years his only studios. His strength and health deteriorated. He participated intensely in artistic circles both at home in Norway and in Paris and Berlin and made friends with many artists who were at the center of the controversies of the day. Both pictorial and literary artists offered him inspiration. He took a stand on the issues of his time, as an artist and as a man. During this time, his art was self-searching and introverted. But in 1909, at the age of forty-six, he returned to Norway and withdrew from contact with most of his friends. He became "the lonely one," a vital and realistic painter. His art became extroverted, even though he continued to use certain old motifs, working them out further.

The primary purpose of his art had been to ex-plain life to himself, but, as he himself said, "I also want to teach others to make life clearer to themselves." The lonely, old Munch also wanted to reach people. He withdrew, but not to an ivory tower. The aging Munch loved life more intensely than at any time before and gave the clearest expression of this in his vital art. Munch had gone through a series of periods, from naturalism via impressionism and symbolism to become one of the fathers of expressionism. In fact, Munch was the only artist in Scandinavia who had any significant impact on the development of world art. Each period developed organically from the previous one. One can almost hear Munch's protest against being placed in the various schools of art. He despised all talk of "isms." "There are no 'styles.' It is the wrong word. There are only tasks." He felt it was a constraint to commit himself to a certain style, "like nailing oneself to the wall." To define Munch's art by means of stylistic analysis—no matter how brilliant and "correct"— perhaps serves a purpose for the art historian, and it may be useful to clarify the chronology. But such a classification does not actually lead to any deeper understanding of his art nor to an appreciation of his actual artistic significance.

Munch wanted something different, something more than to reach certain artistic goals. The important thing was to reach people and tell them something significant about themselves. He therefore sometimes allowed the passion and intensity in the expression to take over to such an extent that it affected the artistic composition. At least in his youth, he felt himself to be a preacher and a prophet, who had to get his message across to people by any means. "All means are equally valid," he said himself. To be able to carry out his ambitious program, "to paint pictures from the modern psyche," he had to immerse himself in his thoughts, build on his own experience, sense intuitively what

fig. 1 *The Empty Cross*, 1897/1899, OKK T 2452, Munch-Museet, Oslo

he might not have been consciously aware of, and then recreate what he had experienced—primarily what he had seen. "I do not paint what I see, but what I saw." One may wonder whether a significant reason for his unusual ability to renew himself was not precisely his incredible visual memory, perhaps a family trait. His admired uncle, the highly gifted historian P. A. Munch, was supposed to have had a remarkably strong visual memory. But Edvard Munch emphasized that "nature is not all that is visible to the eye—it is also the inner pictures of the soul—pictures behind the eye." When he recreated the memory of his mother's death, which occurred when he was five years old, or that of his beloved sister Sophie, it is precisely the pictures of the inner eye that he communicates to us. And when he sat in some hotel room far from Norway, he could recreate the beach in his beloved Åsgårdstrand and relive the fair Norwegian summer night.

He admitted that in spite of nature being the large realm from which art takes its nourishment, it confused him, and he needed to keep it somewhat at a distance. "One has to paint it out from oneself." Some of Munch's strength emanated from the fact that he always stayed in touch with reality, even though he transformed nature. Through his manifold phases, where he experimented with abstract-

ing, or "crystallizing," as he himself called it, he always preserved this contact. And it was practically always a concrete visual image that formed the basis for what he created.

Around the turn of the century, a significant change took place in Munch's choice of motifs and also in his pictorial idiom. One of the main works from his youth, *Spring* (1889), was his break with impressionism and realism. In *Dance of Life* (1899-1900), we may say that he parted with symbolism. He painted himself dancing between two women, a young one and an old one (even though the model was the same for both). Around him, other wanton, dancing couples are whirling about. In the pictures that follow, it is as though he no longer wanted to participate in the witch dance of life. In a series of drawings from 1901 entitled *The Empty Cross* (fig. 1), we recognize him in the monklike figure. (Munch—monk is a word relationship that the artist frequently hints at.) The figure turns away from the loving couples who wallow in their intoxicated state or drown in the swamp at the foot of the steep slope. "It was me here. A blood-red sun shines over the whole scene, and the cross is empty." It was clearly a reckoning with the past and with previous friends. The catastrophe with the pistol shot and the break-up with Tulla Larsen, the woman who is said to have

fig. 2   *Fertility*, 1898, Private Collection

meant much to him occurred the following year.

But the struggle to free himself from his past cost him dearly. He was, as he himself put it, entering into "the most unhappy, but fullest decade" of his life. He went through a serious mental crisis and expressed a fear of going mad. He clearly realized that he showed signs of being ill. His mental split manifested itself strongly in his art. From 1900 until the final collapse (1907-1908), he painted two kinds of pictures simultaneously. On the one hand, he seemed consciously to detach himself more from his motifs than earlier. He became the observer and chose motifs not concerned primarily with Munch the soul searcher, but rather with Munch the *painter*. In certain works, he obtained a realistic harmony unknown in his earlier works, but which is reflected in some magnificent Norwegian landscapes and also in some characteristic portraits from this period. We can witness how this nervous, unstable man, through struggle and crisis, entered into a calmer and artistically fruitful new period. His weapon in the struggle against the menacing illness was precisely his art, which he used very consciously.

On the other hand, especially during the time in Warnemünde and Berlin, he painted a series of pictures that is not very well known. Here Munch the painter mercilessly exposed the human being.

The titles tell a lot: *Lust, Hate, Jealousy.* But most significantly, he painted the subject of the self-righteous woman and the slain man, which he called *Death of Marat* (cat. no. 53). It is he himself lying there, a victim of the woman's vindictiveness. It is as though Munch had to reach the depths of his own psyche to find out what deep and sinister powers held him in their grip. He had earlier told the world about dangerous powers, but at the same time about positive forces—longing, tenderness, devotion. The purpose of the merciless self-scrutiny was probably to survive the crisis that he felt approaching. And he got through it.

Let us look at some of his main works from the period 1900-1908, before he committed himself to the psychiatric clinic in Copenhagen. As a temporary completion of the "Life Frieze" (which, by the way, he worked on until his late years), there is the large picture *Fertility* (fig. 2). There is a monumental quality to this picture which is more pronounced than in any of the earlier ones. This is also a symbolic picture, with the pregnant woman who brings the yield of the soil to the man beneath the tree of life. But the symbolism is not obtrusive, and the mood is far more affirmative of life than in earlier works. The picture has a material, physical richness in the coloring, and it clearly shows joy by the free, broad brushstrokes. The mature Munch now needed to see life, not from the perspective of death, but from a broader point of view. He became more of an observer, but his goal was the same: to communicate his message to others.

In the last part of the nineties, he had worked with a new medium through which to reach a broader public: graphic arts. He continued in the new century to create graphic prints to accompany the paintings. In several of these prints he obtained an even clearer precision and stronger expressive quality than in the painting of the same motif. The painter learned from the graphic artist and the graphic artist from the painter. Moreover, Munch the painter achieved a greater simplicity and monumentality in his painting through his work with lithography.

A main work from the turn of the century is *Girls on the Pier* (cat. no. 49). It turned out to be a fruitful motif which he repeated twelve times in all, as a painting, etching, woodcut, and lithograph. Even in the first version, Munch had found a sure and harmonious composition. The glance is caught by the diagonal railing which continues in the rose-colored road and leads us into the picture. The artist often used such diagonal railings to capture us, indeed, to force us into his world. But in certain pictures, the diagonal races toward us with such force that Munch used it as a means to scare us out of the picture as in *The Scream*, for instance. But in *Girls on the Pier*, we are carefully led into the picture and willingly allow ourselves to be captured by its soft mood. The white, grand house rests in quiet solidity in the summer night. Munch had earlier often used both landscapes and houses to render a mood, and he often used both this particular house and similar ones to create anxiety. But here the house expresses a peace that is underscored by the huge, domed tree. The silhouette resounds deeper in the quiet surface of the water, and the white garden wall that runs parallel to the line of the beach brings balance to the entire composition. There is nothing frightening about the mystical quality of the tree. It merely emphasizes what the small, pale yellow moon tells us: it is a fair, Nordic summer night. With the muted rose, deep green, and blue hues, Munch struck a lyrical tone. But the girls' green, red, and white dresses break into this harmony with a liberating flourish. It was bold but instinctively correct since the clearly defined triad increases the tension without breaking the harmony. "Liebermann considers it my best picture," Munch wrote home to a Norwegian professor in 1902. And he himself was evidently satisfied and felt that this motif could be further expanded. In 1902 he replaced the three

fig. 3   *Women on the Bridge*, 1903, Thiel Gallery, Stockholm

girls with five women. The mood of the summer night was changed to that of sun-filled daylight, but it is still the bridge, the people, and the houses on this particular place in Åsgårdstrand that form the motif. Now we see several houses and find ourselves on the middle of the bridge. Toward us comes Munch's friend from his youth, the woman painter Åse Nørregård. It is a pure portrait and gives this version of the motif a completely different realistic articulation, emphasized by the far more powerful and gay coloring.

About the same time, Munch painted the large summer picture which once was owned by Dr. Linde and which today hangs in the Thiel Gallery in Stockholm (fig. 3). Here Munch composed the group of women in a severe, pyramidal form, in luminous blue, white, and yellow colors. They stand in sharp contrast to the black row of men who are turning their backs to them, untouched by their lively charm, and who stare out over the water, lacking contact. The pyramidal form in the foreground and the row of severe, cubist houses in the background give the picture a taut strength which signals something new in Munch's artistic expression. This motif from 1903 was carried to its utmost articulation a generation later, when Munch painted the last and twelfth version of the motif (fig. 4). Whether the powerful fauve coloring was influenced by Matisse, with whom he several times exhibited, or whether it was related to the fact that in 1930 Munch suffered an eye disease (supposedly affecting the optic nerve), nobody knows with certainty.

During this unhappy but productive time, Dr.

fig. 4   *Women on the Bridge,* 1935, OKK M 30, Munch-Museet, Oslo

Max Linde in Lübeck was one of Munch's many German patrons, as was Judge Gustav Schiefler. Schiefler wrote what might be considered the most useful book about Munch: the catalogue to his lithographic works up to 1926. Munch was very nervous and upset during this time. For several years, Munch had, as Schiefler put it, "invested himself in his art in a *tempo furioso,* with little attention to time, place and exterior conditions." In the two highly cultivated homes in Lübeck and Hamburg, he found people who wanted the best for him and tried to help him against "the alcohol devil" that was increasingly gaining power over him. It was not only refuge and consolation he sought in these homes. He also got important commissions. For a while it appeared as though Dr. Linde had in mind to find a place for at least part of "The Life Frieze." Munch's dream of finding a place for this main work of his was, however, reduced to a commission to decorate the house's nursery. Even this did not work out. Linde did not want all of Munch's "liebende und küssende Menschen. Das Kind weiss noch nichts davon" (loving and kissing people. Children shouldn't know about these things), and he refused the frieze that Munch had painted. Munch's disappointment was enormous. When the great dramatic artist Max Reinhardt gave him the commission to decorate the newly formed theater *Kammerspiele* in Berlin, he accepted with enthusiasm. But it became difficult for him to complete it. "He continued to be a riddle to us," said one of Reinhardt's fellow workers. "He works in the daytime and drinks at night." "The frieze was about to destroy me," Munch wrote

home. He did complete it, but it was later scattered.

He received several other large commissions during this time. "My fame is going away like a snow plough," he said. And in 1907, right before his nervous breakdown, he wrote: "My fame is on the rise. But it has very little to do with my happiness." His suspicious attitude toward his countrymen and some of his old friends grew to border on paranoia, and his roaming life made him rootless and created a painful longing for home. "I feel as though I am losing my country foot by foot." The contact with his home country consisted of his summer visits to the small house that he owned in Åsgårdstrand. He also spent the winter of 1900-1901 in Norway, living in a boarding house right outside Oslo. Here he painted some landscapes that reveal a more immediate feeling for nature than earlier. Previously, the landscape was for Munch more a conveyer of human psychic experiences than an expression of a powerful natural experience. At this stage, however, he sought the Norwegian nature directly, without intending to use it as a background for his soul paintings. In *Winter Night* (cat. no. 51), the dark blue spruce and pine trees stand out against the moonlit, blue snow and create a bewitching mood. The jagged silhouette of the spruce forest in the distance separates sharply and clearly the large, frozen surface of the fjord in the background from the gnarled and troll-like trees in the foreground. Three solitary stars shine dimly in the winter night. In spite of monumental simplification, sharp silhouette effect, and precise rendering of what he sees, or, to be more exact, what he has seen, Munch managed to endow his painting with an almost cosmic feeling. This is increasingly articulated in his intensely experienced landscapes from the turn of the century.

Munch did not go to Åsgårdstrand in the summer of 1907 but rented a small house in Warnemünde—"A German Åsgårdstrand" as he called this small, quiet resort town by the Baltic Sea. Here he spent some quiet and productive months. He still brooded over his personal difficulties and problems, but at the same time consciously sought out new motifs and—what is more important—he was in constant search of new, artistic means of expression. He depicted the small town of Warnemünde with its narrow alleys and cobblestones using broad strokes reminiscent of van Gogh. When he painted Lübeck harbor with its great, medieval gate, he used brilliant coloring and broad brush technique, strongly reminiscent of artistic effects used by a school of Matisse students, the fauves, at this time. Pictures like these were going to mean a great deal to the young German expressionists.

We find a new vitalism expressed in Munch's large, so-called "Bathing Triptych." It is a grandiose counterpart to his *Woman in Three Stages* done ten years before and originally titled *The Sphinx*. It tells us that Munch wanted to express the mysterious qualities in woman; a woman who at the same time is nun, whore, and hopelessly devoted. It is a typical fin de siècle picture. His depiction of men in three stages, on the other hand, belongs to the twentieth century. It is a hymn to healthy, vigorous man. There is no mysticism in this picture painted under a flood of sun at the nudist beach of Warnemünde. It is as if the sick Munch wanted to offer a hymn to the joy and vitality of life, particularly in the large, center panel where muscular men in the full power of their manhood purposefully stride toward us (cat. no. 54). He had seen these men as they stepped out of the ocean and put the impression on canvas. The completely frontal, vertical figures break all the horizontal lines in the almost skyless landscape. There is no attempt to subordinate man to nature here or to let the melodious, soft play of the lines beguile us. The symbolic message of the picture rests entirely on its pictorial theme. In the flood of sun above the beach, a man comes toward us after a renewing swim, while the youth in the panel to the left meets us in a more hesitating posture; but even he has both his feet securely planted on the ground. The very old man in the right panel, with his crossed arms, is filled with the calm of old age. He appears to interest the painter least. Nor does the pictorial articulation have the same vibrating and intense quality as in the two other panels. In these, Munch experimented with some strangely slanted brushstrokes in the first version (Helsinki 1905); the strokes increase the impression of vibrating sunlight above the sky and the ocean surface. Munch had previously painted several pictures with boys bathing. He had also celebrated woman and the female body in his art but had paid only scant attention to naked men. Perhaps we may see this tribute to health and virility as a part of his battle against the threat of his impending illness.

Munch was very eager to learn about the reception of "my nearly last child—the bathing picture." He asked his friend Jappe Nilssen, whose judgment he trusted, to offer an opinion. Another friend, Schiefler, had tried unsuccessfully to include the picture at an exhibition in Hamburg in November 1907. In a letter to Munch, he offered the interesting observation that the jury did not dare exhibit the picture lest the police interfere. "One is no longer offended by naked women. One stands in front of them, in the company of other women, and converses about them. Naked men are still something

unfamiliar. Only if they are painted *à la* Matisse's ocean riders are they a 'main attraction.' In twenty years, we will laugh as much about this as we now laugh about the National Gallery's rejecting Böcklin's *Triton and Nereide* in 1873 as 'indecent'." Schiefler was of the opinion that Munch had never painted anything as powerful and admitted that the picture gave him "ein Rippenstoss" (a punch in the ribs). Munch kept grappling with the subject in related, large sketches, and also painted it in the subsequent versions now in the Munch museum.

As we have seen, Munch experimented a great deal during this period in his search for new painting techniques. In a letter from the 1930s, he commented on his style of the period: "In the beginning of the century I felt a need to break the surface. I felt it might turn into mannerism." He also made it clear why he tried to renew his art in three different ways. When he painted realistic pictures of the children in Warnemünde, he returned to some of the techniques from previous pictures, such as *Sick Child*, using horizontal and vertical lines. He wrote that he "painted a series of pictures with pronounced, broad, often meter-long lines or strokes which run vertically, horizontally, and diagonally. The surface was broken and a certain cubism showed its signs. . . . I chose another way out in pictures like *The Women on the Pier*, which was, as you say, a form of cubism. It was in the air."

We have seen an example of the latter. Let us now look more closely at two other important pictures from 1907: *Amor and Psyche* (cat. no. 55) and *Death of Marat* (cat. no. 53). Both take their motif from Munch's own past and deal with the intimate relationship between man and woman. In the first, he builds on the beautiful myth of Psyche who wants to know the true identity of the man she loves. She lights her lamp in order to see him. A drop from the oil lamp falls on him and awakens him. He must flee because their love was secret, but helps her so they may be reunited. Psyche is lifted up among the gods and becomes Eros' wife. Like countless other artists Munch was inspired by this simple and profound myth during this difficult period when he was trying to come to terms with the past. But there is none of the feeling of hate we find in his pictures of the green bordello room from the same period.

Munch replaced the oil lamp of the myth with a hidden light source placed between the two lovers; this source throws a clarified light over her rose-colored body, while the man, whose back we see, is painted in clear yellow, vivid red, dark brown, and velvet black strokes—precisely those broad, meter-long lines Munch wrote about. In contrast to the vertical lines are the black contours which, together with the vibrating light, model their bodies. The tragic dimension in this motif is not only Munch's own but a universal one, something which touches every man and woman sooner or later in life. It comes out in this way because it was painted in despair. But it is not a malicious or hateful portrayal. Rather, this bold, new vehicle of expression has given him the power to find a release which is totally lacking in his sterile "hate-pictures"—even if these too are painted in a freer idiom than before.

But in *Death of Marat*, the malicious context of the subject and the monomaniacal need to give vent to feelings of revenge have prevailed. Munch said about this picture: "It is not a main work—rather an experiment." But for that very reason it is interesting: the idiom is new and fresh and gives evidence of a conscious will to renewal. The composition within the almost square picture surface is strict. The tension between the horizontal plane and the taut, vertical pose of the woman is underscored by the painting style. She stands paralyzed before the corpse in a collected, statuelike, and self-righteous pose, painted exclusively in vertical strokes. The man who is placed at a slightly oblique angle, extending into the picture space, increases the tension between the horizontal and vertical lines which otherwise would have locked in the composition. His portrayal of Amor and Psyche must have represented a process of liberation for him, in purely human, as well as artistic terms. He also said that "it takes a long time to get one's strength back after this picture." But he was proud when it was hanging at the Salon des Indépendants in 1908.

We have seen how a crisis was in the making, and in the fall of 1908 Munch committed himself to a psychiatric clinic in Copenhagen after an uncontrollable binge "in the heaven of alcohol." The deeper, psychic crisis had, in fact, already come to a head when Munch made this decision. For this reason, his stay at the clinic did not represent an actual break in his development.

His change and renewal, as we have seen, had taken place before the nervous collapse. It is quite another matter that the enforced quiet and care during seven months did him some good. More important than any amount of medical care, however, was that his working capacity was undiminished. "I have always been true to the goddess of art, she is now true to me." His final, overdue acceptance in his native country coincided with the stay at the clinic. When he was made a Knight of The Order of St. Olav, he felt "as if a hand had been extended to me from my country." He began to think about returning home when his old friend Jens Thiis, in his new capacity as director of the

fig. 5 *Omega and the Swine*, 1908-1909, OKK G/1 316-5, Munch-Museet, Oslo

National Gallery, Oslo, forced through the purchase of five main works, under strong resistance from the press.

During his stay at the clinic, Munch painted brilliant portraits of his friends, enchanting pictures of children, and also portraits of his charming nurses. At the same time he created a lithographic series, "Alpha and Omega," in which he fought his last battle with the past and a negative view of women (fig. 5). The series bears witness to a malicious, rather naive, and very revealing philosophy of women. But his work on the series obviously had a healing influence on him: "A strange calm came over me while I was working on this series—it was as if all malice let go of me." Munch decided to return to Norway in the spring of 1909, after great hesitation. He rented a large mansion close to the little coastal town of Kragerø. A new epoch began, perhaps the happiest of his life. His countrymen finally began to celebrate this painter of European fame. But there were probably only a few among them who realized that they were paying homage to the old Munch. Now, a new Munch was about to emerge. No one knew better than he how dangerous stagnation is for an artist.

It was Munch's fortune—and Norway's—that a task as great as that of decorating the University Aula coincided with his move. Fourteen days after his release from the clinic, Munch signed up as a participant in the competition, which he won. But seven years were to pass—from 1909 to 1916—before he saw victory again. It was a hard battle. Munch was filled with a new fighting spirit, and one enormous canvas after the other was created in the many open-air studios he built to have enough room for the project.

fig. 6 *History*, 1915, The University Aula, Oslo

During the years since the 1890s, Munch had dreamed of decorating a great hall. It would perhaps have been natural for him now to want to build on his main work, "The Life Frieze." But the new Munch did not do that. On the contrary, he burned all bridges. He did not paint "a picture of the soul" and did not "interpret the separate individual's sorrows and joys at close range." Now he wanted to "paint the great, eternal powers," and he was equal to the task! He did not use traditional symbols, nor did he fall back on allegories, on ancient or Norse mythology, or history, which so many makers of monumental art had done before him. His stroke of genius was to paint the daily occurrences that he saw around him in the little coastal town of Kragerø. He painted the seaman Børre telling a little fellow about his life of fantastic adventure (fig. 6). They are under a large oak in an ice-blue landscape, and the marvelous thing is that Munch is able to lift the entire scene up from the level of the everyday. The Norwegian fjord landscape with islands and skerries is simplified in the classical manner, distant and timeless. The seaman reminds us of Homer, passing on his experiences to his grandchild. Experience itself becomes a symbol for science. The large canvases were unveiled in 1916 and have been a constant source of contagious joy for those visiting Oslo's most beautiful banquet hall.

Even while he was completing the enormous Aula canvases, Munch painted several large paintings with scenes from the life of workers. He had now become a painter of monumental art and probably had new monumental projects in mind when he plunged into the new motifs. There is really no obtrusive social comment in these pictures. Once more, it is his visual articulation which gives the pictures their strength. He had seen men shoveling snow (fig. 7) in the narrow alleys of Kragerø, others digging in the snow around the steaming asphalt pot, and other workers returning home from the factory. At times, some of these everyday scenes take on a deeper symbolic meaning as when the heavy, dark mass of workers moves slowly toward us like a force of nature. Did Munch want to tell us something more important than the fact that tired workers are returning home? Was this a new class on the march? We know nothing definite about Munch's political views. But we do know that throughout his life he kept a finger on the pulse of the times and that the many scenes from the life of workers were probably not done for casual reasons. A new dream had awakened in him: to decorate the new City Hall to be built in Oslo with scenes from workers' lives. But time ran out on him. When the building finally was completed, Munch was an old man.

In 1916 Munch bought the large property Ekely just outside Oslo. Here he spent the last twenty-eight years of his life in voluntary solitude—"after all, that is the essence of my being." Munch returned to several of the old life frieze motifs at Ekely. At the same time he painted both self-portraits and landscapes in which the color reached a high pitch of boldness.

He painted some winter night pictures at Ekely in which he managed to create a cosmic feeling of space (cat. no. 62). From his veranda, Munch caught

fig. 7 *Workers in Snow*, 1913/1914, OKK M 371, Munch-Museet, Oslo

the landscape in one glance. The perspective of the staircase leads into the picture with mystical shadows in the foreground—are they human shadows? Our eyes wander over the bluish white snow, shot through with rose-colored strokes, from one arched plane to the next, past the illuminated houses under the domed trees, in toward the illuminated city which glitters in the background, to stop by the far hill and finally to be lifted up into the sparkling, starry sky. The picture is filled with a biting coldness. It has been associated with Ibsen's play *John Gabriel Borkman,* a drama Munch is said to have referred to as the "best winter landscape in Norwegian art." It is hardly strange if the lonely Munch, wandering about the many, large rooms at Ekely, thinking back on his stormy life and his difficult relationship to women, may have felt a bitter kinship to Borkman.

He had isolated himself deliberately. The many rooms of the house were working rooms, with great numbers of pictures stacked along the walls and easels everywhere so he could move from picture to picture. He usually worked on several simultaneously. His palettes and brushes littered the rooms, along with stacks of thousands of prints which he neglected terribly. Several of his other "children," the paintings, were often hanging outside on trees, fluttering in the wind, or were exposed to the rain and snow of his open-air studio.

Edvard Munch was to experience having eighty-

two of his works declared decadent and thrown out of German museums. But he shared that fate with the best of his German colleagues and friends and no longer felt so lonely. In the self-portrait *Between the Clock and the Bed* (cat. no. 22), the old Munch depicted himself standing at rigid attention while waiting for death, a death he no longer feared. He is coming from the sunlit room behind him and has stopped. The clock without hands tells him that the hour has struck. His bed is waiting like a sarcophagus covered by the multicolored quilt from his childhood home—the only home he had ever known. His dream of seeing the war end and the Nazis defeated was never fulfilled. A week after Munch's eightieth birthday, Ekely shook because a German ammunition dump had exploded. The windows were shattered, and Munch contracted a bad case of bronchitis which finally killed him. In his last testament he left all his works to the City of Oslo, without conditions—a town which had not treated him well at all.

On January 23, 1944, Edvard Munch quietly moved to what he, with his pantheistic view of life, had called "The Land of Crystal." He envisioned that he would experience delight in passing back into earth, become one with it. For "from my decaying body there will grow flowers, and I shall be 'in' them."

Translated from the Norwegian by Solfrid Johansen

The Hands, c. 1893, OKK M 646, Munch-Museet, Oslo

Love as a Series of Paintings and a Matter of Life and Death

Edvard Munch in Berlin, 1892-1895
Epilogue, 1902

Reinhold Heller

THE YEAR 1893 WAS FOR EDVARD MUNCH one of the most productive and richly inventive of his entire lengthy career as a painter. Except for several summer months spent in Norway, he settled for the time in Berlin, attempting to obtain patrons in the economically prosperous German Empire in the aftermath of the publicity generated by the forced closing of his exhibition at the *Verein Berliner Künstler* (the Association of Berlin Artists) that occurred in November 1892.[1]

For reasons which shall certainly remain forever mysterious, in September 1892, an invitation was extended by the *Verein Berliner Künstler* to Munch, who precisely at that time was having his second one-man show in the Norwegian capital of Christiania. In a building owned by the noted jeweler Tostrup, immediately opposite the Neo-Romanesque structure of Norway's parliament, the *storting*, just off *Karl Johansgate*, the street serving Christiania's burghers for daily promenades, Munch displayed fifty paintings and ten drawings, all created during the previous two years while he was the recipient of national fellowships for study in France. The Tostrup Exhibition, for the twenty-eight-year-old painter, was a public pronouncement of the completion of his studies and of his self-recognition as a mature artist, cognizant of the developments in contemporary art, particularly of French impressionism, neo-impressionism, and the most recently proclaimed "ism," symbolism, a more appealing term for what only recently identified itself as decadence. Each of the various styles was imitated, mastered, and mirrored in various examples of Munch's work, along with the initial stirrings of a personal style and an overwhelming concern with subjective states of mind, the brooding psychology of the soul during moods of anxiety, sorrow, and melancholy. Christiania's uncomprehending and provincial critics found little to like in Munch's French-derived art and almost unanimously opined that he was "making fun of the public's taste."[2] It was this extraordinary and controversial exhibition that was seen by a representative of the *Verein Berliner Künstler's* exhibition committee, Adelsteen Normann, a Norwegian painter making a quite comfortable living by meeting the German public's seemingly insatiable demands for brown-tinged, brooding views of moonlit Norwegian fjords. Inexplicably, Normann immediately invited his radical young compatriot to bring the exhibition to Berlin, where paintings by Renoir were still being described as pictorial anarchism.

Munch arrived in Berlin during the second week of October 1892, and waited for his paintings to arrive. He was introduced by Normann to the *Verein Berliner Künstler* members, who remained ignorant of the true nature of his art, and otherwise busied himself with the sights of the German imperial capital until late in October. Then Munch himself hung his works in the rotunda of the neobaroque *Architektenhaus*, a converted beer hall serving the *Verein* as its meeting and exhibition place. A quick press release announced the paintings as *"Ibsen'sche Stimmungsbilder"*—Ibsen-like mood paintings—invoking the name of the Norwegian playwright whose dramas were being performed with massive acclaim throughout Europe and whose play *Bygmester Solness* (The Master Builder) had just been published and received much publicity. The much-heralded exhibition then opened to the public on Saturday, November 5. The resultant uproar was tremendous: in Frankfurt, a newspaper reported that in Berlin art itself was in mortal danger; Norway's self-righteous critics proudly reported on the "Munch fiasco" in Berlin; and the dean of German art critics observed that there was no reason for wasting one's breath on these paintings because "they have absolutely nothing to do with art."[3]

fig. 1   *Portrait of Stanislaw Przybyszewski,*
1894, OKK M 134,
Munch-Museet, Oslo

Shocked *Verein* members called for a special meeting on November 11, and after lengthy debate concerning Munch's rights as an invited guest, a vote of 120 to 105 determined that the exhibition should immediately be closed and the scandal-provoking paintings be ignobly removed from the *Architektenhaus*' domed Hall of Honor. In the process of this forced eviction, at least one of Munch's works was severely damaged.

Undaunted by these events, Munch wrote home that "the uproar here has been most amusing, and I could hardly have a better advertisement."[4] He was certainly correct. Even the greatest critical success in Berlin would not have transformed the unknown Norwegian painter into the *cause célèbre* and artistic curiosity he immediately became throughout Germany, spreading his name even to Paris, as a result of the events in the *Verein*. Seeking to profit from the publicity, Munch signed a contract with the gallery of Eduard Schulte, who sent the paintings for display to Cologne and Düsseldorf, where they again attracted large and noisy crowds; Munch used his advance on the entry fees to rent a hotel room as his studio in Berlin and prepared to bring his exhibition back there in December. Meanwhile, he was adopted into the circle of Scandinavian, Polish, and German writers and painters who regularly met at Herr Türke's wine cellar on the *Neue Wilhelmstrasse*. Instilling the *Weinstube* with its artistic and bohemian identity was a new name, *Zum schwarzen Ferkel* (At the Black Piglet), bestowed by the group's most vocal member, August Strindberg, who recognized the strange configuration in the form of an old, soot-covered wine sack hung over the entrance door.[5] In addition to the controversial misogynous Swedish playwright, whose portrait Munch quickly painted, the bohemian group included the Swedish novelist and essayist Ola Hansson, noted for his novella *Sensitiva Amorosa* treating various aspects of sexual love; Richard Dehmel, the German poet whose poem "My Creed" loudly proclaimed: "I was conceived during a wild night/and in the greatest ecstacy of passion!/And now I yearn to live only for passion,/just as passion conceived me";[6] and the Polish medical student and Satanist in the process of becoming a writer of novels saturated with the cele-

fig. 2   *Portrait of Hans Jæger*, 1889, Nasjonalgalleriet, Oslo

fig. 3   *Portrait of August Strindberg*, 1892, Nationalmuseum, Stockholm

bration of sensual experience, Stanislaw Przybyszewski (fig. 1).[7] The persistently repeated topic of conversation, shouted out through cigarette smoke and over the sound of Przybyszewski loudly playing Chopin sonatas on an old piano, was naturally the pathology and psychology of human passions. For Munch, it must have appeared as if time were doubling back on itself, repeating the atmosphere and discussions generated during the 1880s in the Kristiania Bohème by the anarchist author Hans Jæger (fig. 2) with his doctrine of free love; this ability to relive in 1893 at age twenty-nine the intellectual and, to a lesser degree, emotional experiences of age twenty significantly accounts for Munch's intense activity and the initiation of his painting series dealing with love and death.

On December 23, 1892, Munch's exhibition returned from its Rhineland journey and, expanded by the Strindberg portrait (fig. 3) as well as numerous drawings, reopened in Berlin, this time in the top-floor gallery rented by Munch himself at the *Equitable Palast*, a palatially ornate neobaroque structure housing fashionable shops at the busy and popular intersection of Berlin's major thoroughfares, *Unter den Linden* and the *Leipziger Strasse*. A large, heavy Norwegian flag was draped outside the building to attract attention, and critics again cooperated by publishing lengthy, violently negative reviews on the front pages of Berlin's newspapers, thereby rekindling interest in the Norwegian wild beast, who meanwhile had declared his intention to settle in the *Reichshauptstadt*. This exhibition was a success outside the press, bringing a total of 1,800 marks income from entry fees, covering all Munch's expenses and providing a slight profit. Three paintings were sold to significant patrons: Dr. Julius Elias, Ibsen's German translator; Arthur and Eugen von Franquet, two Braunschweig coffee magnates who had just written a vocal and impassioned defense of Germany's younger artists under the complex title *The Exhibition Rabble: Stuck, Klinger, von Hofmann etc.: "The Future Heroes of the Woodshed": Glosses on the Conflict of the Old and the Young;*[8] and Walter Rathenau, a young leader of Germany's industrial and monied elite who maintained magnificent visions of an egalitarian future without material worry, collected the art of Europe's younger painters, and, simultaneously, carefully restored the eighteenth-century manor house he had purchased outside Berlin. Likewise visiting the exhibition, but at this time seemingly unimpressed, was Count Harry Kessler, who was introduced to Munch later in the year and thereafter became another of his German patrons.[9]

The sale of his paintings and the exhibitions' *succès de scandale* generated in Munch a rare and overpowering mood of optimism as he sent his exhibition on to Copenhagen. With the paintings, he now also sent specific instructions as to how they should be hung, insisting that eight be singled out and be displayed together and distinctly.[10] Uniting these eight paintings was not subject matter, which ranged from landscape to genrelike interior scenes, but the ability of all the paintings to project a mood of melancholy and contemplative meditation, achieved largely through a dominance of somber tones of blue and green. A sympathetic critic, having been informed of Munch's aesthetic goals, observed that in Munch's works,

> . . . the motif has absolutely no value in and of itself; it ought to play [Munch] says, no more than a purely inspirational role for the artist. . . . Color is everything for him. It is not paintings with recognizable images that are born of his fantasy, but only coloristic moods. His art is its most personal when it consists of vague, melancholy dreams without a trace of materially graspable reality.[11]

The paintings isolated by Munch thus formed a unified group through their coloristic ability to engender a mood or *Stimmung* in the viewer without consideration of the specific motif depicted. The unity of mood was discovered by Munch after the paintings had been created, and bringing them together to form a unit was a willfull fusing of thematically disparate elements into a multi-imaged totality.

> When they were brought together, suddenly a single musical note went through them and they became completely different from what they had been. A symphony resulted. . . .

Munch later wrote and added, "It was in this manner that I began to paint friezes."[12] Seeing his paintings brought together in a single large interior at the various exhibitions in Christiania and Berlin from September 1892 through January 1893 made Munch aware of the emotional identity attained by much of his art, causing him in his exhibitions to divorce images wed to each other through an identical mood from images possessing jarringly disparate emotive content. And in the effusive optimism of the winter months of 1893 as the paintings returned from Copenhagen and went on to Breslau, Dresden, and Munich, Munch determined to exploit the innate serial character of his imagery and to create a number of deliberately thematically interrelated paintings. "At the moment," he wrote to the Danish painter Johan Rohde early in March, "I am busy with studies for a series of paintings. . . . It will have love and death as its subject matter."[13] With these grand themes in mind, Munch set to work in the confines of his hotel room to create a grandiose series of paintings that would embody his personal views on the procreative powers of life and simultaneously aid in the further reform of art away from the limitations of naturalism.

He shared both the themes and the goal with the other members of the Strindberg-Przybyszewski cenacle of the *Schwarze Ferkel*, which now embraced the rebellious Norwegian. During December and January, the group briefly expanded to include from Norway the painter Christian Krohg, the art critic Jens Thiis, and the playwright Gunnar Heiberg, and from Denmark, the poet Holger Drachmann, who accompanied Strindberg in guitar duets. By remarkable coincidence during this time almost the entire Scandinavian literary avant-garde thus collected in the two dark rooms at the corner of *Neue Wilhelmstrasse* and *Unter den Linden*, where the owner prided himself on always having available a selection of 900 liqueurs. From time to time, the group was also joined by somewhat lesser figures: Franz Servaes, a young German literary critic who was befriended by Hansson and who made possible the publication of Przybyszewski's first book; Max Dauthendey, a novice poet recently arrived from the Franconian city of Würzburg and quickly converted into a Scandinavophilic aesthete; Julius Meier-Graefe (fig. 4), an art-hungry engineering student turned novelist and later to become the author of the first book on the history of modern art; and Hermann Schlittgen, a German cartoonist and illustrator who once also brought with him the draftsman of the Berlin proletariat, Heinrich Zille, who observed that "Whoever had, paid." Among those who "had" and thus paid many of the poets', painters', and critics' bills were two doctors: Max Asch and Karl L. Schleich, a noted surgeon, author of an authoritative book, *The Aetiology of Skin Tumors*, and in 1892 a medical renegade who discovered local anesthesia which he used during his operations despite the general ridicule of his medical colleagues. It was a diverse but remarkably gifted group, and from it the shy, reserved, quiet but radically inspired Munch could not fail but draw vast measures of confidence for his ambitious pictorial project. In an atmosphere where artistic and intellectual modesty justifiably had no place, he proudly recognized himself as the equal of Scandinavia's famed writers.

fig. 4 *Portrait of Julius Meier-Graefe*, c. 1895, Nasjonalgalleriet, Oslo

Uniting this uneasy and temperamental amalgam of diverse literary, artistic, and medical egos, ages, and nationalities was rejection of naturalism in literature and art, or, in the sciences, the "naturalist" conviction that everything was measurable and physically definable. Naturalism, they argued, although then celebrating its final glories after a long struggle against the remnants of romantic sentimentalism, had attained a stage of senility and weakness.

Art began to move backward. It was transformed into water and slang. Whoever was able to attract attention by means of many and crude words was declared a poet *par préférence*, and Parnassus was turned into the Canaan of mediocrity, flowing with milk and honey. Literature became a sermon and the brothers of the press sang their Amens and Hallelujah for the monotonous text. Strong spirits, the true talents, the most remarkable personalities were roughly pulled down to stand on the same level as the measure of mediocrity, and the purer tones, the clear harmonies, the good art works were drowned out by the crude sounds of indignant women and the noisy protest of literarily impotent men playing on all imaginable tinny instruments of the opposition.[14]

Thus Ola Hansson characterized the situation of literature at the end of the 1880s; similarly, Munch sarcastically accused naturalism of seeking "the extraction of nature, the square root of nature" and of transforming art into a mechanical trade akin to a shoemaker's automatic pounding of pegs into the soles of shoes.[15]

In his semiautobiographical novel *Overboard*, first of the trilogy *Homo Sapiens*, Przybyszewski recorded Munch's alter-ego, Mikita, likewise excitedly complaining of naturalism's thoughtless dominance:

> In Paris I went to one of the great ones, the chief of naturalists, or whatever they call them there. He pulls in the cash, I tell you! Of course, the public is now starting to buy that stuff, the "fifth column" discovered by Napoleon in Poland, *la boue*—mud—and a few stalks of potatoes on it. Before, they used to buy the gingerbread pictures of His Apostolic Majesty's Court Tapestry Manufacturer. Raphael's his name, isn't it? Well, now it's the potato-painters' turn.
>
> Anyhow, I asked this chief of the tribe why he bothers to paint what nature makes a thousand times more beautiful and, moreover, had absolutely no significance.— "What do you mean, significance? Nature, you understand, is its own significance and meaning."
>
> "But," I said, "certainly not the potato?"
>
> The potato painter got excited. "Yes, certainly, precisely the potato. That is what nature is. All else is nonsense. Fantasy? You talk about fantasy? Nonsense! Nonsense! It is only a crutch!"[16]

In contrast to this mythical "Chief of the Naturalist Tribe," Munch opted for an art based on fantasy and content:

> An artwork's effect consists in what it says. Now art is liberating itself from Impressionism (Manet) and from realism. The soul has evolved beyond the elemental, and Symbolism there found its form, the newer tendencies are taking form.[19]

To the members of the *Schwarze Ferkel* circle, the precise form of the new art was not yet clear; although Munch used the newly fashionable French term "symbolism" to identify his art of subjective content, such definite association with an artistic movement was alien to most of the adamantly individualistic Scandinavians and Poles in Berlin. In *Overboard*, Przybyszewski's self-disguise as "Falk" expounds his philosophy of art at the cafe "The Green Nightingale" and, like Munch, asserts the significance of content at the expense of form:

> What I want? What I want? I want life and its terrible depths, its bottomless abyss. To me art is the profoundest instinct of life, the sacred road to the future life, to eternity. That is why I crave grand thoughts, pregnant with meaning and content, thoughts that will lay the foundation for a new sexual selection, create a new world and a new understanding of the world. For me art does not end in rhythm, in music. Art is the will that out of nonexistence conjures up new worlds, new people.—No, no, my dear friend, what we need is an art whose belly is swollen with ideas. Otherwise, what's the use of art at all? It's superfluous, meaningless.[18]

In the male fraternity of the *Schwarze Ferkel*, that saw women such as Hansson's or Krohg's wives in its midst only with great displeasure, the main topic that would lend art a new sense of profundity was sex, preferably the subjective and personal experience of sex through which the artist could plumb the depths of the nature of woman. For it was the mystery of sex, not the externals of intercourse, that seemed to have survived the deadly onslaughts of

naturalism, Darwin, and Nietzsche against the traditional mysticism of life, against divine creation, and against God. Ola Hansson therefore began his *Sensitiva Amorosa* with slashing visual indications of emptiness and mortal boredom, then presented his solution:

> . . . I now have no more than one interest left for me: to study and use sex. All the tender filaments through which my existence was attached to life and through which it drew its nourishment therefrom, have, one after the other, dried up and shrivelled, all except one, and this one has grown big by itself and saturated itself with sap, dug itself in and spread itself out, and now it is a refined network of branches that alone gives me any attachment to life.

The celebration of sexuality as the final life force is accompanied by a sense of superior resignation, however, an insistence on self-sufficiency that rejects any human affection.

> For men such as myself, there always comes, sooner or later, a time when one is tired of all real attachments to women. There is, in all such attachments, no matter what else they may be, so much that is banal and painful. I have had more than enough of that, and now I use women at arm's length, in the study of them and of myself, and from this point of view I can reject all the trivial aspects of sexual relationship while using the pure essence without all the distasteful accretions.[19]

The primacy of sexuality in human life, and beyond human life as a primal force of all existence, was also preached fervently by Stanislas Przybyszewski, whom Strindberg nicknamed Priapus, and who was completing his first novel, *Totenmesse* (Requiem Mass), during the early months of 1893 while Dehmel corrected his eccentric German for publication. In the novel, again with heavy autobiographical strains accented by the first-person narrative— "in this, the most intimate impulses are best presented, the quietest trembling of the new spirit longing to come forth from the placenta-skins of the unconscious"[20]—Przybyszewski translates a life into its sexual components, from fetal existence to the metamorphosis of death:

> In the beginning was sex. Nothing outside it—everything contained in it.
>
> Sexuality was the endless and limitless *apeidos* of the old Anaximander as he dreamed Me my primeval beginning, the spirit of the Bible that hovered over the waters as nothing yet existed outside of Me.
>
> Sexuality is the primal substance of life, the content of evolution, the innermost essence of individuality.
>
> Sexuality is the eternally creative, transformatory-destructive.
>
> It was the power through which the atoms were piled atop each other by Me,—the blind passion that inspired them to copulate so that elements and worlds could appear.[21]

In this maelstrom of literary sexual obsession, Munch too gave in to thoughts of expressing his own experiences in literary terms, briefly returning to a half-forgotten project to write an autobiographic novel, so that Franz Servaes later recalled:

> Every evening Edvard Munch could be seen there [at the *Schwarze Ferkel*]; he was the creator of the most remarkable imaginative paintings, called a "color symphonist" ... and twice the recipient of the state fellowship, whereupon the young artist—stopped painting, translated his genial ideas into words, and wasted them on the "Schwarze Ferkel" public.[22]

Munch had concentrated on notes for his novel previously, particularly during his stay in Saint Cloud in 1890 and then during a period of illness at a hospital in Le Havre in 1891; in both cases, the situations were ones in which he would not or could not paint. In Berlin, beguiled by the discussions with Dehmel, Strindberg, Przybyszewski, and Hansson, he returned to his literary ambitions as his paintings traveled to Copenhagen in February 1893. The disconnected notes reveal the vivid memory of Munch's first serious love affair. It occurred in the years of delayed adolescent turmoil spent in the company of Hans Jæger and the Kristiania Bohème during the mid-1880s.

> So he thought, he could find a woman, that could mean something to him—outside the bonds of marriage.
> The Era of the Bohème came with its doctrine of free love. God and everything else was overthrown; everyone raced in a wild, insane Dance of Life. A blood-red sun stood in the sky; the cross was atoned for. ... Then the experienced Woman of the World came on the scene and I received my baptism by fire. I was made to feel the entire unhappiness of love ... and for several years it was as if I were nearly crazy. The horrible face of mental illness then raised its twisted head. ... After that I gave up the hope of being able to love.[23]

Thus Munch later summarized his romance with Milly Ihlen, wife of Dr. Carl Thaulow and later of Ludvig Bergh, and identified as "Mrs. Heiberg" in Munch's autobiographical notes.[24] Until the tumultuous affair with Tulla Larsen at the turn of the century, it was the memory of "Mrs. Heiberg" that almost totally formed his conception of the nature of love and of women.

> What a deep mark she has left on my mind, so deep that no other image can ever totally drive it away.
> Was it because she was so much prettier than the others? No, I do not even know if she was pretty; her mouth was large. She could seem repulsive. The other one, tall and pale, was far more attractive, with her dazzling young skin, her blond hair that a slight breeze blew over her eyes, and her eyes that were so full of loyalty. ...
> Was it because we shared the same opinions? We did not really know each other. And yet—
> Was it because she took my first kiss, that she took the sweetness of life from me? Was it because she lied, deceived, that one day she took the scales from my eyes so that I saw Medusa's head, saw life as a great horror? And everything that previously I had seen in a rose-colored mist now seemed empty and grey to me.[25]

The experience of the illicit love of Milly Thaulow seemed justified to Munch in the 1880s from the viewpoint of Jæger's Kristiania Bohème, that, with a beguiling mixture of thoughts derived from Zola, from messianic socialism, from the dialectics of Hegel, and from the futuristic romanticism of Fichte, sought to erect an idyllic social edifice on the foundation of free love:

> An open, free life together for open, free men and women knowing no laws for the organization of society other than freedom and love and happiness on earth; a society in which each single life is able to develop in all its individuality like a fruitful tree planted in fertile soil ... Oh, what people they would be! Godlike people! contrasting to the miserable creatures that now creep around on the earth's surface, hiding themselves, each separate and alone, in the dark cellular holes of decrepit freedom-suffocating institutions and traditions, frightened of the strong, stimulating daylight of the open, free society.[26]

Seeking to destroy the pillars of the old society with its frequently two-faced values that argued, for example, for marriage and monogomy while also supporting legalized prostitution, Jæger believed that in his new society women and men should love without the need for life-long faithfulness, freely separating once love ceased, and that in this manner more and more people would come to truly love one another, thereby ultimately creating a society of total love. The process of sexual love—attraction, seduction, consummation, and separation—became Jæger's obsessive concern, and he inaugurated several experiments with members of his Kristiania Bohème to permit him to observe scientifically and with detached logic the processes of love among the sexes.

One of Jæger's experiments was the love triangle formed with Christian Krohg, his wife Oda, and Jæger himself. The three were to record, each separately, the events, impressions, and emotions of the relationship to reveal a true history of it, a totally unique literary document; only Jæger's third of the trilogy—*Syk Kjaerlihet* (Perverse Love)—was published. Similar experiments, usually not as complex to orchestrate as Jæger's affair which ultimately involved at least three other men simultaneously in love with Oda, were conducted by others among Jæger's following. Sigurd Bødtker conceived of a series of poems, apparently autobiographical and entitled *Elskov* (Love), that naturalistically depicted the events of an affair experienced with a deeply religious "madonna" who passionately satisfied her illicit sexual cravings after dutifully attending Sunday church services. The teen-aged poet Vilhelm Krag, arriving from Stavanger in Christiania and brought under Jæger's influence through Bødtker, sought the experience of a somewhat commercially tinged free love during three days and nights spent

fig. 5 *Portrait of Dagny Juell Przybyszewska,*
1893, OKK M 212, Munch-Museet, Oslo

in Vika, Christiania's prostitutes' quarter. Munch's
courtship of the married Milly Thaulow likewise fits
into Jæger's pattern of consciously entered free love
relationships whose emotional events must be recorded and, to a degree, manipulated to reveal the
nature of "free men and free women knowing no
laws" and therefore happy. Munch's vision of the
head of Medusa in the process reveals the flaw of
Jæger's system: rather than "freedom, love and
happiness" the multipartnered loves of the Kristiania Bohème lead to jealousy, flaunted faithless-
ness, combative confrontations, increasing insensi-

bility, anxious arguments, and debilitating despair.
Jæger himself was forced to the same conclusion:

> There was, after all, no more than one true woman on the
> whole earth—oh, how I trembled! How you coursed
> through me like a perverse anxiety in my blood! And I
> saw you leave in the pale violet coat, a full step ahead of
> me, a bit to the side, with a walk that is so much you; and I
> imagined the form under it, those forms that are so much
> yours; oh, I saw only yours in the entire world—and fear
> ran ever more insanely through my blood; and my entire
> body shook when suddenly you turned your head and
> looked at me with your grave, large-eyed, fatelike face
> from the coupé window—Oh God, my God, how I was
> sick![27]

94

In 1893, in the sex-saturated conversations of the Berlin *Schwarze Ferkel,* for Munch's thoughts to return to those emotions of love, jealousy, and despair that he had experienced during his initiation to a woman's love and the pleasures of her body was an almost predetermined event. To aid in precipitating Munch's return to his obsessively written recollections of "Mrs. Heiberg," Christian Krohg arrived with his wife Oda and her current amorous interest, Gunnar Heiberg, thus literally transplanting the Kristiania Bohème's "system" of free love to Berlin, again forcing it in front of Munch's eyes. At the same time too, from Paris arrived Jæger's novel *Syk Kjaerlihet,* chronicling the paradigmatic Bohème triangle of Krohg-Oda-Jæger. Munch himself contributed the last ingredient to the explosive recipe of freely and easily given love fused with inevitable jealousy that characterized the reexperiencing of his first tragic and illicit love affair, now with different actors and in Berlin rather than in Christiania. On March 9, 1893, Edvard Munch brought into the midst of the heated emotional, artistic, and intellectual egotism of the *Schwarze Ferkel* Dagny Juell (fig. 5), a young Norwegian music student, daughter of a doctor, reputed descendant of Norway's ancient kings, a slender, blond believer in Hans Jæger:

> One day she stepped into the *Ferkel* at Munch's side— blond, thin, elegant, and dressed with a sense of refinement that understood how to hint at the body's sensuous movements but avoided giving too clearly defined contours. Thus tempting a man's robust strength without destroying the fashionable decadent nervous glorification of the head with too much "unmotivated" fleshiness! A classic, pure profile, her face overshadowed by a jumble of curls! . . . A laugh that inspired a longing for kisses and simultaneously revealed her two rows of pearllike white teeth that lurked behind the thin lips awaiting the opportunity to latch on! And in addition, a primeval, affected sleepiness in her movements, never excluding the possibility of a lightning-quick attack![28]

The exclamation mark-dotted description, essentially attributing to Dagny Juell the qualities of a crouching cat, is the recollection of Strindberg's self-appointed biographer, chronicler, and functioning aide-de-camp in Berlin, the Finnish writer Adolf Paul. A similar, but more sympathetic, characterization is supplied by Franz Servaes:

> She was anything but beautiful, and yet she was tempting as few other women are. Tall, thin, supple, with a darkly complexioned brow, and pale eyes behind almost always half-closed, sleepy eyelids. Dry, kinky brown-red hair that crackled when touched like a ripe field of rye before a storm. A mouth, much too large, with thin lips that glowed in such an intense red over her pointy, white, truly Nordic weasel or marten teeth that whoever did not know her well swore that she painted them, something she never did. How, or from what, she lived, none of us knew.

> To tell the truth, we did not worry much about it either. We assumed that she slept her days away, and, to judge from the late hours of the *Schwarze Ferkel* symposia, that was probably true. She spoke little when she was sober, and all sorts of confused, mostly incomprehensible stuff when she was not. But in her eyes there was such spirit, just as in her laughter, in every movement of her subtle form, that whoever spoke to her could not help but be inspired. All she had to do was look at a man, place her hand on his arm, and immediately he found the proper expression for something over which he had been brooding helplessly, unable to give it artistic form for some time. It was she who released the thoughts of these bards struggling to create in pain and suffering. But not one was truly comfortable near her, not even those who desired her most. During the common activities of daily life, kings take off their crowns, but she always wore hers, the iron band forged around her brow by fate. There was no mark, not the slightest blemish marring her smooth skin, and yet as soon as one saw her, one had the impression that she was a doomed woman.[29]

Servaes' description was written with the knowledge of Dagny's ultimate fate: to be murdered in 1901 in Tiflis by a Polish student whom newspaper accounts incorrectly identified as her lover. Munch, also writing a brief memorial to her then, recalled with more reserve that ". . . she moved among us freely and proudly, encouraging us, constantly comforting us, as only a woman can, and her presence alone was sufficient to calm and inspire us. It was as if the simple fact that she was nearby gave us new inspiration, new ideas, so that the desire to create flamed up fresh and new."[30]

Before 1892, Munch had known her, perhaps courted her, in Norway. In Berlin, Przybyszewski, Strindberg, Schleich, Dehmel, Meier-Graefe, Servaes, and Bengt Lidforss all fell in love with her immediately. Masterfully she played their emotions as if they were a psychically controlled musical instrument, eliciting from each living key its desired tone before moving on to the next. Munch, judging from the colored and not fully reliable accounts that narrate Dagny's reign in the *Schwarze Ferkel,* acted much the role of a bass note frequently returned to, but during the intervals anxiously waiting, while Strindberg took on qualities of a grace note, quickly picked up once, then cast off, to his persistent hysterical displeasure. Where previously heated discussions about the nature of sex and women dominated the fraternal tables of the *Schwarze Ferkel,* now dominant was the single emotion of jealousy— jealousy such as only a group of male artists could generate when each was convinced of his own superior genius and equated this with his irresistible appeal to women. The result of this jealousy, obviously, was instant animosity that transformed into perpetual hatred the mutual love of friends and the fellowship of similar artistic convictions. In disgust and disappointment, Adolf Paul wrote home to Finland about his literary idol:

> Strindberg is now the enemy of one of his former friends, and since private slandering seems to be the order of the day among artists in such a situation, so they now reveal each other's small falsehoods to their mutual friends, and since they are falsehoods told with fantasy, you can imagine how they blow up small bagatelles into remarkable major crimes. . . . I've had it up to here with all the humbug and the dirt into which the *entire* former coterie of friends has dissolved.[31]

To Munch, the free love and domineering jealousy of the Kristiania Bohème reappeared as Dagny took on the qualities of "Mrs. Heiberg" and exaggerated them. And once again, just as then, he found himself rejected and cast off by the woman, only to be occasionally reeled back in as Dagny, in her expertly practiced rondelle of free love, fished in the confines of the *Schwarze Ferkel* for suitor after suitor.

The bohemian cenacle of fervent writers, painters, and scientists was unable to bear the strain. By the end of May, less than two months after Dagny's initial charged materialization in the fraternity's midst, the *Schwarze Ferkel*'s members were all fleeing separately and desperately on trains heading north, south, and east: Strindberg to marry Frida Uhl, Lidforss to his parents and a festive reception of King Oscar II in Lund, Schleich and Dehmel to the forgiving arms of their wives, and Munch to his paintings. Przybyszewski alone remained in Berlin, continued to court Dagny, and went to jail: a fugitive Russian anarchist had been found in his home.[34] Love and a woman had triumphed over artistic fellowship, brother artist turned on brother artist, and the *Schwarze Ferkel* turned into an old wine sack again with Strindberg's inspiring transformation gone. At least for a brief time.

After trips with his paintings to Dresden and Munich, Munch returned to Norway late in the summer, after having once again been in Berlin where he took part in an exhibition of "Free Artists" that included many of his supporters from the *Verein Berliner Künstler* conflict of the previous November and December. He exhibited only copies of his own earlier paintings; no significant work had been done during the *Schwarze Ferkel* excursions into writing and then into the debilitating turmoil of jealousy and love. His triumphantly optimistic mood remained, however, and the months he spent back in Norway were months of feverishly intense and inventive activity in preparation for a new Berlin exhibition. During the late summer and fall months of 1893, isolated in Norway and removed from the amorous and artistic turmoil of Berlin, Munch initiated the series of paintings on love and death that he announced earlier to Johan Rohde. It marked the beginning of his "Frieze of Life."

On December 5, 1893, in a second-floor gallery space rented at *Unter den Linden* 19 in Berlin, Munch presented the results of his months' painting in Norway. A total of twenty new paintings was exhibited, along with some thirty watercolors and drawings of varying complexity. Focus of the exhibition concentrated on a large painting entitled *A Death* (now known as *Death in the Sickroom*, cat. no. 41) which was hung at the entrance to the exhibition to greet the viewer coming up the steps. This view of the various members of Munch's own family, reacting in isolation and bewilderment to the process of dying as his sister (unseen by the viewer) dies in the chair next to his praying father, set the underlying tone of the exhibition; the remainder of the paintings were to be seen under domination of the constant awareness of dying, death, and decay biologically fulfilled in a reality where prayer is useless and God fails to be present.

In his fictionalized account of his sister Sophie's death, Munch recalled:

> It was evening. Maja lay flushed and feverish in her bed; her eyes blinked and she looked restlessly around the room. She was hallucinating. My dear, sweet Karleman, take this away from me; it hurts so. Please, won't you: She looked pleadingly at him. Yes, you will. Do you see the head over there? It is Death.
>
> It was night. The Captain stood at the side of the boys' bed. You have got to get up now, my children. They understood, quietly got dressed, did not ask why.
>
> My darling Maja,—I have to tell you this—the Lord will take you for Himself soon. A sudden jerk passed through her body, then death—Then she gathered her energies and smiled weakly.—Would you like to live? Yes, she whispered, I would like that so much.—Why, little Maja?—Because it is so nice here.—Sing a hymn, Maja.—She whispered almost soundlessly. Now we were supposed to come together around her. Would she really die, then? During the past half hour she had felt almost better, after all, than before; the pain was gone. She tried to raise herself, pointed to the armchair at the side of the bed. I would like to sit up, she whispered. How strange she felt. The room looked different, as if seen through a veil. Her arms and legs felt as if they were filled with lead. How tired![33]

Although seeking to project the mood of the dying girl, Munch succeeded best at rendering the sense of absolute helplessness felt by those near her: his own pathetic inability to keep his sister from suffering and, even more tragically, his father's desperate, obsessive, almost manic attempts to comfort his dying daughter with hymns, muttered prayers, and the painful assurance that Jesus wants her. This image of existential desperation is frozen into the painting *A Death*. It is Munch's own experience, not an attempt to experience emotionally the process of death itself as in his earlier masterpiece, *The Sick Girl* (1885-1886).

fig. 6   *Vampire,* pastel, c. 1893, OKK 122 B, Munch-Museet, Oslo

The conviction that his own experience necessarily must form the foundation for the universal content of his new art[34] also determined the formation of the other paintings of the 1893 exhibition, notably what he identified in the catalogue as a "Study for a Series: 'Love' "—love seen in the constant, overpowering presence of death. Its images consisting of oil paintings as well as pastel studies for paintings not yet carried out, "Love" was identified by six titles:[35]

a   *Dream of a Summer Night* [*The Voice*, 1893, cat no. 31]
b   *Kiss* [1893?, cat. no. 43]
c   *Love and Pain* [*The Vampire*, 1893, pastel study, fig. 6]
d   *The Face of a Madonna* [*Madonna*, 1893, pastel study?]
e   *Jealousy* [*Melancholy-Jealousy*, 1891-1893]
f   *Despair* [*The Scream*, 1893, pastel study]

The theme is love, traced from its initial stirrings in the pale and soft light of a Norwegian summer night, to the ecstasy of love's physical consummation, and finally to the—for Munch—inevitability of jealousy and final isolation in despair. It is love as seen by the Kristiania Bohème's members, love as seen by the *Schwarze Ferkel*'s members in their relationship to Dagny Juell, love as experienced by Munch with "Mrs. Heiberg" and with Dagny Juell, and it is the sexual excitation of love played against the setting of the infallible certainty and towering presence of death past, present, and future.

In a poem, "Our Hour Has Come," dedicated to Dagny, Richard Dehmel recreated the mood of overpowering but sublimated eroticism and desperation of this initial phase of Munch's "Frieze of Life":

Already it is getting dark; come, come home,
come! The leafy mass of the chestnut trees reaches
out toward us like sharpened claws.

It is too lonely here, too hot and damp
for us.

Then see: the lines of your hand,
look, they are too much like mine.
You seem, suddenly, so very close to me,
as if known earlier,
perhaps from some other world.

Once I had a sister; she is dead.
Be not so silent, as if you could not speak!
The clouds of evening stream so red
through the young trees,
as if blood-soaked incest threatened us.

Listen! Yes, just as wild and helpless
as the nightingale just sounded
your heart trembles in my hand.
We know it; that suffices
for us.[36]

Mysterious, overpowering sexual attraction fused with *Lebensangst,* with a persistent and ever-present foreboding of doom—this is the content Munch's cyclical representation of love projected onto its viewers in 1893, on the sensitive souls of the Dehmels and Dauthendeys, the Przybyszewskis and Meier-Graefes, who frequented Munch's exhibition, and the impact was so powerful that it colored their own novels, plays, and poems. For Munch, as for them, it was a modern mythology, a quasi-religious representation of the mystical forces of the human soul, fulfilling Munch's own earlier call for depictions of men and women "in that moment when they are no longer themselves but only one of thousands of links tying one generation to another generation." And, he added, "people should understand the sanctity of this and take off their hats as if they were in church."[37]

Throughout the nineteenth century artists strove to answer Winckelmann's demand, made in 1766, that they seek new and modern allegories to depict the mysteries of life, not simply as had been done traditionally but rather in a manner and using imagery that would be meaningful in the altered environment of the modern world.[38] As creator of such modern allegories, the nineteenth-century artist also became an educator and a moral teacher, consciously using his art to teach humanity a life of virtue and nobility and to reveal the eternal, underlying verities of that life. For these purposes, the multiple imagery of a cycle of paintings, prints, or drawings seemed the most suitable means, fusing pictorial imagery with serial narrative; what was not possible for a single image—the calling forth of temporally or conceptually complex events, ideas, or emotions—could be achieved by multiplying the number of images, placing them next to each other, and permitting the process of one painting succeeding the other to generate a single dominant and unifying conception. For Munch the ability of a pictorial cycle to narrate a series of events just as a

poem or novel might was ideally suited to translate into visual form his own attempts at forming a novel from his autobiographic recollections of loves and deaths that concerned him during evenings at the *Schwarze Ferkel* early in 1893.

The content of such a pictorial cycle, particularly in paintings, traditionally transcended the limits of individual biography and anecdote. Only great historical events or great moral teachings were considered proper to fill walls with narration.

> The content of the pictorial cycle consists of the universal and higher fortunes of mankind and the eternally valid world view of the sacred books of Christianity. The activity of divine grace in opposition to the sin of men, the redemption from sin, destruction and death, the triumph of life and of immortality are presented to the eyes of the viewer in noble images that inspire in him the uplifting consciousness of eternity . . . and encourage him to join in the joyful cry of the Apostle: "Death, where is thy sting! Hell, where is thy victory!"[39]

In this manner a more traditional artist than Munch, the German Nazarene Peter Cornelius, projected a "frieze of life" to be placed in the sacred precincts of an ancient burial site where the visitor would become the recipient of the hopeful message of Christian salvation, traced in its effects from the moment of human birth, through the temptations of the sin-fraught material existence of earthly life, finally to lead by way of physical death to the eternal life enjoyed in the spiritual presence of God.

Painfully Munch, however, like many of his nineteenth-century contemporaries inundated with an antitheistic and scientifically oriented rationalism, found himself incapable of maintaining the faith Cornelius still sought to depict. "One became accustomed to the idea of not believing in a god," Munch wrote, "but that was a belief, after all. . . ."

> All this was in connection with that great wave that went over the earth: realism. Things did not exist unless they could be pointed to, be explained by chemistry or physics. Painting and literature consisted only of what one saw with one's eyes or heard with one's ears; it was the shell of nature. One had become self-satisfied with the great discoveries that had been made. . . .[40]

Dissatisfied with this materialistic, shallow optimism and self-satisfaction, Munch, like others of his generation—"The curiosity of the readers and the desire of the writers are again turning from the exterior inward, from the image of things around us to the confession of what is deep within us, from the *rendu des choses visibles* to the *intérieurs d'ames*," wrote Hermann Bahr in Vienna in 1891[41]—sought both a new mysticism to overcome the barrenness of scientific materialism and the emptiness of a world ending at death without the assurance of immortality.

> Mystical qualities will always exist; after all, the more one discovers the more inexplicable things there will be. The new movement whose progress and whose flashes of light

are being felt everywhere, it will give expression to all that which now has been suppressed for an entire generation, all that of which humanity will always have a great quantity: mysticism.[42]

The new mysticism ultimately discovered by him, as by the *Schwarze Ferkel* writers, was the one means by which a deterministically and materialistically oriented mentality seemed still to permit a sense of immortality: sex. Through sex, through the mingling of male sperm and female ovum, new life could be generated by already existing life, thereby guaranteeing the continuation of life so that "the chain binding the thousand dead generations to the thousand generations to come is linked together," and "new life shakes the hand of death."[43] In the processes of love and human reproduction, death was deprived of its sting and its victory.

The series "Love," inaugurated by the image of death, thus becomes a statement on the triumph of life over death through sexuality. The sexual relationship celebrated by Munch was founded on the ideals of the Kristiania Bohème, however, and incorporated the painful, anxious, and inevitable process of attraction followed by possession, followed by jealousy, separation, and isolation. The process of attaining eternal life consisted of a savage battle of the sexes; this was the fundamental dictum of Munch's metaphysics of love. Describing his series, Munch wrote:

> These paintings are the moods, impressions of the life of the soul, that at the same time form a development in the battle between men and women and that is called love.[44]

More dramatically stated, a similar conception forms the basis of Przybyszewski's narration of incestuous love, *De Profundis*, dedicated to "My Friend, My Sister, My Woman: Dagny":

> If I speak of the revelation of the soul in sexual life, then I naturally do not mean the pale, nice, comically piquant eroticism of a Guy de Maupassant . . . nor the saturated boredom of the marriage bed. What I have in mind is the painful, fearful consciousness of an unnamable, gruesome power that hurls two souls into each other and seeks to join them in pain and suffering; I have in mind the intense suffering of love that breaks out in the soul because it cannot fuse with the other; I have in mind the enormous sense of expansion in love as one feels active within the soul a thousand generations, thousands of centuries of suffering and again suffering by these generations that perished in the rage to recreate and in the passion for the future; I have in mind only the spiritual side of love: the unknown, the strange, the great problem.[45]

The conception—whether Munch's, Przybyszewski's, Dehmel's, Strindberg's or Hansson's, and implicitly Jæger's as well—of love is as a process bringing together two inextricably opposite forces, women and men, that mutually complement each other within their antagonism. That fusion necessarily becomes an explosive one in which the stronger partner (since totally equal partners, although possible, are extremely rare) is predetermined to destroy the weaker, and the sole purpose of the entire anxiety-ridden process is the generation of new life, whereby the same process is begun all over again. With a pseudo-scientific terminology, a Norwegian author summarized the process as the "dragging together of he-specimens and she-specimens, so that they can bring forth new specimens that then can be dragged together with harpoon and rope."[46] And Munch, in a less sarcastic but possibly more artificially poetic way, wrote:

> Humans' fate is like that of planets that move in space and cross each other's orbits. A pair of stars that is fated to meet strays toward one another only for a moment, then each disappears to its own region in the vastness of space. Among the millions of stars, there are only a few whose paths collide so that they go up totally in one another in glowing flames.—
> A man seldom meets his ideal.[47]

It is this conclusion and pronunciation of a "modern mysticism" discoverable in the souls of a man and woman meeting in a deadly yet immortality-generating sexual relationship that Munch gave visual form with his series "Love," encapsulating in it the personal experiences of Milly Thaulow and Dagny Juell but translating them into the immutability of a philosophical conclusion about the nature of human life. The universal conclusion reflects the similar conclusions of the men with whom he associated during the 1880s and 1890s, but the source is Munch's obsessive process of self-analysis through which his art reveals himself.

When Munch returned to Berlin in November 1893, with his initial studies and formulations of his series "Love," he also returned to the *Schwarze Ferkel*. The jealousy-ridden atmosphere that he had left there earlier in the year was changed, although most of the earlier actors in the drama with Dagny Juell had returned. Strindberg, newly married to Frida Uhl, returned from his extended honeymoon in the middle of August, now anxious to continue his recently started alchemy experiments at transforming sulphur into gold. The German contingent of the earlier bohemian circle—Dehmel, Schleich, and Asch—were still in Berlin and informed Strindberg of Przybyszewski's imprisonment, and also that in May, Dagny had joined Przybyszewski's household, moving in with his common-law wife Marta Foerder and their infant son. Strindberg reacted in hysterical furor in response to the "seduction" of his "most beloved disciple" by the woman he named Aspasia after Pericles' legendary mistress who also served to inspire Socrates. Nevertheless, he did not prevent or could not prevent Przybyszewski's next act: on September 3, he and Dagny left Marta Foerder and his child, briefly lived together at Berlin's *Unterbaumstrasse;* on the 18th they were legally married and on the 24th, settled at *Luisenstrasse* 6.[48] Przybyszewski sought to justify his actions and mollify his idol by arguing that he had married Dagny to give her a "moral alibi" for her belief in free love, an argument akin to those made in Norway by Jæger and Krohg, both of whom considered marriage an inconvenience through which women could be liberated from the moral and legal strictures that otherwise would brand them as prostitutes, a conviction likewise shared by Munch's "Mrs. Heiberg." To Adolf Paul, however, Przybyszewski wrote differently:

> All the unknown power that slept within me—my soul's greatest mystery—she has released; she gives physical shape to my soul's mystery; for me, she is the height of all intellectual and aesthetic benefits. . . . She is good, infinitely good. I have her to thank for so much, for so very much, and would be totally happy if disaster were not sounding from the next hill.[49]

The disaster was actually double: Strindberg continued to attack Aspasia at every possible occasion, even seeking to arrange her deportation to Norway, and Przybyszewski lost his job as editor of the Polish socialist newspaper in Berlin, *Gazeta Robotnicza.* By November, however, when Munch came to Berlin, these "disasters" had been slightly ameliorated as Strindberg left for England and Przybyszewski's first novel, *Totenmesse,* was published.

It was at the newly created Przybyszewski home, freed of the physical presence of Strindberg if not the written results of his increasing conviction that Dagny and Przybyszewski were attempting to kill him, that Munch arrived as a guest. Bengt Lidforss also briefly came, and Przybyszewski gloried over the presence of his former rivals. Visiting the small furnished suite of rooms on the *Luisenstrasse,* Count Kessler saw it as an environmental symbol of Przybyszewski's bohemian convictions:

> The dramatic contrast between the taste of the landlady and the current inhabitant, apparent immediately in the arrangement of the furnished room, is made comically clear by the conflict between a reproduction of Thumann's *Fates* [a popular late nineteenth-century painting widely available in cheap oil-print reproductions] that decorated the wall and, displayed directly opposite it on an easel, a landscape by Munch; it is a battle that is continued by several prints by Rops appearing on a table covered by a bleached, crocheted tablecloth. . . .[50]

Meier-Graefe's recollections, appearing in slightly differing versions late in the 1920s, recall the domination of the strange interior by the magnetism of Dagny's presence:

> They lived in a furnished room overlooking the yard of a house on the *Luisenstrasse* . . . In the center stood a table with chairs, above it hanging on a wire was an oil lamp with a red lampshade made of crepe paper. The table pushed against a worn, standing screen covered with a rococo pattern and hiding the two beds. They rented an upright piano whose resonance could be turned off with a key so that it was possible, without disturbing the neighbors, to play the whole night through. It sounded like someone hammering cardboard. Then there was the library: a rectangular hole in the floor beneath the window, earlier probably a covered bin for coal but whose lid was now missing, a foot deep and as long as a person. In the hole, other than Stachu's [Przybyszewski's nickname] worn collars and bottles, there were piles of books, magazines, music sheets, all resting where they had been tossed. At the table under the red lamp, there were two men seated; the one was Munch, the other changed, but was usually Scandinavian. The others moved about the room. Those at the table sat like angry bulldogs, never speaking, drinking corn-brandy, and never looking at the others. Stachu pounded on the turned-off piano. Before he began, it was necessary to place a burning candle on a chair next to him to ward off spiritistic hallucinations. Once it was an English woman wearing taffeta and with green eyes made out of pencils. Never have I heard Chopin played like that again, partially because usually one does not play on cardboard, but more because I was dancing with Ducha [Przybyszewski's nickname for Dagny]. Never again have I been able to dance like that. It is necessary to drink a lot. The red lamp is necessary, as are Stachu, the bulldogs and, naturally, Ducha. . . . She actually did nothing but walk, but within this measured rhythm her body found unlimited possibilities of expression. . . . In her walk, her slender body bloomed and attained dreamlike fullness and variety: the playing child, the innocent girl, the mistress. . . . She stepped towards the temple, a Vestal Virgin; she passed through the night, a Euridice; she slithered to the tent of Holofernes, a Judith. Her small head with its short hair bent backward and swam on clouds of smoke. In the smoke, her form glowed like phosphorous.[51]

In this room filled with Ducha's magical charm, Munch painted her portrait, showing her in a vapor of blue, her face glowing and her eyes looking sleepily at the viewer. The painting was included in the December exhibition; placed directly between the image of death of the *Sickroom* and the images of the series "Love," Dagny's portrait served as intermediary between the two worlds of a series on love and death, a record of artistic inspiration. Dagny had been transformed into Munch's muse, a future source for his art just as "Mrs. Heiberg."

At the time of the exhibition, Munch and Przybyszewski initiated plans for a publication of a collection of essays on Munch's art. Przybyszewski wrote the first of these, and it appeared under the title "Psychic Naturalism" in the February 1894 issue of *Freie Bühne,* an avant-garde Berlin periodical otherwise largely an advocate of naturalism. That essay was expanded by further considerations of Munch's art by Franz Servaes and Julius Meier-Graefe, both members of the *Schwarze Ferkel* group,

fig. 7 *Ashes,* 1894, Nasjonalgalleriet, Oslo (cat. no. 47)

velous pictures."[52] Early in July, Stachu visited his "Edzin," who painted his portrait with a "powerful psychic presence" while also painting a "grandiose variation" of an earlier painting, but, Przybyszewski reported, Munch's life remained miserable. In August, Munch was evicted from his studio for failure to pay his debts and was forced to leave behind his new paintings. Baron von Bodenhausen again sent money to bail out both Munch and his paintings, and Munch yearned to return to Berlin, where his existence now seemed brighter than in the "impossible nest of fishermen" in Norway.

Munch did return, but by way of Stockholm, where an exhibition was arranged with the aid of the husband of Dagny's sister. As a catalogue introduction, Munch used a translation of Przybyszewski's earlier essay. Among the sixty-nine paintings presenting an overview of Munch's entire career, there were now fifteen "Studies for a Mood-Series: 'Love' ":

1   *Mysticism of a Summer Night* [*Starry Night,* 1893, cat. no. 32]
2   *Man and Woman* [*Eye in Eye,* c. 1894, cat. no. 35]
3   *In the Forest* [*The Voice,* 1893, cat. no. 31]
4/5 *Kiss* (two versions) [*The Kiss,* 1892; *The Kiss,* c. 1893, cat. no. 43]
6/7 *Loving Woman* (two versions) [*Women and Death,* 1893; *Madonna,* c. 1894, cat. no. 37]
8   *Sphinx* (accompanied by the motto: "All others are one. You alone are a thousand," from Gunnar Heiberg's new play *The Balcony*) [*Three Stages of Woman,* 1893-1895]
9/10 *Vampire* (two versions) [*Vampire,* 1893; *Ashes,* 1894, fig. 7, cat. no. 47]
11 *Hands* [*Hands,* c. 1893]
12 *Jealousy* [*Jealousy (Melancholy),* 1891-1893, cat. no. 39]
13 *Insane Mood* [*Anxiety,* 1893, cat. no. 34]
14 *The Scream* [*The Scream,* 1893, cat. no. 29]
15 *Vignette* [*Man and Woman (Metabolism),* ?, cat. no. 46][53]

and a third by Willy Pastor, a somewhat reluctant participant, possibly convinced to join the venture by Servaes. Not until July was the book published, however, so that it proved useless as a means of generating publicity for Munch's exhibitions in Hamburg, Dresden, Frankfurt, and Leipzig arranged by Munch for the spring of 1894.

Despite Przybyszewski's support and several portrait commissions, Munch's fortunes following the Berlin December exhibition slowly but surely declined. The glorious optimism of the winter and spring months of 1892-1893 disappeared as monetary difficulties increased. Canvas for new paintings ran out; his family in Norway had monetary needs he could only partially fill; Norway's relationship with her sister-state Sweden had deteriorated to a point where war seemed likely; his brother Andreas, recently finished with his medical training, wished to get married to a woman the family deeply disliked and distrusted. In May 1894, using money earned from a portrait of the Baron von Bodenhausen, Munch again returned to Norway. Ducha and Stachu accompanied him; their money had run out even before his, and they spent the summer with her parents while Przybyszewski wrote a trilogy tentatively entitled "Love's Dance of Death."

In Norway during the summer of 1894, Munch painted again, although not without further difficulties. Baron von Bodenhausen commissioned a painting, thereby giving Munch some income and making it possible to rent space for a studio; Przybyszewski described him as sitting in "an impossible fishermen's nest" and painting "the most mar-

In October, having sold only one painting in Stockholm, Munch came back to Berlin, hopeful and eager to resume contact with his friends, as well as to plan yet another exhibition.

The remaining months of 1894 and the initial ones of 1895 did not see the hoped for turnabout in Munch's fortunes, however. Count Kessler recorded that in November, Munch was found wandering the streets of Berlin one morning unable to return to his room from which he had been evicted; for three entire days, he had had nothing to eat.[54] Despite his difficulties, or perhaps because of them, Munch took on a new task and learned how to create engravings and lithographs. Meier-Graefe collected several of these into a portfolio, wishing to sell it in Paris, and Munch announced immediate plans to translate his series on love and death into prints.[55] Prints would make the images more readily available to the public; they would also be cheaper, yet through their large number possibly bring in more money than paintings.

Finally convinced by Bodenhausen and Meier-Graefe to aid in supporting Munch, Count Kessler sat for a lithograph portrait in early 1895. From Kessler's diary entries about these sittings, Munch's affairs and state at the time are clearly revealed:

> 20 January 1895. After breakfast, with Bodenhausen to Munch . . . Munch lives in Charlottenburg, four stories up, in a students' den. He has cleared out the living room and uses it as atelier; the pale winter light falls through two curtainless windows onto large colorful, unfinished paintings that stand about leaning against walls. A bitter smell of turpentine vapors and cigarette smoke rises in one's nose. Munch is still young, but already seems worn out, tired, and, both in a psychic and physical sense, hungry. He receives us in a rather wornout robe; around his neck he had tied a Scottish, blue and green checkered scarf. He was exceedingly happy when I gave him 60 marks for a few engravings.

> 9 February. In the afternoon with Munch, whom Bodenhausen begged me to support. He now lives in a hotel on the *Mittelstrasse* and claims he is sick. A few new engravings that he showed me again were of little value in terms of their execution.

> 13 April. In the morning to Munch for continuation of my lithograph. During the sitting, an energetic shopkeeper-ma'msell came with a helper and, because of 25 marks in debts, carried away the easel. The entire execution lasted two minutes and had something of a quality of being taken for granted about it. Munch at first tried to joke about it, made remarks about the energy of the pretty young lady and continued working by propping the stone in front of himself on a cane chair. Afterwards, he was rather quiet and melancholy, however. But, until he received money, he did not give even the slightest indication of wanting to borrow money or anything like that.

Kessler, not overly appreciative of Munch's art (one diary entry early in 1895 comments on the "certain irony" that he is supporting artists "so little sympathetic to me" such as Munch and Przybyszewski),[56] was ultimately won to Munch's cause by the inherent nobility of the artist's personality, of someone who refused to give in even under the most debilitating adversity and who remained too proud even in obvious poverty to ask for loans. This sense of pride and self-confidence likewise found expression in Munch's desire, just as early in 1895 his fortunes reached one of their lowest ebbs, to expend energy on yet another major project: he initiated the process of translating his "Love" series into graphics, a process never totally finished although its tentative completion as the series "The Mirror" was announced two years later. It was a process too that, incidentally, Kessler helped make somewhat physically less difficult for Munch when he had the German printmaker Joseph Sattler teach the artist the process of transfer lithography, permitting drawing on paper instead of directly on the lithographic stone.[57]

While focusing on his remarkably quick adaptation to the processes of graphics early in 1895, Munch also once more exhibited his painting series "Love," now again consisting of fifteen paintings, displayed March 3-25 at Ugo Barroccio's gallery, *Unter den Linden* 16:

1 *Mysticism* [*Starry Night,* 1893, cat. no. 32]
2 *Two People* [*Eye in Eye,* c. 1894, cat. no. 35]
3 *Two Eyes* [*The Voice,* 1893, cat. no. 31]
4 *Kiss* [*The Kiss,* c. 1893, cat. no. 43]
5 *Vampire* [*Vampire* or *Ashes,* 1893-1894]
6 *The Loving Woman* [*Woman and Death,* 1893]
7 *Madonna* [*Madonna,* 1894, cat. no. 37]
8 *Sphinx* [*Three Stages of Woman,* 1894, cat. no. 98]
9 *Separation* [*Separation,* c. 1894]
10 *Hands* [*Hands,* c. 1893]
11 *Jealousy* [*Jealousy (Melancholy),* 1891-1893, cat. no. 39]
12 *Evening* [*Evening on Karl Johans Street,* 1894, cat. no. 28]
13 *Insane Mood* [*Anxiety,* 1893-1894, cat. no. 34]
14 *The Scream* [*The Scream,* 1893, cat. no. 29]
15 *Vignette* [*Man and Woman (Metabolism),* c. 1894?, cat. no. 46]

This marked the final formulation of the series "Love"; when exhibited again in Christiania in 1895 as "A Loving Woman" (an inexplicable change in title) and in 1897 in Paris at Samuel Bing's *Salon de l'Art Nouveau,* the content remained identical so far as can be determined from incidental critical notices and without the listings of catalogues. It is, moreover, unlikely that Munch would have altered the painted series during this time, as he devoted most of his energy to building up the massive oeuvre of his graphics and, at least compared to the burst of activity during 1893-1895, painted relatively little. Not until late in 1899 did he return his attention to his painted series, when he began the process of providing links between the love-oriented paintings and the paintings, previously not incorporated into the series, of death, thereby changing the character of his series in both content and meaning.

Munch's definitive formulation of the series "Love" contained paintings he had created during the time he was closely associated with the Berlin community of avant-garde artists and writers, a community that actually consisted of a minority of Germans and a plurality of Scandinavians and Poles. The international makeup of this community and its lack of nationalistic limitations in its search for aesthetic ideals found its most easily visible expression in the initial issues of the periodical *Pan.* Edited by Julius Meier-Graefe and the German poet Otto Julius Bierbaum, receiving financial support from Kessler and Bodenhausen, as well as the Bavarian royal family, *Pan*'s first issue appeared just at the time of Munch's 1895 Berlin exhibition. During its first year, *Pan*—the periodical's title was suggested by Dagny during an evening at the *Schwarze Ferkel*—carried literary contributions by Nietzsche, Dehmel, Verlaine, Maeterlinck, Rossetti, Kipling, Garborg, and Obstfelder, and illustrations or original prints by Boecklin, Sattler, Vallotton, Toulouse-Lautrec, Rops, Khnopff, Whistler, and the Scandinavians Gallèn-Kallela and Kittelsen; it was, on a uniquely European scale, a survey of the most significant current artistic developments with a predominantly symbolist orientation.

During the depths of his pecuniary problems, before Kessler and others came to his aid and at roughly the time he was found hungry one morning on the streets of Berlin, Munch wrote home:

> I have the feeling that soon I will have had enough of Berlin, so that I shall either go to Paris or else home to Norway. Berlin is, in any case, not an art center by a long shot.[58]

Although a tone of bitterness dominates this comment and, with the prospect of financial support, Munch remained in Berlin yet another year before returning to Norway and then going to Paris, Munch's observation is certainly correct. For further development of his art in its technical and stylistic characteristics, and notably in his graphics, he would need the impact of Parisian artistic developments, just as his earlier conversion from a Norwegian *plein-air* painter into the artist of symbolist persuasion who first exhibited in Berlin necessitated the knowledge of French contemporary art.[59] What was invaluable for Munch, however, in Berlin, and what was made possible by the brief artistic renaissance of which he himself formed a major part within the *Schwarze Ferkel*, was the intellectual atmosphere provided by Berlin's international artistic community as well as the immense encouragement and support he received from it, particularly for the creation of his painting series "Love." In its individual components, he achieved a unique fusion of French synthetist formal concerns with the concerns for content shared by non-French writers and artists seeking to move from naturalism to a highly subjective, spiritualized art having different names in different countries, but perhaps best identified as international symbolism. As Munch put it:

> These paintings are moods, impressions of the life of the soul, and together they represent one aspect of the battle, between man and woman, called love—
> From its beginnings, where it is almost rejected (3 it[ems])—then paintings No.   Kiss, Love and Pain, where the battle has then begun—Painting No.
> The woman who gives herself, and takes on a madonna's painful beauty.—The mystique from an entire evolution collected into one—Woman in her manysidedness is a

> mystery to man—Woman who is at one and the same time a saint, a whore, and an unhappy person abandoned. Jealousy—a long, empty shoreline.
> The woman's hair has entwined itself and entangled itself around his heart.
> The man is very disturbed by this battle—No. 4 insane mood—nature to him appears as a great scream in which blood-red clouds [are] like dripping blood (No. 6 and 7).
> No.   (Girl with the Hands) Lust.[60]

In his conception of the process of love as a battle, Munch shared the concerns of other *Schwarze Ferkel* members, as already noted, while at the same time founding this concept in his own experiences with women before he came to Berlin. Munch did not derive his thoughts from others such as Przybyszewski or Strindberg, but their similar conclusions supported Munch in the convictions formed earlier and must have been of significance in his remarkable decision to translate his own unsuccessful love life into a universal pictorial statement on the nature of love, an extraordinarily ambitious intention particularly when his prospects in 1893 are considered. It is doubtful that in either Paris or Christiania, where he tended to be far more isolated, Munch would have made that particular decision; the heated atmosphere and inspiration of the *Schwarze Ferkel* was a necessary ingredient, as was also the igniting ingredient of jealousy provided by Munch's introduction of Dagny Juell into the bohemian artistic mixture.

Munch's emphasis on the uniqueness of woman, on her inherent difference from man so that she appears as "an eternal mystery," again reflects Przybyszewski's ideas and certainly is quite unlike Strindberg's or others' wishful projection of male superiority over women. "For me," Przybyszewski wrote, "the problem man-woman is a simple, if also infinitely deep biological question. . . . As a man, I cannot, I am not capable of judging a woman as such in any ethical or any other manner, for she is in a certain sense a diametrically different creature than I am, neither superior nor inferior, only different."[61] If Munch would have agreed with such a position prior to his arrival in Berlin, as is likely, he failed then to bring it to expression in his art; although he had created sexually charged images of women, at no time did he seek to present the "diametrical difference" of women and men. The Berlin experience had to intervene.

The painting *Madonna* (cat. no. 37) demonstrates this process. Munch's first image of the loving woman seen from the viewpoint of her lover during the act of love, as he himself recalled, was the painting *Hulda* (1886), now destroyed, that Hans Jaeger took with him when he was sentenced to prison briefly for his book, *From the Kristiania Bohème*. It is to Jaeger that we owe a rather detailed description, set in the context of a visit to his cell by the prison chaplain:

> He sat there for a while and stared silently and blankly ahead of himself. Then, from the corner of his eye, he became aware of Munch's *Hulda* who hung on the wall behind him, thrown back onto her bed, life-sized, naked down to her hips, both her hands raised up under her head, her elbows stretched out, and her dark hair falling in disarray over one of her naked shoulders—:
> "That should be a good companion for you," he said slowly and pointed up toward her as he nodded knowingly with his head.[62]

As he left, the chaplain argued that he was referring to the clock hung on the wall, failing to convince Jæger, however. Whatever the amusing chaplain's reference may have been, what is significant in Jæger's description of the lost painting's power is the absolute emphasis on woman as a purely physical, animalistically charged object of sexual attraction. Love, in such a context, was necessarily "perverse," as Jæger later described it, concerned only with erotic attraction and the freedom of erotic experimentation between men and women. As Jæger as well as Munch later realized, such love necessarily generated emotions of possessive jealousy, even if the original intention of the free-love ethics propagated in the Kristiania Bohème was to liberate and to found a new anarchist society lacking fettering moral limitations. Under the tutelage of Jæger and "Mrs. Heiberg"—the painting may well have been a celebration, if not portrait, of her—Munch too was learning the lessons of this love, indulging in its pleasures and freely courting the favors of his willing mistress-teacher as she presented her naked body to him in her own bedroom, on beaches, or in his studio. In this hedonistically oriented love, no thoughts extended beyond the moment of physical experience, and it might well be identified, using the title of Jæger's periodical issued while he was in prison, as an "impressionist" philosophy of love. *Hulda*, Munch's first painting to explore the man-woman relationship, similarly totally equated the emotion with momentary physical excitation.

By 1890, as Munch reflected back on his relationship with Milly Thaulow, the focus of his attention was transferred from her breasts and hair to her lies, infidelity, and her destruction of his innocence, and the sensually smiling mouth appeared in the context of the head of Medusa. Dagny Juell's ability to generate vast amounts of jealousy in Berlin in March 1893, likewise reaffirmed these convictions. Significantly, however, no Munch painting corresponds to this one-sided and totally negative view of women, although such images as Félicien Rops' *Mors syphilitica* provided ample precedent. Several factors seem to explain this. Not the least of these, but perhaps the most difficult to evaluate, is the fact that

between 1890 and 1893 Munch's own sisters experienced tragic love affairs, leaving one mentally disturbed and transforming the other into a life-long spinster, two events that would argue strongly against conceptions of women's universal evil and destructiveness. Likewise, Munch's increasing awareness of death and the ability of women to act as links in the chain of physical being, an awareness initiated by his father's death in 1889 and Munch's despondency following that, forced an alteration of perspective in his view of women.

This alteration of viewpoint found further support in Berlin. Richard Dehmel had begun his poetic study "The Transformations of Venus," ultimately to become a series of twenty-two poems presenting Venus in twenty differing, sometimes comical guises, including a Venus Perversa and Venus Adultera, but also such Venuses as Consolatrix, Mater, and Mama, in short, a veritable catalogue of woman's nature expressing itself to man in multiple manners, both positive and negative. Przybyszewski's erotically oriented thoughts likewise sought to plumb the "horrible, cosmic power" that for him was woman in her manifold sexual and life-generative appearances:

> I have sent my mind out to the green pasture, onto the sterile moor of my homeland; now I am totally synthesis, totally concentration, totally sexuality.
> You rest in my arm, and it is night.
> We kiss one another so that our breath is forced out, so that we dissolve in each other, so that we become essentially one.
> I press my lips into your fiery bosom, so that my chest expands from the yearned-for, hotly desired happiness; I press your panther-body so intensely against myself that I can feel your heart beat against my male chest and can count its beats, that I can feel the bloodstream that races through your body rushing alongside of my own, and the shivers of pleasure moving through your body become my own.
> I burrow myself into you; I feel how your limbs arch in the dionysian ecstasy of a spasm of pleasure, how they rise up in the wild eurhythmy of a painful delight.
> Faster—deeper—yet deeper, so that I can grasp your immortal spirit in this unbearable heat of my passion, in this insane force of my sensual pleasure, in the panted Allelujah of my desire.
> And now I am the incarnation of the Logos as it became the gospel of the flesh; now I am the all-powerful pan-sexuality, the meeting point of the past and the future, the bridge between what is gone and what will come, the pledge of a new evolution.[63]

In such passages, with their fusion of extraordinary sensuality, religious vocabulary, identification of sexuality and spirituality, and recognition of the new life resulting from sex, Przybyszewski's paean to Dagny Juell approximates Munch's own thoughts concerning copulation as a forced coupling between past and future generating immortality in a child.

The contrast between Munch's initial recollections of Milly Thaulow and his later commentary on his painting and lithograph *Madonna* becomes a telling indication, moreover, of the transformation of his thought:

> May I? he said. He felt her give in. She let herself be pulled closer and—closer—totally in to him. He took hold carefully of her body. She pushed herself up against him. He felt a warm mouth on his neck, a moist chin near his, and his mouth glided in toward hers.
>
> Trees and air disappeared and he only saw into two large, dark green eyes that looked back into his—until they closed. Oh, he felt as if he wanted to cry—it was so wonderful—he sank as if into a marvelous dream.
>
> A second later he saw her bent shadow disappear into the shrubbery. . . .
>
> He wanted to cry, shout in joy. Tonight he had seen—a new world. He had not imagined before that it was so—so wonderful, marvelous, and she had taught him it. . . .[64]

Although aspects of this text, primarily the setting and the situation of the ever-polite Munch and "Mrs. Heiberg" peering into each others' eyes, are reminiscent of the paintings from the series "Love," the fundamental attitude focused totally on the male and his pleasures is not. The essential emotional interaction between woman and man is lacking, as is any indication of the more universal significance of a sexual embrace.

A later text shifts emphasis:

> Your face contains all the earth's beauty, your eyes, dark as two green-blue seas, draw me toward you. Your mouth has a painful, tender smile—as if you wanted to ask my forgiveness for something—
> Your lips are voluptuous like two bloodied serpents.
>
> There is worship in your face under the lamp of moonlight. Your pure forehead is pulled severely back. Your profile is. . . .[65]

Munch did not complete the final sentence, but the description of his loving woman appears to fit studies, particularly the large pastel of a woman in a nightgown also described in Przybyszewski's essay, for the painting *Madonna*. This pastel, created in 1893 and apparently using a Berlin prostitute as model, points to Munch's quandary at this time. Through the pose, he sought to capture the supravisual meaning, but the imagery, with the portraitlike features of the model and the rather intrusive presence of the white negligée, prevents a final solution, much as the incomplete text hints at but does not fulfill the task of shifting attention from the physical to the metaphysical, from the woman's body to her reproductive function.

In the painting of 1894 the limitations of the pastel are overcome. The woman—now bearing the more meaningful features of Dagny Przybyszewski or possibly her sister, then expecting a child—is now nude, deprived of all time-bound clothing, and, instead of on a rumpled bed, she appears in a vague, fluid like ambiance suggesting the form of a womb in which the woman is enclosed. By being viewed frontally instead of in profile, her communication with the viewer is heightened to the point of forcing the viewer's participation, transforming the viewer from observant voyeur into her sexual partner. Her pose is a traditional beauty pose arching her back and lifting her breasts while totally opening up her body, but it is also the classical pose of a dying Niobid seeking to remove from her back an arrow shot by Apollo. This reference to death through the symbolism of the pose was, in 1894 and in the 1895 lithograph based on the painting, clarified by symbolic imagery painted on a frame. The forms of embryo and sperm on the frame, the embryo having a skeletal face, also appear surrounding the *Madonna*'s pendant painting *Loving Woman*, today known as *Woman and Death*, a depiction of a woman embracing death as he presses his bony leg between hers. It is in this multiple imagery within the symbolic frame that Munch's conception of a woman's role as grantee of immortality to the human race became clear:

> The pause as all the world stops in its path. Moonlight glides over your face filled with all the earth's beauty and pain. Your lips are like two ruby-red serpents and filled with blood, like your crimson red fruit. They glide from one another as if in pain. The smile of a corpse. Thus now life reaches out its hand to death. The chain is forged that binds the thousands of generations that have died to the thousands of generations yet to come.[66]

Both in text and image, the transition from personal experience and a focus on Munch's own reaction to the process of making love has been completed, as the focus now is on the woman, still seen through the man's eyes, at the moment she becomes pregnant and herself embraces death to triumph over it. The Norwegian poet Sigbjørn Obstfelder, also in Berlin in 1894-1895, summarized this new content as "the world's Madonna, woman who gives birth in pain. . . ."

> That which lies at the bottom of life is not clearly seen by our eyes, either in form, color or idea. Life has surrounded itself with a mysterious beauty and terror, which the human senses cannot, therefore, define, but to which a great poet can pray. The desire to concentrate on this human quality, to understand in a new way that which our daily life has relegated to a minor position, and to show it in its original enigmatic mystery—this attains its greatest heights here in Munch's art and becomes religious.
>
> Munch sees woman as she who carries the greatest marvel of the world in her womb. He returns to this concept over and over again. He seeks to depict that moment when she first becomes conscious of this in all its gruesomeness.[67]

There is, in the final painting of the *Madonna*, a desire by Munch to empathize with the emotions and feelings of the woman, much as in Przybyszewski's evocation of copulation. Since, as Przybyszewski also noted, woman remains forever an other for the man, Munch's attempt is ultimately marked for failure, and his *Madonna* remains, in the midst of her sexual ecstacy and in her absolute function as maternal genetrix, very much a male-oriented view of woman. Nevertheless, the attempt is significant and again reflective of an aesthetic ideal indigenous to the Berlin *Schwarze Ferkel* cenacle.

"In love," Lou Andreas-Salomé, muse to men such as Nietzsche, Freud, and Rilke, wrote during Munch's stay in Berlin, "persons are driven to persons as if to a second, unduplicatable ego only in order to fulfill themselves in a mutual interchange with the other person, not as a means of love, but for the sake of oneself. . . . Thereby love becomes the most bodily as well as the most spiritualistic, ghost-believing quality spooking about within us; it focuses totally on the body, but absolutely and totally on it as symbol, as a corporeal language of signs for everything that may find a way to the soul through our senses in order to wake the soul to its most intense dreams."[68] From such a point of view, man's love for woman or woman's love for man consists not of a yearning for another, but an egocentric desire to rediscover one's self in another person, an expression of self-love and a desire to fuse with oneself, thereby generating an immortal image of oneself. Przybyszewski too adhered to this principle, drawing from it more extreme conclusions, suitable to the art-oriented ethos of symbolism:

> Why do I love woman?
>
> . . . The woman that strikes the finest and deepest strings of my being slips without objection into my brain, and I love her with the deep, undetermined feeling of acceptance with which I love the land that has formed my soul.
>
> I love in the woman my self, my own ego raised to its greatest intensity; my fragmented states, napping in all the corners of my mind and in which the most inner secret of my existence rests, have collected around this woman like iron shavings around a magnet. . . .
>
> And the woman that I love, that is I, my most intimate and inner ego, my ego as *arrière-fond*, as distant background, myself seen from a bird's eye view, me, the objective of a mirroring plain.[69]

The process of love therefore involved a man's absorption of the qualities of the woman, generating an androgynous ego of creativity from the male and female spirits:

> Now I no longer know my own suffering; I suck at your spirit; constantly deeper, I draw it into myself, and in this unity of being and fusion of beings, in this dissolution of my existence in your existence, in this meshing of the cogs of our deepest and most intimate feelings, in this superhuman, ruthless, supremely triumphant victory of sexual freedom as my will attains an ecstacy of the future and immortality, in this I have grabbed hold of your spirit with my trembling, shaking fingers.[70]

This I-Thou creature, the androgynous result of a man's absorption of a woman's spirit, was the artist. He was capable now of generating his own immortality through his work, thereby triumphing over death and depriving it of its victory without the intercession of woman. "I have no other children than my paintings," Munch observed in an androgynous self-identification with woman's ability to give birth. *Madonna* ceases thereby to be solely a representation of woman's insemination and becomes an artist's self-portrait.

The process through which the painting *Madonna* was created is symptomatic of all the paintings in the series "Love." They originated in the anecdotal autobiographies of the Kristiania Bohème, in recollections of the sensuality and infidelity of Milly Thaulow, Munch's ultimate muse depicted in his "diaries" and in drawings of genre scenes recreating the love affair with her. The influence of the concepts of symbolism and decadence in France during his studies there from 1889 to 1892 generated in him the intention to create, not naturalistic genre scenes, but rather symbolic images rendering the mysteries of life and death. That ambition was not realized, however, until the experience of Berlin's *Schwarze Ferkel*. It was the atmosphere there that provided Munch with the ultimate suprapersonal content and means of depiction for the series expressing his philosophy of love. Born at the tables of Christiania's cafés, Munch's symbolic imagery and content attained its maturity in the international, pan-European ethos of the two small rooms of Herr Türke's bar on Berlin's *Neue Wilhelmsstrasse*.

Epilogue

After 1895, Munch did not return to Berlin for any extensive time during the 1890s. Paris, where the techniques of lithography and woodcut were finding new application by artists, proved the stronger attraction, and certainly provided his art with far greater resources than could Berlin at that time. Munch's disastrous affair with Tulla Larsen likewise occupied much of his time, causing him to seek refuge in the Kornhaug Sanatorium in Norway's Guldbrandsdal during the winter of 1899-1900. During this time, his thoughts concerning his series of paintings on love and death also underwent transformation, in large part due to his personal experiences.

Woman's role as mediator between life and death was played down, and her infidelities asserted more emphatically. Death and anxiety likewise became significantly greater powers than in the series

fig. 8   Munch exhibition at P. H. Beyer & Sohn, Leipzig, 1903

"Love." This altered emphasis was achieved largely by expanding the series so that, rather than appearing as a single background or introductory image, death and motifs related to it dominated half the paintings. It was in this new revision that the series was next seen in Berlin in 1902.

"Max Liebermann [the dean of German impressionist painters]," Munch wrote to Norway, "has suggested that, in addition to my other six paintings, I exhibit at the [Berlin] Secession all of my so much insulted cycle of paintings that treat love and death."[71] Munch had returned to Germany where now several patrons were offering support, and portrait commissions became available in a quantity he had not previously experienced. Germany also provided a haven for him, following his termination of the affair with Tulla Larsen with a shot through the joint of a finger of his left hand,[72] from his real

and imagined Norwegian enemies, so that instead of the bohemian and avant-garde circles he frequented during the 1890s, he now found refuge from his sense of persecution by visiting fashionable spas or finding shelter in the homes of his wealthy patrons.

At the Fifth Berlin Secession Exhibition, opening in March 1902, Munch's paintings were hung high on the wall, according to his instruction, in the Sculpture Hall in the center of which stood a maquette for Max Klinger's melodramatic, polychromed figure of Beethoven. For the German public, there was no contest, and the much admired and adulated Klinger received most critical attention, while Munch's paintings, hung just below the hall's ceiling as a room-encircling frieze—the catalogue for the first time identified the series as "Frieze"—were easily ignored. He received little more than polite but largely negative mention from the critics.

Nevertheless, the exhibition of the completed Frieze was a significant achievement for Munch.

> Three horrible years had passed. New life—New hate. His great, finished Frieze hung at the Berlin Exhibition.
>
> There all the paintings hung, in the grand foyer to the Secession.
>
> Man and woman are attracted to each other—Love's underground cable led its currents out into their nerves. Wires tied their hearts together.
>
> My words to accompany it:
>
> There was Kiss, Vampire; there was Jealousy. In the middle, the large painting I painted that summer. I danced with my very first love; it was a recollection of her. In comes the smiling, blond-locked woman who wants to take away the blossom of love, but it does not permit itself to be plucked.
>
> Over on the other side she, dressed in black, looks in sorrow at the dancing pair. She is an outcast, like I was cast out by her dance; and in the back, the raving mob caught in wild embraces.
>
> Then The Scream — — — —
>
> It ends in the Death painting, the eternal background for the Dance of Life.[73]

For the "Frieze of Life," the "Cycle of Moments from Life" as the Secession catalogue identified it, of the 1890s, this was the final and definitive form, consisting of twenty-two paintings subdivided into four conceptual groups:

Left Wall: *Seeds of Love*
    187 *Evening Star* [*The Voice*, cat. no. 31]
    188 *Red and White*, cat. no. 36
    189 *Eye in Eye*, cat. no. 35
    190 *Dance* [*Dance on the Shore*]
    191 *Kiss*, cat. no. 43
    192 *Love* [*Madonna*, cat. no. 37]

Front Wall: *Flowering and Passing of Love*
    193 *After the Fall* [*Ashes*, fig. 7]
    194 *Vampire*
    195 *Saint Hans Night* [*The Dance of Life*]
    196 *Jealousy*, cat. no. 39
    197 *Sphinx* [*Three Stages of Women*, cat. no. 98]
    198 *Melancholy*, cat. no. 45

Right Wall: *Life Anxiety*
    199 *Red Clouds* [*Anxiety*, cat. no. 34]
    200 *Street* [*Evening on Karl Johan Street*, cat. no. 28]
    201 *Autumn* [*The Red Vine*, cat. no. 50]
    202 *Last Hour* [*Crucifixion*]
    203 *Scream of Anxiety*, cat. no. 29

Rear Wall: *Death*
    204 *Death Battle* [*Fever*]
    205 *Deathroom*
    206 *Death* [*The Girl and Death*, Munch Museum version]
    207 *Life and Death* [*Metabolism*, cat. no. 46]
    208 *The Girl and Death* [Bremen version]

With the exception of *The Dance of Life* (1899-1900), *Dance on the Shore* (c. 1900), and *The Red Vine* (1898), all the paintings had been completed by 1895; their new ordering projected a far greater pessimism about the nature of life and death than Munch did

during his *Schwarze Ferkel* association. The optimism of youth, optimism despite adversity, was forever gone.

Munch offered the entire Frieze for sale, not wishing to break it apart into its components. There were no buyers. Instead, he sent it to Leipzig, Christiania, and Prague to be exhibited while he dreamed of finding a permanent exhibition space for it (fig. 8). To Franz Servaes, his former *Schwarze Ferkel* associate, he wrote on January 29, 1903:

> B. Cassirer [the Berlin art dealer] tells me that you would like to have one of my prints. Then I say, that you should right away have three and choose them since I have regarded you as an old friend and companion in arms for so long and wanted to give you something. . . . Soon I will have an exhibition in Prague — — . . . I will exhibit my Frieze from the Berlin Secession. I would like very much to show this Frieze in Vienna sometime, since I consider it my most significant work. The Viennese artists are the only ones who could help me display the Frieze well in an architectonic setting — —
>
> With hearty greeting to you and your wife,
>
> Your old Edv. Munch[76]

It is the sole indication known of how Munch wished his "Frieze of Life" to be displayed.

The Vienna Secession had attained renown for its semiannual exhibitions and their architectural setting in the Secession Building. In 1902 they attracted particular attention for their display of Max Klinger's sculpture *Beethoven*, building for it a sanctuarylike *Jugendstil* space and placing into the accompanying rooms large painted friezes visualizing Beethoven's music. It was this type of pristine Viennese *Jugendstil Gesamtkunstwerk* that would have formed the proper setting for Munch's Frieze, giving it a somewhat more grandiose appearance and quasi-religious significance than the otherwise remarkably suitable interior by Henry Van de Velde in which the Frieze was displayed in Leipzig in 1903. The Frieze never found such an architectural home. In 1905 Munch began selling its components separately, and since then the 1890s Frieze has never been brought together again. Munch did create later versions of many of the Frieze paintings, bringing those together in 1918 and writing a vociferous defense of his new "Frieze of Life," but the product of the *Schwarze Ferkel*, that he himself identified as his greatest achievement, has been forever dispersed.[75]

NOTES

1. Concerning the history of Munch's *Verein Berliner Künstler* exhibition, see Reinhold Heller, "Affæren Munch, Berlin 1892-1893," *Kunst og Kultur*, 52 (1969): 175-191, and Ragna Stang, *Edvard Munch: Mennesket og kunstneren* (Oslo, 1977), 88-94.

2. *Morgenbladet*, Sept. 14, 1892.

3. Adolf Rosenberg, "Eine Ausstellung von Oelgemälden," *Kunstchronik*, N.S.4 (1892/93): 75. Rosenberg's deprecatory reference to, not an art exhibition, but an "exhibition of oil paintings," without reference to the name of the painter, should also be noted.

4. Edvard Munch, letter to Karen Bjølstad, dated Berlin, Nov. 17, 1892, in *Edvard Munchs brev: Familien, et utvalg*, ed. Inger Munch, Munch-museets Skrifter I (Oslo, 1947), no. 129, p. 122.

5. Among the most objective histories of this international group of writers and artists who met briefly at *Zum schwarzen Ferkel*, a group subject largely to myth-tinged accounts, is that in George Klim, "Die Gestalt Stanislaw Przybyszewskis im Rahmen der deutschen Literatur der Jahre 1892-98, mit besonderer Berücksichtigung seiner Weltanschauung," Ph.D. diss., Australian National University, Canberra, 1970, p. 60f. I have not had access to the thesis by Carla Hvistendal Lathe, "The Group *Zum schwarzen Ferkel*: A Study in Early Modernism," University of East Anglia, 1972.

6. Richard Dehmel, "Bekenntnis," *Erlösung* (Berlin, 1891), as in *Gesammelte Werke in drei Bänden* (Berlin, 1913), *1*: 11. Dehmel's primary occupation at this time was as an insurance agent.

7. Throughout this essay, details of Przybyszewski's writings and career are based on Klim's study unless otherwise noted.

8. Eugen von Franquet, *Das Schau-Pöbel: Stuck, Klinger, Exter, von Hoffman, usw.: "Die künftigen Helden der Rumpelkammer": Glossen zum Streit der Alten und Jungen* (Leipzig, 1893). The artists named in the title were controversial, symbolist-oriented painters in Germany at the time.

9. In his diary entry of Dec. 24, 1892, Count Kessler lists the "special exhibition of Munch's paintings at the Equitable," but makes no further comment concerning the exhibition. At the time of Munch's *Verein Berliner Künstler* exhibition, Kessler was just completing a trip around the world. For the opportunity to examine and to cite the unpublished portions of Count Kessler's diaries, I wish to thank the Deutsches Literaturarchiv, Schiller-Nationalmuseum, Marbach a.N.

10. Edvard Munch, letter to Johan Rohde, dated Berlin, Feb. 8, 1893, Rohde Archives, Copenhagen. Photocopy in Ingrid Langaard, *Edvard Munch, modningsår* (Olso, 1960), 182-183. The paintings listed in the letter can be identified as follows:

  1 *The Lonely Ones* (Destroyed)
  2 *Melancholy: The Yellow Boat* (Munch-museet, Oslo)
  3 *Spring* (National Gallery, Oslo)
  4 *The Mystic Shore* (Private Collection, Munkedal)
  5 *Night* (National Gallery, Oslo)
  6 *Despair* (Thiels Gallery, Stockholm)
  7 *Portrait of Hans Jæger* (National Gallery, Oslo)
  8 *Portrait of Karl Jensen-Hjell* (Private Collection, Oslo)

11. E. H. (i.e., Emil Hannover), "Edvard Munch," *Politikken*, Feb. 23, 1893. This review was kindly made available to me by Trygve Nergaard.

12. Munch-museet ms. N 45, written c. 1933.

13. Edvard Munch, letter to Johan Rohde, undated (c. March 1893), Rohde Archives, Copenhagen. Here cited according to transcript in Munch-museet.

14. Ola Hansson, *Das junge Skandinavien* (Dresden and Leipzig, 1891), 10.

15. Munch-museet ms. N 59, written c. 1892/1893.

16. Stanislaw Przybyszewski, *Homo Sapiens: A Novel in Three Parts*, tr. T. Seltzer (New York, 1915), 18. *Overboard*, the first novel of the trilogy, was originally published in a Danish translation in 1896; a German edition appeared in 1898. I have altered the Seltzer translation to approximate more closely Przybyszewski's original German text.

17. Munch-museet ms. N 59, c. 1892/1893.

18. Przybyszewski, *Homo Sapiens*, 32-33.

19. Ola Hansson, *Sensitiva Amorosa* (Uppsala, 1957), 3-4.

20. Stanislaw Przybyszewski, *Totenmesse* (Berlin, 1893), 6.

21. Przybyszewski, *Totenmesse*, 7.

22. Anonymous, "Das Schwarze Ferkel," *Berliner Tageblatt*, June 17, 1901, as reprinted from *Neues Wiener Tageblatt*. Written shortly after the murder of Dagny Juell by Wladislas Emerik at Tiflis on June 5, 1901, the article was also published in various Scandinavian newspapers, bringing a response from Munch in the *Kristiania Dagsavis* ("Dagny Przybyszewska," issue of June 25, 1901). Publication of the anonymous article in *Svenska Dagbladet* (June 21, 1901) and the Swedish Socialist paper *Arbedet* (June 19, 1901) has caused attribution to be given to Bengt Lidforss, a young Swedish botany student in Berlin in 1893 (cf. Erix Vedefelt, *Den unge Bengt Lidforss* [Lund, 1962], 200). This attribution has no supporting evidence, however. Considering the article's apparent origination in Vienna (I have not seen the original publication), it appears most likely that Franz Servaes would have written it since he then lived in Vienna and, moreover, was a regular contributor to the *Neues Wiener Tageblatt* at the time.

23. Munch-museet ms. T 2759 (E.M. III). The date of this manuscript remains uncertain; events discussed in it fix a date *post quem* of 1903.

24. The true identity of "Mrs. Heiberg" was determined by Trygve Nergaard in his immeasurably valuable thesis, "Refleksjon og visjon. Nautralismens dilemma i Edvard Munchs kunst, 1889-1894," Universitetet i Oslo, 1968, p. 77 and note 163.

25. Munch-museet ms. T 2770 (E/M II). The entry prior to this is dated by Munch, Feb. 4, 1890.

26. Hans Jæger, as cited by Carl Nærup, *Illustreret Norsk Litteraturhistorie* (Christiania, 1905), 233.

27. Hans Jæger, *Syk Kjærlihet* (Oslo, 1969), 49.

28. Adolf Paul, *Strindberg-minnen och brev* (Stockholm, 1915), 90-91.

29. See note 24.

30. Edvard Munch, "Dagny Przybyszewska," *Kristiania Dagsavis*, June 25, 1901. The article is an impassioned and somewhat misguided defense of Dagny Juell against rumors of immorality engendered by her murder and seemingly supported by the Servaes article.

31. Adolf Paul, letter to Axeli Gallèn-Kallela, c. June 24, 1893, as cited by Göran Söderström, *Strindberg och bildkonsten* (Stockholm, 1972), 400.

32. Klim, p. 48-51.

33. Edvard Munch, memories of his sister Sophie's death, in *Brev*, no. 82, p. 89-90. Although dated 1890 by Inger Munch, this semifictional recollection was certainly written later, possibly c. 1891-1893. In the text, Munch uses the name "Maja" for Sophie, "Captain" for his father, and "Karleman" for himself.

34. Concerning the origins and premises of Munch's ego-centered aesthetic, see my article on Munch's *Night in Saint Cloud*, to be published in *Arts Magazine*, Oct. 1978.

35. Cf. catalogue: *Edvard Munch * Gemälde-Ausstellung—Berlin. Unter den Linden 19*[i]:

No. 4. Studie zu einer Serie: "Die Liebe"
   a   *Sommernachts-Traum.*
   b   *Kuss.*
   c   *Liebe und Schmerz.*
   d   *Das Madonna-Gesicht.*
   e   *Eifersucht.*
   f   *Verzweiflung.*

The titles and dates in brackets are those generally accepted today.

36. Richard Dehmel, "Unsere Stunde," *Lebensblätter* (Berlin, 1895), 57.

37. Edvard Munch, *Livsfrisens tilblivelse* (Oslo, c. 1929). The text was probably originally written in 1890.

38. Cf. Johann Joachim Winckelmann, *Versuch einer Allegorie, besonders für die Kunst* (Dresden, 1766).

39. Peter von Cornelius, *Beschreibung der Campo Santo-Entwürfe* (Munich, 1848), as cited by Alfred Kuhn, *Peter Cornelius und die geistigen Strömungen seiner Zeit* (Berlin, 1921), 219.

40. Munch-museet, ms. T 2760 (The Violet Book), entry dated Nice, Jan. 8, 1892.

41. Hermann Bahr, *Die Ueberwindung des Naturalismus* (Leipzig, 1891), p. 196.

42. Cf. note 40.

43. Munch-museet, ms. T 2547. The content is similar to that of other texts written c. 1893-1894, although as cited here derives from Munch's portfolio of graphics now entitled "Kunskapens træ på godt og ondt" and probably written during the late teens and twenties.

44. Munch-museet ms. N 30, c. 1894-1896?

45. Stanislaw Przybyszewski, *De Profundis* (Berlin, n.d. [1896]), 11.

46. Arne Garborg, *Trætte mænd* (Oslo, 1970), 84. Garborg's impressionistic novel was first published in 1891.

47. Munch-museet ms. N 30, c. 1894-1896?

48. The events of the summer and fall, 1893, are recounted by Klim, pp. 72ff. and pp. 48-51.

49. Paul, pp. 128-129.

50. Kessler, diary entry dated Dec. 7, 1894.

51. Julius Meier-Graefe, *Geschichten neben der Kunst* (Berlin,

1933), 152-154. The name "Ducha" derives from the Polish word meaning "soul."

52. Information concerning Munch's and Przybyszewski's stay in Norway during 1894 is derived from their correspondence with Baron von Bodenhausen, Deutsches Literaturarchiv, Schiller-Nationalmuseum, Marbach a.N.

53. Catalogue, Konstföreningens Lokal, Stockholm, *Edvard Munch* (October 1894), nos. 55-68.

54. Kessler, diary entry dated Dec. 9, 1894.

55. "He is now planning to create engravings and lithographs of his entire cycle Love, that is now almost finished in paintings." Julius Meier-Graefe, introduction to *Edvard Munch: Acht Radierungen* (Berlin, 1895), 19.

56. Kessler, diary entry dated Feb. 9, 1895.

57. Kessler, diary entry dated May 10, 1895.

58. Letter to Karen Bjølstad, dated Oct. 24, 1894, *Brev* no. 166, p. 146.

59. This issue is discussed further in my study of Munch's *Night in Saint Cloud*, cf. note 34 above.

60. Munch-museet ms. N 30, c. 1894-1895. It should be pointed out that the numbers to which Munch refers seem not to correspond to the numbering of any known catalogues of his exhibitions. However, up through the title *Sphinx*, there are eight paintings listed in the identical order as in the 1895 Berlin exhibition, suggesting there is correspondence here. Moreover, if one divides the exhibition listing into two sections, the first ending after *Jealousy*, and if the painting *Hands* is excluded (as it is separate in the handwritten listing), the numbers again correspond, with *Insane Mood* as no. 4.

61. Stanislaw Przybyszewski, *Erinnerungen an das literarische Berlin*, tr. K. Staemmler (Munich, 1965), 183.

62. Hans Jæger, "Fra distrikts fængslet," *Impressionisten* (1886), no. 1, p. 4.

63. Przybyszewski, *Totenmesse*, 32-33.

64. Munch-museet, mss. T2781o and T2781n, both c. 1893.

65. Munch-museet, ms. T2782 au/1, c. 1893.

66. Munch-museet, ms. T2547 ("Kunskapens træ på godt og ondt"), compare note 43.

67. Sigbjørn Obstfelder, "Edvard Munch, et forsøk," *Samtiden*, 7 (1896): 21.

68. Lou Andreas Salomé, *Erotik* (Berlin, 1903), 15 and 27.

69. Stanislaw Przybyszewski, *Zur Psychologie des Individuums, II: Ola Hansson* (Berlin, 1892), 12-14.

70. Przybyszewski, *Totenmesse*, 33.

71. Letter to Andreas Aubert, Mar. 18, 1902, Oslo University Library, Letter Collection no. 32.

72. For an extensive and accurate account of this usually incorrectly recorded, legendary event, see Arne Eggum, "Det gröna rummet—The Green Room," in catalogue, Stockholm, Liljevalchs & Kulturhuset, *Edvard Munch 1863-1944*, March 25-May 15, 1977, pp. 62 ff.

73. Munch-museet, ms. no. T2759 (EM II), after 1903.

74. Letter to Franz Servaes, Jan. 29, 1903, Private Collection, Vienna. Servaes' response (Munch-museet Archives) indicates that he had lost contact with his former "companion in arms"; he asks Munch if his *Fries* is a large portrait!

75. Concerning the later frieze variations and their composition, see Arne Eggum, "Munchs sena Livsfris—Munch's Late Frieze of Life," in catalogue, Stockholm, 1977, pp. 19ff. Eggum makes the proper observation that the specific term "Frieze of Life" seems not to have been used by Munch before 1918; prior to that, his friezes bore the titles "Love" (1893-1897), "Cycle of Moments from Life" (1902-1903), "From the Life of a Modern Soul" (1902), and "Life" (1905). I cannot agree with Eggum's conclusion that this is ". . . an unclear concept, pointing in a definite direction but not precisely delimitable" (p. 33), since during the periods 1895-1897 and 1902-1905 Munch definitely did give precise limits and content to his Frieze conceptions; the "lack of clarity" appears only after Munch disbanded the original Frieze and, during the later teens and twenties, created variants of his earlier paintings that he willfully combined with new compositions in a constant process of alteration and experimentation. While it is true, as Eggum and other Norwegian scholars point out, that there is a continuity of motifs, themes, and concerns in Munch's work from the mid-1880s to the time of his death, it should also be emphasized that after c. 1900 his major concerns shift from the symbolist orientation and stylistic characteristics of the 1890s to what might best be described as neo-naturalism, a concern with a celebration of the visual and hidden forces of nature, which found its greatest expression in the central image of Munch's paintings for the Oslo University Aula, *The Sun*. While this aspect of Munch's work is art historically (art history seen in the usual deterministic and linear conception of influences and an avant-garde—rear guard antithesis, a conception that, incidentally, is historically incorrect) less significant than his work of the 1890s, Munch's defenders do disservice to its inherent quality by seeking to justify it through an association and total equation with Munch's symbolist paintings and prints.

Evening/Melancholy, 1896. OKK G/t 571-23, Sch. 82, Munch-Museet (cat. no. 136)

Despair

Trygve Nergaard

"I PAINT NOT WHAT I SEE, BUT WHAT I SAW" is an often cited statement by Edvard Munch, which invites a biographically based interpretation of his pictorial themes. The past is, of course, not something which is established once and for all. What the memory selects from the past and the way in which this is interpreted is also determined by the situation one finds oneself in, as well as by one's projects and hopes for the future. One can only achieve a partial understanding of the theme of despair in Munch's art by considering the biographical background which forms the basis for the paintings. We might gain a fuller understanding by viewing the despair at the time he was creating the art as a reason for his selection of pictorial themes from his memories. In the following pages I will consider the theme as a sense of despair rising out of Munch's self-awareness as an artist and projected onto his recollected images from the past.

In 1891 Munch received the National Fellowship for Artists for the third time. At the end of November, he returned to Nice where he had spent the winter and summer of 1891. Soon after his departure, Bjørnstjerne Bjørnson wrote a newspaper article entitled "Misguided Fellowships for Artists" in which, among other things, he criticized Munch's being selected, as well as Munch's decision to use the fellowship in Nice.

> This probably means the Munch will remain in Nice—in other words that he is ill and will stay at the health resort. It was rumored, when he received the fellowship for the third time, that it was because he was and still is ill. However, our few and extremely modest fellowships for artists are absolutely not meant as health insurance . . . private contributions must be collected for a sick man; the fellowship should be awarded to one who would make full use of it for his art.[1]

In an ironic reply to Bjørnson, Munch attempted to explain why he was reawarded the grant. At the same time he refuted a stipulation which was im-

plied in Bjørnson's article and which was generally accepted as a necessary requirement for a fellowship award, namely, that the fellowship should be used in one of Europe's major art centers:

> I became seriously ill the last time I was abroad and therefore was not able to benefit fully from my stay. I was reawarded the fellowship partially to make up for the lost time, not because I was still sick . . . Furthermore, I would like to reassure you that I am in excellent health, that I have not yet availed myself of any treatment at the health resort, and I would like to inform you that Nice is not at all a health spa but a rather large city on the Mediterranean which attracts many painters because of its natural beauty. . . . In addition, I believe that when a painter is awarded a fellowship, he should also be trusted to have good enough sense to decide where he should use it. He certainly ought to be able to determine best where it is most advantageous to work for his development.[2]

In the meantime, the painter Frits Thaulow had wholeheartedly rallied to Munch's defense. Thaulow referred to the fact that Erik Werenskiold "buys paintings by Munch" and that Fritz Uhde in Munich stated that Munch is "the most interesting painter in Scandinavia," and rebuked Bjørnson on behalf of his colleagues:

> Yes, this is what *we* think and this is what *we* see because we work every single day with the difficult language of colors and lines. We have progressed a bit in the difficult task of developing good taste—we have paid our tribute! That you have not done! Therefore you have no right to interfere when it comes to awarding fellowships to painters. In this case, it is *you* who is misguided![3]

Even though Thaulow had some personal reservations about certain aspects of Munch's art, he found that there were "qualities in his work which undeniably award him first place among the younger artists" and he felt that all his colleagues would support a suggestion that:

> Munch should be allowed to retain the fellowship indefinitely, even if it meant sending him to a health resort in order to keep his art alive—this rare and beautiful flower.

Ørebladet supported Bjørnson's views in an editorial. Slighting artistic expertise, the paper chose to be a spokesman for the general public's opinion about Munch's art and about the purpose of fellowships for artists:

> The great number of people who can't understand the extraordinarily remarkable qualities in the paintings Munch exhibited this year [The National Art Exhibition], and who have not been made much wiser by Christian Krohg's explanation and defense, have in all humility and simplicity thought and expressed that it is rather peculiar that this man should once again receive the art fellowship. . . . We, on our part, have thought the same. However, we also have believed that what is still lacking in Munch's talent—the inability to paint in such a manner that, if not everyone, at least the majority can understand and value his works—This defect could perhaps be resolved if Munch continued to live and work abroad.[4]

Through these articles we can sense the tension-filled gap between artist and public which had come about as a result of the gradual liberation of art during the 1800s. The artist-oriented aesthetic had become so generally accepted that artists, as a group with common interests, powerfully asserted their absolute competence in opposition to the opinions of all nonexperts. On the other hand, "the free artist's" work was relegated to the art market where it could only hope to gain acceptance from an anonymous public. This hope hinged on the public becoming familiar with it. The art work had to be acknowledged as "art" to fit the traditional art categories. And the life it represented had to be recognized by the bourgeois public as its own life.

Munch's article foundered against both sides of this conflict. He did not refer to the point of view of an artistic group but insisted on the individual artist's absolute authority over his own development and art. To the extent that Munch sought support for his development from the public or from his painter colleagues, he had to reconcile himself to their expectations for his future. As long as these expectations were unfulfilled, there remained a conflict in which his hopes for acceptance were countered by the expectations of the public. In Thaulow's review of Munch's paintings at the National Art Exhibition, we sense that he had an inkling that a reconciliation of this conflict could only be achieved through a redefinition of the concept of art.

> It was almost a corner of the future up there where his paintings hung. I was constantly drawn there by a singular power—the marvelously new color contrasts, a vibrating nervous "ganz-bei-der Sache" art and a noble disdain for banal taste. This bold "courage de defaut" gave me an uneasy feeling that I was witnessing the germination of an art which would eventually kill ours—our nice, respectable, and precise realism.

The tension between his own intentions and others' expectations and demands, the hope for a reconciliation of the conflict through future artistic practice, and the despair at the possibilities for such a reconciliation became a central theme in Munch's art. In the following pages, we will examine more closely these hopes and expectations, which revealed themselves in his public appearances in connection with the fellowship applications and his exhibitions.

There were no detailed instructions for awarding or using the national grants for "Researchers' and Artists' Travels Abroad," as it was listed in the parliamentary budget. But the intentions and stipulations of the authorities granting the award surfaced in the recommendations of the budget committee and in parliamentary debates concerning the alteration of the budget, especially in 1880 and 1884. Bjørnson referred to these parliamentary debates in his reply to Thaulow's article.[5] In these debates, there was substantial agreement that the public had a duty to advance the development of the pictorial arts and that this important national task had long been neglected. The tight economic situation did not allow any improvement of artistic education in Norway. The travel grants were regarded as a temporary compensation for this:

> As long as we have not established an art academy, aspiring and talented artists should apply, on the strength of their abilities, to their fellow citizens for economic support toward their further advancement.

It was also made clearer how the individual artist should use his fellowship. He was expected to study and develop further within established traditions:

> He must first of all, if possible, put his talents in touch with real life in the entire civilized world; here he should visit art collections, which can provide him with the artistic models, and attend studios where experienced masters can guide and instruct him.

During the period from 1884 to 1890, it was also decided, in consultation with the artists, to require fellowship holders to donate one of their works to the National Gallery—a decision which was not carried out in practice. The committee report reads:

> These art works should preferably be copies—in original size—of excellent works of non-Norwegian art.[6]

When Munch applied for the national grant for the fourth time, in 1889, he did so with full support from established artists. At that time he was holding a large one-man show of 110 items which constituted a representative selection from his production. It is rather curious that his two latest pictures at the exhibition, the portrait of Hans Jæger and the large painting *Spring,* were more complete and closer to the prevailing naturalism in pictorial arts than most of the works he had exhibited at the Autumn Exhibitions of previous years. In the catalogue, *Spring* was labeled "unfinished," as though Munch wanted to emphazise that he mastered the techniques of his Norwegian teachers, even without finishing the work. Just as in terms of motif, *The Sick Child,* 1886, implicitly referred to his teacher Christian Krohg, *Spring* is a reference to Hans Heyerdahl's large compositions *The Dying Child,* a success at the Paris Salon, and to *The Worker's Death* from the Autumn Exhibition of 1888.[7]

Munch's one-man show functioned in a way as "supporting documentation" for his fellowship application, and it contained an implied request to travel abroad to develop further. This objective of the show was emphasized by two long newspaper articles written by Munch's supporters, Christian Krohg and the art historian Andreas Aubert. Krohg used as a point of departure how he and his generation had broken with the late romantic, German-academic painting of the previous generation, and how the realistic painting of the "second generation" had gradually become established. He then looked for those who were to carry Norwegian painting tradition further:

> Where are they? Where is the third generation? The leaders of the second generation still remain unchallenged on their throne. . . . Finally we have found it. Edvard Munch is the third generation. For the time being, he is all of it. . . . *Munch* is therefore the Norwegian artist on whom we place our greatest hopes.

Krohg defended the "unfinished" quality in Munch's pictures against the judgment of both the public and the art critics, and he promised that "one of these days he will master it all, and express what is important to him without necessarily giving up sketching, etc.," adding:

> It is a shame that Munch has never had the opportunity to undergo a rigorous program at an Academy, as all French painters have. Munch is sufficiently independent that this experience would not have harmed him as it has so many others.

Krohg further maintained that the principal new quality in Munch's art was the artist's subjective interpretation of the motif.

> It is not only the *plein air* painting that is so important for the third generation—but he certainly has been able to communicate: "How wonderful this is!" Precisely that which he has spontaneously felt at the time he perceived it. He is an impressionist, our only one so far![8]

Andreas Aubert wrote "on request" an article about this exhibition. He stressed the "stroke of genius in his talent" but at the same time warned against Munch's neglect of traditional technique. Aubert's reaction represented a compromise between the spontaneous enthusiasm of Munch's colleagues and the criticism by the bourgeois public for his breaking with traditional art criteria. With this, Aubert gave an accurate description of Munch's situation with its surrounding expectations and demands:

> In assembling together a great number of his works, Munch has invited a public evaluation. He ought to receive it without reserve and without beating around the bush. . . . Even if the exhibition as a whole reveals a lethargic aspect in his self-development and an indifference to form and composition, all the more disappointing in an artist who has so much talent for depicting the human being, it does demonstrate an important development, strongest in the life of the colors, but also expressive in form and spiritual in suggestion. If we seek the reasons for Munch's irregular development, we must consider how little we do to educate our artists at home. Munch's poor health is also an excuse. But he must also share of the guilt himself. . . . However, more important than placing the guilt is finding an appropriate remedy. I have said before and will repeat it now: a fellowship could hardly be more timely and significant for any of our other young painters. Munch should be one of the first to receive one of our two-year grants, but with the expressed condition that he should study under a leading master of life drawing and moreover submit samples of his work after the first year.[9]

By a "leading master of life drawing," Aubert probably referred to Leon Bonnat. He was so highly respected that even mature, established artists sought out his studio. Werenskiold, for example, studied there for several months in the spring of 1889. Krohg had made serious plans to attend in January 1890. Munch began to receive instruction at the studio as soon as he arrived in Paris in October 1889. At first he did what was expected of him. He worked conscientiously at the studio every day and used his spare time to study at the World's Fair. From letters home to his family, it is evident that he felt he would benefit from working at Bonnat's studio and that Bonnat liked his drawings very much.[10] After three months, however, by the winter of 1889/1890, the situation had changed drastically. He stopped attending Bonnat's studio, isolated himself more and more from his friends and colleagues, and immersed himself in constant self-reflection. Memories going back to his early childhood appeared, and he tried to preserve and organize them in a series of literary notes that in some respects resemble a diary. Thoughts about death and the transitory nature of things dominate, and suicide presents itself as a concrete and close possibility.

> Every day is the same—my friends have stopped coming. . . . they see I can't be a part of them, that their laughter

fig. 1 *St. Cloud,* 1890. OKK T 126-28, Munch-Museet, Oslo

fig. 2 *St. Cloud,* 1890. OKK T 126-29, Munch-Museet, Oslo

disturbs me—tortures me. . . . Goldstein, who held out the longest, has also given up. . . . My long daily walks around the old castle are becoming shorter and shorter—it tires me more and more to take walks—The fire in the fireplace is my only friend—The time I spend sitting in front of the fireplace gets longer and longer. . . . When I suffer most I lean my head against the fireplace—then I can suddenly feel a desire overwhelm me—Kill yourself and then it is all over, why live? . . . When I light the candle I suddenly see my huge shadow across half the wall, clear up to the ceiling—And in the large mirror over the fireplace I see myself—the face of my own ghost (T 2770, p. 3; see figs. 1 and 2)[11]

The future seemed meaningless. Confronted with total uncertainty, Munch became paralyzed with desperation. He turned toward the past, as if to find there an explanation for his loneliness and despair. In his memoirs, which are marked by a constant longing for reconciliation and contact, we can see how he searched his thoughts for past relationships which could have offered the possibility of contact. But on all levels, his search only led him back to his own despairing loneliness.

He explored the distance between himself and his family in his thoughts about his father's death, of which he was notified in the beginning of December. Munch wrote about their separation at the time he went to Paris:

We were a little embarrassed in front of each other—We didn't want to show how hard it was to part—how much we loved each other despite everything—How he suffered for my sake, for my life—*during the nights*—because I couldn't share his faith. (T 2770, p. 4)

And in another note he wrote:

What I wanted he didn't understand. What he valued the most I didn't understand. God *separated* us. (N-18)

Religion, like his life as bohemian and artist, also presented an insurmountable barrier between him and the rest of the family:

Those at home, my aunt, my brother and my sisters believe that death is only a sleep—that my father sees and hears our sorrow—that they will meet him again up there. . . . I sit alone with a million memories. (N-18)

A drawing from this period (cat. no. 109) shows an old man walking on a path that leads into an endless, desolate landscape. Since Munch drew two sketches of his father on the other side of the paper (together with his mother, or aunt, and two small children), it may be assumed that the old man on the path also represents his father and that the landscape is meant to evoke the emptiness of death.

He turned toward his relationships with women and reread old letters:

There were letters from various women—there were photographs . . . I am looking at a photo—this gentle beautiful face with the smile of spring. . . . She was more beautiful than the other—why couldn't I care for her? (T 2770, p. 4)

"The other" returned to him in a series of recollections of short moments of togetherness and fervent passion. But he dwelt mostly on the painful separation, on the husband who stood between them, and on the gradual dissolution of their relationship.

The Path of Death, 1889. OKK T 250 A, Munch-Museet, Oslo (cat. no. 109)

His relationship with the public and art colleagues emerged in his recollections of the Autumn Exhibition of 1886 where he exhibited *The Sick Child*. Even though he met some who spoke well of the picture (like Christian Krohg and Hans Jæger), he regarded himself mostly as the lonely outsider.

> He saw the picture hanging straight in front of him in a prominent place—how strongly the streaks stood out—he looked with anxiety at the people standing around—there was a crowd in front of the painting—he walked quickly through the cluster—"Frightful," he heard—There was a ringing in his ears.

He tried to explain his intentions to a group of younger colleagues, but was not understood:

> I think it's crap. . . . What the hell are all these streaks for?—it looks like its raining. Everyone laughed—Now we return to Brandt's painting again—he only talks about his own paintings—he doesn't care about others—Go to hell, said Brandt. (T 2771, p. 34)

The feeling of artistic isolation and uncertainty was significant. The experience released the desperate search for companionship revealed in his notebooks. His daily work became increasingly meaningless in light of the goals he had for his art. The work was arranged according to the expectations accompanying the fellowship, and after a while it became a strain:

> I work at the studio in the morning, stretch out my arm and use my pencil to measure relationships in the body of the naked model who stands in the middle of the room. How many heads per body, how wide is the chest in relation to the length of the body. It bores me, it tires me—it dulls me. (T 2770, p. 11)

The goal of the art that the activity in the studio centered around seemed to be the practical work itself. The recognition which he sought had to be articulated through an art which did not consist merely of slavery to a traditional technique. When

Man and Woman in Bed, 1890. OKK T 365, Munch-Museet, Oslo (cat. no. 110)

Munch pictured how this art was to come about, he did so in a negative manner, through a denial of the practical aspect of the work. In the so-called St. Cloud Manifesto, Munch expressed a hope for an art that was to spring forth mystically from himself—and that this art would be totally his own but at the same time capable of moving others.

> I was going to do something—I felt it would be so easy—it would form itself under my hands like magic—and then they'd see.[12]

But this was at best a hope for the future. In daily work the miracle hadn't happened. And the hope was soon undermined by memories of how things had been earlier.

> I remember how many times before I had felt something similar—and when I had finished the picture—they just shook their heads and smiled.

Nevertheless, he imagined conjuring forth such pictures that would unite him with his public through a reconciling experience of a shared feeling. And when he described how he imagined this artistic articulation in practice, the theme of the work dealt, characteristically, with closeness to "the other" in total mutual acceptance.

A strong naked arm, a tanned powerful neck—a young woman rests her head against a broad chest. She closes her eyes and listens, with open quivering lips, to the words he whispers into her long, flowing hair. I would give form to this as I now see it, but envelop it in the blue haze— These two in that instant when they are no longer themselves, but only one link in the thousands of links that bind generations to one another. People should understand the sanctity, the might of this, and remove their hats, as if in a church.

The picture of mutual devotion which he imagined here was never realized except in a small ink sketch (cat. no. 110). On the contrary, at the time when the note was written, the resulting painting (cat. no. 26) shows a contemplating, melancholy figure who sits lonely "in the blue haze." It has been suggested, perhaps correctly, that the model for the pensive figure at the window in *Night in St. Cloud* was Munch's friend, the Danish poet Emanuel Goldstein. It may be more accurate to consider the painting as an expression of Munch's own situation, as evidenced by the notes quoted above. Loneliness and lack of contact are emphasized by the window which opens onto the life, passing at a distance, outside. Desire for contact with this life is implied by the contrast between the light, alluring colors outside and the dark, closed feeling of the room. One of the critics at the Autumn Exhibition of 1890 captured the mood in the picture rather well when he wrote that the lonely man by the window

> looks like a "decadent" in the true sense of the word; he relives his life in his thoughts, while he stares blindly down into the dark Seine outside, which has softly closed over so many wasted lives.[13]

Another picture from the same period, *Une Confession*, which later disappeared, depicted two men engaged in an intimate conversation over glasses of absinth. About this picture, the same critic commented that "it is only the absinth that is effective." There is an ambiguity implied here which throws doubt on the possibility for fellowship and camaraderie. Contact and the ability to confide in others are artificially brought about by alcohol.[14]

The longing for fellowship, reconciliation, and recognition characterized both his notes and pictures from this period. But there is also a despairing gap between hope and reality that cannot be bridged in practice. Munch fulfilled his duty of accounting for his fellowship year by submitting no less than ten pictures to the Autumn Exhibition. The underlying tone in the conservative papers was that Munch's paintings were still unintelligible and that they were, for the most part, unfinished sketches and experiments. Several also emphasized that he had not proved himself deserving of the fellowship, and that he had not, in any case, developed his art in a favorable direction.

It is noteworthy that several critics commented on the peace which dominated the exhibition. There was no longer a struggle between tendencies and factions. The realism and *plein air* painting of the new generation had become completely established and recognized. As the art critic for the newspaper *Verdens Gang* put it:

> The mood cannot be better described than as mutual respect between the artists and the public. . . . The new trend is now accepted together with other trends. There are no longer factions. They are dissolved into individual artists. Each artist has become a faction who is fighting, not for his trend, but for his individuality.[15]

This description of each artist's individuality is a general formulation of the subjective situation which Munch experienced. Munch experienced this situation as despair; he could not find a practical way in which to go beyond his own individuality and obtain a feeling of fellowship. Individuality was experienced as isolation from society. The condition for enduring this isolation was a consensus to engage in a mutual project which was to reunite the individuals in the society. It is a characteristic idea in bourgeois society that art is a medium through which isolated individuals recognize themselves and learn to recognize others. It is precisely in art that concepts of fellowship, such as nationality, lineage, race, or humanity, are formed and explained. A good example of this ideology is expressed in the introduction to a petition, in 1884, from "almost all Norwegian artists" to the Parliament, concerning the establishment of a yearly, subsidized art exhibition (the Autumn Exhibition):

> Artistic work in the context of the people's common goals should not be regarded as luxurious decoration on a completed building. It is an integral part of the structure, without which the work could never be complete. For it is only through art that the people reach total self-awareness. . . . By holding up for consideration the grandeur of Nature and Human Life . . . the infinite variations of life, the artist enables people to understand themselves. . . . The pictorial artist is, therefore, a participant in the common task of creating the people's happiness. . . . By looking at their work, people arrive at a higher understanding of themselves, as they take part in the beauty that the artist has managed to create through the strength and refinement of his conception.[16]

Toward the end of the eighties, increasing emphasis was put on the idea that the more the artist turned to his own personal experience, the one he would know best, the more accurate society's image of itself in art would be. This turning to the subjective was expressed especially well by the Danish art historian Julius Lange:

> We shall learn to know one another through art . . . recollections of what is very personal . . . something so pri-

vately and personally experienced . . . is precisely what others would understand best, the truly universal. . . . Even if a society is rather fragmented into atoms, it weaves together a mask of unity through reciprocal personal communication. In this way, we catch a distant glimpse of the great Social Art and the Canaan of the great style.[17]

As an understanding of the self, the experience of this ideology can be rather painful for the artist. Precisely because art is supposed to be the conciliatory medium that dispels the fragmentation within society, the artist must to a certain extent *live* loneliness in a different way than others. He must remain outside and alone in order to continue to express individuality, as a continuation of the tradition of realism. He must assume the sufferings on behalf of others in order to lead them into a reconciliating fellowship. It is not surprising that biblical expressions are common in the art discussions from this period, nor that artists are often identified with such figures as Moses or Christ.

For Munch, such discomfort did not lie only in the unavoidable loneliness but particularly in the demand for a common objective basis for the artistic idiom which was to transcend individuality and teach the atoms of society to know each other. Such an art would have to be based on a common ability to recognize the object. This would require a certain faithfulness to the rules of perspective, local color, and objects' relationships and consistencies. In short, the idea of a socially reconciling art was dependent upon a practice of realism. For Munch, however, the possibility of creating a personal and individual art depended precisely on breaking with the practice of realism. In a note dated January 2, 1891, probably prompted by the reaction to his pictures at the Autumn Exhibition of 1890, Munch objected especially to the demand for the recognizable object. In the end, he directed a despairing invocation to the future:

> It would be fun to preach a little to all these people who for so many years have looked at our pictures—and have either laughed or shaken their heads—They can't comprehend that there might be the smallest ounce of reason in these impressions—these momentary impressions— That a tree can be red or blue or that a face can be blue or green—They know this is wrong—They've known since childhood that leaves and grass are green and that skin color is rosy. They can't imagine that this is seriously meant—it must be a sham, done out of laziness—or in insanity—most likely the latter—They can't get it through their heads that these paintings are made in earnest—in suffering. . . . Yes, for this is the path to the painting of the future—to the promised land in art. For, in these paintings the painter gives what is dearest to him. . . . his soul—his sorrow, his joy—he gives his heart's blood. He gives the human being—not the object. These pictures will, they must, grip stronger—first the few—then more—then everyone. (T 2760, p. 9f)

During 1890 Munch tried various ways of developing new painting techniques, from a unifying coloring to a decomposed, impressionistic blotched painting. The general reaction at the Autumn Exhibition was that he hadn't developed beyond the experimental phase. Several critics pointed out that Munch was trying to cling to "the latest"; that he had eagerly been studying Pissarro and Monet. That was easily demonstrated since they both participated in the exhibition.

In the autumn of 1890, Andreas Aubert wrote a long series of articles entitled "Idealism and Realism in Art," in which he introduced Julius Lange's ideas to the Norwegian public, and he used this series as the basis for an equally long series about the Autumn Exhibition where Munch was treated in a separate article.[18] It was important for Aubert to depict the new idealism in art as an extension of the realistic tradition. For Aubert, the dominant goal was the development of a national art which would mirror the people's life and distinctive character. This art was to be based on a detailed study of reality, so that the public might recognize their own lives. Several spokesmen for the new idealism in art had recently aimed fanatic attacks at realism. These attacks, which were primarily directed at literature, but which also applied to the pictorial arts, declared realism dead.[19] Its objectivity and its close ties to artisan traditions were considered destructive precisely to those emotional and spiritual qualities that the new idealists regarded as most important in art. Instead of countering or spurning these attacks, Aubert tried to reconcile the new idealism with the realistic tradition. Through Lange's concept of an "art of memory," Aubert found an acceptable interpretation of the strivings of the new idealists. He also maintained that Lange "regarded the realistic art of our time as the natural passage to the Ideal Art which he is on the lookout for." Aubert explained this "natural passage" by considering impressionism as a mediating trend. He viewed impressionism as an attempt to

> grasp the *totality* in order to retain it in the mood of the moment with the intensity of immediate impression. . . . And this training of the soul to retain the image as a totality in the moment of perception is precisely the best training for retaining the picture in *memory* and for grasping the *inner* picture, which will emerge from the depths of the soul as an "art of memory."

In addition, Aubert maintained:

> Impressionism's *other* perculiarity—which is closely related to its emphasis on the impression of *totality*—is that it places far more weight on the *subjective* than did the older form of realistic art. Therefore, it will be able to let *fantasy* play a more important part. . . . By emphasizing the subjective with greater strength, impressionism is preparing for a new ideal art.

Aubert found his ideas confirmed by Arne Garborg, who on behalf of literature

here in *Dagbladen*—has traced in detail the same movement away from the objectively descriptive through the *impressionistic* and subjective toward "intuition"—toward a new idealism.[20]

According to Aubert, the new, personal ideal art or "art of memory" had to be based on realism. A detailed study of nature and models was necessary to make the new ideal art "healthy and viable." On this basis, Aubert found that the "rich promises" of Munch's unique talent had not yet been fulfilled. He believed that the reason could be found in Munch's temperament and in his relation to practical work.

If I've called Wentzel's ability healthy, powerful and capable, I'd call Munch's nervously delicate and self-indulgent to the point of sickness. . . . He has been said to typify the "fourth [sic] generation" of a new period which is supposed to be on its way. There is some truth in this: Munch is the artist whose whole temperament embodies most of the *neurasthenic*. He belongs to those natures with refined, sickly sensitive nerves . . . who often obtain a certain satisfaction in calling themselves "Decadents": children of a refined, overcivilized period. . . . there is something of a pleasure-seeking self-admiration in his temperament. This is one of the greatest dangers that a great talent with introspective tendencies must fight: the danger of enjoying oneself, *without being fertile in one's own ability.* This is intimately connected with a characteristic of Munch, that he has too often and too strongly demonstrated a *disdain for the public*, which is not healthy. . . . But I hope that in this following fellowship year, Munch will show a far more concentrating and self-denying ability to work—not only all these landscape sketches of a fine *impression*, but more serious and thorough *nude studies.* For the sake of his development, I would rather he had done a single, serious and thoroughly worked out drawing or study of a model. It's possible that he has done such studies. But then he should have exhibited them. And even if he hasn't done any, I will not pass any judgment, if, for instance, health precautions have prevented him from carrying out the academy exercises.[21]

There is something striking about the manner in which Aubert pointed out the "sickly" tendencies in Munch's art—an inner sickness—and in which he implied that an external, physical weakness may have hindered a positive development. His choice of words seem to be more than an accident. A mutual relationship between psychological and physical misery manifested itself directly in Munch's self-understanding, in his pictorial themes and in his notes. The abnormal state of being "deadly ill" was interpreted as a necessary condition for, and source of, the genuine artistic experience of reality.

Let us first examine the role that considerations of health played in connection with his fellowships and his sense of duty toward the authorities who awarded them to him. On December 27, 1889, he wrote to the Ministry of Culture to say that he "had used the first half of his National Fellowship in Paris that autumn under the tutelage of Bonnat" and to request payment of the second half of the fellowship.[22] It is not explicitly stated that he intended to continue studying with Bonnat, but we should probably interpret the letter as a concession to public and official expectations. At the same time, he wrote in the notes quoted above that the work at the studio "bores, tires, and dulls" him, and in a letter to his family, on January 2, 1890, he stated: "I am going to leave Bonnat's studio soon." He chose to follow his own path since he felt outright physical discomfort at fulfilling his duties. However, his pictures at the Autumn Exhibition did not elicit any particular recognition in regard to this self-chosen path. In fact, the expectations tied to the next fellowship year were emphasized. In his request for payment of the fellowship, dated October 21, 1890, Munch wrote, "I intend to travel to Paris on the 28th to continue my studies." On the way to France, he became ill and was hospitalized in Le Havre until New Year's, 1891. Afterwards, he went to Nice. In a letter from there of January 22, 1890, he requested payment of his fellowship, "to continue my studies. They have been interrupted for a short while because of sickness, but I will probably be able to resume them soon in Paris." However, he remained in Nice and wrote home on April 13 that he would be traveling to Paris "in about two weeks." On March 24, 1891, he applied for the national fellowship for the following year and explained that sickness had hindered his work and that only now could he resume his studies and consider traveling to Paris. Furthermore, he wrote:

Under these conditions, the benefits of my stay cannot be great—and it would be tremendously important for me now to receive the support of the fellowship, insofar as a year's study in Paris or Florence next year would enable me to consolidate what I learned in Paris last year.

Referring to the fact that sickness had reduced the benefits of his studies, a majority of the committee recommended that he should be granted a third fellowship year. When Munch again traveled to Nice, in the autumn of 1891, Bjørnson insinuated that this was a misuse of the fellowship. Munch answered that when a painter received a fellowship, he would know best how it ought to be used. His reply to Bjørnson may give the impression that he had made a final decision concerning his development and that he had raised himself above the expectations, advice, and demands of others. But, even so, this decision was soon to be undermined by doubt. As from the St. Cloud period, we also find from this winter in Nice a series of notes which bear witness to a similar despairing situation. The notes are again characterized by a longing for fellowship

By the Fireplace, 1892. OKK T 1990, Munch-Museet, Oslo (cat. no. 111)

and recognition and by despair over the practical difficulties which hindered his artistic plans. Reflections about his uncertainty in this situation led him to turn back to the past in search of companionship and reconciliation. On January 14, 1892, he wrote:

> He—you shall create great works—eternal masterpieces shall fall from your hands. I—yes—I know it—but can they get rid of that worm that lies gnawing at the roots of my heart. (T 2760, p. 38)

Shortly afterwards, in some notes and in a drawing (cat. nos. 111 and 112), he expressed themes of loneliness and despair in a way that refers back to the St. Cloud period.[23]

> Most of the time I sit by the fireplace—sick and feeble—I haven't worked at all recently—How the thoughts are working in my poor head—memories gnawing deeply in my breast—It seems as though I can point at the exact place where *that* wound is—the open wound. Memories of the dead—why did you do this—why didn't you do that—Never being able to right the wrong one has committed—Sometimes I get a sudden absurd feeling of thankfulness for individuals who have been more or less gracious in the past—An old captain who once showed me such a gentle face—I almost get tears in my eyes from the thought. Then I began to think about the women I have cared for—began to think about the others. (T 2760, p. 39)

Some of the notes describe, in a sort of retrospective diary, events which occurred earlier that autumn. The imminent confrontation with the public at the Autumn Exhibition produced doubts as to whether his work could possibly fulfill their expectations. If his failing health had hindered him in his practical work, as can be inferred from his correspondence regarding the fellowships, the opposite situation is expressed here. The sickness, in both the

By the Fireplace, 1892/1893. OKK T 291A, Munch-Museet, Oslo (cat. no. 112)

spiritual as well as the physical sense, seemed to be induced by his experience as an artist:

> Since Thursday I've been terribly weak—I have occasionally visited the framer's shop and looked at my paintings—I feel that I am distancing myself more and more from the public's taste—I feel that I am going to

fig. 3 *Despair*, 1892. Thielska Galleriet, Stockholm

fig. 4 *Despair*, 1891/1892. OKK T 126-10R, Munch-Museet, Oslo

offend them even more. I have been so fatigued that I have dragged myself through the streets—The day before yesterday I had to go to bed at 8 p.m., I slept straight through until 11 a.m. the next day; I woke up tired—The whole time I've had a disgusting feeling of indifference to everything—to paint is not important enough. Most of the time I've been sitting in the Grand Café—I've been so tired that I could barely hold my head up—I've not been able to think—I've felt like I was going mad.[24]

Christian Skredsvig, who traveled with Munch to Nice, and with whom Munch stayed for a while, described their life together in his memoirs. Even though they may have been written down much later, Skredsvig's descriptions seem authentic and give a very striking characterization of Munch's situation. He commented on the background theme of *Despair/The Scream* as follows:

For a long time, he [Munch] wanted to paint a sunset he remembered. Red like blood. No, it *was* clotted blood. But no one would experience it like he did. Everyone would think about clouds. This had made him sad and had filled him with fear. Sad because the painter's humble means were never sufficient. "He is yearning for the impossible, and despair is his religion," I thought, but I advised him to paint it.—And he painted his remarkable "The Scream."[25]

The painting Skredsvig refers to must be the *Despair* now in the Thiel Gallery in Stockholm (fig. 3). In the first edition of the catalogue for his one-man show in the autumn of 1892, the painting was entitled *Mood at Sunset*. In the second edition of the catalogue, the title was changed to *Deranged Mood at Sunset*. The title *Verzweiflung* (Despair) was first used at an exhibition in Berlin in 1893/1894.

In one of his sketchbooks, we find a drawing of what must be the first version of this motif (fig. 4). A road, strongly foreshortened, recedes to the left. The landscape is rather similar to the view from Ljabruveien, the road from Oslo toward Nordstrand, where the Munch family lived as of 1889. This topographic characteristic is preserved in all the later variations, even though the road is raised to a higher level to increase the effect of the dizzying depth below.[26] After indicating two possible placements of the figure in the drawing, Munch placed him leaning over the characteristic railing into the landscape. As may be seen in the painting, Munch created a dramatic distance between the main figure and the two figures walking on the road. He obtained this by moving the main figure clear out to the edge of the frame, and by an exaggerated foreshortening of this distance. This dramatic distance is related to Munch's work with the pictorial theme *Evening*, and with a pictorial structure from earlier paintings. This is particularly true for the picture *Evening* from 1888 (fig. 5), in which Munch's sister Laura is the model. It is easy to see that this painting has been overpainted. There had been a woman's figure standing beside Laura,

fig. 5 *Evening/Laura*, 1888. Private Collection, Oslo

fig. 6 *On the Couch*, 1892. OKK T 2761-37, Munch-Museet, Oslo

almost in the center of the painting. There had also been a woman standing on the steps leading into the house. By removing these figures from the middle ground, Munch created a tension throughout the entire picture. Laura becomes more isolated and stands out in monumental solitude. This distance from "the others," which emphasizes the despairing solitude, became a pictorial formula which Munch used in many paintings. The window motif, which shows life outside, used in *Night in St. Cloud,* for instance, functions in the same way. A couple of drawings from one of Munch's notebooks are characteristic examples of how these pictorial formulas are always at hand (figs. 6 and 7).

The loneliness of the foreground figure in *Despair* is produced precisely by the undefinable distance between it and the background figures, which are walking away. Their function is to distance themselves from the foreground figure. They represent a possibility for companionship which is disappearing. This distance is also characteristic of the written formulations of the theme. The first version is probably the one dated "Nice, 1/22/92"

I went down the road with two friends—the sun went down/behind the hill over the city and the fjord/—I sensed a gust of sadness—The sky suddenly turned bloody red. I stopped, leaned against the fence, dead tired—/My two friends looked at me and then continued/—I looked at the flaming clouds/over the fjord/like blood and sword,/and the town/—the blue black fjord and town—My friends continued—I stood there trembling with fear—and I felt as though a great, infinite scream went through/the infinite/nature (T 2760, p. 38)[27]

fig. 7 *On the Couch*, 1892. OKK T 2761-57, Munch-Museet, Oslo

"The friends" continue, unaffected by the drama in nature. For them it is only a normal sunset. For the one who remains behind, deadly tired, the experience is so strong that it affects him physically. The source of the despair, as Skredsvig implied, lay in the fact that it was precisely this experience (and other similar ones) which separated him from "the others," and pointed to his loneliness.

Despair, 1892. OKK T 2367, Munch-Museet, Oslo (cat. no. 113)

It appeared as though he had been chosen by nature herself, or by his own inner "nature," to have a special insight that "the others" didn't have. It was this stigmatization that made him an artist. But it was also this which distanced him from life and condemned him to loneliness. The experience was filled with a mystical cognition of a unity with nature. Communicating this cognition to "the others" presented itself as an important task, but the possibility of succeeding, of having his view recognized seemed hopeless. His experience was bound to seem abnormal to "the others."[28] "The painter's humble means were never sufficient," as Skredsvig said, because "the painter's means" were temporarily defined within a realistic tradition. It is also rather striking how Munch exploited other means to express this particular idea. At the exhibition of 1892, he probably exhibited a drawing where the sky was painted on with thick, red brush strokes (cat. no. 113). The drawing has a text which is very similar to the above cited note. Moreover, both the lithographic version of *The Scream* and the frame of a painting from 1895 have text fragments.

When Munch painted this "memory of a sunset," the painting expressed the same moment of reflection as the text. The foreground figure is isolated in loneliness. The pictorial structure which expresses this isolation had been developed in his work with

the pictorial theme of *Evening*.

Munch sent six pictures to the Autumn Exhibition in 1891. Three of them were listed under the section "Drawings, Pastels, and Watercolors" in the catalogue. We shall focus on one of these, *Evening* (cat. no. 114), which Christian Krohg praised in a very enthusiastic article. With the exception of one critic, *Evening* and the other two pastels were described as exceptionally ridiculous. *Dagbladet*'s critic, who had been favorably disposed to the three oil paintings, wrote:

> A critic, who enjoys every pencil stroke, every line which raises our art and carries it forward, would like to ask each member of this year's selection committee, why Edvard Munch's humoresques, the catalogue numbers 229, 230, 231, have been accepted and even received such important places in the exhibition.[29]

Part of the answer lies in the fact that Munch was chosen as deputy juror on the selection committee. Because he participated in the selection, his own pictures were, according to the rules, exempt from the selection process.[30]

There are several versions of the pictorial motif in *Evening (Melancholy)*, and some have doubted whether the Munch Museum's version was the one which was shown at the Autumn Exhibition, especially because its quality doesn't seem to merit Christian Krohg's enthusiastic article. The other versions are a picture in Rasmus Meyers' collection in Bergen, another one in a private collection in Oslo, which in size and inner proportions is almost identical to the Munch Museum's version, and finally the National Gallery's version.[31] To argue that the Munch Museum's version was *not* the one which was exhibited, one has to assume that the picture was mistakenly described as a pastel in the catalogue and that two critics therefore mistakenly thought that it was a pastel. The Munch Museum's version is the only one which is executed almost totally in pastel and crayon. On the selection committee's list, notes on the techniques of Munch's entries are added in pencil. Three are marked "oil," and three are marked with the monogram "PL," which must mean pastel. Furthermore, another jury member, Erik Werenskiold, in a letter to Aubert, described Munch's entry in a way which matches the Munch Museum's version well:

> Munch leaves most of his work barely half-finished. He mixes together oils and pastel, and leaves large portions of the canvas bare. This bare canvas is supposed to help depict or express daylight, sunshine, evening mood, moonlight, or whatever. The one [picture] that Krohg wrote his stupid article about is, despite all this, a very beautiful suggestion, and demonstrates a change of direction similar to my own. Moreover, Krohg was *not* so moved by the picture when we—Eilif (Peterson), he, and I—looked at it as it was being hung . . . I then used the

Evening/Melancholy, 1891. OKK M 58, Munch-Museet, Oslo (cat. no. 114)

fig. 8 *Evening,* 1891. OKK T 2760, Munch-Museet, Oslo

Evening/Melancholy, 1891. OKK T 2355, Munch-Museet, Oslo (cat. no. 115)

words—which he used in his article—that there was more progress in this picture than in his others—and Krohg went wild.[32]

There is a series of drawings that must be seen in connection with the theme of *Evening*, but only a few can be considered as preparations for the picture at the Autumn Exhibition. Two of them in particular are usually considered to be the first sketches (cat. no. 115 and fig. 8). But it is impossible to maintain with absolute certainty whether these two drawings were done before the pastel, even though this hy-

pothesis is probable, since the landscape has not yet been given its final form. The concentration on the figures and the anecdotal character of the drawings could also imply that they are closer to an actual event which may have been the origin of the motif. The drawing with the figure standing with its back toward the viewer seems to be the earlier one. It is easy to conclude that Munch later placed him in the characteristic "melancholy" posture, which runs through subsequent versions. The drawing with the seated figure is found in the so-called Violet

fig. 9 Frontispiece for Emanuel Goldstein's *Alruner*, 1892, Munch-Museet, Oslo

fig. 10 *Study for Vignette*, 1892. OKK T 128-25, Munch-Museet, Oslo

Notebook. It is drawn on a page immediately preceding notes from the autumn of 1891. These notes deal especially with the unhappy love that Munch's friend Jappe Nielsen felt for Christian Krohg's wife Oda. None of the notes describe a scene which corresponds to the drawing, and it is difficult to determine exactly when the notes were written.[33] However, it is possible to argue that Jappe Nielsen and his love affair served as a sort of model for the pictorial theme. But to insist exclusively on this interpretation would deprive the motif of its most significant meaning. As will be discussed later, Munch identified himself with the lonely figure on the beach to the extent that he described the scene in the first person singular. He also discovered that the theme could be used as an illustration for situations of other artists.

The majority of the other thematically connected drawings which can be dated before the autumn of 1892 were probably done in connection with Munch's commission to draw a vignette for Emanuel Goldstein's collection of poetry *Alruner* (Mandrakes) (fig. 9). The most important ones are a series of pen and ink drawings in the sketchbooks T 128 and T 129 (figs. 10-12). Five pencil sketches of the landscape turn out to be more problematic (in T 129, fig. 13). Only one of them includes barely suggested figures. They could be considered as preparations for the pastel, but most likely, they are not. The pencil drawings are probably the first attempts to recall the main features of the pastel *Evening* in his memory and to give form to the *Alruner* vignette. Munch received the commission in a letter from Goldstein dated December 12, 1891. Munch, who had been in Nice since the beginning of December, decided quickly that he would use his *Evening* theme. By December 30, Goldstein stated:

> The idea behind your picture from the Autumn Exhibition was excellent. If you could portray the format of "Vekselspillet" (Interplay), I would be extremely happy.

Vekselspillet was the title of the *Alruner* collection of

fig. 11 *Study for Vignette*, 1892. OKK T 129-39, Munch-Museet, Oslo

fig. 12 *Study for Vignette*, 1892. OKK T 129-40, Munch-Museet, Oslo

poetry when Goldstein first published it in 1886. What Munch had written about the "idea behind the picture from the Autumn Exhibition" is unfortunately not known since the letter in question is lost. Munch attempted several drafts for the vignette but ran into difficulties, as can be seen from his letter of February 8th:

> My will exceeds my ability—If I were back in Norway, it would be much easier. I would simply copy the painting—but if it turns out well now, it will just be by chance.[34]

The pencil drawings were an attempt to strike upon such a "chance." They seem to be based on his

experience with the pastel, and at the same time they point forward to the later pen and ink drawings and the vignette. For example, the line of the hill ridge becomes increasingly steeper toward the upper right-hand corner, and the line of the beach and the hill ridge gradually merge toward a diagonal. Both of these characteristics are typical of drafts for the vignette. The more elongated format which gradually develops in the drafts is facilitated by the foreground figure being cut off at a higher level. This aspect and the figure facing out of the picture plane are again characteristic of a series of drawings where we find the same paralyzed, melancholy figure, but in a different landscape (figs. 14-16). The landscapes are variations of the view over the Oslo fjord in *Despair,* and of a painting from the Munch family home at Nordstrand. The framings indicate that these drawings were also intended to be illustrations, either for Goldstein, or for the authors Vilhelm Krag and Sigbjørn Obstfelder, for whom Munch had also planned to create vignettes.[35] If this is correct, it implies that Munch saw a certain similarity between the ideas of these poets and his own themes. In any case, the fact that he repeatedly shifted the "Jappe" figure in various backgrounds implies that this figure's special biographical background cannot be of decisive importance in the interpretation of the pictorial themes.

The use of a figure facing out of the picture, a significant change between the pictures *Despair* and *The Scream,* also seems to have been the fruit of his work with the vignette drawings (fig. 17). However, the important difference between the two formulations of the theme lies in his relationship to the artistic means. The despair and paralysis due to the inadequacy of the artistic means, which is the theme of *Despair,* is to a certain extent conquered in *The Scream.* The moment of reflection in *Despair* has, in *The Scream,* given way to an immediate expression of

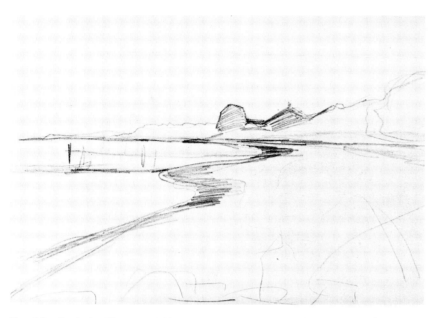

fig. 13 *Study for Vignette,* 1892. OKK T 129-51R, Munch-Museet, Oslo

fig. 14 *Study for Vignette,* 1892. OKK T 128-30R, Munch-Museet, Oslo

fig. 15 *Study for Vignette,* 1892. OKK T 129-32, Munch-Museet, Oslo

the experience, in the conviction that the artistic techniques—the colors and the total enveloping form which subordinates the foreground figure to the curvature of the landscape—will transmit the experience to the viewer.[36] This moment of reflection may have had its origin in the theme of *Evening.* The particular biographical origin, which characterized the first drawings, was gradually being put aside during the work with the pastel. This must have happened in the following way: the lines along the ridge and beach out toward the horizon were drawn in quick, sketchy pencil strokes. The head of the foreground figure was outlined somewhat too

high. After the main features of the landscape were sketched in, the head was moved downward, so that it didn't break the almost horizontal line leading from the beach and out toward the horizon. The figure was drawn in firm outline with pencil, and the head was then begun in oil. Several strokes of the same colors used in the face, hair, and cap were drawn along the hand and the contours of the torso, in the beach area around the head, and in the treetop in the background. The remainder of the work was done with colored chalks, apparently very quickly. Compared to the initial sketching in pencil, the line of the beach had been pulled back slightly

fig. 16 *Study for Vignette*, 1892. OKK T 129-33, Munch-Museet, Oslo

fig. 17 *Study for Vignette*, 1892. OKK T 129-38, Munch-Museet, Oslo

and the boat had been moved out further. Both are aspects which Munch retained in the two later versions of the motif.[37]

The people on the wharf have no trace of individual, distinguishing colors. Since neither Krohg nor the others mention these figures, they were probably less visible in 1891 than they are now. The yellow, blue, and violet tones of the sky and sea seem to have faded a great deal. The green ridge of the hill makes the lower half of the people less visible than the upper half. The yellow and blue colors in the sky, which are barely noticeable now, must originally have covered the figures much more. We must assume that Munch did not consider it worthwhile to emphasize here the anecdotal aspect so characteristic of the first two drawings. The landscape is constructed around the tension-filled distance between the individuals, but the aim of the work seems to have been the loneliness of the foreground figure in the landscape.

In December 1893, the National Gallery's version was exhibited under the title *Eifersucht* (Jealousy). This more precise definition of the meaning of the pictorial theme, served as the background for Stanislaw Przybyszewski's very vivid and suggestive description of the painting,[38] which has been the basis for the majority of later interpretations of both the National Gallery's and other versions of the theme. As a result, interpretations of the motif have too often overemphasized the theme of jealousy and the significance of Jappe Nielsen's love affair. Neither Krohg, who should have understood the biographical origin, nor others who mention the painting before 1894 found any reason to mention that a triangular love drama is being played out on the lonely beach. To the extent that the picture was found to be worth commenting on, the interpretations are far more open. On November 28, 1891, the art critic for *Verdens Gang* wrote:

> His best picture is the bare, long beach in the evening, where a young man sits with his hand under his chin. Munch has been moved by the stillness of the evening, just as that young man sitting there. And therefore, those who can ignore the unimportant, unfinished details are moved by the same evening silence as Munch. Thus, the artist has communicated what he wanted, and therefore the picture is art.[39]

Most of the critiques concentrated precisely on the unfinished aspects of the work and therefore concluded that it was not art. Munch's artist colleagues in a way agreed with the critics. Their defense was based on the idea that Munch's picture was a break with tradition and that Munch wanted to create a new art. They did not, however, give any concrete description of what this new art would be because they did not believe that it was a fully formed alternative yet. They defended Munch's intentions more than his work. Thaulow said, as quoted earlier, that he had witnessed "the germination of an art which would eventually kill our nice, respectable and precise realism." Werenskiold said that Munch's picture was beautiful "as a suggestion," and that it showed "a change in direction." Krohg had difficulty defining the picture as painting:

> It may be that this work is closer to music than it is to painting, but it is in any case brilliant music. Munch should have the national grant for composers.[40]

Werenskiold felt that there was noticeable improvement in the picture *Evening,* and he maintained that his very same words had been used in Krohg's article (see note 32). Krohg, however, defined much more clearly what was new in Munch's painting:

> When one has looked at that picture "Evening" for a while and then turns to the others, even to those by Munch himself, one recognizes a huge gap between them. No connections—no tradition, no bridge—no influences.

When Krohg wished to emphasize the qualities of the painting, he did so by showing how it broke with the prevailing realistic practice. He found the use of lines to be "harmonious" because Munch had left out details. He found the overall coloring to be magnificent precisely because Munch ignored local coloring. And he defined the directions in which Munch's art was heading:

> And the over-all color! A violet charm with a few poisonous green spots in it, which inspires devotion. Spots that one can lose oneself in and become a better person by looking at, that move one like a story of young love, that remind one of something fine and soft in one's own life, and that foreshadow almost ominously a new view of art. Serious and severe. It is related to Symbolism, the latest trend in French art—He, who has been viewed here in Norway as the least developed of all realists. . . . He is the only one, the first one who turns to Idealism, who dares to make nature, the model, etc. subject to the mood and to modify them to achieve more.

The recognition which Munch received was continually expressed in terms of expectations of his future work. More precisely, the expectations rested on his inner qualities, his sensitivity and ability to experience, and on the hope that in the future he would be able to give an outer form to these experiences and hereby awaken others' sensitivities. This split between the inner and the outer qualities, between spirit and body, or between the actual experience and the artistic articulation of it, led to despair. This despair stemmed from the distance between the intensity of his own experience and the cool indifference of others, which his own notes and Skredsvig's memoirs so accurately describe. The sense of despair gradually affected Munch's interpretation of the theme *Evening.* If the picture had originally been a depiction of a mood with erotic overtones, it gradually developed into an image of the artist's isolation and despair. Let us look at the possibilities for such a reinterpretation.

If we attempt to "complete" the pastel *Evening* on the basis of color traces, we must assume that the ocean, which is suggested in blue in the foreground, was gradually transformed into the yellow and violet tones of the sky as it approached the horizon. The pictorial space is about to be enclosed by a complete merging of sky and ocean. But this closed quality of the pictorial space is broken by the narrow bluish or blue-green stripe of the horizon, which suggests an infinitely deep, mutual reflection. The horizon presents a double vision. We can view it as a border for that which *is*: the world *is* that which exists within our field of vision. Or, we can view it as an indication of something beyond itself: beyond the reach of the picture, one might imagine something, perhaps a goal for our aspirations. But the picture can't express anything except an unending, deep emptiness, an abyss. The picture is structured as a drifting flight out toward the horizon. It is as though the entire articulation of the painting consists in a denial of the particular objects. Lines and colors glide over the surface toward the horizon without a single point for the viewer to fix his attention on.[41]

The boat is one of the few objects that could capture the viewer's attention. But the boat has a dual function also. In terms of color, it harmonizes with the evening sky, as if the yellow stripes of the sky were distant echoes of the golden-brown tones of the boat. Iconographically, it underscores the ambiguity of the horizon. The boat lies close to shore, but at the same time it represents the possibility of drifting away from what is immediate and close.

Surrounded by the plane of the beach and held within an outline which is closed and turned inward, the foreground figure appears isolated and introspective. But the isolation from the surroundings is not total. Through articulation of the pictorial surface, he is at the same time brought into contact with the flowing movement of the background. His concave front and the convex back partially reflect the character of the major lines of the landscape and subordinate him to the dominant movement in the picture.

Our impression of the painting is a constantly renewed flight toward the horizon, which repeatedly leads us back to the picture plane. The foreground figure serves as a natural starting point for a renewed flight inward. From this point of view, the figure becomes a constant reminder of ourselves, the actual basis for our observations. Our contemplation of the picture becomes an analogy to his inner self. In his self-searching, he can find no fixed point or motive for practical action. The only thing he can find is a longing away from himself, toward a goal which he seems to have given up trying to reach. The undefined goal of the longing is beyond the reach of the picture, which is limited by the horizon. The flight, or longing, emerges to the extent that the picture is devoid of objects. The depiction of longing becomes, at the same time, an emptying out of the landscape into a dizzying abyss, or into an image of death, as we saw in the drawing of the old man on the road.

A note, dated Nice, December 12, 1891, gives a literary statement of the horizon's ambiguity and the dizzying chasm that opens up in the landscape.

> Waves rush toward the shore in endless succession. The ocean opens its mysterious, green-blue abyss as if it wanted to show me what lives down there in the depths. . . . But out there,—out there—beyond that azure blue line—behind the sparkling clouds—is the end of the world. What is there—Once I believed it was the end of the world—Now I don't know what's there. Now I know nothing! (T 2760, p. 36)

A note written later, in July/August 1892, demonstrates Munch's identification with the lonely man on the beach. Erotic overtones dominate, but at the same time, the symbolic character of the landscape is also apparent:

> One evening, I walked alone by the water—the water sighed and swished between the stones—there were long gray clouds along the horizon—it was as if everything had died out—as if in another world—a landscape of death—but then, there was life out there by the wharf— there was a man and a woman—and another man came with oars on his shoulders—and the boat over there— ready to leave. . . . They walk down there—he and she—on their way out to that island over there—They will walk between the trees arm in arm in the light summer night. The air is so soft—it must be wonderful to make love now. The boat got smaller and smaller. The paddling of the oars still echoed over the water—He was alone—the waves rolled toward him monotonously—and lapped and lapped among the stones. (T 2782 bw)[42]

In another note from the same time, Munch described the landscape as a symbol of his own life situation. He can only observe life from a distance. But it is precisely this distance, separated from life by the abyss of death, that seems to give him a unique insight into the connection between life and death:

> Down here by the beach, I feel that I find an image of myself—of life—of my life. The strange smell of seaweed and sea reminds me of her. . . . In the dark green water I see the color of her eyes. Way, way out there the soft line

where air meets ocean—it is as incomprehensible as life—as incomprehensible as death, as eternal as longing. And life is like that silent surface which reflects the light, clear colors of the air. And underneath, in the depths—it conceals the depths—with its slime—its crawling creatures—like death. We understand each other. It is as though no one understands me better than the ocean. (T 2782 j)

On his way to Nice in the autumn of 1891, Munch visited in Copenhagen his friend from the St. Cloud period, Emanuel Goldstein. They kept in constant touch through correspondence until late summer 1892, when Munch sent the final vignette for Goldstein's collection of poems. The letters dealt mostly with artistic matters. Both men were in general agreement, and they made plans for further cooperative efforts. Among other things, they had considered publishing together their literary notes from the St. Cloud period. They also intended to publish a new journal. Goldstein stated in his first letter (December 12, 1891) that he was in the process of publishing a collection of aphorisms entitled *Kameratkunst* (Comrade Art). ("This could be a sort of introduction to the journal we've considered publishing.") On December 30, he sent Munch a preface to the aphorisms and mentioned that "some of the things we talked about while you were here have slipped in." Munch himself found that "there are a lot of good things in the preface." The journal never materialized, but Goldstein published the preface and some of the aphorisms. They expressed a symbolistic, antinaturalistic attitude. Munch's notes from that time are very consistent with the thoughts he expressed in his letters to Goldstein.

> If only one could be the body through which today's thoughts and feelings flow, that's what an author ought to be. A feeling of solidarity with one's generation, but yet standing apart. To succumb as a person yet survive as an individual entity, this is the ideal. . . . An artistic program should sound like this: In the same way that a situation has at a certain moment impressed itself upon your brain in a certain mood, at that moment, it became true. More precisely, it was true for you. Not for others. The objective novel consists merely of the rules of perspective.
>
> Inspiration is thought—Naturalism is craft . . . salvation shall come from Symbolism. By that I mean an art where the artist submits reality to his rule, which places mood and thought above everything and only uses reality as a symbol. . . . Naturalism was Nature dead. Impressionism was more of an attempt to put life into the style without breaking with the visible world. . . . Symbolism, however, crowned the two previous artistic directions. It has walked over the corpses of Naturalism and Impressionism, and it contains both of the previous directions.[43]

When Munch received the commission to draw a vignette for Goldstein's collection of poetry, he did not have the older edition of the collection *Vekselspillet* (Interplay) with him. Goldstein had mentioned

fig. 18 *Flower of Pain*, front page of *Quickborn*, 1897. OKK T 2541, Munch-Museet, Oslo

fig. 19 *The Flower of Pain*, in the "Folkedal" Sketchbook, 1897. Private Collection

bloodflowers to which the title poem refers.

> In the mountains, where my tears flowed/flowers grew, one for each tear/ They sway in the wind, blood dripping red/ and a pulse beats through the veins of the leaves/ It sounds like a heavy yearning at night/ like the sobbing of tearless crying/ like a struggle of death of a life which is young/ And when I pull out a bloodflower by the root/ your name is heard, born in damnation/ with heavy sighs from the womb of the earth.[44]

that the title of the new edition would be *Alrune* (Mandragora). It is impossible to know whether Munch remembered the title of the poems in the older edition. In the same letter, he must have suggested using "the picture from the Autumn Exhibition." He also asked Goldstein to send him a picture of a mandrake. When Munch later wrote (March 8, 1892), "the drawing could probably be placed over the poem," he obviously had the poem "Alrune" in mind.

Munch probably used the theme *Evening* to illustrate Goldstein's overall artistic intentions, rather than linking it to one particular poem. Although the vignette is generally associated with the poem "Alrune," it doesn't change matters much. Goldstein chose this as the title poem precisely because it embodied the artistic intentions of the collection. It expresses his view on the relationship between life, the artist, and the work of art. The final title of the collection, *Alruner*, expresses in its plural form that all the poems should be understood as the

Munch and Goldstein considered the theme *Evening* to be representative of the thoughts in the collection of poems and the title poem, probably because they interpreted the lonely man on the beach as a symbol of the artist's situation. There is no poem in the collection that directly corresponds to the beach scene. Munch's further development of the theme, however, clarified the vignette's relationship to the poem. Munch must have considered using the rather overworked metaphor of flowers growing up from artists' tears at a relatively early stage, because in the reply to the earlier mentioned lost letter from Munch, Goldstein wrote:

> I cannot send you a drawing of a mandrake. Where would I find one? It resembles, in any case, a mad woman who is totally covered by her own bright yellow hair. But you don't need to draw it.[45]

At first, Munch did not include any flowers in the picture. But in his later production, bloodflowers abound. When he received a commission in 1898 to illustrate an edition of Strindberg texts, he returned to the *Evening* theme and prepared a new variation for the cover (fig. 18). The relationship between this picture of a man dying in pain (who has Munch's

Separation/Salome Paraphrase, 1894. OKK T 337, Munch-Museet, Oslo (cat. no. 116)

features), with the lily of art growing out of his heart's blood, and the original motif becomes clear when we examine one of the drafts for the Strindberg illustration (fig. 19).

There are also many other variations of the theme. Even though Munch never gave the flower the shape of a mandrake, Goldstein's description of the plant as a mad woman totally covered by her own hair had an impact on Munch's articulation of the flower (cat. no. 116). The woman-flowers in the outer area of this triptychlike drawing have their roots fastened to the man's heart and suck nourishment from his blood. The "Separation" theme in the mid-panel is a further development of the "Evening" theme. In other versions of *Separation,* as in *Woman in Three Stages,* we can still observe a massive and lush plant near the feet of the rejected man. It is, for the most part, bloody red. The *Separation* theme itself, where the woman's hair flows across the picture surface and takes root in the man's chest, influenced Goldstein. In the *Alruner* edition of 1916, he added a poem entitled "As Strong as Death." It begins:

A cluster of strands led from you to the roots of my heart/
It tore open my wound when you left me.[46]

The despairing gap between reality and the ideal is expressed in a drawing which must also be understood as a development of the beach theme (cat. no. 117).[47] Physical death is represented in concrete and immediate terms in the lower portion. The view over the beach and sea toward the horizon is only vaguely implied, as if the pen could not quite cap-

Metabolism, 1894. OKK T 405, Munch-Museet, Oslo (cat. no. 117)

ture it. "The artistic means" can only hint at "the promised land" of reconciliation represented in the upper portion. One can only hope to arrive there. And this hope, only to be fulfilled through a further development, is symbolized by the fragile plant which grows from the rotting corpse. In another drawing, where we can also barely discern an ideal landscape, a stripe of the horizon and a naked female form, the idea is made clear by the title *Art* (cat. no. 118). The artist succumbs in his confrontation with life. But out of the bearded man's head in

Art, 1894/1895. OKK T 1380, Munch-Museet, Oslo
(cat. no. 118)

Harpy, 1894. OKK G/r 4-1, Sch. 4, Munch-Museet, Oslo
(cat. no. 119)

Self-Portrait with Skeleton Arm, 1895. OKK G/1 192-54, Sch. 31,
Munch-Museet, Oslo (cat. no. 120)

the mid-section, the flower of art triumphs over the
transitory nature of things.[48]

It is in this context that we should understand the
remarkable etching *Harpy* (cat. no. 119).[49] The
woman-bird on the deserted beach of death should
not merely be interpreted as a beast of prey. It is true
that she nourishes herself, like a vampire, on the
heart blood, but she is at the same time an image of
triumph over death. As a vehicle for the soul of the
dead, which she has incorporated within herself, she
elevates it beyond the transitory. She is a symbol of
the living element in art, which is not bound to the
practical, material, and perishable. The skeleton
who is drawing or writing in the background represents the dead aspect of art, the technical aspect of
the inherited traditions. "Art" consists of surpassing
this, which the individual artist cannot do, except by
sacrificing himself to "Art" and perishing. The
bearded head, which apparently lies loose in the
sand, is a portrait of Christian Krohg and thus depicts the dead tradition from which Munch's own art
stems. However, since this visionary head has not
succumbed to the ephemeral, it stands for those
thoughts that live on and for that insight into the
process that Krohg spoke of in a lecture in 1886:

Harpy, 1893/1894. OKK T 2291, Munch-Museet, Oslo (cat. no. 121)

We, this generation of Norwegian painters to which I belong . . . We can only stand on the mountain and look into the Promised Land. . . . But there are already new legions ready to emerge, workers on society's image of itself. We salute these new legions. Arise! Replace us, disdain us![50]

The unbridgeable gap between body and spirit, or between technique and idea, which is the artist's curse, is perhaps most clearly and strongly expressed in the lithograph *Self-Portrait with Skeleton Arm* (cat. no. 120). The face, "the mirror of the soul," emerges from the darkness with visionary force. It obscures the ephemeral body and triumphs over the dead and powerless artistic means symbolized by the skeletal arm.[51]

The head in the etching *Harpy* (cat. no. 119) should be seen as an homage to Christian Krohg. In the preparatory sketch, however, it should be understood as a general portrait of the "artist" (cat. no. 121). It raises itself over the decomposing body, as if he were looking out over his own ephemerality. This rather obscure symbolic detail has an origin similar to the lonely man on the beach and the bloody red sky. An actual event which Munch experienced in Hamburg, on his way to Nice in the autumn of 1891, developed during the course of the year into a new symbol for the "artist's" situation.[52] The momentary experience of seeing a swan swimming in the Alster Lake one dark evening, gradually became a mystical insight into the interrelationship of life and death (fig. 20). He viewed this picture as an interpretation of his own situation as an artist. In the picture *Vision, an Illustration* (cat. no. 122), shown at the exhibition

fig. 20 *Vision,* 1891/1892. OKK T 128-21R, Munch-Museet, Oslo

of 1892, he tried to give a visual formulation of the experience. It met with little understanding, to put it mildly, both then and later. There were later variations on the theme in a series of drawings (cat. no. 123). In these, we are led to see a contrast between the area above and below the water, and we are led to interpret the head as a general portrait of the "artist" rather than as a self-portrait. In this way, the picture becomes the expression of a visionary insight just as in *Harpy,* and in the above-mentioned ideal landscapes, or, in the picture *Symbolic Study* (cat. no. 124).[53] One of the many literary versions, written in the autumn of 1892, describes the event which inspired the motif:

She was a swan which glided, with its long, delicate neck, through the water. . . . Its fine profile was reflected in the water—together with the clouds in the sky.—I lived down there; I crawled around among the bluish black creatures—greenish brown slime—all sorts of horrid animals. . . . Then I was frightened by my own shadow, and I had to swim up to lighter colors. I forced my way

Vision, 1892. OKK M 114, Munch-Museet, Oslo (cat. no. 122)

Vision, 1892. OKK T 2347, Munch-Museet, Oslo (cat. no. 123)

up—it became dazzling bright—There was the swan. I reached toward it, it came slowly toward me and I thought I could hold it, press its white breast to mine—rest my head in its down. The water was murky around me, and I caught a reflection of my face, it was terribly pale—I saw that it was frightened—I heard a scream—and I knew it was me who had screamed—The swan was far away—where the clear water reflected its delicate lines and the pale clouds of the sky. (T 2782 ae)

The metaphors and pictures in which Munch depicts the loneliness of the artist, his longing for reconciliation, and his visionary insight into nature emphasize the distinctive and unique character of the situation. But precisely this unique element is the most characteristic aspect of the self-understanding of the new idealistic, rebellious generation, or, in Krohg's words, "the third generation." Munch found confirmation of his thoughts and visions in many current authors in addition to Goldstein. However, the companionship which he

could have enjoyed, never materialized in a group project as it had for the second generation, but rather in an association of isolated individuals sharing the same fate. A few literary examples which Munch's pictorial themes could easily have illustrated,[54] are cited below.

In a prose fragment from about the same time as the pictures *Despair* and *Vision,* Sigbjørn Obstfelder described the moment of inspiration during which he was surprised to discover that he was able to observe his own thoughts:

And out of the darkness, I saw a flock of swans float in toward the shore. The first one was so tall and white, its breast stood out as an arch emerging from the darkness, and the ones behind merged with the darkness. I hardly heard a ripple, it was silent. Suddenly I felt as though a train rushed through my breast—There were thoughts, noble, proud and majestic, which had never been mine. Are your thoughts like that? Is that the way they flow through your breast?

Symbolic Study, 1893. OKK M 1033, Munch-Museet, Oslo (cat. no. 124)

The swans had hidden themselves between the rushes. There was no light, there were no more ripples. Everything was darkness and silence. But far away, as I felt everything die away and fall asleep around me, it became very silent within myself, so silent. But suddenly a scream sounded over the earth and rushed through the sky.[55]

Another friend of Munch, Vilhelm Krag, described, in a long prose poem "Nat" (Night), a wandering, where he meets life, love, and death in a series of visionary scenes. The book was written in the autumn and winter of 1891/1892 and published in May 1892. The imagery is strikingly reminiscent of Munch's notes, but it is impossible to determine whether the prose poem had influenced Munch. Like many of Munch's pictures and notes, "Night" is a characteristic statement of the artist's isolation and despair.

Above the water and land, above the plains and roads, above the world's huge sphere lies the burning sun, stinking and suffocating, and the earth gasps and groans, withers and rots. Until the red clouds down near the horizon rise quickly and silently up into the sky—behind them are glimpses of blue and streaks of gold:—it was as if a red, blistered skin grew over the heavens; and as if deadly sick blood pulsed through its veins.—And then, suddenly, a streak of lightning raced over the heavens and long, rumbling thunder rolled over the plains.

Another description states:

As depressing as a life which cannot be lived, the plateau spreads out toward the river, and here I am, lonely in this huge world. ... Death, dull silence. And I leap up in inexpressible anguish, press my hands to my head, and scream far out over the dusky plain.

Finally, in the following passage, the scream in nature is interpreted as the poet's own desire to express himself, his inner feelings:

Why can't there be a scream, piercingly sharp, rending the moon's veil into long, bitter strands, smashing the silence, an infernal scream from heaven to earth . . . Do you know what that is? Yes, you see, the scream—*that* is what lies in here smoldering, that never gets air, that has been strangled for all these long years . . . Oh, God, it is the longing, the endless, sobbing longing. . . .[56]

The bourgeois society's self-understanding as a fellowship of isolated individuals could not be endured if the fellowship could only be experienced through the abstract ideas of race, nationality, etc. As a counteraction to the isolation of the sacred and inviolable quality of private life, public life offered various forms of social intercourse through which individuals could meet each other in freedom and acknowledge each other as equal. These public leisure activities, such as café life and strolling through the streets, quite naturally became central themes in the art of that period. Munch was no exception, as

Evening on Karl Johan Street, 1892. OKK T 2390, Munch-Museet, Oslo (cat. no. 125)

he demonstrated in his pictures of Karl Johan Street, the most popular street among strollers in Oslo. But with the picture *Evening on Karl Johan Street* (cat. no. 28), he transformed this theme from a confirmation of society's fellowship to a powerful expression of despairing loneliness. In this work, there is no longer any distinction between "the artist" and "the others." Fellowship on the public level is revealed as an empty ritual. The mass of people have no contact with each other. Even in the midst of public intercourse, individuals are bringing their private loneliness to a public gathering. The intercourse merely consists of everybody passing one another in the same public space. Companionship is only experienced as momentary instants of contact within prescribed rituals of recognition and acknowledgment.

Evening on Karl Johan Street, like the other pictures we have discussed, had its origin in a concrete experience which is recounted in a series of notes. These describe an expected meeting with a woman, who constantly seems to emerge from the crowd. But each time, it turns out to be someone else. When she finally comes, she walks past very quickly and leaves behind only a crushing emptiness.

And then she finally came. . . . She smiled softly and walked on. I was about to stop. But that old stubbornness prevented me for an instant, and by then she was gone. Everything became so empty, and he felt so alone. . . . He almost went into a trance. And then it was as though

fig. 21 *Workers on the Way Home,* 1913/1915. OKK M 365, Munch-Museet, Oslo

everything became so silent. The noise from the street became so distant, seemed to come from above. He no longer had any sensation in his legs, they wouldn't carry him any further. Everyone who went by looked at him, stared at him, all of these pale faces in the evening light. He tried to hold on to a thought but couldn't. He felt nothing but emptiness in his head. . . . Then he looked at the window up there where it shone yellow against the dark sky—he stared at it steadily as if he wanted to hang onto it—and as he fell, it sounded so strange, it grated on his ears. (T 2761, p. 17 f)

In a drawing, which probably dates from the autumn of 1892 (cat. no. 125), Munch tried to capture the fleeting quality of the meeting, as he described it in the notes. In the painting which was probably finished the next year, he removed the anecdotal element, and we meet the mass of people, ourselves, face to face. In the picture *Anxiety* (cat. no. 34), the mass of people streaming by is transferred to the landscape from *Despair.*

If art is supposed to be the reconciling medium through which people "will learn to understand each other," the lesson to be learned here is that everyone is in the same situation as the artist, helplessly lonely. In this way, the picture becomes a critique against bourgeois ideology, even though negatively formulated. The positive formulation, which implies a community where people actually get to know one another, was first expressed many years later, as in the oncoming mass in the picture *Workers on Their Way Home* (fig. 21).[57]

Translated from the Norwegian by Einar Petterson
Edited by Solfrid Johansen and Jorge Salazar

NOTES

1. "Kunstnerstipendierne paa Afveje," *Dagbladet,* December 16, 1891.

2. "Til Bjørnstjerne Bjørnson," *Dagbladet,* January 4, 1892.

3. "Vore Kunstnerstipendierne paa Afveje," (Answer to B.B.), *Dagbladet,* December 17, 1891.

4. "Kunstnerstipendierne," *Ørebladet,* December 17, 1891; concerning Christian Krohg's article, see note 40.

5. "Vore Kunstnerstipendier paa Afveje," *Dagbladet,* December 22, 1891.

6. The first two quotations are from representative J. Sverdrup's speech, *Stortingstidende,* No. 60, 1880, p. 549. The third quotation is from the budget committee's proposal in 1884, Indst. S. No. 115, St. F., 1884, p. 400. See also St. F., 1890, p. 914 and St. F., 1891, p. 484.

7. Søknader og innstillinger (Applications and requests) Statsarkivet, Oslo, Kirkedept., Kontor D, *Journaler* 1886ff. About the pictures cited, see Arne Eggum's article.

8. "Tredie Generation" (Third Generation) reprinted in Christian Krohg, *Kampen for Tilvaerelsen* (The Struggle for Existence) (Copenhagen, 1920) vol. 1, p. 188ff.

9. "I Anledning af Edvard Munch's Udstilling" (On the Occasion of Edvard Munch's Exhibition), *Dagbladet,* May 19, 1889. It is not known who encouraged Aubert to write the article.

10. *Edvard Munch's brev, familien,* "Munch-museets skrifter I," (Oslo, 1949), nos. 56, 58, 67, and 73.

11. Note dated "Saint Cloud, February 4th, 1890" in a book with notes. The Munch Museum's registration number T 2770 and the page reference to the museum's typed copy, p. 3. In the following pages, the museum's registration number and the page number of the museum's copy will be cited in parentheses after the quote. The drawings in the sketchbook T 126, one being very similar to the painting *Night in St. Cloud,* should be viewed in connection with these notes. Compare note 23.

12. This and the following two excerpts are quoted from notes by Munch in the brochure *Livsfrisens tilblivelse* probably published in connection with the exhibition in 1929. See Reinhold A. Heller "Edvard Munch's Life Frieze," Ms., Indiana University, 1960, p. 52-61. The note is found in a copy in the Munch Museum entitled "St. Cloud 1889 Copi," which must be assumed to have been transcribed from a note from the St. Cloud period. The theme of the drawing cat. no. 111 is used as an illustration to the note in *The Origin of the Life Frieze.* See the Munch Museum's catalogue A 3, 1973 and Ragna Stang, *Edvard Munch: Mennesket og kunstneren* (Oslo, 1977), 287.

13. "Statens Kunstudstilling" (The State Art Exhibition), *Kristiania Intelligenssedler,* October 9, 1890. The theme will be discussed by Reinhold A. Heller in *Arts Magazine,* October 1978.

14. The theme of the lost picture is probably repeated, with the addition of two figures (to the left and in the background) in the etching *Christiania-Boheme I,* Sch. 10. The etching *Christiania-Boheme II* demonstrates even more clearly the isolation of each individual in the midst of a social gathering. The six men sitting around the table are isolated in their separate little hells of jealousy. They have no contact with each other. The only thing which has brought them together in this imaginary gathering is the relationship of each to the woman in the background. For the interpretation and the biographical background, see Trygve Nergaard, "Refleksjon og Visjon," 1968 (ms. in the Munch Museum), p. 27 and note 52.

15. "Høstutstillingen" (The Autumn Exhibition), *Verdens Gang,* October 7, 1890. Compare "Statens Kunstudstilling," *Kristiania Intelligenssedler,* October 9, 1890 and "Statens aarlige Kunstudstilling," *Faedrelandet,* November 10, 1890.

16. See Indst. S. No. 115, p. 399ff and Document No. 18 (from the Budget Committee) 1884. Even though the artists of the Düsseldorf generation also signed the petition, it is clear that the dominant artists were the generation from the period of realism. Erik Werenskiold probably wrote the document.

17. "Studiet i Marken. Skilderiet. Erindringens Kunst" (The Field Study. The Picture. The Art of Memory) in Julius Lange, *Bastien Lepage og andre Afhandlinger* (Copenhagen, 1889), 57ff.

18. "En Bog af Julius Lange: Idealkunst og Virkelighedskunst," *Dagbladet,* September 7, 14, 17 "En Vending i den danske Malerkunst" (A Turn in the Danish Pictorial Arts) and September 21, 1890. "Høstudstillingen," *Dagbladet,* October 11, 26, November 1, 2, 5 (Edvard Munch), and November 9, 1890. I thank Niels Messel, Oslo, for the references to these articles.

19. See for instance Johs. A. Dale, *Litteratur og lesing omkring*

1890 (Literature and Reading in the 1890s) (Oslo, 1974) for further references. A particularly interesting study is Peter Kirkegaard, *Knut Hamsun som modernist* (Knut Hamsun as Modernist) (Copenhagen, 1975).

20. "Idealkunst og Virkelighedskunst II" (Idealism and Realism in Art II) *Dagbladet,* September 14, 1890. Garborg tries, like Aubert, to view the new ideal art as a continuation of the realistic tradition. Arne Garborg, "Den Idealistiske Reaktion," *Dagbladet,* June 22, 25, July 2, 6, and 7, 1890, reprinted in Arne Garborg, *Tankar og utsyn. Artiklar, 2* (Thoughts and views. Articles 2) (Oslo, 1950), 104ff.

21. *Dagbladet,* November 5, 1890. The underlining here and in all other quotations is the author's own.

22. Statsarkivet, Oslo, has the following letters to the Department of Culture. The arrangement by which semiannual reports were due before the fellowship was paid had been abandoned. It does not appear as though Munch sent in any report after the end of his fellowship year, as was stipulated.

23. Compare figs. 1 and 2. Cat. no. 111, where the lonely, melancholy figure sits and stares into the fire in the fireplace, must be dated to this winter in Nice on the basis of the characteristic violet ink and the style of the drawing. It is reasonable to date the other drawing, cat. no. 112, to the first winter in Berlin 1892/1893. In the upper plane, we see Munch staring into the fireplace while the lower plane depicts what he "sees with his inner eye." This clarification of earlier pictorial motifs through more direct symbolic language is characteristic of the first Berlin years after 1892, as we shall see in other pictorial motifs. The conversation which is suggested in the quotation by Munch's use of "He-" and "I-" perhaps refers to a conversation with Christian Skredsvig.

24. The note in the book T 2760, p. 25, is dated Saturday, August 31 (1891). The day of the week must have been incorrectly rendered. See note 33.

25. Christian Skredsvig, *Dagr og Nætter blandt Kunstnere* (Days and Nights Among Artists) (Kragerø and Copenhagen, 1908), 117.

26. In a list of pictures, written on the back of a letter from Vilhelm Krag (July 1, 1892), obviously intended as the first plan of the exhibition choices, is the word "Ljabruveien." This is probably a private designation for the picture before the title *Mood at Sunset* had been conceived.

27. / / indicates here and in the following Munch's deletions in the text.

28. The version of *The Scream* in the National Gallery, Oslo, has a note written in pencil on one of the red stripes in the sky: "Can only have been painted by a madman." Reinhold A. Heller (*The Scream,* [London, 1973], 87) maintains that Munch himself added this note. However, the language and orthography appear more Danish than Norwegian. Munch would probably have written "malt" (painted) instead of "malet." Within bourgeois ideology, the connection between creative artistic work and insanity was an established truth, most completely and systematically developed in Cesare Lombroso's writings, as in his *Der Geniale Mensch* (Hamburg, 1890). About the pathological side of "the scream in nature" and Munch's pictures, see Hans Burkhardt's writings, especially "Die Wahnstimmung als pathologisches Kommunikations-Phänomen," *Der Nervenarzt,* (September, 1964): 405ff, which also refers to a number of literary examples. However, a search for literary models for Munch's formulations is bound to fail. The possibilities are many, especially in the period around 1890. See, for instance, the passages from Sigbjørn Obstfelder and Vilhelm Krag, cited later.

29. "Kunstudstillingen II," (The Art Exhibition II) *Dagbladet,*

November 15, 1891.

30. The Norwegian Artists' Association, *The Proceedings 1889-1909,* The Artists' House, Oslo, meeting October 31, 1891, p. 47f: "Jury for Maleri: Krohg, Soot, Sinding, Werenskiold, og Eilif Peterson. Suppleanter: Munch, Homboe, Munthe, Gløersen, Borgen." Munch was exempted from the judgment of the jury at the meeting November 5, 1891.

31. Arne Eggum has demonstrated in a very intelligent analysis that the National Gallery's picture appears in a photograph from the exhibition in Berlin in 1892/1893. I do not, however, share his opinion that the other version, which is barely seen in the photograph, is the picture which is now in a private collection in Oslo.

32. Letter dated December 1891, Universitetsbiblioteket, Oslo, Brevs. 32. Quoted in Ingrid Langaard, *Edvard Munch, Modningsår* (Edvard Munch, Maturing Years) (Oslo, 1960), 138.

33. "Fiolett bok," (Violet Book) T 2760. The first part of the book was written during the first stay in Nice. The rest was written in the autumn and winter of 1891/1892. Of the twelve diary entries one is out of order, one is without an indication of the day of the week, and four falsely indicate the day of the week. This implies that the "diary" was written in retrospect. But it is difficult to determine whether it was written after Munch came to Nice.

34. Correspondence in the Munch Museum. See Trygve Nergaard, "Emanuel Goldstein og Edvard Munch," *Louisiana Revy* (October 1975): 16ff.

35. Sigbjørn Obstfelder, *Breve til hans bror* (Letters to His Brother), ed Solveig Tunold (Stavanger, 1949), 144. Letters from Vilhelm Krag to Munch, July 1, 1892, the Munch Museum. The drawings, p. 20, 21, and 22 in sketchbook T 129 are the only ones which, with certainty, can be said to have been done with Krag's poems in mind. The view over the Oslo Fjord: compare the picture *Fra Nordstrand,* 1891, Rasmus Meyers' Collection, Bergen.

36. About the difference between *Despair* and *The Scream,* see Heller, *The Scream,* p. 78ff.

37. The technical curator at the Munch Museum, Jan Thurmann-Moe, does not share my opinion that all the pencil drawings must have been executed first. However, it is not possible to demonstrate even with the help of powerful magnification that the lines of the pencil have anywhere overlapped the crayons.

38. Stanislaw Przybyszewski, "Psychischer Naturalismus," *Die Freie Bühne* (January 1894): 150ff. Reprinted in S.P., ed., *Das Werk Des Edvard Munch: Vier Beiträge* (Berlin, 1894). During the first few years, the theme was exhibited under the titles *Evening, Sad Evening,* and *The Sorrow.*

39. A contributor to *Kristiania Intelligenssedler,* September 19, 1892, was of the opinion that "this beach line is simply masterly. It lies there so secure and dependable, it disappears more and more; it is like a symbol of loneliness." That the beach can also be a symbol of jealousy is demonstrated by the note where Munch, in a few words, characterized the various pictures that were a part of the series "Die Liebe" in 1895. He writes: "Jealousy—a vast, deserted beach—."

40. "Munch," *Verdens Gang* and *Dagbladet,* November 27, 1891. Reprinted with the title *Evening* in *Kampen for tilværelsen,* vol. 1 (The Struggle of Existence), p. 193f.

41. The work process itself where he seeks to renounce realistic art's clinging to the individual object, becomes in a way a confirmation of the despairing emptying of the world which characterizes the experience of loneliness, which is the basis for a series of written memories. Compare, for instance, the later quoted T 2782 bw and T 2761, p. 17f. In the first note, he wrote,

"It was as if everything was exterminated . . . a landscape of death." The second describes the Karl Johan Street: "Everything became so empty. . . . He tried to hold on to a thought but couldn't. . . . Then he looked at the window way up there . . . stared intensely at it as if he wanted to hang on to it." But the experience of despair, which the pictures attempt to transmit, consists of his inability to *hang on to* anything.

42. The title of this note "Melancholy/At the Beach" was added much later, probably in connection with the organization of his papers in the 1920s. There is no indication that the title *Melancholy* was used in the 1890s. Another version of the cited note is, like T 2782 bw, published in the Munch Museum's catalogue A 3 1973. The dating to the late summer of 1892 of these and the note cited later is based on a study of paper and ink types.

43. The first part is quoted after the aphorisms, published under the title "Tankefosfor. Kunstneren, Naturens Befuldmæktigede" in the newspaper *Kjøbenhavn*, February 20, 1892. The other part is quoted after the preface, in *Kjøbenhavn*, February 8, 1892, under the title "Kameratkunst." The Munch Museum's library lists an offprint of "Kameratkunst" which seems to be lost. Goldstein sent the offprint to Munch. The book, however, was never printed because of the publisher's reservations.

44. "Mandragora" in Hugo Falck (pseudonym), *Vekselspillet, Psykologiske Digte* (The Interplay, Psychological Poetry) (Copenhagen, 1886), 10, and in E. Goldstein, *Alruner Psykologiske Digte* (dedicated to the painter Edvard Munch) (Copenhagen, 1892), 10. / and / / indicate lines and stanzas in the poem.

45. The letter is dated Copenhagen, December 30, 1891. The picture with the flowers which spring forth from the poet's tears has its classical formulation in another "Dichterliebe," that of Henrich Heine, where the second song begins: "Aus meinen Tränen spreissen/Viel blöende Blumen hervor." (Out of my tears, many blossoming flowers bloom forth.) The roots of the mandrake were traditionally depicted as a human body (both masculine and feminine). See, for example, Otto Pächt, "Die früheste abendländische Kopie der Illustrationen des Wiener Dioskurides," *Zeitschrift für Kunstgeshichte* (Munich, 1975), 39, figs. 7 and 8. Such depictions could easily have contributed to Munch's formulation of the *Metabolism* theme. According to a widespread popular belief, the mandrake screams when being plucked. Goldstein's poem also refers to this.

46. *Alruner* (Copenhagen, 1916), p. 39. Compare the notes about the "Separation" theme, for instance, in "The Tree of Knowledge." (See Gerd Woll's article.) *The Woman in Three Stages* was exhibited with the title *Alrune* (Mandrake) in an exhibition in Copenhagen in 1904. See the critique in *Nakskov Tidende*, September 5, 1904.

47. The drawing is possibly a sketch for an illustration of Maurice Maeterlinck's *Pelléas et Mélisande* (3rd act, 3rd scene). See Trygve Nergaard, "Refleksjon og Visjon," ms. 1968, p. 49f.

48. The head must be understood as an idealized representation of "the artist." The type is influenced by Przybyszewski's features in the same way as "Jappe" became a type of an ideal, or the way Krohg was presented in *Harpy*.

49. A more thorough treatment in Trygve Nergaard, "Kunsten som det evig kvinnelige—en vampyrgåte," (Art as the Eternal Feminine—a Vampire Riddle) in *Kunst og Kultur* (Oslo, 1974), 251ff. The man's, or the artist's, meeting with death in *Harpy* and his further life in the development of art, has a counterpart in *The Maiden and Death* which depicted woman's meeting with death and her life being passed on through the development of her offspring. The themes were at the same time developed as etchings, and the first sketch for the etching

The Maiden and Death is found on the back of the drawing for *Harpy* (T 2291). These two themes could almost be thought of as a diptych. Compare Pål Hougen's discussion of the connection between *The Flower of Pain* and *Madonna* in "Kunstneren som Stedfortreder (The Artist as Substitute), in *The Yearbook of the National Museum* (Sth, 1968), 123ff. The thought about art's generational development in *Art, Harpy, Symbolic Study*, etc. is well illustrated by a comparison with *The Family Tree* (T 338), where the lineage grows forth from Christian Krohg's head.

50. Christian Krohg, "Om den bildende kunst som led i kultur-bevæg elsen" (On the Pictorial Arts that Suffered in the Cultural Movement) *Den frisinnede studenter-forenings foredrag og diskusjoner IV* (Kristiania, 1886), 15. Munch had a copy of the lecture.

51. The brother P. A. Munch wrote about the lithograph: "A wide, black frame with dull silver borders on the inside would probably go best with Edvard's picture—I think it would fit best with the meaning of the picture, it is a peculiarly profound image of the soul—this portrait—his own mood of the soul captured on paper." *Edvard Munch's brev, familien*, no. 176, September 6, 1895.

52. The first note, which was possibly written during his journey to Nice, is found in sketchbook T 128. There is also a pen and ink drawing (21R) which shows a swan and a high horizon line. The theme is more thoroughly treated in Trygve Nergaard, "Edvard Munch's visjon: Et bidrag til livsfrisens historie" (Edvard Munch's Vision: A Contribution to the History of the Life Frieze), *Kunst og Kultur* (Oslo, 1967), 69ff. and in Reinhold Heller, "Edvard Munch's Vision and the Symbolist Swan," *Art Quarterly*, 36, no. 3 (1973): 209ff. Since there were probably more swans in art than in nature in the 1890s, I believe it is hopeless to try to trace a definite influence for Munch's theme. A discussion of the meaning of the theme ought to concentrate on the artists that Munch had a connection with or interest in, during the actual period. In regard to the formulation of the picture and Munch's eagerness to include it in the "Life Frieze" in its first groupings, it is possible that Max Klinger's *Untergang* from the series "Ein Leben" can have been of some importance. (Wolfgang Singer, *Max Klingers Radierungen . . .*, [Berlin, 1909]), nos. 138 and 144. It is also tempting to suppose that the etching *Night* which introduces the series "Vom Tode, Erster Teil" (Singer no. 171) has influenced the development of the theme *Evening/Mandrake/The Flower of Pain*. One finds few works which more closely resemble Munch's variations of the theme in the rich tradition which follows Dürer's *Melancholia I*.

53. The reference back to *Evening* becomes clear in the left panel of the diptych. The head, which represents thoughts and ideas, is here, as in the drawing *Time, World, Marriage* (T 1380) immortal, in contrast to the body.

54. Sigbjørn Obstfelder, manuscript in the University Library, Oslo. Ms. 8° 1424, No. 15. / / indicates Obstfelder's deletions. The manuscript is not dated, but must be from the beginning of the 1890s. In a manuscript with the text "Written for the first time in 1892" for the play *Ester*, the following monologue occurs: ". . . It roared. It was so overwhelming, so spectacular. And then they came—Something black swept by. . . . Something black swept through my brain (like in "The Scream" where he places his hands to his ears and shakes his head.) In here!" The University Library, Bergen, ms. 790 A 49.

55. Vilhelm Krag, *Nat: Digte i Prosa* (Night: Poems in Prose) (Bergen, 1892), 20, 55, 90.

56. The picture *Evening on Karl Johan Street* is mentioned by Franz Servaes in Przybyszewski, ed., *Das Werk des Edvard Munch*, p. 44ff. The description of the work implies that Munch himself informed him. Since there are no earlier descriptions of this picture, it seems probable that the picture was painted in the winter of 1893/1894 and that Servaes had seen it in the studio.

The Sick Child, 1894. G/R 7-2. Munch-Museet, Oslo (cat. no. 149)

The Theme of Death

Arne Eggum

The Life Frieze Deals with Inheritance as a Curse
Edvard Munch

Sick Child

THE FIFTH FALL EXHIBITION OF ARTISTS opened to the public on October 18, 1886 in the Museum of Sculpture. The picture which attracted the greatest attention at the most important art event of the year in Christiania was Edvard Munch's *Study*. Throughout the entire period of the exhibition, people gathered before the picture reacting with laughter and indignation. Among artists, the reaction was mixed. The painter Christian Krohg had pushed the picture through the selection committee under pressure. Munch later expressed his gratitude by making Krohg a present of the picture.[1] According to the conservative *Morgenbladet*,[2] a certain group of those in the know held the opinion that *Study* was the best picture at the exhibition. But the majority, including the younger artists, must have had a negative reaction. In a retrospective note from the 1930s Munch wrote this about the reception of the picture:

> No painting in Norway has caused such offense—When I came into the hall on opening day where people were hanging about tightly packed before the picture—yells and laughter were heard—When I went back out into the street the young, naturalistic painters were standing there with their leader Wenzel—He was the celebrated artist of his time—Wenzel was then having his best period and there are several fine paintings by him from that time in our museum—Humbug painter! he yelled into my face—[3]

In his review of the Fall Exhibition, the young and influential art historian Andreas Aubert expressed an attitude which was very representative:

> There is genius in Munch. But there is also a danger that it will go to the dogs.
> I therefore wish, for Munch's own sake, that his Sick Child had been rejected. Not because it speaks less succinctly about his talent than his previous works. But because it shows that he is lax about his own development.
> As this "Study" (!) now appears, it is merely a discarded, half defaced rough draft. He himself has grown tired while working on it. It is an abortion, one of those which Zola so brilliantly has described in l'Oeuvre."[4]

Munch's position as the most modern but also the most controversial and individualistic, among modern Norwegian painters was definitively established in the reviews of *Study* in 1886. It was further ascertained that there was an insuperable chasm between his art and the public's taste and that he would not lift a finger to meet its taste half way. A journalistic but reliable description of the public's reactions may be found in the following newspaper account:

> "What smearing!" says one. "No, this is really too awful!" says another. Number three in an indignant tone, as if he were the interpreter for all of the thoughts and inner feelings of that entire segment of humanity which truly understands art: "It is a scandal that something like this be permitted to hang here!" Number four is mildly ironic:
> —Tell me—what do you say about that arm over there?
> —I suppose it belongs to an orangutan or a polyp?—And say! . . . that thing couldn't possibly represent a hand, that thing there—It's forcemeat of fish in lobster sauce, that's what it is!—"[5]

A review by the author and anarchist Hans Jæger was intended as an introduction to Munch's *Study*. The article was refused by *Dagbladet* but printed on October 20 by *Dagen*, along with a remark by the editor that the newspaper's regular art critic hardly shared Hans Jæger's view of Munch's picture. The article was written as a conversation between the writer and a "frail fellow of the arts," easily identified as the influential professor of art history, Lorentz Dietrichson.[6] Hans Jæger called attention to the beautiful coloring of the picture, while the other was of the opinion that the sketch was too loose to be exhibited. The conversation quickly turned to what was the focus of everyone's attention in regard to *Study*:

> What are those odd streaks down across Munch's picture," asked the fellow after a while; he had started looking at it again. "It's the genius that has been running in big streaks down across it."
> The fellow laughed derisively.[7]

The picture that hides behind the designation *Study* is *Sick Child* from 1886, now in the National Gallery, Oslo. In this picture, the streaks are no longer visible, a fact that has been completely ignored by everyone who later has written about the picture. For this reason, Munch's own statements and the criticism of the time have been poorly understood.

In his review Hans Jæger went on to explain the genesis of the picture. In this he almost certainly found support in the artist's own comments:

> First the man made a rough draft and in it he brought out what he wanted—: a certain mood which you apparently do not perceive. Now the sketch had to be executed. But during the execution the mood was lost and so Munch painted the whole thing over again with great energy and managed to catch the mood once more. Wanted to execute it again but destroyed the whole thing once more. And did this another twenty times or so. And finally he had to give up and be content with the sketch. In it there is genius which has not been able to find its form, this is true; big streaks have been running down across the poor, unsuccessful picture. But what Munch has given us in his sketch is something no one can learn to give; that which he has not been able to paint is at least something that can be learned.[8]

Munch was hardly satisfied with his *Study*. In a literary diary from 1890, it is evident that he was particularly anxious about the streaks. In the Museum of Sculpture some hours before the opening of the exhibition, an artist told Munch he thought the picture was "rubbish," without "substance." To this Munch (Brandt in the diary) replied:

> What the hell do I care about substance said Brandt.—
> What I wanted to bring out—are things that cannot be measured—I have wanted to bring out the tired movement—in the eyelids—the lips are supposed to whisper—he is supposed to give the appearance of breathing—I want life—the stuff that lives—what the devil do I care about the well-made chair—
> He spoke enthusiastically—made motions in the air with his skinny fingers
> —His voice was hoarse
> You'll go crazy if you keep this up—
> What the devil is the purpose of all those streaks—it looks as if it were raining—
> They all laughed—
> Go to hell said Brandt—[9]

When the exhibition opened his worst apprehensions came true. In the previously mentioned diary he wrote:

> He saw the picture hanging just before him in an excellent spot where the stripes were brought out forcefully—he looked anxiously at the people around him—there was a dense crowd of people before the picture—he walked quickly through the crowd—dreadful—he heard—it whizzed before his eyes. . . .[10]

Munch depicted himself as an artist who talked incessantly about his own pictures and never cared about those of others. He was immensely preoccupied with what he felt had been entrusted to him: a completely independent and personal view of art and its function. The fact that the public was not moved by the motif in the way he himself had been moved while at work came as a shock, even if an expected shock. At this time, Hans Jæger was the person who meant most to Munch in his formulation of an artistic vision. According to Jæger, a work of art was supposed to move the public to the same degree the artist himself had been moved by his subject. In the spirit of Kierkegaard, it was the intensity and the inwardness that mattered. That Munch had the ability to be moved in such a way and that he had been particularly moved by the subject of *Study* is something Jæger must have been convinced of. According to Jæger, the rule that the motif in a work of art was to be experienced and lived through by the artist was absolute and unalterable. The fact that Jæger devoted a separate article to Munch's picture can be explained by his having felt that this picture had been created in the spirit of that aesthetic of personal experience which he himself defended. But even Hans Jæger could not accept the final result because the public was not moved by the motif. He concluded his article:

> Munch, Munch! No more pictures of this kind. Not until you have learned to affect all of them, from the artists all the way down to long and skinny art fellows, not until then will you have found your way to a whole art, a great art.[11]

There is every reason to believe that Munch accepted Jæger's judgment.[12] He did not exhibit similar, experimental works at the subsequent fall exhibitions. During the latter half of the 1880s, Munch in fact became more conservative in his pictorial idiom. In a note from the 1930s, Munch explained the psychological reason that *Study* was abandoned in a most unsatisfactory fashion:

> I act either in haste or upon inspiration or after long deliberation—and anxiously—the result is then often weaker and may fail—the result may become the destruction of the work—This is true for me as a painter and as a human being—
> The Sick Child and Spring were both results of long years' efforts—in my most perfect Spring I had been able to make use of a number of happy moments—
> It was less nervous and was not spread out or ruined by interfering, rash moods—
> Sick Child was a more intense mixture of thoughtless work—inspired—and nervous deliberation over a long period—It was finished through a series of inspired and rash revisions—The work abandoned in a most unsatisfactory fashion—
> In this lay its more violent, intense effect—[13]

Munch, then, exhibited a study which had taken him more than a year to complete. The main purpose of exhibiting it must have been to present the intentions he invested in his art, well aware of the risk he would run of being slaughtered. His immediate family did not dare come to the opening because they were afraid it would turn out to be a painful situation.[14] Munch must have been completely aware of the kind of reception his piece would receive—provided it was accepted by the selection committee—but he had hardly anticipated such a conspicuous location "where the stripes were brought out forcefully."[15] He was therefore hardly prepared for the force of the reaction. A more modest placement would, in all likelihood, have caused no more than an academic debate among artist colleagues and the public.

Another bit of circumstantial evidence that Munch did not altogether vouch for the result of his *Study* is the completely ignored fact that the picture was later heavily overpainted.[16] The proof for this is found in some photographs in Munch's photo album of individual pictures

fig. 1 *The Sick Child*, 1886, Nasjonalgalleriet, Oslo

fig. 2 *The Sick Child*, 1892/1893, Nasjonalgalleriet, Oslo

from his exhibition at the Equitable Palace, 1892/1893. There is good reason to believe that all the photographs were taken at the exhibition, at the request of the artist himself. If we compare the photo of the painting *Sick Child* (fig. 1) with a later photo of the same painting (fig. 2), we discover that the right side of the painting is conspicuously overpainted. Originally the lower part was distinctly marked by thinned paint or paint thinner which had run down the picture surface in a close configuration of stripes. It appears as if a liquid had been applied to the picture surface with a rag or sponge in the field which adjoins the barely visible face of the collapsed woman, and that the artist had then allowed the liquid to run freely. Munch did not perfect the use of running paint as a conscious artistic means of expression until after the turn of the century. Even then it was considered a radical vehicle of expression. It is important to note that this revolutionary technique originated in *Study* of 1886. The original *Study* must have had a more pronounced avant-garde character than the *Sick Child* now in the National Gallery. A further comparison of the two photographs also reveals that the glass in the lower right-hand corner of *Study* has been moved and changed through the subsequent overpainting. The articulation of light falling into the picture from the right has also been changed. In the original *Study* it was far more diffuse. The other overpainted parts of the picture in the National Gallery are also easily identified. A comparison between photo and painting reveals that the overpainting was executed with long, swift strokes in contrast to the original surface which was built up meticulously with a palette knife. The color of the overpainting is, moreover, less sensitive and

constitutes a heavy, somewhat mushy mixture of red and green tones. Compared with the original gentle, gray, shimmering surface, the overpainting appears as scrapings of the palette. Even if Munch sporadically also scratched these areas with the spatula, he did keep them coloristically neutral. As a whole, *Study* must have had a far more pronounced atmospheric quality. The tactile elements were veiled, and the general impression must have been unreal—immaterial. The figure of a collapsed woman—the mother—also had a far more unreal quality.[17] The blurred and evanescent tone of the picture, particularly pronounced in the streaked areas in the lower half, must also have given the picture the distinct quality of a technical experiment.

Perhaps Munch originally used thinning solution to veil the unfocused areas in the painting and the resulting streaks were not intended. He may then have perceived them as a new way of veiling the surrounding areas so that the focused area—the face of the sick girl—emerged more clearly. When the streaks were later removed, intentionally or by accident, the problem of making the child "breathe" had to be solved anew. The dark area to the right contrasts with the pale face of the girl and draws attention to it. At the same time it limits the picture surface, while the overpainting in the lower part of the picture amplifies the volume and creates more space. The subject thus became less incorporeal. This also concentrates our attention on the sick child. Explained in this way, it seems natural that Munch gave the overpainted areas a more neutral and diversionary expression.

Leif Østby has shown that the picture in the National Gallery has cubistic characteristics and is built up according to a geometric plan consisting of several squares. This is not so conspicuous in the original formulation but may be perceived as an underlying structure.[18] The two-dimensional character of the picture and the predominant tone of gray must originally have been more pronounced. In a letter to Jens Thiis, written in connection with Thiis's biography, Munch offered a characterization of the painting along these lines:

> I think the sick child is diametrically opposed to Krohg—After all, it is an altogether nervously constructed (cubistic) and colorless picture.[19]

According to Jens Thiis, Munch used Betsy Nielsen as a model for the sick girl and his aunt Karen Bjølstad, who managed the house after his mother's death, as model for the weary-looking woman.[20] Who the models were constitutes no problem. There is a question as to what they represent, however.

In a later memorandum to Jens Thiis, Munch gave an exhaustive account of what he had sought to express in this painting:

> —As far as the sick child is concerned I might tell you that this was a time which I refer to as the "pillow period." There were many painters who painted sick children against a pillow—but it was after all not the subject that made my sick child.
> No, in sick child and "Spring" no other influence was possible than that which of itself wells forth from my home. These pictures were my childhood and my home. *He who really knew the conditions in my home*—would understand that there could be no other outside influence than that which might have had importance as midwifery.— One might as well say that the midwife had influenced the child.—This was during the pillow era. The sick bed era, the bed era and the comforter era, let it go at that. *But I insist that there hardly was one of those painters who in such a way had lived through his subject to the last cry of pain as I did in my sick child. For it wasn't just I who sat there, it was all my loved ones.*[21]

In the same note he wrote:

> In the same chair in which I painted the sick one I and all my dear ones, from my mother on, have been sitting, longing for the sun.[22]

In other words, Munch stressed heavily that he found the subject as such conventional and that he did not wish to compete with other "pillow painters" in having experienced illness and death in his immediate family. For Munch the point was that he *himself* lived this event to the last cry of pain. Munch primarily identified himself with the sick child, but he also emphasized that all his siblings and his mother had been through the same ordeal. Seen in this light, the picture becomes a concentrated expression of the tubercular infirmity of Munch's family.

The reviewers described the subject as a mother-child relation; a young, deathly ill girl with an emaciated face and a sorrowful mother bending down toward her. A preliminary study in the collection that Rolf Stenersen gave to the City of Oslo depicts the mother as the central person, throwing herself on the floor with her hands over her face in despair. The sick girl is here of secondary importance and hardly visible in the picture. In this study

Edvard and His Mother, 1886/1889, OKK T 2273, Munch-Museet, Oslo (cat. no. 141)

the daylight is caught by a carafe on the table before it fades into the darkness where the mother and the sick girl are found, not touching each other.[23]

A large pencil drawing from the 1880s may be interpreted as a comment on the "family in the sick chair." On the back his sister Inger wrote: "Childhood reminiscence. Edvard Munch and his mother" (cat. no. 141). We see here the mother with the same hair in a bun, sitting in the same sick chair, dressed in a similar high-necked, dark dress.[24] The powerful light outside contrasts with the subdued light inside. The mother is totally absorbed in her knitting. The boy is leaning toward the mother, stretching his arms up to her. It is as if the little boy is seeking a contact he is not given. Each of the participants is alone with his destiny. In *Sick Child* there is also an unrelieved tension in the mother's hands and in the area of contact they establish with the child. It is unclear what the mother is doing with her hands.

In an article signed "H." in *Norske Intelligenssedler* an

fig. 3 *Am Strom* 53, Warnemünde, 1907

interpretation was suggested. Later writers have not touched on the problem.

> Munch's picture depicts a young girl—who appears hopelessly ill—perhaps in her last moments. She is sitting in an easy chair with a quilt covering her. The mother is kneeling down by her side with one of her daughter's hands in both of hers, and she is bending her head so that we see nothing of her face. The young girl is looking down at her as if she were trying to whisper some word of consolation, but cannot find the words.[25]

Even if this description may well be correct, it is not immediately obvious that the mother is holding the daughter's hand in both of hers. We may perhaps explain the posture by assuming that the mother's hands are lying on the armrest of the chair and that the left hand of the child is meeting hers but is hidden through a heavy foreshortening behind the mother's clutching hands.

By means of an automatic timer and conscious use of double exposure, Munch made a photograph in the summer of 1907 in the hallway of his house Am Strom 53 in Warnemünde (fig. 3). In the picture he is standing in front of an almost finished copy of *Sick Child*, among other objects. In symbolic fashion, Munch lets himself become one with the subject. Parts of the painting which is actually behind him are visible through his body. This photograph from Warnemünde may be read as a statement by Munch that he also is present in *Sick Child*, and he may consciously have put his left hand over those of his sister and mother in the way we see it in the photograph.

In a pamphlet entitled *The Genesis of the Life Frieze*, which Munch wrote and probably published in conjunction with a studio exhibition in 1929, he gave a full description of the genesis of *Sick Child* and its importance for his art. There is much to suggest that neither Thiis

nor Gauguin had access to this pamphlet when they wrote their biographies of the artist. Munch probably did not want the biographers to transcribe material but rather to put forth alternative points of view on his art. As Munch's "official version," the entire account ought to be read:

> Three years later I gathered several drafts and pictures into a frieze—which was first exhibited in Berlin 1893. It was Scream—Kiss—Vampire—Loving Woman etc. It was in the time of realism and impressionism.—I would occasionally, either in a sick, agitated frame of mind or in a happy mood, find a landscape I wanted to paint.—I fetched the easel—set it up and painted from nature.—
> The picture turned out well—but it was not what I wanted to paint.—I was not able to paint it the way I saw it in my sick mood or in my happy mood.—
> This happened often.—On similar occasions I then began to scratch out what I had painted—in my recollection I was trying to recapture the first picture—the first impression—and I sought to bring it back.
> When I saw the sick child for the first time—the pale head with the vividly red hair against the white pillow—it gave me an impression which disappeared while I was working.—
> I managed to bring out a good but different picture on the canvas.—I repainted the picture numerous times in the course of a year—scratched it out—let it become blurred in the medium—and tried again and again to catch the first impression—the transparent—pale skin against the canvas—the trembling mouth—the trembling hands.—I had done the chair with the glass too often, it distracted me from doing the head.—When I saw the picture I could only make out the glass and the surroundings.—Should I remove it completely?—No, it had the effect of giving depth and emphasis to the head.—I scraped off half the background and left everything in masses—one could now see past and across the head and the glass.
> I also discovered that my own eyelashes had contributed to the impression of the picture.—I therefore painted them as hints of shadows across the picture.—In a way, the head became the picture.—Wavy lines appeared in the picture—peripheries—with the head as center.—I made frequent use of these wavy lines later.
> —I finally quit, tired out.—I had achieved much of that first impression, the trembling mouth—the transparent skin—the tired eyes—but the picture was not finished in its color—it was pale grey. The picture was then heavy as lead.—
> I went back to it in the course of 1895 and 1906[26]—I then succeeded in bringing out more of the stronger color I had wanted to give it.—I painted three different ones.—These are all dissimilar and each contributes toward bringing out what I felt in that first impression. In Spring—the sick girl and her mother at the open window with the sun streaming in I bid farewell to impressionism and realism.
> —In the sick child I broke new ground—it was a breakthrough in my art.—Most of what I later have done had its birth in that picture.[27]

The art of Christian Krohg and Hans Heyerdahl provided the closest model for Munch's painting. Munch was influenced by both of them, but in *Sick Girl* the dissimilarities are far more interesting than the similarities. Krohg and Heyerdahl were both anchored in a purely naturalistic tradition. With his *Study*, Munch put a distance between himself and this tradition, bringing himself closer to a more emotionally charged and individualistic art where psychic realities became the governing motif. Even comparison with Heyerdahl's picture, *Family Scene*, 1881, which in my opinion is more related to Munch's *Study* than any other Norwegian picture, does not alter this fact.[28] To explain why Munch put such distance between himself and his contemporaries in Christiania, Thiis looked to Paris where Munch stayed for a few weeks in 1885. We know that Munch was impressed by the Rembrandts, at the Louvre, which he visited often. Jens Thiis wondered whether Munch may have seen some of the pure impressionists, but is uncertain. Thiis believed the clearest models for Munch's *Study* were Rembrandt's self-portraits, and I am in full agreement with this observation.

Two more painters, one Danish and one French, should however, be mentioned in this context. Kristian Zahrtmann, a Dane, later influential in the development of Norwegian art, became famous because of his painting, *The Death of Queen Amalia,* from 1883.[29] The mirror image of the painting is almost identical to Munch's *Study*, as far as the grouping of the figures. The use of strong colors and the realistic details in an overcrowded luxurious room show how peculiar Munch's picture is in comparison.

Albert Besnard had just finished his decorative panel in L'Ecole de Pharmacie in Paris when Munch visited Paris in 1885. He was then generally accepted as the most successful in adapting modern impressionistic techniques to naturalistic motifs. Munch must have had the same intentions when painting *Study*. Especially in his etchings, Besnard depicted air as if it were solid. His large etching *La Fin de Tout,* 1883,[30] shows an arrangement of figures similar to that in Munch's *Study*[31] and the air is depicted in the same way as in Munch's etching *Sick Child,* 1894, using parallel vertical and horizontal streaks.

The Graphic Versions

In the graphic arts Munch found a medium well suited to the dissemination of his motifs to a larger audience, but the graphic techniques also challenged him to vary and clarify his motifs.

One of the first subjects Munch executed as an etching was *Sick Child,* done in 1894. It is a mirror image of the painting *Study*. Munch made a number of proof impressions,[32] and on close inspection, one can discern a first stage (type A), which corresponds to the original *Study*. He later overworked the plate, changing the image in the same way the painting was changed when overpainted (type B). Type A has a flowing, vibrating character where everything is seen as in a fog (fig. 4). The stooping woman appears to materialize out of nowhere, and the tactile elements in the picture, such as the table and the chairs, are only suggested. The sophisticated technical elements are an important part of the picture's expression. The horizontal lines give the impression of steady rain, as in *Study*.

Type B is characterized by stronger contrasts and by

fig. 4 *The Sick Child,* 1894, OKK G/r 54-1, Sch. 7, Munch-Museet, Oslo

fig. 5 *The Sick Child,* 1894, OKK G/r 7-5, Sch. 7, Munch-Museet, Oslo

the fact that the picture possesses tactile qualities to a far greater degree (fig. 5). The stooping woman figure is more clearly separated from the atmosphere. The upper part of the chair back which supports the pillow is now much more forcefully accentuated. None of the formulations, however, suggests a light source which corresponds to the triangular area in the painting, but type B corresponds to the overpainted version. Since the glass has not been moved, it is plausible that Munch had not overpainted the painting before he started work on the copperplate in 1894. The overpainting may have been done in connection with this work, but it may also have been done as late as 1896 when Munch once more took up the motif in another connection.

Munch had already drawn the base, with its light summer landscape, summer clouds, and the solitary, leafy tree, as a pencil sketch superimposed on the first known proof.[33] This makes it clear that from the beginning Munch had intentions that went beyond a pure reproduction of the painting.

In her 1960 book, Ingrid Langaard sums up the various interpretations which until then had been offered about this landscape.[34] She wonders if Munch wanted to give a synthesis of the emotional content of *Sick Child* and *Spring*. In the painting *Spring*, there is an outside/inside dimension as strong light is falling into the sickroom, filtered through a curtain.

When Munch took up graphic techniques in Berlin in 1894, he was a central figure in a rich, literary milieu with strong interests in psychology, spiritism, mysticism, and alchemy. According to Stanislaw Przybyszewski and several others, Munch at this time was unusually well read for a painter. He devoured the spiritist literature Przybyszewski gave him.[35] Munch may have had an interest in spiritism as early as the 1880s, in view of the strong belief in the existence of the soul after death which prevailed in his childhood home.

When Munch did the etching *Sick Child*, he had already done important works based on recollections of death and sickness in his childhood home. He had earlier written down his recollections in the form of literary notes. There is, therefore, reason to believe that its sketchlike, light landscape is not due to a chance impulse but is the result of mature deliberation. The simplest way to interpret the base is to emphasize the conspicuous contrast between outside and inside, between awakening and withering away; in a deepest sense, between life and death.[36]

Another possible interpretation points to other death motifs by Munch. Thoughts about life and death within the framework of a metabolic religion had been formulated by Munch as early as 1890 in St. Cloud. Given his beliefs the landscape base becomes a symbol of resurrection and eternal life:

> I felt it as a sensual delight that I should become one with—become this earth which is forever radiated by the sun in a constant ferment and which lived—lived—
> —and which was to grow plants from my decaying body—trees and plants and flowers
> and the sun would warm them and I would exist in them
> and nothing would perish—that is eternity.[37]

fig. 6 *Berta and Karlemann*, c. 1888/1890, OKK T 2761-6, Munch-Museet, Oslo

In an illustrated diary written around 1890 is a drawing *Berta and Karlemann* (pseudonyms for Edvard and his sister Sophie) in which the small children walk into a virtually desolate landscape (fig. 6). They are lonely children—he carries a cane, she has a doll. To the left is a dead tree tattered by the wind; to the right is a tree which is alive and luxuriant. It is hardly an accident that the "living," right half of the landscape has features in common with the landscape base. The cloud formations resemble one another in the two pictures, and the dark cloud which encircles the tree in the drawing corresponds to that part of the etching where the cloud is covering part of the tree. In the early drawing on the print which Munch gave Jens Thiis, the tree formation is also similar. It is interesting to note that the drawing is found in the diary account in the context of a childhood recollection in which Edvard and Sophie are awakened at night to learn of their mother's death.

In the drawing *Berta and Karlemann* Munch surrounded Sophie with a set of vertical lines in waving patterns, giving her a somewhat trembling, uncertain quality. By contrast, Edvard is standing there, manly and steady, with a cane. Similar wavy line patterns, although less obtrusive, are also seen in the etchings. Like the painting *Sick Child*, the drawing does not make it clear how the children are grasping each other's hands. In another little drawing from the same sketchbook, Sophie's hand which might have touched Edvard has simply not been finished (fig. 7).

One detail of *Sick Child*, the girl's profile against the pillow, appears in an 1896 etching. It was also done as a color print with reddish brown in the hair and green on the body and the background. This little etching does not have the same power of expression as either of the stages of the etching from 1894. The black-and-white prints have a hard quality, and we miss the sensitivity. The color prints become pieces of candy. Munch printed only a limited number of the motif. He did a much more con-

fig. 7 *Sophie and Edvard,* c. 1888/1890, OKK T 2761-8, Munch-Museet, Oslo

fig. 8 *The Sick Child,* 1896, Private Collection

vincing lithograph of this pictorial element the same year and also made a handsome pastel probably at the same time, now in private hands (fig. 8).

In 1896 Munch was given an assignment by a patron, a factory owner named Olaf Schou, to paint a copy of *Sick Child* for his collection. The result was the version which now hangs in the Gothenburg Art Museum. The "copy" turned out just as smoldering with color as the original had been gray-upon-gray in its tonal values, implying a completely new coloristic interpretation of the motif. While the original *Study* appears heavy because of the thick, partially scraped-off layers of paint, the 1896 copy was painted in a thin, light, and flowing idiom. The striping in the paint done with a spatula is repeated—as in all subsequent versions—but in the Gothenburg painting the execution is far more sophisticated than in the original.

Munch used the 1896 version as a direct model when he drew the motif with a lithographic crayon on stone to create a lithograph (cat. no. 154).[38] The locks around the girl's forehead from the Gothenburg version were followed, and the more elegant scoring which characterized this version had its counterpart in a sensitive scoring with needle in the stone. From this stone, a few prints survive—in part colored—in the Munch Museum. Munch later used this stone mainly for the green or bluish tones in his multicolored prints and must have drawn the main motif on another stone with a dryer lithographic crayon (cat. no. 159). The first stone, however, has a much greater fullness of expression than was attained with the new, main stone. For its part, this stone has a quality of elegance and evidences sophisticated use of the lithographic pencil. Separate prints from the main

stone also exist, most in monochromatic red, but also black ones. These are occasionally enlivened by overprints from other stones done in india ink which color only a part of the girl's red hair.[39] A fourth toning stone is often used for yellow or gray tones. The rich possibilities which multistone prints offered were the foundation for what is perhaps Munch's finest graphic work. It was this sheet which artistically and financially became the most highly valued property while Munch was still alive, and it remains his most highly valued standard print.

An intimate cooperation with the printer Auguste Clot became the prerequisite to fulfilling Munch's intentions. Clot had previously printed color reproductions for Degas, Renoir, and Cézanne and printed graphic works for such young avant-garde artists as Bonnard, Denis, Signac, and Vuillard. It was particularly in his refined use of the lithographic pencil that Munch approached his French peers in sophistication of expression. He had already perfected the technique of combining india ink, lithographic crayon, and needles before he came to Paris in 1895.

It is fascinating to follow how Munch varied the coloristic possibilities of the motif using one to four plates. By means of this technique and the assistance of the printer Clot, Munch could create an almost unlimited number of variations.[39] Most of the colored versions were done in relatively small editions, often printed on different and rare qualities of paper. The number of variations also says a great deal about the importance of this motif for Munch. Erich Büttner wrote a lively account of how the prints came to be made, which was published as a postscript in Jens Thiis' German edition of the Munch biography:

The Sick Child, 1896,
OKK G/L 203-13, Sch.
59, Munch-Museet,
Oslo (cat. no. 154)

The Sick Child, 1897,
OKK G/L 203-7,
Munch-Museet, Oslo
(cat. no. 159)

Paul Herrmann tells about the making of the wonderful lithographs of the "Sick Girl" as follows: I wanted to have some printing done at Clot's when I was told: don't go, Mr. Munch's coming has been announced. The lithographic stones with the great head were already lying next to one another, neatly lined up, ready to print. Munch arrives, positions himself before the row, closes his eyes firmly and begins to direct blindly with his finger in the air: "Go ahead and print . . . gray, green, blue, brown." Opens his eyes, says to me: "Come, drink a Schnaps. . . ." And so the printer printed until Munch came back and gave another blind order: "Yellow, rose, red . . ." And so on another couple of times. . . .[40]

There are two interesting lithographs in the Munch Museum, both with a drawing of the mother's head superimposed as in the painting. On one of them the head is painted with india ink in a sketchy manner. On the other there is heavy overpainting of gouache. The first sheet shows the woman's head heavily bowed in profile; on the other she is less bowed and her face is in three-quarter profile. In both sheets the woman's eye is formed as a deeply sunken, deathlike, cranial depression. The deathlike quality is most pronounced in the gouache. The overpainting gives strong effects of contrast. Munch did nothing to reconcile the two worlds and deliberately introduced a pall of death into the picture.

The Painted Repetitions

Munch did his first painted "copy," as mentioned above, for Olaf Schou in 1896.[41] Coloristically speaking, the painting was given a completely independent expression. Schou was satisfied but hardly overly enthusiastic about the picture. In a postscript of an undated letter in which he thanked Munch after having received the painting, he wrote:

> I think you have been lucky with the copy, it resembles the original even if not quite as well done. But you should not do any more to it, I am satisfied the way it is.[42]

This painting was exhibited for the first time at Le Salon des Indépendants in 1896. The distinctive qualities of the picture were discussed by Ivan Angueli:

> M. Munch. Son tableau, représente une enfant malade midebout sur son lit se détachant contre l'oreiller blanc et, à droite, une femme qui s'incline; il systhétise un drame de la vie humaine avec une si profonde émotion, que l'on sent que la mort y assiste en personne spectrale, comme une troisième acteur, caché. On dirait que cet enfant au profit effacé—que l'on restitue pourtant si bien—ne se meut que par une force d'outre-tombe, et le geste des épaules et du bras stigmatise le désir de s'en aller de la vie. Les cheveux roux brillent comme dans une vision, et tout en bas, à droite, un liquide rouge dans un verre projette un rayon du poupre le plus pur. Le deuil en prières muettes courbe la tête de la femme, et au-dessus de tons vert-mousse plane un nuage gris-perle à la fois profond et léger, comme l'inconnu. Une analyse des moyens serait un sacrilège.[43]

This picture was given to the National Gallery in Oslo by Schou in 1910, where it was accorded the place of honor until 1931. In that year it was sold to the Gothenburg Museum of Art because the National Gallery needed

money to acquire the original version which was then on the market. Munch went along with the transaction. He wanted the original to go to the National Gallery because, as he expressed it in a letter to the then owner, Harald Nörregård:

> I am certain you will understand me when I think that my first sick child ought to go to the National Gallery—It is perhaps my most important picture and at any rate my breakthrough into expressionistic painting—[44]

Munch made still another copy in Warnemünde in 1907 on assignment from the patron Ernest Thiel. At this time he was going through a radical reevaluation of his style. That same spring he had painted a few harbor scenes. In those pictures he was defining himself in relation to French fauvism. At about the same time he painted a picture from Dr. Linde's garden with a version of Rodin's *Thinker* as the main motif.[45] Here we see for the first time Munch's use of long, parallel, vertical and horizontal strokes, a technique that was to characterize a number of his main works done that year and the following at Warnemünde. In the new version of *Sick Girl* commissioned by Thiel, he demonstrated his newly developed technique. In a 1933 letter to Thiis, Munch wrote:

> At the beginning of the century I felt a need to break the plane and the line—I felt it might turn into mannerism—I then followed 3 paths: I painted some realistic pictures such as the children at Warnemünde—Then I took up part of the technique from "Sick Child" again. At that time I was copying this picture for Olaf Schou; it later came to our gallery and thereafter to Gothenburg. This is, as one may see from "Sick Child" in the gallery, built up from horizontal and vertical lines—and inward-moving, diagonal strokes[46]

We must suppose that Munch had photographs from Am Strom 53 before him when he wrote this. The version of *Sick Child* he "stands in front of" in the photograph was the copy he painted for Thiel (fig. 3). The painting was not yet completed. *The Children in Warnemünde*, from the same period, is placed to the left of *Sick Child*. This and *Old Man Warnemünde* (the motif is from the backyard of the same house) prove that Munch had developed such technical innovations as painting directly on the canvas with the tube of paint by the summer of 1907.

Thiel was very enthusiastic when he received the picture. In an undated letter he wrote to the artist:

> 'The Sick Child' has the effect of a revelation. My Munch wall will be the most stately in all of Europe—I can see that even now.[47]

In the photograph featuring Munch before his pictures in Warnemünde, to the left is part of a newly begun canvas of *Sick Child* with a triangular field to the right which defines the source of light. No other known work by Munch has a similar field in that part of the picture plane. It agrees, as far as I can see, in detail with only that version which is now in the Tate Gallery. It is therefore reasonable to assume that this version was also painted in Warnemünde. In the new version of *Sick Girl* commissioned by Thiel, he demonstrated his newly developed poses.[48] The picture was sold to the State Gallery of Paintings, Dresden, in 1927.[49] In a letter to the director of the Gallery in Dresden, Munch gave an account of why he had hesitated to let go of the painting:

> You know the partial reasons why it was difficult for me to accept your great and honorable offer—You know it was the first picture and the main picture in the Frieze of Life[50]

The two versions of *Sick Child* painted in Warnemünde in 1907, have widely different coloristic qualities. While the version in the Thiel Gallery has a golden, glowing, overall coloring, the Tate Gallery version is characterized by bold red/green contrasts. Although the vivid green colors, bordering on the garish, resemble tones Munch used ten years later, the stroke technique indicates that the picture was painted in Warnemünde in 1907. Besides, there is a similar coloring in the painting *Rodin's "The Thinker" in Dr. Linde's Garden* which may be dated 1907 with certainty. Yet another reason that Munch did not want to send *Sick Child* to Dresden immediately may have been that he needed it when he was painting a final version in 1927. In a letter to Thiis from the early 1930s, Munch wrote a further commentary on this picture and touched on the criticism he had received for painting so many versions of this motif:

> Apropos "The Sick Child"
> I painted it (during my exhibition at the National Gallery) for the fifth time—Since I needed it for the forever fleeced life frieze—It was removed from Lerolle to Carnegie—exhibition and is reproduced in the Catalogue—I think it has a naive and simple power in the midst of all the pale, glib classicism which has sprung up after Picasso. The picture is also being called attention to in the press—There are loud cries of complaint because I have painted it several times. But a picture and a motif which I have struggled with a whole year is not concluded in a single picture—Why cannot a motif which is so important to me be painted and varied five times when we see how painters paint apples, palms—church steeples and haystacks *ad infinitum*—?[51]

It is clear from a photograph of an exhibition arranged by Carnegie International Exhibition in the U.S. in 1933 that the picture was neither signed nor dated at that time. The picture was later signed and dated 1926. It was not unusual that Munch remembered incorrectly when post-dating his works.

There is still another version of the motif, signed but undated, in the Munch Museum. At exhibitions after Munch's death this canvas has been dated 1927. On a photo of one of Munch's studios at Ekely, which can be dated Christmas 1929, this version is seen. It is probably this painting that is referred to in a letter to A. Rütschi from late 1928 as "die 5te Fassung von 6 Jahre gemalt." Thus we should date this version 1921/1922.[52] The Munch Museum's two versions of *Sick Child* have clear differences, the version from 1921/1922 being far more brilliantly colored than the later one, which I date 1927.

THE DEATH MOTIFS FROM THE 1890s

The Literary and Theoretical Origin

In the 1890s, Munch became extremely careful not to overwork a rough draft in which he had captured an essential side of a motif, be it a mood or an expressive quality. Instead of continuing to work on a draft, he often painted a new study. In this way there are a number of versions which represent mood variants on most of his central motifs.[53] Each rendition formed the basis for testing formal and artistic qualities. But it was the crystallizing of the motif which was crucial to the effort. The death motif posed the problem of giving a number of profound childhood experiences a form which could also communicate the feelings that accompanied the recollections.

Munch frequently exhibited several final versions of the same "Life Frieze" motif. When he had the opportunity, he also simultaneously exhibited drawings of the motif.[54] The exhibition style in which sketches, studies, and more finished works were exhibited together emphasized the great significance of the motif in relation to the artistic effort. At the same time, the artist clarified to the public what the result had cost him in terms of work and concentration.

Before Munch began the final formulation of the individual motifs in the "Life Frieze," he had developed an art theory which both reflected Hans Jæger's views and established connections with contemporary French avant-garde theories of art. In a note dated January 2, 1891, Munch considered it a condition for an expressive art that the artist expose himself in his work:

> For in these pictures the painter gives his dearest—it gives his soul—his sorrow his joy—it gives his heart blood—He gives the man—not the object. These pictures will affect more strongly—first those few—then more then everyone.[55]

The process of creation was also conceived of as being as painful as giving birth. He did not doubt, however, that the end result would mean the total victory for his art. It is important to note that Munch in this and the following passage evidently referred to his purely impressionistic works:

> . . . that these pictures are done in seriousness—in suffering—that it is a product of waking nights—that it has cost one's blood—one's nerves.[56]

The fervor of these quotes and the decisively existential stress on intense inwardness, seriousness, and suffering point back to the Scandinavian tradition whose central figure was Sören Kierkegaard. Later in life Edvard Munch also strongly emphasized points of similarity between his own views and those of Kierkegaard, particularly as expressed in the book *The Concept of Dread*.

Munch's views were probably also strongly influenced by the author Hans Jæger (see Gerd Woll's article). Jæger's demand that the artist lay himself and his art ruthlessly bare was a principal Munch followed.[57] Similar sentiments had also been formulated by van Gogh in letters to his brother Theo.[58] There is a distinct possibility that Munch knew of van Gogh's views through the Dane, Johan Rohde, as early as 1888.[59]

In a note from approximately 1890, it is evident that for Munch the subject of an impressionistic picture was secondary to the mood which is expressed as a result of a need to communicate with a fellow human being:

> Art, generally speaking, is born from a person's need to communicate with another—
> All means are equally good—
> In painting as in literature we often confuse the means with the goal—Nature is the means, not the goal—If we can achieve anything by changing nature—we must so—In a state of strong emotion a landscape will have a certain effect on us—by reproducing this landscape we will come into a picture of our mood—it is this mood which is the main thing—Nature is merely the means—Whether or not the picture then resembles nature is of no consequence—
> Explaining a picture is impossible—It is precisely because we cannot explain in any other way that it has been painted—We can merely give a small hint as to the direction we had in mind.
> I do not believe in an art which has not forced its way out through man's need to open his heart
> All art, literature, as well as music must be brought about with our heart blood.
> Art is our heart blood.[60]

In keeping with prevailing symbolist and synthetist theories from around 1890, Munch reacted against an art program in which the personality of the artist did not have a central place. For Munch, the external motifs were interesting to the extent that they were able to induce a distinctive, strong mood in him or call forth recollected images. The image of recollection included in the accompanying mood or the emotion was, according to Munch, the proper subject of the artist. It was therefore impossible to recover the motif in external nature when the artist was emotionally cold. The image of recollection, on the other hand, was always before one. The light, airy, impressionistic paintings Munch did in France between 1890 and 1892 are most often "pictures of recollection." It was only after more than a year of formulating his expressionistic theory that Munch began to paint "Life Frieze" motifs. The statement, "I do not paint what I see, but what I saw"[61] must also be applied to Munch's so-called impressionistic phase.

The emphasis on memory at the expense of the immediate was not peculiar to Munch but something he shared with the entire continental opposition to naturalism. The strong emphasis he put on the depiction of recollections, on the other hand, was distinctly his own. Gauguin, for an example, recommended that one ought to paint according to memory so that the picture would have a personal character. While Gauguin sought harmonies, not contrasts, Munch preferred to paint dissonances to recreate strong emotions. Munch further analyzed the picture of recollection to explain physically as well as psychically why it turned out differently from a "photographic" rendering of nature. If an individual, for example, stares intensely at a green billiard table and then moves his glance upward, he will see black clothes as crimson. If this picture is to be painted, those dressed in black must be painted wearing crimson. Another source of error is the mental state of the beholder. A quote from one of Munch's diaries from 1890/1891 shows how Munch combined extreme subjectivism with an almost scientific argumentation:

> During a drinking bout one sees things in another way. The drawing often becomes blurred and everything has more the effect of chaos. We may then, as is well known, see wrongly.
> But then one must—that seems crystal clear—also paint the drawing wrongly.
> If one sees double one must for example paint two noses. And if one sees a glass as lopsided, one will make it lopsided. Or one wishes to bring out something one has felt in an erotic moment when hot and amorous. At that moment, one has found a motif, then one cannot reproduce it exactly as one sees it another time when one is cold. It is obvious that the first picture one has seen must appear quite different from the last. One perceives everything quite differently when one is warm than when one is cold. And it is precisely this, this and this alone, that gives art a deeper meaning. It is the person, life, one must bring out. Not dead nature. It is true that a chair may hold as much interest as a person. But the chair must be seen by a person. It must have moved him in one way or another and one must make the viewers become moved in the same way.
> It isn't the chair which is to be painted, but that which a man has felt by seeing it.[62]

Munch's example of a chair suggests that he knew van Gogh's paintings from 1888 with a chair as the main motif. In the publication *The Genesis of the Life Frieze*, 1929, the effect of distance in time on the image of recollection is also discussed:

> I painted then only what I recalled without adding anything—without details I no longer saw.
> —Hence the simplicity of the pictures—the apparent emptiness.—
> I painted impressions from my childhood—the indistinct colors from that time.—
> By painting those colors and lines and forms I had seen in an agitated mood—I once more wanted, as in a phonograph, to make the agitated state of mind tremble forth.—
> In this way the picture in the life frieze came about.

When it came to painting living people, Munch also stressed memory. In the 1889 "St. Cloud Manifesto," later printed in *The Genesis of the Life Frieze*, we find his famous program.

> A strong, naked arm—a brown powerful neck—a young woman puts her head up to the arched chest.—She closes her eyes and listens with open, trembling mouth to the words he whispers into her long, flowing hair.
> I should shape in the way I now saw it but in the blue haze.—These two in the moment they are not themselves but only a link in the thousands of generations that tie generations to generations.—
> People would understand the holy, the powerful in this and they would take off their hat as if in a church.—I should want to depict a series of such pictures. Interiors should no longer be painted, people reading and women knitting.

They should be living persons who breathe and feel, suffer and love.

The original manuscript is lost so we must take into account that the program is somewhat edited. It may also be added that at least one year passed between the time Munch wrote the manifesto and his work on paintings for the "Life Frieze."

While he was familiarizing himself with French avant-garde art on a fellowship trip to France and writing fragments of a theory of art, Munch, began an intense literary activity, with plans for speedy publication. In all likelihood, he worked from memoranda and notes already formulated in Christiania from the middle of the 1880s. An illustrated diary may have been written in Christiania before his fellowship trip to Paris in 1889. For the next couple of years Munch wrote a series of diaries and an incalculable number of notes of recollections on loose sheets. The diaries consist partly of passages in which he recalled experiences of death and illness in his childhood home. Other sections deal with recollections of his first love experiences as an adult. Interspersed are impressions of current experiences and reflections on the goals and meaning of art.

Munch let the sections stand separately, with no attempt at connection. This was probably done deliberately. More than twenty years later, he started to edit his loose notes by inserting them in a book divided into the following chapters: Art, States of Mind, Moods, Recollections of Youth, Love, Amours, Lunacy.[63] Particularly interesting and moving are the long, detailed descriptions of dread and despair in connection with the death of his mother and sister and experiences of fear of death during his own illnesses. There seems to be an unusual precision in his recollections, some of them dating back more than twenty years. A paragraph from a very long description of one of Munch's illnesses as a boy, dated St. Cloud, February 5, 1890, gives an impression of the intensity of the scenes:

Daddy, the stuff I am spitting is so dark—
Is it, my dear boy—
He found a light and looked at it—
I saw he was hiding something—
The next time he spit on the sheet and he saw it was blood—
It is blood Daddy—
He stroked my head—don't be afraid my boy
I was going to die from consumption—he had heard so much about it that when one spit blood, then one got consumption
I am walking up to you—his heart beat—
He crawled out to his father as if to seek protection—
Don't be afraid my son the father said once more—[64]

Munch had a sensitive mind, and the agonizing experiences of illness and death in his childhood home left their mark on him. That in itself is not so remarkable; it was a fate he shared with many others. The remarkable thing is that he so consciously and intensely relived these events and later recreated them in stirring images. There are aspects of depth psychology in this which have new implications for the pictorial arts. Similar tendencies were already present in literature; Ibsen's *Rosmersholm* and *Ghosts* are examples, in which the suspense lies in the process by which the past is gradually revealed to the audience and brought to the surface of the consciousness of the characters through a process of recollection. Such authors as Bourget, the brothers Goncourt, and Ola Hansson in Sweden were working simultaneously on the problem of how subconscious, repressed experiences determined the pattern of behavior and sexuality in adults. In Paris, the psychiatrist J. M. Charcot gave his famous lectures on psychology and used hypnotized young women as subjects. These lectures were well known and respected by the Norwegian colony in Paris. The lectures were followed by Sigmund Freud during the 1880s. Munch's favorite authors were Dostoevski and Edgar Allan Poe—authors whose main interest lay in uncovering the nocturnal and shadowy sides of the psyche. In his interest in childhood experiences and their significance, Munch is a contemporary of Freud's in the most profound sense. When Munch later analyzed his agonizing childhood experiences, he saw them as causes for his nervous disposition. In a note from approximately 1903, Munch wrote:

My art found its roots in that reflection where I sought an explanation for this disparity in my relation to life—Why was I not like others? Why born to something I had not asked for. The curse and reflection over this became the undertone of my art and its strongest undertone and without it my art would have become something else—
But in the reflections about this and in the release through my art lay a need to and a wish that my art may bring me light—darkness and also light for men[65]

The diary entries about his adolescent experiences of love and his erotic experiences as an adult have the same richness of detail. In his youth, Munch must have been very frustrated in his need for love and his natural drives. And yet, a great many of the love motifs from the "Life Frieze" are present in embryo form in these literary diaries. Munch was obsessed with his relationship to "Mrs. Heiberg," a pseudonym for a woman married to a ship's physician. She was three years older than Munch and had the reputation of being unfaithful to her husband.[66]

The interesting thing is not whether Munch had a sexual relationship with her (we know nothing certain about this), but rather that Munch dwelled on all the circumstances that led to the meeting between the two, all the details that preceded the first kiss, and everything that happened after this innocent kiss. Munch wrote that it was his first kiss; it happened in 1885, when he was twenty-one years old. As a submotif, a young, blond girl appears, the girl he really loved but never attached himself to because he was attracted to "Mrs. Heiberg," who prevented him from forming a more natural relationship with women. A typical example of his recollections may be found in the following excerpt from a diary dated 1890:

He was walking along Karl Johan at dusk—a soft, mild winter evening—two days had passed since he had been together with—he was going to meet her Sunday—that

155

would be the day after tomorrow—He was full of longing for her—the day after tomorrow was so far away—he looked at the yellow air behind the King's Castle—dark shapes were passing him. The soft melancholy of dusk—gave him a sickly longing after her He felt someone who glided up towards him And then she was there next to him wrapped in her fur coat—it gives her a more wifely appearance than usual—he felt her arm against his—she was a bit chilled—It was as if a flood went through his blood a flood of joy he had never felt before—a weakness in his limbs—in his cheeks, could almost not say a thing He was so happy at just being able to walk next to her without saying a word. They walked down Karl Johan. You must go now because here comes someone I know—she said suddenly. Goodbye then she said and turned off It was sad to leave her now but he was going to see her tomorrow And he drifted about while the light disappeared more and more—filled by her he had just left—This chance meeting.
But then a thought suddenly came up in him which appalled him—was he supposed to have left her—had he not heard wrong.[67]

Munch began his illustrated diary with an exhaustive description of personal recollections of his mother's illness and subsequent death. These portrayals move directly into descriptions of his unresolved relationship with "Mrs. Heiberg," and he was hardly unaware of the connection. Associative psychology was much used in contemporary literature. Ola Hansson's *Sensitiva Amorosa* from 1887 must have been an important influence for Munch. A theme in this book is precisely how the image of recollection is associated with experienced events, often destroying human relationships.

"Mrs. Heiberg" was, like Munch's mother, most beautiful when she was pale, suffering, and dressed in black. Like his mother, she also had dark hair. She is depicted as being married to a military physician of captain's rank, like Munch's father. Already as a thirteen-year-old, Munch had admired her husband because he was the most dashing lieutenant in the military. Munch's father was also an elegant gentleman.

In this literary vein, Munch conveyed the impression that the memories of his mother colored his relationship to women. His farewell to his mother, intensified through later illnesses and the death of his sister, became for Munch an explanation of why he experienced life from its nocturnal side. By laying himself bare through his art he also wished to help others find the truth about themselves. Most of the later "Life Frieze" motifs may be illuminated by scenes from these notes and diaries. In a letter to Jens Thiis from 1933 we read:

> You don't have to go far to explain the genesis of the life frieze—After all, it has its explanation in the bohemian period itself—What I wanted was to paint the living life and my own life—
> Furthermore I also had the life frieze finished for some time in poetic form so I assume that it was already in a prepared state many years before I came to Berlin.[68]

Outside the Gate, 1891/1892, OKK T 2261, Munch-Museet, Oslo (cat. no. 137)

Childhood Memories–The Mother Image

A photograph of Munch's exhibition at the Equitable Palace, Berlin, December 1892, shows a number of drawings carelessly mounted on a wall (fig. 9). On the far left are two delicately executed pencil drawings placed above and below a drawing of *Melancholy,* now lost. The motif of the two drawings is Munch's deathly ill mother when he was four-five years old. In *Outside the Gate,* mother and son are standing in a richly illuminated street outside a dark entranceway (cat. no. 137). The street leads in a vigorously diagonal perspective inward and toward the left. The drawing recalls an experience which took place when Munch was four and a half years old. In *By the Double Bed,* the mother is leaning toward the bed in a tired attitude (cat. no. 142). The light is falling on her from a window to the left of the bed. In the darkness, at the end of the large, double bed, the five-year-old Edvard is huddled closely with his sister Sophie, then six. Exactly in the middle above the bed, the cross of the window frame is

fig. 9 Munch exhibition at the Equitable Palace, Berlin, 1892

outlined as a symbol of impending death. To the right of *By the Double Bed*, the photograph of the exhibition shows a motif which is difficult to identify. The most obvious guess is that it is a drawing of the motif *Vision*. The drawing *Outside the Gate* is flanked by yet another death motif, *Death Raking Leaves:* death, represented by a woman raking autumn leaves in an avenue lined by trees. This montage plausibly records the first attempt by Munch to group together his important motifs of death, love, and anxiety in an exhibition.[69]

The literary diary which Munch probably wrote first is illustrated by a number of drawings in the text. We shall here call it "Illustrated Diary" and tentatively date it 1889.[70] It is introduced by a short, pastoral description which leads up to a scene in which a group of farmers brutally kill a "small and very white" lamb. Then follows the text of the motif we have called "By the Double Bed":

By the lower end of the large double bed were two small children's chairs, placed closely; the tall figure of a woman was standing next to them, large and dark against the window.
She said she was going to leave them had to leave them—and asked if they would be sad when she was gone—and they must promise her to stay with Jesus and then they would meet her again in Heaven—
They did not quite understand—but thought it was terribly sad and then they both cried,—sobbed—[71]

The text for "Outside the Gate" follows immediately:

It was dark and gloomy in the stairwell. I held her hand and pulled her, I could not get out fast enough. Then I asked her why she walked so slowly. She stopped at every tread and drew her breath.
But outside the gate the daylight blinded us—everything was so bright, so bright.
She stopped for a while and the air was so strangely warm with a few cold gusts. The grass shot up among the cobblestones and light green grass; it was spring.
She had a pale blue hat on and the band fluttered with every breath of air, hitting her in the face.
then we went down castle street to the fort and looked out at the sea.[72]

The next, crucial childhood memory is from Christmas of 1868; his mother died on December 29 of that year.

There were many white lights all the way to the top—some were dripping—it was shining in all the light colors but mostly red and yellow and green. It was almost impossible to see for all the light.
The air was saturated with the heavy odor of stearin and burnt spruce. Nowhere any shadows, the light crawled into all nooks and crannies. She sat in the middle of the sofa in the large black dress (silk) which seemed still blacker in this ocean of light, quiet and pale. Round about her sat or stood all five. Father was walking up and down the floor and sat down by her over in the sofa and they whispered together and bent down towards one another. She smiled and tears ran down her cheeks. Everything

By the Double Bed, 1891/1892, OKK T 2358, Munch-Museet, Oslo (cat. no. 142)

fig. 10 Edvard and his Mother, 1864

was so quiet and bright.
Then Berta sang Silent night holy night all is calm all is bright.
Then something opened and one could see far far into the heavens and Angels could be seen descending, smiling with long robes. And we were all of us so enraptured, so enraptured.
She in the sofa looked at us from one to the other and stroked our cheeks with her hand.[73]

Immediately following is the description of Edvard's and Sophie's farewell to their mother. We have called this childhood memory "The Mother's Farewell Kiss":

We were supposed to leave
A man dressed in dark clothes was standing at the end of the bed praying.
It was dim in the room and the air heavy and gloomy. We were dressed in street clothes and the maid who was to accompany us was waiting by the door.
Then each of us had to go over to the bed and she gave us a strange look and kissed us. Then we left the room and the girl brought us to some strange people.
They were all so kind to us and we were given cookies and toys as much as we wanted.
We were awakened in the middle of the night

We understood immediately
We dressed still half asleep.[74]

Laura Cathrine Bjölstad married the military physician Christian Munch, twenty-one years her senior, in the fall of 1861. At this time her father was still relatively well-to-do but later went bankrupt because of unfortunate business transactions. She was very religious and even from the beginning of her marriage was inclined toward a thrifty, puritanical way of life. Both she and her sister Karen who helped her in the house were very sickly. The religiosity of their upbringing and the disposition of both sisters dictated that they accept their fate. Before Laura Cathrine died at thirty, she gave birth to five children during seven years of marriage. At their mother's death, Inger was eleven months, Laura two years, Peter Andreas three, Edvard five and Sophie six. The two eldest children, Edvard and Sophie, experienced the death of their

fig. 11 The Artist's Mother and her Children

Childhood Memory/Christmas, c. 1895, OKK T 2266, Munch-Museet, Oslo (cat. no. 145)

mother in close solidarity. Sophie is always "the sister" in Munch's literary notes. The others are the small children.

Munch's mother was stately, dark-haired, and beautiful. As the middle class style of the time dictated, she generally dressed in black and wore her hair parted in the middle and piled high on her head. In a photo of her with Edvard as an infant on her lap (fig. 10) she has an active, open look and is staring directly into the camera. If we compare this photo with one of the paintings or lithographs of *Madonna*, we find a great similarity in the features.

Some weeks before Edvard's mother gave birth to her youngest child, Inger, February 5, 1868, she wrote a letter of farewell to Sophie. She did not expect to survive the birth. In the letter she urgently asked Sophie and the other children to keep to the Lord and renounce the Devil. She was afraid that the children would turn their backs on the Lord.

> I am often full of worry that I shall be missing some of you who are my heart's treasure here on earth, in Heaven, but trusting the Lord who has promised to hear our prayers, I shall beg for your souls as long as the Lord grants me life.[75]

In the above farewell letter she addressed Munch as "my dear, pale Edvard," and in a separate letter to him she called him "my dearly beloved son." Mutual illnesses

must have tied the two of them closely together.

Even if his mother survived the birth by almost a year, she did not write another letter of farewell. During her convalescence another photo was taken of her surrounded by all her children (fig. 11). On her lap she holds Inger as a baby, to the right is Edvard with hands lifted in an uncertain gesture, and to the left Sophie holds a doll. Edvard was then four and a half years old, Sophie almost six. The photograph communicates a sadness and quiescence not unlike the mood of Munch's later pictures of "death in the family" motif. In the photograph it seems as if the mother already has retreated from the world and that Edvard and Sophie understood they were participants in a farewell portrait.

Munch later used this photo as a model for drawings of the childhood recollection *Christmas* (which in reality took place approximately half a year later). One of the drawings of this childhood memory depicts Christian Munch bending over his wife who is dressed in a black silk dress (cat. no. 145). Both have their attention directed to her lap, which is empty, although she may have been pregnant. In the far background to the right is a Christmas tree, and before this are three children with their heads to one side as if they are singing. They look like overgrown embryos, and the background figure in particular reminds us of the foreground figure in *The Scream*. In a sketchbook drawing from the 1930s with a motif from Christmas 1886, Edvard is standing to the right in a stiff posture, while the other children are walking around the Christmas tree.[76] Edvard here seems bald, and the articulation of the head has similarities with the personification in *The Scream*.

A group of drawings on a sketch sheet, probably from 1901, may refer to the mother's pregnancy (fig. 12). A naked, pregnant woman is standing in front of the same bed found in the drawings of the childhood memory *By the Double Bed*. This type of bed is otherwise found only in

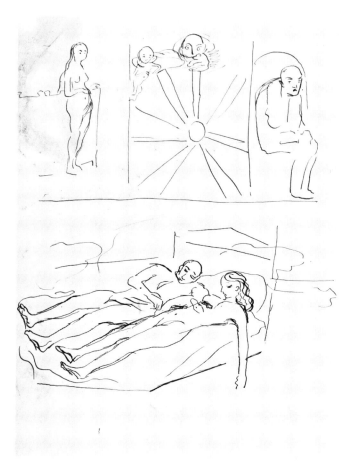

fig. 12 *The Dead Loving Couple*, 1896/1897, OKK T 373 (left side of triptych), Munch-Museet, Oslo

motifs directly associated with recollections from the childhood home.[77]

In the upper part of another drawing sits a man bent forward, Munch himself, staring into a fireplace (cat. no. 112).[78] He is looking into another plane of the picture where a woman is buried with a child that seems to be growing out of her. The subject of metabolism may be found in its embryonic form in this picture. The particular point of departure for this drawing may have been Munch's notions about an unborn child, or it may have reference to a more general notion about the fetus as a murderer.

The question of when Munch began writing literary sketches of recollections is an unsolved problem. We know that he wrote a good deal in St. Cloud during the winter and spring of 1890, but we know little about what he may have written before that time. Munch's active participation in the circle of the Kristiania Bohème where the slogan was: "You shall write your own life," makes it plausible that Munch was writing literary notes even at that time. A number of these probably were included in his literary diaries.

The most detailed drafts for "Outside the Gate" and "Christmas" most likely date from the winter of 1887/

1888. The drafts were originally written on the same sheet, but Munch cut them apart, probably in connection with his later editing of the material for "The Moss Ledger" in 1915 or later.[79] On the back of the sheets, in the same ink as that used for the text, Munch made drawings which must be the first studies for the painting *In the Rented Room* of 1888. The painting has been lost, but is preserved in the etching *Christiania-Bohemian I*.[80] These sketches prove that the texts were written during the winter of 1887/1888.

An important detail was later deleted from this datable text for "Christmas." It is Munch's reactions to Sophie's singing hymns. In this draft of "Christmas" the description ends:

> The melody and the words were so well suited
> and Karlemann seemed taken
> opened up so that he looked into
> the heaven and he saw the angels who descend
> and descend with white shining
> robes and so friendly and smiling and
> he could see so far into the heavens
> and brighter and brighter it became—Oh he felt
> enraptured—he did not know what
> to say only stood there laughing—[81]

We know nothing about the family's reaction to Munch's laughter, but it must have been an emotionally charged situation. A short time later his mother was dead.

The childhood recollection "Outside the Gate" is illustrated by a large number of almost identical drawings and sketches (cat. no. 138 and figs. 13-15). In all versions, mother and son are placed in a space with a strongly articulated perspective. The mother is passive; it is difficult to determine whether she is walking or standing. Her son's relationship to her varies in the different drawings, however. In some of them it seems as if he wants to pull her along with him. In others he is crawling in toward her skirt and almost merges with her visually.

One variant is the placing of the scene in a symbolist frame (fig. 16). In the lower part is sprouting grass; in the upper, well-defined cloud formations are seen. The clouds reflect and repeat the movements of the hat ribbon. On the side panels of the frame we see roundish, floating forms which, like other symbolist frames by Munch, must be intended as embryos or sperm cells. In the drawing with the frame, the son is placed inside his mother's skirt. A larger sketch done in oil on cardboard repeats this grouping and was possibly intended to have the same type of symbolist frame (cat. no. 139). This type of frame was otherwise exclusively reserved for depictions of the motifs *Madonna*, *The Girl and Death*, and probably *The Scream* during the early nineties.[82]

fig. 13 *Outside the Gate,* early 1890s,
OKK T 2637, Munch-Museet, Oslo

fig. 14 *Outside the Gate,* early 1890s,
OKK T 245, Munch-Musęet, Oslo

fig. 15 *Outside the Gate,* early 1890s,
OKK T 2260, Munch-Museet, Oslo

fig. 16 *Outside the Gate,* early 1890s,
OKK T 2264 B, Munch-Museet, Oslo

Outside the Gate, c. 1915, OKK T
2263, Munch-Museet, Oslo (cat. no.
138)

Outside the Gate, early 1890s, OKK M
137, Munch-Museet, Oslo (cat. no.
139)

The Scream—*A Picture of a Death Vision*

There are clear parallels between Munch's description of the memory which is the basis for *Outside the Gate* and his longer comments on *The Scream*. Both texts reflect, among other things, the theme of not being able to go on, of weariness to the point of death, and an unusually strong, visual experience of light. The main difference is that the childhood memory only registers facts, while the texts of "Scream" also render feelings.

In *The Scream* (cat. no. 129) the Akershus headland, viewed across the Oslo fiord, makes the setting of the experience easy to identify. The boats with crosslike masts and the church in the city are suggestions of death. This was the place mother and son visited when they "looked out on the sea" in the childhood recollection "Outside the Gate." Akershus was also his father's place of work. As a military physician, he was stationed at the Akershus garrison, and the family therefore belonged to the garrison congregation. The funeral service of the artist's mother, and later those of his father and sister, took place in the Akershus Palace Church. The church depicted in *The Scream*, with its cupola and steeple, is located behind Akershus, in the city proper, and therefore hardly refers to the Akershus Palace Church. The only church in Oslo which it could represent is the Trinity Church.

In a private collection in Oslo there is a painting of this church cupola (fig. 17). Painted around 1833, the church, is seen from the family residence in Foss Street. The cupola, which fills the upper half of the picture, has an almost threatening character. It is a picture charged with expression. In a watercolor, also privately owned, the church is framed by smoke from chimneys (fig. 18). The steeples to the left and right belong respectively to the Church of our Savior and St. Olav's Church. In the Munch Museum there is yet another drawing with the cupola of the Trinity Church as background, but it has a burial motif in the foreground (cat. no. 148). The drawing suggests an open church, of which only the back wall is standing. Turned away from us, the pastor is officiating behind the casket. The part of the churchyard which is depicted in the drawing still exists. It was the military churchyard of the garrison congregation—the Churchyard of Christ, established in 1860 and closed in 1930. Here Christian Munch had established a family plot which was located exactly where the funeral service in the drawing is taking place. The grave is marked by a puritanical low stone frame. Seen from this location, the cupola of the Trinity Church gives the impression of encompassing the entire churchyard with its arches. The psychological charge this motif must have had for Munch made it natural for him to give it a central place in *The Scream*. Trinity Church, in part defined through its single staircase tower, was used by Munch in this and other contexts as a symbol of Christiania.

I would like to point out another parallel between *Outside the Gate* and *The Scream*. In the Munch literature, there have been several suggestions as to where Munch may have found inspiration for the exaggerated perspective in the picture.[83] Two versions of *Outside the Gate*, the

fig. 17 *Trinity Church*, c. 1883, Private Collection

drawing which was exhibited at the Equitable Palace and the one which accompanies the text in "Illustrated Diary," both have an articulation of perspective which is almost identical to that in *The Scream*. Munch worked with the two simultaneously. There is therefore reason to ask whether or not Munch did not consciously interpret his anxiety in the deepest sense as a reaction to his mother's premature death.

Taking the theme of death into consideration two possible points of departure for Munch's *The Scream* are Max Klinger's *Tod auf der Schienen* from his portfolio "Vom

fig. 18 *Trinity Church,* c. 1901, Private Collection

Trinity Church, Funeral Scene, c. 1901, OKK T 293, Munch-Museet, Oslo (cat. no. 148)

Tode I," 1889, and Albert Besnard's *La Suicide* from his portfolio "La Femme," 1886/1887. Klinger's obvious symbolism, his technique, and interest in detail place him in an older generation than Munch, and it is questionable whether he actually could have influenced Munch.[84] The frightening masks in the frame in *Tod auf der Schienen* might, however, have given Munch inspiration for the foreground figure in *The Scream*. The perspective of the railings in this picture is similar to that in Munch's.

Besnard's large etching, plate XI in "La Femme" has so many features in common with Munch's *Despair/Scream* that it can hardly be accidental. Note the town in the background. The carriage which is analogous to the "friends" in *The Scream* moves into the depth, while the foreground figure stands still. Besnard's cycle "La Femme" has clear resemblances to Munch's idea of a "Life Frieze." When Munch integrated the death motif into his "Frieze of Life" at the Secession exhibition in Berlin, 1902, he, like Besnard, ended his series with a picture of a dead woman, but Munch's had a far greater psychological impact.

Madonna in the Churchyard

In the drawings which illustrate the childhood recollection "By the Double Bed," Munch's mother is depicted as a serious, stately woman standing by the bed, while the children are sitting huddled by the bed with the window frame's cross as a symbol directly above them. In a 1916 lithographic version a personification of death was added behind the mother (cat. no. 144). The important watercolor *Madonna in the Churchyard* has an analogous structure, with a statuesque woman with some kind of halo behind her head and with long, dark hair falling over her shoulders (cat. no. 146). Her figure has the same expression of sadness as the other mother figures from the childhood recollections. The little cupid skeleton is placed low and to the left, just like the children in *By the Double Bed*, and the cross on the headstone corresponds to the window frame's cross in the childhood recollection. This interpretation is further substantiated by the fact that the tombstone to the right is the same as the stone erected over Munch's brother Andreas' grave in Christ Churchyard, in 1895. His wreathed tombstone is a mirror image of the family grave in the watercolor. If we imagine the madonna figure standing on the grave where

By the Deathbed, 1916, OKK G/L 510-2, Munch-Museet, Oslo (cat. no. 144)

Madonna in the Churchyard, 1896, OKK T 2364, Munch-Museet, Oslo (cat. no. 146)

Family Tree, 1894/1895, OKK T 391, Munch-Museet, Oslo (cat. no. 189)

fig. 19 *Death in the Sickroom*, 1896, OKK G/1 217-7, Sch. 73, Munch-Museet, Oslo

Munch's mother, his sister Sophie, and his father were buried and she sees herself in a mirror in the churchyard, the mirror image may be explained.

Dr. Svenaeus commented on a compositional similarity between the watercolor *Madonna in the Churchyard* and the composition *Death in the Sickroom* (fig. 19).[85] Munch

may also have reversed the image to achieve this similarity. According to Svenaeus, the woman in the churchyard is placed in the same relationship to the headstone by the poplars as Inger is placed in relation to the group around the chair with the dead person in the picture of the interior. His observation gives us a basis for another line of argumentation. The "skeleton Cupid" may most simply be interpreted as a symbol in which love implies death or love may be coupled with death. Cupid's bow, furthermore, is broken. One arrow points to the Madonna figure; the other points behind her, but to what?

In the different versions of *Death in the Sickroom*, Edvard is standing close to his sister Inger, looking diagonally into the picture toward the dead person in the chair. Behind the halo shape, as a kind of bulge extending from it, there is a dark crescent which does not have an immediate explanation in *Madonna in the Churchyard*. With reference to the juxtaposition of Munch and Inger in *Death in the Sickroom*, the shape may simply be interpreted as a small section of Munch's own head. He then stands looking in toward his brother's cemetery plot and is practically merged with his mother.

In the painting *Inheritance*, 1897/1899, the woman is wearing a light skirt with an autumn leaf pattern. We see the same pattern of falling leaves in *Madonna in the*

fig. 20 *Family Tree*, 1894/1895, OKK T 387, Munch-Museet, Oslo

fig. 21 *Family Tree*, 1894/1895, OKK T 388 A, Munch-Museet, Oslo

Churchyard. In *Inheritance*, "skeleton-Cupid" is represented by the infant. As in Munch's *Madonna*, the infant is lying naked against a sheet with one hand toward the hip and the other under its neck. Here too the presence of death is evident.

A group of three drawings of *The Family Tree* gives depth to this interpretation (cat. no. 189 and figs. 20, 21). The common feature of the drawings is a tree which grows out of a city street. Its root is the head of Munch's father seen in profile; the trunk is his mother's body seen from the front. Out from this figure shoot wilted, slack branches with children's heads. It is indeed a sad family portrait, in which only the mother and the father are individualized. In a large watercolor version,[86] the street has a violent perspective. In the background can be seen a church cupola. In one of the drawings,[87] there is a huddled fetus on a thin branch which shoots directly out of the mother's back. This may be interpreted as the symbol

of an unborn child. The family tree is, like the tree in the churchyard, practically without leaves.

Madonna: Pregnancy means Death

We shall not discuss the various interpretations of *Madonna* as a motif of love here but merely touch on those elements which are relevant to the subject of death. The account here will therefore be deliberately slanted. Sigbjörn Obstfelder knew Munch well when he wrote his interpretation and worked with problems similar to Munch's in his poems. Obstfelder wrote about the picture:

> For me his Madonna picture is the quintessence of his art. It is a Madonna of the earth, the woman who bears her children in pain. I believe one must go to Russian literature in order to find a similarly religious view of woman, such glorification of the beauty of pain.[88]

Munch's own texts which deal directly with the motif can most frequently be interpreted as encompassing the entire mystery, from conception to birth. In all of Munch's text fragments dealing with this motif, the presence of death is an essential element:

The pause when the entire world stopped its course
Your face holds all the beauty of the earth
Your lips crimson as the coming fruit glides apart as if in
pain
The smile of a corpse
Now life extends its hand to death
The chain which binds the thousand generations which
are dead to the thousand generations to come is joined.[89]

It is the lips of woman that produce the associations of death. In one formulation of the text we find this cryptic remark:

In her mouth is something painful—in one corner of her mouth sits a dead man in two lips the joy of life—[90]

In a description of his much later relationship with Tulla Larsen, Munch wrote the following:

One night
I dreamt that
I kissed her.
I felt the
narrow cold
lips against mine
—and I felt the
cold teeth
against my lips—
—I had . . .
kissed someone dead

such was the kiss—
and I discovered that
it was a dead
face—I awakened
in terror—[91]

When Munch later kissed her, according to other notes, his experience was colored by an association of the death kiss experienced in his dream. A similarly private motif may lie behind those experiences which led up to *Madonna*. It may also have been a dream, and a dream which colored his experiences with women, analogous to one described in Przybyszewski's novel *Vigilien*. The scene which gave the novel its name is a long dream of a death mass, experienced by a fourteen-year-old boy and his mother. The scene can be interpreted as showing a mystical union between mother and son. Przybyszewski finished his manuscript on November 13, 1893, and Munch's exhibition, including the first showing of *Das Madonna-Gesicht* opened a few weeks later. When *Vigilien* was published in 1894, it had a drawing of a *Madonna-Gesicht* on the cover. Munch thus let this motif illustrate a satanic death mass with sexual mother fantasies.

In Félicien Rops's *Het offer*, 1883, one of four pictures on his series "Suite des Sataniques," there is a naked woman with gestures and features similar to Munch's *Madonna,* lying on an altar resembling a grave stone. She is obviously absorbed in sexual ecstasy, having intercourse with Satan himself. The Cupid to the left resembles the unborn child in the frame of Munch's lithograph *Madonna*, and the face of the one on the right is not unlike the skeleton-Cupid in *Madonna in the Cemetery*. Munch gave Madonna's features to the woman in the lithograph *Lovers in Waves*, 1896. Death and sexuality are also present in this picture. In a letter from Dr. Linde to Gustav

Schiefler it is titled *Tot in Wellen*, and it might therefore be linked to Jean Delville's *Tristan and Isolde*, 1887, and other works of this artist, where sensuality and death fantasies are mingled.

There is a long tradition of depicting the sensual aspects of death in the nineteenth century. Munch's *Madonna* has historical precedents in such Pre-Raphaelite works as John Everett Millais's *Ophelia*, 1852, and Dante Gabriel Rosetti's pictures of his dead wife.

The Infirmary at Helgelandsmoen, c. 1882, OKK M 185, Munch-Museet, Oslo (cat. no. 197)

A Retrospective View of the 1880s

The first picture Munch painted with an illness motif is a portrait from the infirmary at the Helgeland Drill Grounds where his father was stationed with his regiment; the children often visited him there during summer vacations (cat. no. 197). The picture communicates a sure use of subtle shading in an intricately built composition. The interplay between the prone position of the ill person and the sitting visitor is a main point in this otherwise very matter-of-fact picture. More essential in our context are the family portraits Munch painted throughout the 1880s (cat. no. 199). As a group, they communicate a very depressed mood; deep melancholy flows through most. His father is most likely to be reading, the aunt knitting. No contact—no communication.

The series of paintings from the medieval Old Aker Church, painted from the apartment in Foss Street, have

The Artist's Father and Sister Inger, c. 1885, OKK M 627, Munch-Museet, Oslo (cat. no. 199)

a memento mori quality. In several of these studies there is an exceptional power of expression, a stillness of death which has its origin in the romantic landscapes of Friedrich. On a sketchbook leaf from 1892, Munch gave the title *Place Morte* to a drawing of the motif.[92]

In *Sick Child* Munch used death as the theme in an exceptionally expressive work.[93] But toward the end of the 1880s, he treated the motif in a new way. In 1888, Munch's grandfather Andreas Bjölstad was lying on his deathbed, and the family was called. On this occasion, Munch painted a study of his grandfather which, even if unfinished, was exhibited in his exhibition in Christiania in 1899, under the title *In the Sickbed* (cat. no. 198).[94] Shortly thereafter, Munch noted the circumstances surrounding the painting of the portrait. He did not refer to his feelings; his attitude was more that of the professional man of science:

He tried to sit upright.
My aunt and the maid managed after great efforts to place him in a chair with pillows stacked around him. He looked even more poorly then. His head sank down to his chest and one could see that he had difficulty holding his eyelids open.
He shook his head a little.
It was strange how tired he was—he wanted to return to his bed—
Oh I who was so clever he said. How strange that fate should single me out—
Can't get down any food—had a desire for food before.
Well well, I suppose I may recover.
I was to paint him.
He wanted to tidy up a bit first. My aunt had to comb his hair. He did not think that was sufficient, his hair smoothed out by *hand*. His hand trembled and he almost did not have the strength to hold his arm up.
He got some of the same expression he had in the photograph where he was so gruff.
But then he did not have the strength any longer—the tired distracted expression returned—and he fell into a slumber.
The pains in his back returned—awakened with a startled expression as it were
He saw me paint.
Stop the painting he said somewhat sharply.
I quickly put my things together.[95]

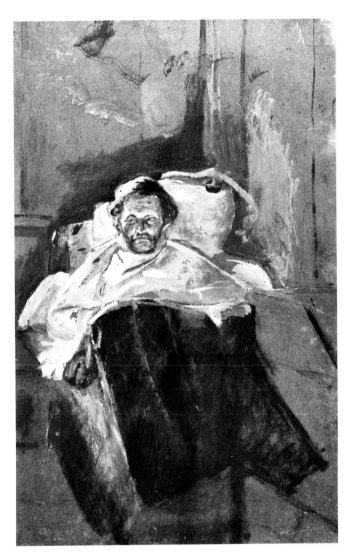

The Death-bed of Andreas Bjølstad, 1884, OKK M 1094, Munch-Museet, Oslo (cat. no. 198)

The reason why Munch did not complete the picture was, we understand, because he was stopped by his grandfather.

Shortly thereafter Munch was given an assignment to paint Mr. Hazeland, an attorney, socialist, and atheist, on his deathbed (fig. 22). The portrait was painted in the morgue of the state hospital. Hazeland is lying in his casket which is pointed at a slightly oblique angle into the picture. The deceased has a flower and green leaves in his hands. In the right corner is a dark brown, square field which indicates a closed window. Munch used his experiences from this painting for *The Dead Woman*.

Munch also documented this assignment in diary entries. As so often in his writings, the notation is found in two versions, one a condensed version of the other. Omitted in the final edition are references to Munch's own feelings, which were reported as follows in the first notation:

I was first captivated by this strange, clammy sensation one gets from a corpse.

fig. 22 *Hazeland Dead,* 1888/1890, Private Collection

fig. 23 *Death at the Rudder,* 1893, OKK M 880, Munch-Museet, Oslo

The Dead Mother and the Angel of Death, 1892, OKK M 756, Munch-Museet, Oslo (cat. no. 205)

Then I was seized by the great, powerful gravity that lay in these congealed features.[96]

In the final version this was deleted:

Among the dead
It was in the morgue
Directly across the yellowish figure of Christ made from plaster of Paris with blessed outspread hands stood the casket.
The face of the dead man was uncovered. The old lovely head with the almost white hair lay gray-yellow against the shining, blue-white sheet
There was a powerful gravity about this old head
The eyes closed the large forehead from which the hairs so neatly were brushed aside the equally modelled nose and the firmly closed mouth which as it were shut off a great enigma
A bouquet of red and white flowers lay on his chest next to his hands which lay smoothly side by side.
—he died without a God—[97]

Munch probably drew the Christ figure in the square field to the right but later overpainted it, since Hazeland was an atheist and the figure of Christ therefore would be inappropriate. The possibility that such a figure may have existed in this picture is perhaps supported by the fact that a similar figure—an angel—is depicted in one of Munch's versions of *The Dead Woman.*[98]

The portrait of the deceased Hazeland is quite pale, with dominant tones of blue and yellow. The combination of blue and yellow recurs in *The Dead Woman* and *Death at the Rudder* (fig. 23). At Munch's exhibition in *Unter den Linden,* December 19, 1893, the two motifs of the dead woman were displayed. The paintings had much more force in the 1890s than they have had later.

The painting which Willy Pastor considered the more notable of the two is *The Dead Woman and the Angel of Death*[99] which was called *A Corpse* in the exhibition catalogue (cat. no. 205). It has very rarely been exhibited. The impressionistic technique makes it difficult to believe that the picture was painted as late as 1893. On the other hand, there are no compelling reasons to reconsider its date. Also, when it comes to *The Dead Mother with Spring*

Landscape, also called *Lying in State,* the powerful color contrasts offer associations with Manet's art and are evidence of a wish on Munch's part to give color greater power of expression (cat. no. 207). Similar considerations come to mind in the case of *Death at the Rudder.* This picture was described in great detail by Franz Servaes in *Vier Beiträge.* He compared the picture with *The Storm* and found that the experience of a mood in nature must have turned into an experience of something deeper.[100] In analogy with the foreground figure in *The Scream,* the skeleton in *Death at the Rudder* extends the mood. The experience of death in vivid yellow and blue has associations with van Gogh's late pictures of grain fields. Parenthetically, it might be mentioned that the painting proba-

The Dead Mother with Spring Landscape, c. 1893, OKK M 516, Munch-Museet, Oslo (cat. no. 207)

Death and the Child, 1899, OKK M 420, Munch-Museet, Oslo (cat. no. 204)

bly was exhibited as catalogue number 13a, *Yellow Sunset*, at the one-man exhibition in *Unter den Linden*, December 1893. Catalogue number 13b was *A Corpse*. Two kinds of death fear were juxtaposed here: fear of death in life, symbolized by the skeleton in *Death at the Rudder*, and death outside life in *A Corpse*.

Death and the Child

The motif expresses, perhaps more nakedly than anywhere else in Munch's art, his despair and angst over something completely incomprehensible. When Munch took up the motif in 1898 or 1899, it is reasonable to believe that he wished to include it in the "Life Frieze." The Munch Museum version of *Death and the Child* is most likely the first one he painted (cat. no. 204). The picture is constructed in a somewhat dry, classical idiom; in the foreground is the despairing girl, in the middle ground the dead mother, and in the background the five family members. In the version which is now hanging in the Bremen Hall of Art, the motif was radically simplified (fig. 24). An important difference is that the girl seems to be a portrait. It is plausible that the children kissing their mother farewell is reflected in the painting. In the etching of the same motif, a new submotif is introduced: the contrast here is between the matter-of-fact shroud of the corpse and the elaborate dress of the child (fig. 25). The face of the child has a distorted, suffering quality and expresses naked, unconcealed angst and despair. She is depicted at the moment when she discovers that the mother really is inaccessible. The face is completely deformed to express these strong feelings, while the face of the mother is drawn with hard, angular lines, sharp and inaccessible. The contrast between the lifelessness of the mother and the vehement inner life of the child is much more strongly accentuated here than in the painted versions. In the etching, the same dissonance between life and death, between profile and full face, and between vertical and horizontal, is expressed.

fig. 24 *Death and the Child*, 1899/1900, Bremen Kunsthalle

The attitude of the child has often been compared to the attitude of the foreground figure in *The Scream*, and these pictures do share a basic mood.[101] But while *The Scream* has a greater degree of recollective quality, of symbolism, the etching *The Dead Mother and the Child* has a more immediate and direct effect. While the entire expression of *The Scream* is made concrete in the deformed landscape, the dead mother in the etching serves only as contrast. The child might have been depicted without changing the context; the mother becomes an explanation of the object of the anxiety. If we use the psychological/biographical line of argument, we might say that

fig. 25 *Death and the Child,* 1901, OKK G/r 54-13, Sch. 140, Munch-Museet, Oslo

fig. 27 *The Dead Mother and her Child,* before 1899, OKK T 301 A, Munch-Museet, Oslo

fig. 26 *Country Trade in Vengen,* 1888, Lillehammer Bymuseum

in the etching *The Dead Mother and the Child,* Munch created a picture of a cause for his anxiety, unambiguously explained through a child's reaction to his dead mother.

As early as 1888, Munch painted a picture in which a child's face fills the foreground, looking directly at the viewer (fig. 26). When Munch did the etching *The Dead Mother and the Child* more than ten years later, he was probably highly conscious of similarities with Klinger's etching *The Dead Mother,* 1889, and therefore defined his own intentions by stressing the dissimilarities. Within the symbolist movement, Klinger's work comes across as exotic, rich in detail, elegant, and dry. In Munch's etching, however, the setting is one of poverty, not unlike Antoine Bourdelle's etching *L'Amour Agonisé,* 1886. The bed in which the mother dies is coarse wood, as is the case in Albert Besnard's *La Mort,* 1882. This picture could also have been a source of inspiration for Klinger in his version of the motif.

Munch may have begun the work as early as 1896; there is a pencil study of the dead mother and the child on

the back of a pencil drawing for *Les Fleurs du mal* from 1896 (fig. 27). It is a moving study with great expressive power. In the childhood memory *By the Double Bed,* Edvard and Sophie are crouching together in the shadow of the bed's footboard. Both clasp their heads tightly in their hands. The gestures are the same as those in *The Scream* and in *The Dead Mother and the Child.*[102]

Memory of Youth—Sister Sophie

As touched on above, Edvard and Sophie experienced the death of their mother in close solidarity. They were Berta and Karlemann. Their mother's death bound them together. In the "Illustrated Diary," where the siblings walk into the wide landscape hand-in-hand, it is clearly he who is leading his older sister into the world. Whether or not this solidarity lasted during the next nine years is not known.[103] With Munch's literary notes as background, on the other hand, we know about the two of them during the summer of 1877. The winter before Munch had been extremely ill, and when he began to recover during the spring, it was a great relief to him and his family. This summer, when he was thirteen and she fifteen, they both experienced childhood romances.

In a note dated St. Cloud, February 26, 1890, in one of his literary diaries, we find the following sketch which must refer back to an experience from the summer of 1877:

I was 13 years and she was 14
She was well developed for her age—full—Her eyes blue and mild and her mouth sensuous—
I had never spoken with her she was my sister's girl friend—
My sister had once "introduced" me to her—but I had turned away at once
Then we met each other on the street—it happened that she turned red—when we had to pass each other—we turned each to our own side—but when we were walking on opposite sidewalks we looked at each other—

My sister was 15 years—She had found "girl friends"—
They had fine parasols—and had a certain cut in their
dresses—They walked arm in arm—sauntering along and stand-
ing on the street corners—
My sister had a modest purple dress—which had a lighter color
where the sun had been shining on it (Bleached it most)—
Her girl friend knew so many young fellows—[104]

Immediately following are particulars about how interested Sophie was in this new business with boys. The
following is a description which Munch must have had
clearly in mind when he painted *A Spring Day on Karl
Johan* a few months after writing the note.[105] His sister
took a walk with her girl friends, and Edvard followed
them, walking behind the girls in the company of several
friends:

I gave the girls a terribly bashful greeting—I took care
always to be as far away from "her" as possible—*walked a
little distance behind for the most part*
It was warm—the ladies unfurled their parasols bright red and
white—My sister opened hers as well—it was an old one with
fringes—the handle had been broken once—the pieces had been
joined together—
Edvard was so good—take my shawl
I was surprised it never occurred to her to ask me to do
things like that on other occasions—
No thanks I said curtly
My sister turned red
I felt like offering my services but was ashamed
You should see how polite—Miss Greenhild's brother
is—she whispered to me. Gentlemen always carry ladies'
clothes—
I saw she was embarrassed before her girl friends
A while later I walked over to her. Let me have it then—I
said at loss. Never mind now she said[106]

Following is a description of Munch's advances to a Miss
Gren while the children were playing "touch" in the
woods. Finally Edvard screwed up his courage and offered to climb a spruce tree to get some cones for the girl.
When he did this, he was teased by the girls:

Emma and Edvard, Emma and Edvard, they love each
other

Edvard's reaction is fairly timid:

I crawled into the dense foliage and hid myself—dizzy
with bashfulness—and copper red in my face

Another diary entry completes the summer recollection by putting it in a context. While Edvard recovered,
his sister became ill and died after a relatively short
period that fall:

As spring wore on he gradually recovered—
The sun came with its first beams of light on the walls to
the west—at noon-time—It grew larger and larger and he
let the sun shine on him—There was a strange and sick
twinkly in the red chest of drawers and in the bottom
boards—it glittered in the golden frame—He began to
take small walks outside—How sharp the air was—
—When the sun warmed icy gusts of wind came—
The birch trees took on a light green—
The summer will come—perhaps he would be well then—
Bertha coughed faintly—she had red spots on her
cheeks—
—Let me have a look—Your cheeks are red

—Be careful—
She went out with girl friends and stood at the street
corners.
There was a draft there—
—The faint cough continued—
She was being irascible—and often impatient—
I wonder if you may not become ill too said the Doctor—
Careful in drafts—
Summer and fall came—He was recovering and was to
have private lessons—Bertha had been coughing faintly
the whole time and she was red in her cheeks and irasci-
ble. One fall day she jumped up and threw her arms
around her father's neck—
She was spitting blood—
Then she was put to bed—
Heavy days—

A Spring Day on Karl Johan–*A Key Image*

By the spring of 1890 Munch had, through a series of
pictures of scenes viewed from the window of his room in
St. Cloud, developed a free-flowing pointillist style. In
May he went home to Norway and painted *A Spring Day
on Karl Johan*,[107] which was displayed in the fall exhibit
that year. In spite of being placed in a disadvantageous
spot, it was one of the most discussed pictures in the
exhibit. Shortly before he painted the picture, he had
spent a lot of time on his writing and had postulated his
main theses: "I do not paint what I see, but what I saw."

The scene is Karl Johan Street seen from Løvebakken
below the Parliament, looking towards the Royal Palace
in Christiania. Karl Johan was the city's parade street;[108]
everyone of importance met here. In the center foreground is a severe, darkly dressed woman with a red
parasol behind her head. The parasol is like a geometric
sign. To the left of the woman, the foreground is completely empty, and to the right are three figure of youths.
We see only their heads and hats, and such details as eyes
and ears are not defined. The collective motion that the
three figures convey provides a contrast to the austere
shape of the woman. To the left and in the middle
ground two children are standing under the lush vegeta-
tion, looking out toward us or at the woman in the foreground. Aside from two long shadows falling from the
left, the middle ground is empty. To the right in the
middle ground three women are moving into the picture
space. The one on the left repeats the attitude of the
"gateway figure," and thus creates suspense. She is as fair
and light as the gateway figure is dark and heavy. The
women in the middle seems sturdy and strong in contrast
to the girl on the right, who is dressed in a faded bluish-
purple dress. While the two women on the left proudly
carry open parasols, she holds a closed, dark parasol
which points down to her shadow. In contrast to the two
other women, she has an almost sickly look. In the background the people along the rows of houses to the right
and along the groups of trees to the left are crowded
together. This causes the three girls, through isolation, to
stand out as a group. Like Seurat's *La Grande Jatte*—or
rather, the studies for that picture—Munch's painting
has a dreamlike timelessness.[109]

There is a sketch which may be a rough study for *A
Spring Day on Karl Johan*. It portrays the scene from the

Royal Palace looking toward the Parliament. Here too, the centrally placed woman figure lends an element of unity to the picture. *A Spring Day on Karl Johan* is a completely mute picture; only the light vibrates. I believe it can be interpreted as an attempt by Munch to tie together what he leaves as separate paragraphs in his "literary diaries:" hypersensitive impressions from his daily life, memories from his childhood and adolescence. The picture, thus, contains a hypersensitive impression; the dazzling daylight over *la vie moderne* in Christiania. It also holds a memory from his childhood if we see Berta and Karlemann in the two children and his mother in the gateway figure. In addition, there is a memory from puberty in the picture. The girl with the closed parasol, which is "ancient black with fringes" and points down toward her shadow, is a reference to his recollection of Sophie's walk in the sunshine with her friends.

Puberty *and* Consolation

There is no more information about his sister's illness than the phrase "heavy days." But two works, *Puberty* (cat. no. 38) and *Consolation,* may refer to these heavy days. These works stand entirely isolated and have received casual treatment in the literature. *Puberty,* for example, has been interpreted, without argument, as an expression of the young girl's menstruation.[110] During his sister's illness, Munch's family had five children between the ages nine and fifteen, and besides the adults, at least one maid always lived in the house. The apartment was quite modest in size and in its bathing and washing facilities. Nudity was hardly mysterious in this family. Nudity, however, might be an adequate basis for creating a visual picture of spiritual nudity and chill of the soul. The external causes of Sophie's illness and death were a draft and inadequate clothing.

To the degree that Munch followed his program of painting experiences he himself had lived through, his fear of death during puberty was a central theme. He had lived through this fear himself and later experienced it through his mortally ill sister. In both of the painted versions of *Puberty* from the 1890s,[111] as well as in the 1894 lithograph and the 1895 etching, there is a threatening shadow behind the young girl who anxiously and shyly hides her lap and stares ahead with wide, fearful eyes. The shadow of death that follows her explains her fear.

In *Consolation* there is a similar shadow behind the young woman. It is a young boy who warmly puts his thin arms around her. He looks over her and puts his head softly against her hair. The picture has few, if any, sexual overtones, but it transmits deep human contact. It is quite unique in Munch's art of the nineties, because in it a man and a woman seek contact with each other without any trace of conflict or nervous tension between them. The young girl sits almost exactly as "Berta" sat under the large double bed in the drawing *By the Double Bed.* Here also she presses her hands against her face, with the doll held tightly against her. Another variant of the motif is the watercolor *On the Bed.* This analysis opens the field for new interpretations of the motifs *Puberty* and *Consola-*

tion. In this context they may be perceived as picturing a virtually naked fear of death.[112]

By the Deathbed–*Agony*

There is a lengthy memoir of Sophie's death, most likely written in the period 1890-1892. Here we can read how her father prepared her for death and comforted her with the thought that she would be reunited with her mother in heaven. After Sophie received Extreme Unction, a situation occurred that illustrates one of Munch's most moving motifs:

> It was evening—Maja lay red and burning hot in her bed, her eyes shone and traveled restlessly around the room—she was delirious—
> You dear sweet Karlemann take this away from me it is so painful—won't you do that—she looked at him imploringly—yes you will—Do you see that head over there—it is Death[113]

Sophie (Maja) asked her brother (Karlemann) to do the impossible—to rescue her from her suffering. This scene produces spontaneous associations with Christ in Gethsemane. The responsiblity that Sophie placed on Munch must have made a strong impression on him. In *By the Deathbed* Munch put himself in her place.[114] Seen in this way, the picture becomes an expression of Munch's vicarious experience of his sister's suffering.

By the Deathbed, 1892, OKK T 286, Munch-Museet, Oslo (cat. no. 169)

In a small india ink drawing, which must be Munch's first study for this work, his objectives concerning the composition and content are most evident (cat. no. 169). Three layers of reality are placed next to each other here. The left part consists of a bed where all we see is the feverish person's delirium depicted on the wall. We are standing, as participants, where the artist is standing and are led to a vicarious experience. In the middle, the picture is completely dominated by the imploring father who is silhouetted by the bed. He constitutes the axis in the family group as well as in the picture. A skeleton with its arms folded across its chest like the fetus in the frame of the lithograph *Madonna* is on the right. The skeleton

By the Deathbed, 1893, OKK M 121, Munch-Museet, Oslo (cat. no. 181)

By the Deathbed, 1892/1893, OKK T 2366, Munch-Museet, Oslo (cat. no. 173)

has a faint halo. The narrative element in the picture predominates.

In the large pastel, which must have been done shortly after the india ink drawing, the picture is concentrated and saturated with expression, and the composition is again a kind of triptych (cat. no. 181). This is achieved by moving the skeleton behind the woman at the end of the bed to the right. The woman in the pastel is much older than the one in the india ink drawing and represents Munch's aunt, Karen Bjølstad. In the pastel, the man, who stood behind his father in the drawing, has been moved to the right of the father; he represents Munch's brother, Andreas. The skeleton and the aunt have thus been isolated from the family group, even if the aunt is partly tied to them through the threatening, joint shadow. In a larger drawing, most likely from the same period, the skeleton is no longer to be seen, but Karen Bjølstad is isolated from the others through a shadow of her own (cat. no. 173). Munch maintained the three layers of reality of the triptych in this way but avoided the narrative elements. The result of the change is that his father's originally dominant role is reduced, and the woman who represents the aunt has been given an increased importance. She now also represents the presence of death which the skeleton previously represented. Noting how the aunt is standing in the drawing, with her arms folded across her chest and her own shadow sneaking up on her from behind, we suspect that the skeleton with the halo and the folded arms in the india ink drawing literally is creeping into the aunt. The best explana-

By the Deathbed, 1896, OKK T 296,
Munch-Museet, Oslo (cat. no. 172)

By the Deathbed I, 1896, OKK G/L
214-12, Munch-Museet, Oslo (cat.
no. 176)

tion for this fusion is Munch's wish to let his mother
figure be represented in the picture as a psychic reality at
Sophie's deathbed. We know that both his father and
Sophie were convinced that, after her death, Sophie
would meet her mother.[115]

Munch's home was, according to Munch himself, colored by his father's exaggerated piety. In the first india
ink drawing *By the Deathbed,* everything centers around
his father's prayer. Whether she will go directly to heaven
or only after a stop in purgatory, or in hell, is an open,
existential question,[116] even if Sophie actually was gen-
tleness itself. After having given her Extreme Unction,
the minister can positively say:

> —this is a child of God he said—so innocent and
> lovable—she will go straight to heaven.[117]

The picture also can be analyzed as showing a struggle for
Sophie's soul taking place between the forces of light and
the forces of darkness. The delirium then shows the
forces of darkness contrasted with the heavenly reality
symbolized by the "Madonna" to the right, thus placing
the picture in a religious context.

By the Deathbed II, 1896, OKK G/L 214-19, Munch-Museet, Oslo
(cat. no. 179)

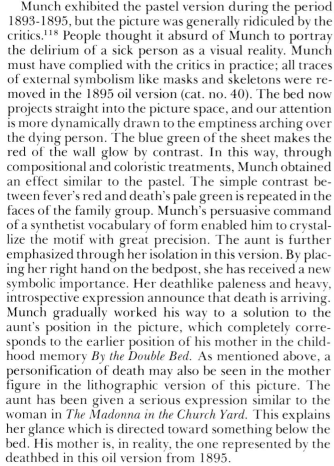

By the Deathbed III, 1896, OKK G/L 214-11
Munch-Museet, Oslo (cat. no. 175)

By the Deathbed IV, 1896, OKK G/L 214-18, Munch-Museet, Oslo
(cat. no. 178)

Munch exhibited the pastel version during the period 1893-1895, but the picture was generally ridiculed by the critics.[118] People thought it absurd of Munch to portray the delirium of a sick person as a visual reality. Munch must have complied with the critics in practice; all traces of external symbolism like masks and skeletons were removed in the 1895 oil version (cat. no. 40). The bed now projects straight into the picture space, and our attention is more dynamically drawn to the emptiness arching over the dying person. The blue green of the sheet makes the red of the wall glow by contrast. In this way, through compositional and coloristic treatments, Munch obtained an effect similar to the pastel. The simple contrast between fever's red and death's pale green is repeated in the faces of the family group. Munch's persuasive command of a synthetist vocabulary of form enabled him to crystallize the motif with great precision. The aunt is further emphasized through her isolation in this version. By placing her right hand on the bedpost, she has received a new symbolic importance. Her deathlike paleness and heavy, introspective expression announce that death is arriving. Munch gradually worked his way to a solution to the aunt's position in the picture, which completely corresponds to the earlier position of his mother in the childhood memory *By the Double Bed*. As mentioned above, a personification of death may also be seen in the mother figure in the lithographic version of this picture. The aunt has been given a serious expression similar to the woman in *The Madonna in the Church Yard*. This explains her glance which is directed toward something below the bed. His mother is, in reality, the one represented by the deathbed in this oil version from 1895.

Munch redefined the function of the mother figure a year later when he created a lithographic version of the motif. The woman is placed full face. In two drafts preceding the lithograph, Munch experimented with the use of vertical and horizontal lines as a substitute for colors in the background (cat. nos. 172, 173). The figures are sketched quite realistically in his first experimental draft (cat. no. 176). In his second experimental draft he created suspense by emphasizing the contrast between black and white surfaces (cat. no. 179). The face of the mother figure is quite precisely sketched in this stage. Munch must not have been pleased with the expression; the face is erased in the third experimental draft (cat. no. 175). The face is completely changed in the final print (cat. no. 178). She now looks straight at the spectator, whereas before she looked out at an angle. Her body is completely swallowed up by the darkness, her hands are resting on the bedpost. In contrast to the painting from the year before, she here looks like an unpretentious, tired woman who is physically present and looks us straight in the eye. This mother figure resembles his aunt, Karen Bjølstad.

It is difficult to talk about a particular motif in the picture *By the Deathbed*. As I see it, Munch's pictures containing this subject are most easily analyzed as a link in a memory process where different aspects of the same thing compete. Recollected pictures are not final pictures. The nervous tension is replaced by pure artistic interest in two of Munch's versions of this theme painted as late as 1915. It is obvious that the woman by the headboard represents his aunt. Her function is clear; she is arranging the medicines on the table by the bed. Munch no longer drew so heavily on his memories as a resource, but instead used his pictures as a source of inspiration at this time.

A drawing which later developed into *By the Deathbed* can be found in a sketchbook Munch used in 1885 and 1886 (fig. 28). The bed is in the corner of an empty room, and a praying man kneels by the bedpost. In another drawing from the same sketchbook, Munch portrayed

fig. 28 *By the Deathbed*, 1885/1886, OKK T 2571-23 R, Munch-Museet, Oslo

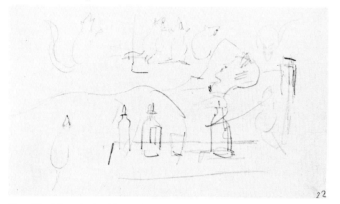

fig. 29 *Munch in his Sickbed*, 1885/1886, OKK T 2571-22, Munch-Museet, Oslo

By the Deathbed, 1894, OKK T 2381A, Munch-Museet, Oslo (cat. no. 182)

By the Deathbed, OKK T 2470, Munch-Museet, Oslo (cat. no. 183)

himself lying in bed with bottles of medicine on the table in front of him (fig. 29). A favorite theme of the 1880s was the artist portrayed in his room, sleeping, sick, or with a bad hangover. What makes Munch's version unique is the simultaneous portrayal of his dream visions. Rats run on the top of the bed and on the wall behind. The mood and symbolism of the drawing are connected with one of Munch's favorite writers, Edgar Allan Poe.

The Covenant with God

Munch's longest coherent childhood recollection describes an illness he experienced at the age of thirteen, during the winter preceding Sophie's death. In the chapter on Munch's theory of art, we quoted from his recollection of how he sought comfort from his father. His father implored God during this crisis to let his son live; he was not prepared to die. His father promised God, on his son's behalf, that Edvard would always serve Him. Edvard took this seriously, and when the crisis was over, he declared:

> He had a covenant with God now—he had promised to serve him—if he became well—if he did not get consumption—he could not enjoy himself as before—[119]

Munch created two sketches of this event, one a drawing and the other a gouache. The drawing has a fantastic play of shadows; the figures seem to leave after-images (cat. no. 182). Edvard lies in his bed praying. His father concentrates on praying, while a woman throws herself on the bed. Three of his sisters are represented in the gouache, where the tension is even more vividly expressed (cat. no. 183). This "family portrait" also refers to a clearly defined situation described in the same recollection:

> Jesus Christ. Jesus Christ.
> He folded his hands—

Daddy I'm dying—I can't die—I don't dare—
Jesus Christ—
Don't talk too loud, my son—I will pray with you.
And he folded his hands over the bed and prayed—
Lord help him if that is your will—don't let him die
I implore you dear Lord.
We turn to you in our distress.
He was interrupted by a new attack of coughing—a new
handkerchief—blood colored almost the whole cloth—
Jesus help me I'm dying—I must not die now.
Berta lay stretched out on the bed next to him and prayed,
while crying loudly, and all the others around the bed,
some red in the face from crying others white—[120]

Sophie (Berta) is the one throwing herself on the bed, according to this passage. This reference and the pictures deepen our understanding of the close relationship between the two siblings.

Death in the Sickroom

This motif is one of Munch's most central formulas in expressing human relations. The figures, depicted full face, in profile, or looking out at an angle, establish contact with each other and the spectator, as if they were actors in a dream play. The actors are members of Munch's family, just as in his work *By the Deathbed*. Munch was almost fourteen years old when Sophie died; his sister, Inger, was nine, Laura was eleven, and his brother, Andreas, twelve years old. The actors in the picture are without doubt older.[121] Munch portrayed the family members as they were when he painted the picture. He may have remembered the scene in that way[122] or he may also have wanted to express a dimension of simultaneity with the event. It is possible he thought, for example, that his family was forever marked by what happened and was, therefore, still "present" in the sickroom.

The first version of this motif must be a pastel, signed and dated 1893 (cat. no. 167). On the right we see his aunt caring for the dying person who is hidden from us. His father stands praying in front of her. Laura sits in profile in the foreground. Inger stands behind her, full face, and behind her Edvard looks at what is happening in the chair. Andreas stands on the left with his arm raised as if to open a door. This pastel became the basis for a charcoal drawing with an outlined frame (cat. no. 162); it was, perhaps, not until 1896 that Munch did another sketch of this motif in red crayon (cat. no. 165). In tune with modern synthetist ideals of form, the motif is far more deliberately composed and crystallized in the drawing. But the clarity of the motif has been achieved at the expense of its expressive range. The charcoal drawing is a direct basis for the large painted version in the Munch Museum (fig. 30), which includes a couple of new elements; a print and a plaque[123] are hanging over the night stand. A reddish stripe on the wall marks a door on the left in the picture. We also see medicine bottles on the night stand and a bedpan under the bed. It looks as if the figures are standing on a slanted stage. In a 1895 version, now in the

Death in the Sickroom, 1893,
OKK M 214, Munch-Museet,
Oslo (cat. no. 167)

Death in the Sickroom, OKK T 297A, Munch-Museet, Oslo (cat. no. 162)

fig. 30 *Death in the Sickroom*, c. 1893, OKK M 418, Munch-Museet, Oslo

Death in the Sickroom, 1896 OKK G/L 215-18, Munch-Museet, Oslo (cat. no. 165)

fig. 31 *Room in Number 7 Fosveien*, 1878, OKK T 54, Munch-Museet, Oslo

National Gallery, Oslo, and undoubtedly his main version (cat. no. 41), the steep perspective is even more heavily stressed. The figures in the foreground are closer to the spectator and give the impression of being unusually large. Had Laura stood up from the chair in this picture, her head would have reached far beyond the picture frame. This version was most likely painted after a visit to his home; the image of Christ over the bed is quite like a print owned by his family (fig. 31). Andreas is now completely separate from the other children, and Edvard and his aunt also stand more freely in the enlarged room. His father is clearly portrayed, full face, and repeats Inger's strict frontality.

When he developed a lithographic version in 1896, Munch went back to the original, i.e., the pastel in the Munch Museum (cat. no. 166) and most likely developed the red crayon drawing as a rough draft for this. He no

longer needed the deep room of the 1895 painted version in the lithograph, and the relation between floor and wall is reduced to one to one. Now that the wall was enlarged he needed a rectangular picture on the wall over the bed. The figure of Inger has completely changed character. Her hair is in a distinct bun, which was only hinted at in the pastel version. Her face also has a completely new expression. It is no longer as heavy as in the large painted versions. The compositional similarity between this pic-

Death in the Sickroom, 1896 OKK G/L 215-19, Munch-Museet, Oslo (cat. no. 166)

ture and *Madonna in the Church Yard* indicates that the mother image may again interfere with the experience. Munch wanted to find a place for his mother in this family portrait and tentatively used Inger's figure to represent her. On the back of the red crayon drawing, for example, is a drawing of the children—Sophie and Edvard—in front of the bed with the dead mother. Below this drawing is a lengthy text, unfortunately unreadable. We can also analyze the picture as a family portrait. Munch may have wanted to express his growing attachment to his two other sisters when Sophie left him, while Andreas went his own way.

Three versions of the motif were exhibited in December 1893 at Munch's show in *Unter den Linden* 19. Catalogue number 2, *Ein Tod*,[124] had the dominant spot in the exhibit and caught the eye even before one stepped into the room. According to newspaper reviews, this picture was the reason many turned around and left, feeling that such art could not be worth the price of admission. It created a certain interest among the audience for the fact that the dead person was not portrayed. From a lengthy discussion by Willy Pastor in *Vier Beiträge*[125] it is evident that the pastel, now in the Munch Museum, was ex-

hibited, in addition to a drawing that most likely was the hasty, framed charcoal mentioned previously. Pastor was of the opinion that the pastel and charcoal were far more successful than the large painting, in which the narrative elements had disappeared. In this way, he showed that he did not quite understand Munch's intention.

Even contemporary criticism in the 1890s pointed out the closeness between literature and Munch's art, especially because he freely juxtaposed recollected pictures and fantasy images. Critics also pointed out the high degree to which Munch's art invited aesthetic speculation, since it expanded the boundaries of art and its functions. What do we actually know about the external world? Przybyszewski linked Munch's art to Maeterlink's as early as his essay in *Vier Beiträge*. The version of *Death in the Sickroom* belonging to the National Gallery, Oslo has traditionally been linked to Maeterlink's play *L'Intruse*.[126]

Postscript

My goal in this essay has been to analyze Munch's most important death motifs through systematic use of the artist's childhood memories of his mother and sister. This approach proves productive; motifs other than the death motifs attain new and unexpected meanings. I have not brought my analysis to its natural conclusion concerning the metabolic motifs, where Munch created a complete eschatology with its basis in the life that grows from his mother's dead body. Treating this problem here would require many references from the occult tradition, from alchemy, and also from such "modern" religious movements as "Rose et Croix." The main picture *Metabolism* (cat. no. 46), which Munch believed to be as important for the "Life Frieze" as "a buckle is to a belt," is Munch's last commentary on this eschatology. Our analysis of the death motifs allows us to see immediately that the upper part of the wooden frame in *Metabolism* (fig. 32) is not a picture of a heavenly Jerusalem but a symbol of Christiania, the city of Trinity Church under the shadow of which his mother and sister are buried.

Translated from the Norwegian by Gregory P. Nybo

fig. 32 *Metabolism* (detail), 1898/1918, OKK M 419, Munch-Museet, Oslo

NOTES

1. Krohg's ownership of the painting was later questioned. In his sketchbook, OKK T 2571, Munch wrote the name Krohg beside the title *Sick Child* in a list of pictures in preparation for his exhibition of 1889, which indicates that Munch regarded Krohg as the owner of the painting at that time. The friendship faded, however, and Munch sold the painting to Olaf Schou, who could not accept it as the ownership was not clear. Not until the painting came to the National Gallery in 1931 did this dispute come to an end. See Jens Thiis, *Edvard Munch og hans samtid; Slekten, livet og kunsten, geniet* (Oslo, 1933), 138.

2. "U.E.P. Kunstutstillingen," II, *Morgenbladet*, October 28, 1886.

3. Munch Museum, ms. N 78.

4. Andreas Aubert, "The Artists 5th Fall Exhibition," *Morgenbladet*, November 9, 1886.

5. "H. Fra Kunstutstillingen," *Norske Intelligenssedler*, October 25, 1886.

6. Hans Jæger's honesty and his training as a professional stenographer makes his report of the conversation very reliable. Dietrichson was at that time the most influential conservative "fellow of the arts" in Norway. Jæger was the spokesman and leader of the radical artists. For important data about the relationship between Munch and Jæger see: Arne Brenna, "Hans Jæger og Edvard Munch," *Nordisk Tidsskrift* (1976): 89-115, 188-215, and Arne Brenna, "Hans Jægers fengselsfrise," *St. Hallvard*, 50, no. 4 (1972). Brenna, however, does not identify Dietrichson as a participant in the conversation.

7. Hans Jæger, "Utstillingen," *Dagen*, October 20, 1886.

8. Ibid.

9. Munch Museum, ms. T 2771.

10. Ibid.

11. Hans Jæger, "Utstillingen," *Dagen*, October 20, 1886.

12. At the Fall Exhibition, 1885, Hans Jæger praised Erik Werenskiold's picture *Burial of a Peasant* as a masterpiece, which crystallized the efforts of Norwegian artists for a decade. See Hans Jæger, "Høstutstillingen," *Norske Intelligenssedler*, October 28, 1885. Art, thus, had to start fresh experimentation; a year later Jæger must have felt that Munch was introducing a new art.

13. Munch Museum, ms. T 2734.

14. Ibid.

15. Ibid.

16. In a recent study, Leif Plather has published the results of his x-rays of the painting. He did not, however, discern the overpainted parts. See Leif E. Plather, "Det syke barn og Vår; Røntgenundersøkelse av to Munch-bilder," *Kunst og Kultur*, 57, (1974): 103-115.

17. The photograph of *Study* has a striking resemblance to the popular transcendental photographs of the period, which showed people together with their deceased relatives. The following much neglected information about Munch is given by Stanislaw Przybyszewski in *Erinnerungen an das literarische* (Berlin, 1965), 222: "Darüber hinaus interessiert ihn der Okkultismus, und als ich ihm Aksakows Buch 'Spiritismus und Animismus' gab, verschlang er es buchstäblich in einer Nacht und war beglückt, als ich für ihn bei der Staatsbibliothek Swedenborgs 'De coelo et inferno' (in deutscher Übersetzung, Tübingen, dritte Auflage 1873) entlieh."

18. Leif Østby, *Fra naturalisme til nyromantikk; En studie i norsk malerkunst i tiden 1888-1895* (Oslo, 1934), 125f.

19. Munch Museum, letters to Jens Thiis from Edvard Munch.

20. Jens Thiis, *Edvard Munch*, p. 135. According to Thiis the painting was done in a bedroom in the family's flat at Schous plass 1 in Christiania.

21. Munch Museum, ms. N 45. My italics. After Munch's death, his sister Inger systematically burned diaries, letters, and notes to hide any references to unpleasant conditions in the home, which, according to her spinsterly moral code, would harm the honor of Munch and his family. It is therefore no longer possible to reconstruct in detail the circumstances in Munch's home.

22. Ibid.

23. On the reverse of *Sickroom, Study* is a painting, using the same palette, of a cabaret scene. The two paintings, probably from 1885/1886, were separated in the 1930s. The carafe in *Sickroom* has a similar pictorial function as the bottle in *Cabaret Scene*. Munch probably wanted to symbolize opposite worlds. Arne Eggum, *Rolf E. Stenersens gave til Oslo by—Akersamlingen*, Katalog A 6 (Oslo: Oslo Kommunes Kunstsamlinger, 1974).

24. Axel Romdahl records a visit to Munch at Ekely in his *Edvard Munch i Konstmuseet, Særtrykk* (Göteborg, 1944), 93.
   "In his home at Ekely by Skøien he kept an old black and yellow wicker chair. He once showed it to me and said: 'This is the chair of the Sick Child. In that chair we have all been sitting, been ill, and died.'"

25. "H. Fra Kunstudstillingen," *Norske Intelligenssedler*, October 25, 1886.

26. 1895 should be 1896. 1906 should be 1907.

27. Edvard Munch, *Livsfrisens tilblivelse* (Oslo, 1929 [?]).

28. Hans Heyerdahl's drawing *Family Scene*, 1881, was published in the portfolio "Artistes Scandinaves; Dessins Originaux" (Paris, 1881). He repeated this picture in the painting *Death of the Worker*, in 1888, the only important change being that the woman in the original was now depicted as a man. In a notebook (Munch Museum ms. T 2571) which Munch used between 1885 and 1889 he wrote: "Heyerdahl is der beste von der norwegischen Malern. Krohg ist besser als Wernskiold."

29. *The Death of Queen Amalia*, 1883, Hirschsprungske Samlinger, Copenhagen.

30. Roger Marx, "Paul-Albert Besnard I," and Hermann Helferich, "Besnard II," *Pan*, 3 (1895).

31. Leif Plather has shown by an x-ray that the woman in Munch's painting probably was originally placed higher up. See Leif Plather, "Det syke barn." Munch's first arrangement of the figures could thus have been even closer to Besnard's *La Fin de Tout*.

32. The different known proof editions were recorded by Gustav Schiefler in his *Edvard Munch's Graphische Kunst* (Dresden, 1923), and by Sigurd Willoch in his *Edvard Munchs raderinger* (Oslo, 1950). These authors, however, failed to recognize the main stages of the print.

33. Munch later made a present of this print to Jens Thiis, who he thought had written most adequately about *Sick Child*.

34. Ingrid Langaard, *Edvard Munch, Modningsår, En studie i tidligekspresjonisme og symbolisme*.

35. Stanislaw Przybyszewski, *Erinnerungen an das literarische Berlin*, p. 222ff. The passages in Przybyszewski's original manuscript which most directly dealt with his belief in the dark sciences were omitted by the German publisher.

36. An analogous use of a landscape to contrast death can be seen in Max Klinger's etching *The Dead Woman*, 1889. Here, however, the landscape is part of the composition beneath the corpse, not part of the frame.

37. Munch Museum, ms.

38. Pål Hougen, *Farge på trykk*, Munch-museet, Katalog nr. 5

(Oslo, 1968). The information here that Munch used the first version as a point of departure for this stone and that the stone was drawn with india ink is not correct. Technical curator Jan Thurmann-Moe has convinced me that this stone must have been drawn with a fat lithographic crayon.

39. It might be mentioned that the main lithographic stone exists in three versions: one without signature, one with the signature *E. Munch* in the lower right-hand corner, and one with the signature *E. Munch 1896*.

40. Jens Thiis, *Edvard Munch, Mit einem nachwort von Erich Büttner* (Berlin, 1934).

41. According to Thiis, p. 132, the painting was made in Paris, and the artist did not have the original at hand; thus, the freer brushstrokes. This information is contradicted by the fact that Munch, in a letter to Axel Romdahl, wrote that in Paris in 1894 (sic; should be 1897) he had both versions in his hotel room: "Monfreid, a friend of Gauguin's, advised me to exhibit the sick child of the Gothenburg Museum at the L'Indépendence and not the other one. I had both in my hotel room in rue la Santé . . . ."

42. Munch Museum, letters to Edvard Munch from Olaf Schou.

43. Ivan Angueli, "Le Salon des Indépendants," *L'Encyclopédie Contemporaine*, May 10, 1896.

44. Munch Museum, letters to Harald Nørregård from Edvard Munch.

45. Arne Eggum, "The Linde Frieze," unpublished manuscript, Oslo, Munch-Museet, 1972.

46. Munch Museum, draft of letters to Jens Thiis from Edvard Munch. Munch probably remembers incorrectly. He copied a picture for Thiel in Warnemünde, not for Schou, as far as is known. The picture to which Munch refers in the draft of a letter is, we have reason to believe, the version he copied for Thiel in 1907.

47. Munch Museum, letters from Ernest Thiel to Edvard Munch.

48. The Tate version is commonly assigned the date 1907, which agrees with catalogue information for the picture. After Munch's death, the date of this version was given as both 1916 and 1920, without discussion.

49. As part of the Nazis' "cultural policy," the Tate version was sold from Dresden during the 1930s. Their argument was that paintings by non-German artists were unnecessary in their museums. There were more than enough pieces of domestic art. Munch's art was not openly characterized as degenerate in Germany, even if his works generally were removed, but he was bitter about the treatment of his and other expressionist painters' works. See letter from Edvard Munch to Jens Thiis.

50. Munch Museum, letters from Edvard Munch to Staatliche Gemäldegalerie, Dresden.

51. Munch Museum, letters from Edvard Munch to Jens Thiis.

52. Munch Museum, letters from Edvard Munch to A. Rütschi.

53. It is often stated that Munch painted a new version when he sold the original one. This might be, but we do not have specific information about a single case.

54. A good example is Munch's exhibition in Stockholm in 1894. See Arne Eggum, "Edvard Munch's First Exhibition in Sweden," *Edvard Munch, Malmö Konsthall*, Katalog nr. 1, (Malmö, 1975).

55. Munch Museum, ms. T 2760.

56. Ibid.

57. For quotations from Jæger's works, see Gerd Woll's article in this catalogue. An example of an influence from outside the Scandinavian art milieu for a concept of art as a depiction of one's life is found in Jean Marie Guyau, "L'Estétique contemporaine," 1884.

58. Vincent van Gogh, *Correspondance complète de Vincent van Gogh enrichie de tous les dessins originaux,* (Paris, 1960).

59. Arne Eggum, "Edvard Munch i Danmark," *Louisiana Revy* 1 (1975).

60. Munch Museum, ms. N 29.

61. Edvard Munch, *Livsfrisens tilblivelse.*

62. Munch Museum, ms. T 2761.

63. Munch Museum, ms T 2782.

64. Munch Museum, ms. T 2771.

65. Munch Museum, ms. T 2748 b.

66. Trygve Nergaard identified her as Mrs. Milly Bergh (born Ihlen) in his *Refleksjon og visjon, Naturalismens dilemma i Edvard Munchs kunst 1889-1894* (Trondheim, 1968), note 163.

67. Munch Museum, ms. T 2771.

68. Munch Museum, draft of letters from Edvard Munch to Jens Thiis.

69. In his *Edvard Munch's Life Frieze: Its Beginnings and Origins* (Indiana University, 1969), 33ff., Reinhold Heller made the point that Munch discovered an interrelationship among his works in the exhibitions of 1892. There is, however, no evidence that Munch "at each of these exhibitions . . . sought to hang his works in easily comprehensible manner which would demonstrate what he sought to achieve." No critic recognized these "easily comprehensible" intentions. The photograph from the Equitable Palace shows, on the contrary, that Munch showed his paintings there in an extremely disorderly manner. Heller also states that Munch for the first time intended to group together his pictures in a meaningful way at the Kleis exhibition in Copenhagen, 1893. The sole argument for this supposition is a sentence in a letter from Munch to Johan Rohde, who organized the exhibition, in which Munch asked that nine paintings (among them two portraits and a picture of a girl looking out of a window) should be given a prominent place. He used the phrase "Disse Billeder vilde jeg gjerne skulle have god plass," which Heller interprets to mean "with the exception of the two portraits, which were included in the list because Munch regarded them as his best ones and thus wished them hung in a prominent place, all these paintings deal with or project a melancholy mood of despair, and are thus all unified through this theme. It was Munch's intention that the mood should be intensified and clarified by placing the paintings side by side." However, the most obvious meaning of this phrase is that each of the paintings should have a good place on the wall. Furthermore at least one of the paintings in Heller's proposed identification is in my opinion hardly correct. *En Syg* (cat. no. 15) must have been *Sick Child* and not *Spring*, which was exhibited under the title *Foraar* (cat. no. 14), this being the Danish word for spring. See letter from Edvard Munch, February 8, 1893, Royal Library Copenhagen, Rohde archives.

70. Munch Museum, ms. T 2761.

71. Ibid.

72. Ibid.

73. Ibid.

74. Ibid.

75. *Edvard Munch's brev. Familien. Et utvalg ved Oslo Kommunes Kunstsamlinger*, Munch-museets skrifter 1, (Oslo, 1949).

76. Munch Museum, sketchbook T 245.

77. The drawing is part of a triptych. In the central field is the figure of a man steering a sun wheel (?), and to the right an emaciated, older man is sitting. Under the triptych is the first

rough draft of the etching *The Dead Lovers,* which, parenthetically, does not feature a family recollection. Besides, the figures are lying in a different type of bed. This triptych could possibly be interpreted psychologically as a conscious statement by Munch that the mother image destroyed the artist's natural intercourse with women.

78. The idea of a picture representing both a person and his imagination is also found in Albert Besnard's etching *Dans les Cendres,* 1887. The vision in the ashes is the girl in the background. The foreground figure has a striking resemblance to the corresponding figure in Munch's drawing. See also John Henrik Füssli's *Milton's Vision of his Second Wife,* 1789/1790, now in a private collection, Basel, where this tradition originated.

79. Munch Museum, ms. T 2782.

80. About the first exhibition of this painting, see Arne Eggum, "Munch i Denmark," *Lousiana Revy,* no. 1, 1975.

81. Munch Museum, ms. T 2782 f.

82. According to Jens Thiis, *Edvard Munch, The Scream* was exhibited with a symbolic frame in Berlin in the mid 1890s. This frame was later lost.

83. Heller has observed that in *The Scream* there is an expression of despair related to suicide. See Reinhold Heller, *The Scream* (London, 1973), 91ff. Heller's references to Georg Büchner's short story from 1839 is unnecessarily intricate, however. In the novel *Kristiania-Billeder,* 1889, by Hans Jæger, there is a description of a scream in nature in connection with a suicide attempt.

84. See Werner Tinn, "Das Beispiel Max Klinger, Felix Vallotton, Felicien Rops," In his *Edvard Munch, Graphik* (Berlin, 1969).

85. Gøsta Svenæus, *Im männlichen Gehirn* (Lund, 1973), 163.

86. *Family Tree,* Munch Museum, T 391.

87. *Family Tree,* Munch Museum, T 388 A.

88. Sigbjørn Obstfelder, "Et forsøg," *Samtiden* (Kristiania, 1896), 17.

89. Munch Museum, ms. T 2547.

90. Munch Museum, ms. T 126-44.

91. Munch Museum, ms. T 2737.

92. Munch Museum, sketchbook T 121-13.

93. *Spring,* which was exhibited in Munch's first one-man show in 1889 and marked as unfinished in the catalogue, is a dead-end in Munch's art. It is a concession to the academic taste of the time, which Munch detested. It was primarily meant for the World Fair in 1889 and was included in Munch's international exhibitions in the beginning of the 1890s, probably to show that if he wanted to make concessions, he had the ability. The painting is of no consequence in regard to Munch's important death motifs and is therefore not analyzed in this essay.

94. The catalogue was recently discovered and was most kindly given to the Munch Museum by Rolf Kirkengen.

95. Munch Museum, ms. T 2781.

96. Munch Museum, ms. N 27 b.

97. Ibid.

98. *The Dead Woman and the Angel of Death,* 1892, Munch Museum, M 756.

99. *Das Werk des Edvard Munch: Vier Beiträge von Przybyszewski, Servaes, Pastor, Meier-Graefe* (Berlin, 1894).

100. Ibid.

101. Stanley Steinberg and Joseph Weiss, "The Art of Edvard Munch and its Function in his Mental Life," *The Psychoanalytical Quarterly,* no. 3, 1954. The likeness between these two figures is the main point of this article, which comes to the same conclusion as this essay regarding the mother image in Munch's art. It

is my point however that Munch was conscious of the nature of this image. In his *Close-up of a Genius,* 1944, Rolf Stenersen suggested that Munch's difficulties with women were caused by the image of his dead mother, even to the degree that the smell of women was the smell of death to Munch.

102. See also Henri Dorra, "Munch, Gauguin and Norwegian Painters in Paris," *Gazette des Beaux-Arts* (November, 1976).

103. In a letter to Thiis, Munch said that Sophie, his brother Andreas, and himself had prevailing characteristics in common with the Munch family, while the two younger sisters had more in common with the Bjølstad family.

104. Munch Museum, ms. T 2770. My italics.

105. *Spring Day on Karl Johan,* 1890, Bergen Picture Gallery.

106. Munch Museum, ms. T 2770. My italics.

107. The painting was wrongly inscribed 1891 by Munch, as it had been exhibited at the Fall Exhibition in 1890. Camille Pissarro was represented by two paintings at the same exhibition. Munch's painting was thoroughly treated by the critics. It is wrongly identified by Ingrid Langaard, *Edvard Munch,* p. 113ff.

108. See also Per Jonas Nordhagen, "Impresjonismen og det moderne bymenneske," *kunst og Kultur,* no. 3 (1968): 129.

109. Gøsta Svenæus has pointed out that Munch could very well have seen Seurat's *La Grande Jatte* and the sketches for it in the spring of 1890. See Gøsta Svenæus, *Edvard Munch: Das Universum der Melancholie* (Lund, 1968). He did not, however, identify *A Spring Day on Karl Johan* as the one exhibited at the Fall Exhibition, 1890.

110. Langaard, Ingrid, *Edvard Munch,* p. 28ff.

111. *Puberty,* 1895, National Gallery, Oslo; *Puberty,* 1893, Munch Museum, OKK M 281.

112. The first time that this shadow appears as a menacing element in Munch's art is in a drawing of his sister Inger in 1888/1889: *Inger with Shadow,* pencil and charcoal, OKK T 2271.

113. *Edvard Munch's brev,* p. 89.

114. In the 1890s the painting was called both *Agony* and *Fever.* At the Blomquist exhibition, 1895, the final version was exhibited under the title *Agony;* before that the motif was called *Fever.*

115. We are thus led to the interpretation that, as in *Sick Child,* the dead mother is present in the aunt figure. In a letter to Thiis, Munch wrote about the relationship:

My wonderful aunt who came to us after her [my mother's] death, was during the first years rather distant to me. That is, the memory of my mother was vivid and my aunt was for a long time a stranger. More and more she became a permanent member and the female head of the family. It was different with my sisters. They did not remember their mother and to them my aunt became the mother and their feelings for her were like those for a mother.

116. See also Rolf Stenersen, *Close-up,* which records the dispute between father and son as to the reality of hell and purgatory.

117. *Edvard Munchs brev,* p. 89.

118. *Morgenbaldet,* December 7, 1893. *Bergens Tidende,* December 12, 1895.

119. Munch Museum, ms. T 2771.

120. Ibid.

121. Langaard, Ingrid, *Edvard Munch,* p. 152.

122. A most consistent analysis in this respect is given in Stanislaw Przybyszewski, "Ein Unbekannter," *Die Kritik* 3, (Berlin, 1896).

123. A framed, biblical quote or proverb, often embroidered.

124. *Death in the Sickroom,* Munch Museum, OKK M 418.

125. *Das Werk des Edvard Munch,* pp. 62, 63.

126. Ingrid Langaard, *Edvard Munch,* pointed out that Munch could have seen *L'Intruse* on stage before he left Paris in 1892. See also the brilliant analysis in Hans Dedekam, *Kunst og Kultur,* 1911, where attention is drawn to the likeness between the painting and the Maeterlinck scenario. In an article in *Pan* 2, (1895): 202, about the Norwegian artist Gerhard Munthe, Andreas Aubert states "unter den Dichtern nennt er mit Vorliebe besonders Maeterlinck." Thus Munch was not the only artist influenced by Maeterlinck. Werner Timm, "Das Beispiel," p. 26ff., has drawn attention to F. Valloton's woodcut *The Big Funeral,* 1892. The differences between this and Munch's lithograph are, however, more fundamental than the likenesses.

Attraction I, (cat. no. 218)

The Mirror

Bente Torjusen

Are you continuing your lithographic album, in which you wanted to mirror all the different phases of your life's— soul's life—or have you been painting?

William Molard in a letter to Munch, Paris, March 7,1898

EDVARD MUNCH'S VAST LIFE WORK IS NOTABLE for its variety of content and expression. And yet another of its most striking characteristics is its unfailing inner continuity. Intense personal experiences and Munch's reflections on them were a constant source of creativity, and many of the resulting works came to be important sources of inspiration for further work. So it is not surprising that Munch early felt a need to present his pictures in meaningful groups —as *series*. At the same time, Munch also wanted to reach as many people as possible with his art, and in this his graphic work played an important role. Later in his life, Munch wrote, "My intention in working with graphics was to bring my art into many homes."[1]

The characteristic continuity of Munch's works began to appear in the early 1890s. In the spring of 1893, Munch mentioned in a letter to the Danish painter Johan Rohde that he was working on a series of pictures that were to deal with love and death, and that pictures which earlier had been "rather incomprehensible" would probably be easier to understand when displayed together.[2] Later that same year, in Berlin, Munch for the first time exhibited a number of paintings as a cohesive group. The exhibition catalogue, however, makes it clear that the collection was not complete. In Munch's own words, the six paintings in question were presented as "Outline of a series: 'Love.' " Munch worked hard in the following years to put together a series of pictures dealing with love, anxiety, and death. "The Frieze of Life," a name first used by Munch in 1918, has become the collective title for the series of works that he produced around these principal themes.

In Berlin, in the spring of 1895, Munch exhibited fourteen paintings about love and anxiety under the title "Series: Love." By 1902, when it was presented at the Berlin Secession, the series had grown to twenty-two paintings and for the first time included paintings about death. In the years that followed, the series was exhibited under various titles and with a varying number of paintings; the three main themes remained constant, but within these three principal groupings, Munch often made editorial changes. During this time, he looked for an appropriate place where "The Frieze of Life" could be exhibited in a manner that would emphasize the relationships among the pictures as well as clarify the meaning of each individual work. But this idea was never realized. By 1910, "The Frieze of Life" as Munch imagined the series about the turn of the century had been split up into smaller units and dispersed among various museums and private collections.

In Berlin, toward the end of 1893 and at about the same time that he first exhibited paintings in a series, Munch also began to experiment with graphics. In the course of the next two years he produced a number of important drypoints etchings and black-and-white lithographs. Munch's first graphic portfolio appeared in 1895 and consisted of eight etchings, the so-called Meier-Graefe Portfolio.[3] However, the etchings in this portfolio had no clear inner relationship. The following year, in Paris, he made his first pioneering experiments in the art of woodcut and began as well to print in color, in all techniques. In the course of this stay in Paris, which lasted from the end of February 1896 until into the spring of 1897, Munch created a number of graphic works that are closely tied thematically to the paintings in "The Frieze of Life."

"I must have money for my work, which I believe may come to be of importance—at least in initiating an art form that is not known at home, namely, the reproductive," Munch wrote from Paris in the early summer of 1896.[4] His emphasis on the reproductive nature of graphic art and his simultaneous efforts to recreate the subject matter of "The Frieze of Life" must of course be seen in conjunction. Now the way lay open for Munch to spread his message to a large audience.

In Norway, a few months after his return from Paris, Munch announced plans to publish a graphic portfolio with the title "The Mirror." Most of the lithographs and woodcuts in this portfolio were done in Paris in 1896-1897.

"The Mirror" as announced by Munch in 1897

In Christiania, from September 15 to October 17, 1897, Munch held a large exhibit at the Diorama Hall, number 41 Karl Johan Street. According to the catalogue, 180 works were displayed: 85 paintings, 64 prints, and 30 sketches and studies.[5]

The graphic works are grouped together under the common title, "Lithographs, Etchings, and Woodcuts." The lithographs (catalogue numbers 85-116) are listed first, by title alone, while in the case of woodcuts (117-125) and etchings (126-144) the title is followed by the technique.

After catalogue number 144, the catalogue contains the following information:

"No. 94, 95, 96, 97, 98, 99, 100, 101, 102, 103, 104, 105, 106, 107, 108, 113, 114, 116, 121, 124, 118, 118 [sic] belong to a series of portfolios, 'The Mirror,' which will appear in the near future."

These catalogue numbers represent the following titles, listed here only with the information contained in the 1897 catalogue, i.e., the title—often different from the one in use today—plus, in some cases, the technique:

94	*On the Other Side*
95	*Funeral March*
96	*Metabolism*
97	*Death Throes*
98	*Death*
99	*Hands*
100	*Waves*
101	*Loving Woman,* hand-colored
102	*Two Heads,* hand-colored
103	*Stars,* hand-colored
104	*Jealousy*
105	*Vampire,* hand-colored
106	*The Urn*
107	*Loving Woman*
108	*Separation*
113	*A Street*
114	*A Plant*
116	*The Scream*
118	*Evening,* hand-colored woodcut
119	*Evening,* woodcut
121	*The Mirror,* hand-colored woodcut
124	*Anxiety,* hand-colored woodcut

Without trying to identify these prints exactly, we can see from their titles that "The Mirror" as exhibited in 1897 consisted of the principal themes from

"The Frieze of Life"—death, love, and anxiety. But it is also clear that "The Mirror" placed a greater emphasis on the so-called transmutation themes (e.g., catalogue numbers 94, 95, 96, 106, 114) than "The Frieze of Life" was to do in the years that followed.

According to the 1897 catalogue, "The Mirror" was made up of twenty-two graphic works (eighteen lithographs and four woodcuts), but of only twenty different subjects, since *Loving Woman* and *Evening* occur in two versions each, one black-and-white and one hand-colored. In all, according to the catalogue, seven prints were hand colored—four lithographs and three woodcuts. It seems reasonable to suppose that these hand-colored prints were intended to be prototypes of the works Munch planned to print in color for the soon-to-be-issued "Mirror" portfolio. However, there is nothing to indicate that portfolios of "The Mirror" were ever actually published or that the series was ever exhibited again under this same title.

Catalogue Number 121—The Mirror

Munch's numerous notes, letters, and diaries contain no direct references to a portfolio called "The Mirror." None of the newspaper notices of the 1897 exhibit mentions either "The Mirror" or any other of the graphic works. Consequently, the 1897 catalogue itself is a primary source, since "The Mirror" is mentioned in it twice: as catalogue number 121 ("The mirror, hand-colored. Woodcut") and in the announcement of the intended publication of "a series of portfolios, 'The Mirror.'"

Naturally, it is of particular interest to try to identify the title picture of this portfolio. In the introduction to the catalogue of the Epstein Collection, Reinhold Heller wrote in 1972 that this title print, *The Mirror,* was identical with a woodcut entitled *The Voice* (Schiefler 83).[6] Earlier, however, the Munch Museum in Oslo had come to the conclusion that *The Mirror* must be identical with the woodcut called *Man's Head in Woman's Hair* (Sch. 80). This conclusion was based on two items in the Munch Museum—an empty portfolio, the cover of which is imprinted with this motif (OKK G/t 569-11, fig. 1), and another copy of the same print, with the motif positioned on the left side of the print paper in such a way as to suggest that some text was intended for the right half of the sheet (OKK G/t 569-33). On the upper left-hand corner of this sheet Munch has written in pencil, "A portfolio, 19 prints, Love."

The only solid evidence in the case is to be found in a series of twelve prints that Kaare Berntsen, Sr. and Jr., of Gallery KB in Oslo, discovered in the hands of a Norwegian collector in 1973. These twelve prints—nine lithographs and three woodcuts—have several striking features in common.

All the prints have been trimmed, the paper cut away close to the edges of the pictures themselves. Great irregularities in several cases suggest that this trimming was done in great haste and probably with a dull knife or scissors. The prints have then been pasted onto considerably larger pieces of heavy brown cardboard. The pasting shows signs of haste—many of the prints were not pressed smooth; in some cases the cardboard was spread too generously with paste leaving a broad dark band around the edge of the print. All except one are signed either "E. Munch 1897," "Edv. Munch 1897," or "Edvard Munch 1897" in pencil on the cardboard directly beneath the right-hand corner of the print. Five of the prints are hand colored, chiefly in tones of red and blue watercolor.

Without question, the most surprising of these graphic works is a unique version of *Man's Head in Woman's Hair*. Here Munch did not simply cut along the edge but encroached upon the print itself. He cut out the shape of the man's and woman's heads from an impression of the woodcut and pasted it onto the coarse brown cardboard, which he afterward painted dark red with watercolor. He also used red and gold paint in several places on the woman's hair. Across the whole breadth of the cardboard and across the subject itself Munch has written in large letters in transparent black watercolor, "THE MIRROR—SECOND PART—1897." This too must have been done in great haste—originally he started to write the numeral 2 for "second part." The 2 can still be seen under the first letter. This special variant of *Man's Head in Woman's Hair* can hardly be anything but catalogue number 121, *The Mirror*, as exhibited in the fall of 1897.

The KB Series

The twelve prints in this recently discovered series, hereafter referred to as the "KB prints" or the "KB series" are the following:

Attraction II, Sch. 66, hand-colored lithograph
Attraction I, Sch. 65, hand-colored lithograph
Jealousy, Sch. 58, black-and-white lithograph
The Urn, Sch. 63, black-and-white lithograph
Madonna, Sch. 33, black-and-white lithograph
Separation, Sch. 68, black-and-white lithograph
The Flower of Love, Sch. 70, black-and-white lithograph
Man's Head in Woman's Hair, Sch. 80, 1896, hand-colored woodcut
Anxiety, Sch. 62, hand-colored woodcut
Vampire, Sch. 34, black-and-white lithograph
Ashes, Sch. 69, hand-colored lithograph
The Kiss, Sch. 102B, hand-colored woodcut

With the exception of the black-and-white version of the lithograph *Vampire*, the hand-colored lithograph *Ashes*, and the hand-colored woodcut *The Kiss*, all of the KB prints can be linked to the "Mirror" series as listed in the 1897 catalogue. Munch often varied his titles widely from one exhibit to another, and therefore the exhibition catalogues are poor evidence on which to base the identification of any particular work. A title like *Two Heads*, for example, is so unspecific that it might fit any number of works. Here, it must refer to either *Attraction I* (Sch. 65) or *Attraction II* (Sch. 66). In an undated draft of a letter to August Clot—probably from late summer, 1897—Munch did a sketch of *Attraction I*, beside which he wrote the title *Deux Têtes* (Two Heads). Nevertheless, the most likely supposition is that, in "The Mirror," *Attraction I* was exhibited under the title *Stars*. The stars in the sky above the young couple are of vital importance to the meaning of the print; moreover, this is the only work in the series which the title *Stars* would fit. *Attraction II*, in essence an enlarged detail of the man's and woman's heads from *Attraction I*, must therefore be the *Two Heads* of "The Mirror." The hand coloring in *Anxiety*, *The Mirror*, *Attraction I*, and *Attraction II* agrees with the entries "hand-colored" in the catalogue.

There is every reason to believe that the twelve KB prints were part of the original "Mirror" series as presented in the fall of 1897, and that the prints are still in the original mountings Munch made for them in haste at that time. The approximately square shape of the brown cardboard on which the prints are mounted is unique. That prints from 1895 and 1896 are here dated 1897 merely points up the importance Munch ascribed to the presentation of his works—the prints are dated to accord with the special mounting that gives them their distinctive character and emphasizes their interdependence. The hand coloring was undoubtedly done at the same time, for in a few cases a little of the paint extends over the edges of the print onto the brown cardboard.

The fact that Munch indicates in the 1897 catalogue that numbers 94, 95, etc. "belong" to a portfolio called "The Mirror" does not rule out the possibility that other prints were to be included in the portfolio as well. In his opening-day notice of the exhibit, *Dagbladet*'s Rosenkrantz Johnsen wrote, "There were, when the exhibit opened this morning, no catalogues." Together with a number of typographical errors, this information confirms the impression that the catalogue was put together at the last minute directly from Munch's hurried notes and without time for proofreading. Quite possibly, as was often the case with Munch's catalogues, it was also incomplete.[7]

The three prints in the KB series not named in the catalogue—*Vampire, Ashes,* and *The Kiss*—must nevertheless have been part of "The Mirror" at this exhibition. It is quite possible that Munch added them after seeing the other works collected. Thematically, they fit. It is worth noting that he included a black-and-white variant of the lithograph *Vampire* even though he already had a hand-colored version. It is especially interesting that the woodcut *The Kiss* (Sch. 102B, and dated by Schiefler to 1897/1898) was included, and indeed there is reason to believe that the print was actually made for this exhibit. But the most important indication that these three prints were part of the original presentation of "The Mirror" is simply the fact that they have been trimmed and mounted and signed in the same manner as the rest of the KB series.

Except for the title work itself, all the KB prints have the initials H.S. on the cardboard by the lower left-hand corner of the print. These are the initials of Dr. Heinrich Stinnes of Cologne. In the supplemental volume of *Les Marques de collections de dessins & d'estampes,* Frits Lugt notes that Dr. Stinnes put his initials only on prints that he considered to be among the best in his collection.[8] As a collector, Dr. Stinnes placed particular emphasis on prints that were unique, such as an artist's earliest work, trial pulls, or different stages in the development of a single print. After Dr. Stinnes's death in 1932, his collection of some two hundred thousand prints (chiefly concentrated on German art from the last decades of the nineteenth century, but also a significant number of French impressionists and other well-known foreign artists) was sold and dispersed in a series of auctions held in Germany and Switzerland in the 1930s. A search of those auction catalogues shows nothing to indicate that any of the other Munch prints listed in them may have been part of "The Mirror." The twelve KB prints were acquired by a Norwegian collector from an art dealer in Berlin not long after Stinnes's death. We do not know how and when Dr. Stinnes came into possession of the prints, nor whether his collection ever included "The Mirror" in its entirety.

"The Mirror" as exhibited in 1897

To judge from the exhibition catalogue and the KB series, "The Mirror" as displayed in the Diorama Hall in the fall of 1897 appears to have consisted of twenty-five graphic works and of twenty-two different subjects. Of twenty lithographs and five woodcuts, nine—five lithographs and four woodcuts—were hand colored. Three of the twenty-five

prints were not listed in the catalogue.

In an attempt to reconstruct the complete "Mirror" based on information from the 1897 catalogue and on the KB prints, catalogue number 113, *A Street,* is among the more uncertain cases. None of the KB prints fits this title. *A Street* could refer to the lithograph *Evening on Karl Johan* just as well as to *Carmen* (or *Stealth* or *The Alley,* as it is also known—Sch. 36). The painting *Evening on Karl Johan* was in several exhibits of "The Frieze of Life" around the turn of the century with titles such as *Street* or *A Street.* Still, the lithograph *Evening on Karl Johan* (not registered by Schiefler) is known to exist in only one copy, which is hand colored, while, according to the 1897 catalogue, *A Street* is not hand colored.

On the other hand, we have reason to believe that *Carmen,* too, was exhibited under the title *A Street.* An 1895 copy of the satirical monthly *Tyrihans* contains a series of caricatures of Munch works then on exhibit at the Blomquist Gallery. The titles written under these simple sketches are surely identical with the exhibit titles, and here the title *A Street* occurs under a print that corresponds to Schiefler 36.[9]

Aside from the title work, discussed earlier, and the works just mentioned, the catalogue titles of 1897 give enough information to make positive identifications. With a reconstruction of "The Mirror" in mind, we are, however, confronted with an additional problem. Since it is known that the impressions varied from print to print, it is difficult to establish in all certainty which of these variations Munch included in the 1897 exhibition of "The Mirror."

In the following outline, each print is listed by its modern English title but in the order and with the catalogue number that it had in the 1897 catalogue. The Norwegian titles are given in parentheses, followed, in those cases where the original title differs from the one in use today, by the 1897 Norwegian title and its English translation. The indication of hand coloring is also from the 1897 catalogue. Titles of prints from the KB series are set in bold type.

94 *In the Land of Crystal. (I krystall-landet.* 1897: *Hinsides; On the Other Side.)* Schiefler 93, OKK G/1 225. Lithograph, 1897.

95 *Funeral March. (Sørgemarsj.)* Sch. 94. OKK G/1 226. Lithograph, 1897.

96 *Metabolism. (Stoffveksling.)* Sch. 95, OKK G/1 227. Lithograph, 1897.

97 *By the Deathbed. (Ved dødssengen.* 1897: *Dødskamp; Death Struggle.)* Sch. 72, OKK G/1 214. Lithograph, 1896.

98 *Death in the Sickroom. (Døden i sykeværelset.* 1897: *Døden; Death.)* Sch. 73, OKK G/1 215. Lithograph, 1896.

99 *Hands. Lust for Woman. (Hendene. Begjær etter kvinnen.)* Sch. 35, OKK G/1 196. Lithograph, 1895.

100 *Lovers in Waves. (Elskende par i bølger.* 1897: *Bølger; Waves.)* Sch. 71, OKK G/1 213. Lithograph, 1896.

101 *Madonna. (Madonna.* 1897: *Elskende Kvinde; Loving*

Woman.) Hand colored. Sch. 33, OKK G/l 194. Lithograph, 1895.

102 **Attraction II.** (*Tiltrekning II.* 1897: *To Hoveder; Two Heads.*) Hand colored. Sch. 66, OKK G/l 208. Lithograph, 1896.

103 **Attraction I.** (*Tiltrekning I.* 1897: *Stjerner; Stars.*) Hand colored. Sch. 65, OKK G/l 207. Lithograph, 1896.

104 **Jealousy.** (*Sjalusi.*) Sch. 58, OKK G/l 202. Lithograph, 1896.

105 *Vampire. (Vampyr.)* Hand colored. Sch. 34 a, OKK G/t 567. Lithograph, 1895.

106 **The Urn.** (*Urnen.*) Sch. 63, OKK G/l 205. Lithograph, 1896.

107 **Madonna.** (*Madonna.* 1897: *Elskende Kvinde; Loving Woman.*) Sch. 33aI, OKK G/l 194. Lithograph, 1895.

108 **Separation II.** (*Løsrivelse II.* 1897: *Adskillelsen; Parting.*) Sch. 68, OKK G/l 210. Lithograph, 1896.

113 *The Alley, Carmen. (Smuget. Carmen.* 1897: *En Gade; A Street.*) Sch. 36, OKK G/l 197. Lithograph, 1895.

114 **The Flower of Love.** (*Kjærlighetsblomsten.* 1897: *En Plante; A Plant.*) Sch. 70, OKK G/l 212. Lithograph, 1896.

116 *The Scream. (Skrik.)* Sch. 32, OKK G/l 193. Lithograph, 1895.

118 *Melancholy. (Melankoli.* 1897: *Aften; Evening.*) Hand colored. Sch. 82, OKK G/t 571. Woodcut, 1896.

119 *Melancholy. (Melankoli.* 1897: *Aften; Evening.*) Sch. 82, OKK G/t 571. Woodcut, 1896.

121 **Man's Head in Woman's Hair.** (*Mannshode i Kvinnehår.* 1897: *Speilet; The Mirror.*) Hand colored. Sch. 80a, OKK G/t 569. Woodcut, 1896.

124 **Anxiety.** (*Angst.*) Hand-colored. Sch. 62, OKK G/t 568. Woodcut, 1896.

Not in the catalogue:

Vampire. (*Vampyr.*) Sch. 34aII, OKK G/t 567. Lithograph, 1895.
Ashes. (*Aske.*) Sch. 69, OKK G/l 211. Lithograph, 1896. Hand colored.
The Kiss. (*Kyss.*) Sch. 102BI, OKK G/t 577. Woodcut, 1897. Hand colored.

"The Mirror—Second Part"

The so-called KB prints raise a number of different sorts of questions. One of the most obvious is why the title print bears the inscription "Second Part." Did there exist a "Mirror—First Part?" And if so, then what—and where—is it?

One possible explanation is that Munch was thinking of issuing "The Mirror" in two versions—a portfolio of black-and-white prints and a portfolio of colored prints. As mentioned earlier, nine of the twenty-five prints in "The Mirror" are hand colored, and three subjects—*Madonna, Vampire,* and *Melancholy*—exist in black-and-white as well as in color. "Second Part," therefore, may represent a purely technical division.

It appears that Munch was experimenting avidly with color printing at the time of the 1897 exhibit and immediately afterward. In an undated draft of

a letter to Julius Meier-Graefe from November or December 1897, he wrote:

> I am at work on various woodcuts—and will—soon send you some of them—If you're to have colored woodcuts they will have to be printed here—as I am having the color printed with lithographic stones—.[10]

Here we have the startling information that as early as 1897 Munch was already working with a combined form of lithography and woodcut. What prints were involved, however, is unclear.

In another undated draft of a letter to Meier-Graefe, probably from March 1898, Munch writes of the difficulty of printing woodcuts and of how he has to print them all himself: "I have my own small press—on which I print lithographs and woodcuts—." And he continues: "Later I will send you a small portfolio of my color woodcuts—They will interest you greatly—This portfolio will be made in only twenty or thirty copies and will therefore be very expensive—." Like so many of Munch's other plans at this period, this one was never realized. But his work on "The Mirror" was probably what gave him the idea for a portfolio of color woodcuts. This conjecture is born out by the fact that on the back of the previously mentioned portfolio in the Munch Museum—the one with *Man's Head in Woman's Hair* on the cover (OKK G/t 569-11, fig. 1)—is the following inscription in Munch's handwriting: "*Woodcuts:* 'Kiss,' 'Meteors' [i.e., *Meeting in Space*], 'Girl with Heart' etc." But such a plan must have originated after the exhibit in the Diorama Hall, for both *Girl with Heart* (Sch. 134) and *Meeting in Space* (Sch. 135) are traditionally dated to 1899.[11]

There is, however, another, perhaps more convincing explanation of the title "The Mirror—Second Part." And this is to be found in the manner in which we might assume Munch exhibited these prints. We know that Munch usually listed works in his catalogues in the order in which he hung them. As the 1897 catalogue shows, the "Mirror" series began with motifs of transmutation and death.

At the Berlin Secession in 1902, Munch exhibited the paintings of "The Frieze of Life" under the title "Darstellung eine Reihe von Lebensbildern" (Presentation of a Series of Images from Life). According to the catalogue, the twenty-two paintings that then made up the Frieze were divided into four subgroups, each with its own subtitle. The series began with "Keimen der Liebe" (The Germination of Love), followed by "Blühen und vergehen der Liebe" (The Blossoming and Decay of Love), "Lebensangst" (The Fear of Life), and, finally, "Tod" (Death). In the light of these titles, it seems natural to assume, bearing in mind the subject of the

fig. 1 Portfolio cover, OKK G/t 569-11, Munch-Museet, Oslo

title print, that "The Mirror—Second Part" represents the themes of love and anguish, while the unknown "Mirror—First Part" must have represented the themes of transmutation and death. But why begin a series with decay and death?

The very word "mirror" suggests reversal, and in the particular case of Edvard Munch it would have been especially appropriate to begin a series of pictures, mirrorlike, with images of decay and death, for these can be said to have had life-giving significance for Munch, as a person and as an artist. As he was growing up, Munch was repeatedly confronted with sickness and death. His mother died of tuberculosis when he was five; his sister Sophie, one year his senior, died of the same disease when he was fourteen. As a child he was several times so seriously ill that there was doubt he would survive. These early and tragic encounters with illness and death encouraged his solemn reflections on the meaning of life. Thus sickness and death came to be principal themes in his work and positive elements in his life, in the sense that they became absolutely decisive for

his creative expression. Death gave life to his art. "My home was a home of sickness and death," Munch once wrote. "Indeed I have never overcome its disasters. And it has also had decisive importance for my art."[12]

Consequently, it would have made perfect sense for Munch to begin a mirror series with works about transmutation and death, which would then have comprised the first part of "The Mirror." According to the catalogue, the series begins with *In the Land of Crystal,* and in one of his notebooks Munch once wrote that "Death is the beginning of life—of new crystallization." In attempting any interpretation of "The Mirror," it is essential to bear in mind that Munch began the series with the themes of transmutation and death.

A closer look at the existing prints from "The Mirror," on the other hand, can lead to the perfectly reasonable conclusion that "The Mirror—First Part" need never have existed at all. The twelve KB prints show signs of having been done in a great hurry, and it seems probable that Munch had no opportunity to see the series as a whole until it had been hung in the Diorama Hall. Then, however, he would have been able to see that "The Mirror" actually contained subject matter that he could divide into several subgroups, as he later did with "The Frieze of Life." So it could well be that he abandoned the idea of subdividing "The Mirror" at that time and decided that the series as exhibited was a hasty, private document that he would work on further before publishing.

"The Mirror" as a Title

The Norwegian word *speil* (mirror) derives from the Latin *speculum,* a word used in the titles of any number of medieval manuscripts. An interesting example is the medieval Norwegian *Speculum Regale* (The King's Mirror) from the thirteenth century. In the prologue, the author explains the book's title by saying that he wants to show proper conduct as if in a mirror, adding that the king in particular should look into this mirror so that he and his army may become examples for others to follow. This moral handbook was first printed in 1848, and Edvard Munch's uncle, the well-known historian P. A. Munch, was one of its publishers.[13] Without drawing any broad conclusions, it is worth noting that Edvard Munch himself was very family conscious, and that Munch's father often read aloud to his children from historical writings. In any case, it is interesting to remember this medieval *Speculum Regale,* for in many ways Munch had similar intentions for his own "Mirror." Later in life Munch wrote, "In my art I have tried to elucidate my life and its meaning. And I have wanted to help others to elucidate theirs."[14]

Words such as "mirror" and "mirror image" were favorite symbols of the writers of the 1890s. Sigbjörn Obstfelder's "Can the Mirror Speak," for example, is one of his most well-known poems. (Obstfelder was one of Munch's many literary friends in the nineties, and the points of contact between Obstfelder's poetry and Munch's art have often been discussed.)

In Munch's notes about his own work, as well as among his more consciously literary writings, the expression "mirror image" occurs in several places. But as the title for a series of pictures, "The Mirror" is found only twice: in the 1897 catalogue and written across the title print of the KB series. Why didn't Munch make use of the same title on other occasions, say, in later exhibitions of "The Frieze of Life?" Primarily because later he exhibited his principal themes in another order than in "The Mirror," namely, with transmutation and death at the end

instead of at the beginning. And thus the name "Mirror" lost the relevance it had once had.

The Beginnings of the "Mirror" Portfolio

Another reason for there being so few references to a portfolio entitled "The Mirror" is that Munch originally planned to publish the portfolio under the title "Liebe" or "Die Liebe" (Love). As mentioned earlier, the Munch Museum has a portfolio with *Man's Head in Woman's Hair* on the cover and another copy of the same work printed on heavy paper with the inscription "Eine Mappe, 19 Blätter, Liebe" (A portfolio, 19 prints, Love).

In 1896, in Paris, when Munch began work on a number of prints related to "The Frieze of Life," it would have been natural to give a planned series of graphics the title "Die Liebe." That was what he had called his "Frieze of Life" when it was displayed as a series of fourteen paintings in Berlin in 1895.

A somewhat special contemporary reference to Munch's plans for a portfolio called "Love" is found in a poem by the French symbolist Marcel Réja, whom Munch must have known in Paris in 1896. The poem, "La Plante," (The Plant) exists in two handwritten copies in the Munch Museum. The two copies, which are identical, are both inscribed to Munch—"pour E. Munch"—and one copy also has the inscription "D'un album sur l'amour" (For an album on love) above the poem's title. There is little doubt but what the subject of this poem is the 1896 lithograph *The Flower of Love* (Sch. 70), which in 1897 was included in "The Mirror" with the title *A Plant.* (It is also part of the KB series.)

A letter from Munch to the art historian Julius Meier-Graefe, dated "Åsgårdstrand 26/6 97" and never sent, is particularly interesting in this connection. (Meier-Graefe was in Paris at the time, where he had been living since the fall of 1895.) In the letter, Munch asks to borrow money to pay the freight on what he calls his "things," such as "studies and equipment for lithography and woodcut," which, since his return from Paris, have been held at the railway station on account of the unpaid charges. In return, Munch promises that Meier-Graefe shall have fifty new prints of *The Sick Child.* Moreover, he writes, "I will give you two or *3 portfolios of Die Liebe, 2 smaller paintings and other original* sketches and studies as a deposit." (The italics are Munch's own.)

To judge from this letter, it would appear that in the summer of 1897 there existed several copies of a portfolio called "Die Liebe." On the other hand, it is not unreasonable to conjecture that the "two or 3 portfolios of Die Liebe" used here to entice Meier-

Graefe were in fact only a plan, which Munch hoped to realize as soon as he had the necessary equipment to continue his graphic work. The correspondence between Meier-Graefe and Munch contains a number of examples, especially from the period 1898-1900, of Munch's promising to send Meier-Graefe prints that were either never produced or greatly delayed.

At all events, it seems clear that at the end of June 1897, Munch had plans to publish a graphic portfolio to be called "Die Liebe," and to use *Man's Head in Woman's Hair* as its title print. Over the summer of 1897, however, the series was apparently enlarged to include the "death" works of 1896 and the 1897 lithographs *In the Land of Crystal, Funeral March,* and *Metabolism.* Once these had been added, the title "Love" was no longer appropriate, and, that September, Munch exhibited the portfolio at the Diorama Hall under the title "The Mirror."

The planned publication of a "Mirror" Portfolio

On March 7, 1898, William Molard, a Franco-Norwegian who was a secretary in the French Ministry of Agriculture and a composer in his spare time, wrote to Munch: "Are you continuing your lithographic album, in which you wanted to mirror all the different phases of your life's—soul's life—or have you been painting?" Molard's question does in fact describe the basic idea behind "The Mirror," and we can fairly assume that Munch had described his planned portfolio in similar terms on his frequent visits to the Molard family in Paris in 1896-1897.

Everything suggests that Munch was indeed occupied with his "lithographic album" at the very time he received Molard's letter. There are several indications that he was thinking of printing a larger edition of some of the works in "The Mirror" and that these were to be included in a portfolio. In a letter written in early March 1898 to the Danish painter Johan Rohde in connection with Munch's participation in "The Free Exhibition" in Copenhagen, Munch lists the lithographs he intends to submit: "1) Self-Portrait, 2) Portrait of Strindberg, 3) Loving Woman, 4) Waves." And he goes on, "The last two lithographs are part of a portfolio I hope to publish soon—anyway the lithographs won't be printed in more than 200 copies."

Since both *Loving Woman (Madonna)* and *Waves (Lovers in Waves)* were included in "The Mirror" at the Diorama Hall six months earlier, the portfolio Munch refers to here can hardly be anything except "The Mirror."

In a letter written about the same time to August

Clot, who had printed most of Munch's lithographs during his stay in Paris, Munch asks how much it would cost to make one hundred prints from a lithographic stone and how much to make two hundred.

One of the earliest indications that Munch had begun thinking along lines that would lead to "The Mirror" is in a letter he wrote to his aunt, Karen Björstad, at the end of December 1896: "I may possibly publish some lithographs that might earn me some money. . . ."[15] That he wasn't merely talking about "some" lithographs, but about a portfolio, is evident from a letter to Munch from Richard Mengelberg, dated Berlin, March 15, 1897. After apologizing for taking so long to answer Munch's letter, Mengelberg writes, "Has the publication of the portfolio taken place? If so, reserve a copy for me and bring it with you." (Incidentally, the first of Munch's graphic works registered by Schiefler—Sch. 1—is a portrait of Mengelberg.)

One year later, to judge from his letter to Rohde, Munch was planning to publish a graphic portfolio in an edition of two hundred copies. But a month before "The Mirror" was exhibited at the Diorama Hall, he was evidently thinking of a smaller edition. In a draft of a letter to Clot, probably from August 1897, he asks Clot to print *"pour commencer"*—to begin with—fifty copies each of *Attraction I* and *Lovers in Waves,* both of which are included in "The Mirror."

Nevertheless, there is nothing to indicate that the portfolio of "The Mirror" ever actually appeared, not even in the smaller edition. There are several explanations. During Munch's stay in Paris in 1896-1897, his letters often mentioned the future he thought graphics would have. Back in Norway, however, he wrote to Meier-Graefe in the summer of 1897, "Here people still have no understanding or interest in prints—No one wants to spend money on them—"

He concludes the letter on a note of resignation: "On the whole I often have the urge to give the whole thing up—money is a problem—and I despise these Norwegian peasants—." Munch's negative view of Norwegians—all of whom were peasants in his eyes—was probably not nearly so decisive for the future of "The Mirror" as the fact that he could not find the financial support he needed to bring the project to fruition. Reproduction of the prints in "The Mirror" would involve numerous problems of a practical as well as technical nature. To produce color prints that would even approximate in tone and expression those that had been colored by hand would be an enormously complex and time-consuming task, both for the printer and for

Munch. Nor were things made any simpler by the fact that Munch's lithographic stones and woodcut blocks were in various countries in Europe—some in France, others in Germany and Norway.

In addition to steadily deteriorating health, Munch suffered great economic and personal difficulties in the years after 1897. Not long after the exhibit in the Diorama Hall he became acquainted with Tulla Larsen, and thus began a conflict-filled relationship that reached a dramatic conclusion in 1902. Vastly increasing use of alcohol did not improve matters. Just after the turn of the century, however, Munch appears to have come a little to his senses again, and in a number of letters to Tulla he appeals to her repeatedly to try to respect his need for solitude and the opportunity to work undisturbed. In an undated letter, probably from the winter of 1900-1901, he writes that he is now in a working period and that she has no right to upbraid him for not giving her enough of his time. He writes that for her sake he has given up a planned trip (probably to Berlin), and that he had hoped to be able to finance the trip "through the sale of my pictures—among other things by printing my great lithographic work—which I have struggled for four years to accomplish." This "great lithographic work" can hardly be anything but "The Mirror."

Another possible explanation of Munch's failure ever actually to publish "The Mirror" may be that he never considered it finished, even if the prints were presented as an apparently completed series in 1897. But that exhibit is more likely to have given a restless, creative personality like Munch the impulse to enlarge and alter the series than to conclude it.

Today we know only a fragment of "The Mirror" as we believe it was originally exhibited. Yet this fragment contains some of the finest and most characteristic qualities of Munch's entire artistic production. Boldness and spontaneity—in certain cases an almost primitive power of expression—are combined with exquisite subtlety and an absolute control of technique and media. That the prints are all mounted on identical brown cardboard serves to emphasize their relationships to one another, and the very manner of their mounting produces an immediate, direct impression of the freshness of the moment. We stand here before one of the rare cases where a number of Munch's graphic works still exist in the same "frame" in which the artist himself originally chose to present them. The pulse of the creative process can be felt behind every one of these prints, and as a result their message comes across with all the greater force. This special immediacy would have been virtually impossible to retain in a larger edition of "The Mirror."

Yet obviously Munch did not abandon the idea of publishing a portfolio of his most important lithographs and woodcuts. Schiefler has written how Munch and he discussed the possibility in Warnemünde in 1908 and how they finally decided to print his large lithographs and woodcuts on expensive paper and publish them as a portfolio, a sort of graphic "Frieze of Life."[16] But as we know, nothing came of these plans either.

Texts to "The Mirror"

As late as 1929, Munch mentioned in a letter to the Swedish Dr. Ragnar Hoppe that he had once had plans to produce a portfolio on themes from "The Frieze of Life." And he added an interesting piece of information. "A long time ago it was my intention to produce a large portfolio of the most important works in the Frieze of Life with accompanying text—mostly poetry—prose—." The letter goes on to say that Munch has been looking through various notes made in the course of forty years—he calls them "notes from a diary of the soul"—and remarks that they might accompany his paintings and prints "arm in arm, and, in a single work, be joined to my prints."

The draft of another letter to Dr. Hoppe from about the same period also mentions Munch's notes. "They include—for all of the paintings in The Frieze of Life and for most of my lithographs with their contents of the soul—small poems in prose— or notes." He adds, "I have also had plans to join these notes to my drawings and prints."[17]

Such a combination of words with drawings and graphic works is exactly what Munch did produce in "The Tree of Knowledge," his private album of his most important works, many of them pasted into the thick, heavy volume, others on loose sheets. A number of the works are similar to motifs in "The Mirror." Several have been very closely trimmed, like the prints in the KB series. To many of the works in "The Tree of Knowledge," Munch has added texts, often written in capital letters in different colors. It is uncertain when Munch began to collect his works in this book—maybe not until after the turn of the century, though a number of the texts, like a number of the pictures, are of earlier origin. It is quite possible that some of these texts may have been written while Munch was working on "The Mirror."

We have several indications that Munch was much taken up with his own writing in 1897-1898. In the spring of 1898, he wrote to the German poet Max Dauthendey to thank him for two books he had recently sent. Munch writes that he likes them very much but that he has not quite finished reading them because he himself is busy writing "I am writing poems—that is to say, concentrated thoughts and experiences—." It is interesting that Max Dauthendey, whom Munch got to know in Berlin in 1892-1893 and who visited Paris while Munch was there in 1896-1897, was an ardent spokesman for an art form that strove to achieve a fusion of all the senses. Among the painters of the time, Dauthendey regarded Munch as the foremost exponent of this idea.[18]

Another reference to the writing that occupied Munch at this time comes from no less than August Strindberg. (Munch's and Strindberg's friendship in Paris in the spring and summer of 1896—interrupted by Strindberg's "inferno crisis" and his flight from Paris—will be discussed later.) In the middle of August 1897, that is, a month before Munch exhibited "The Mirror," Strindberg wrote to Gustaf af Gejerstam to report that his publisher had offered to publish *Inferno*. The letter goes on to say that a mutual acquaintance "who has just returned from Christiania, ran into Edvard Munch, who said that he had temporarily abandoned painting in order to write a book that is to be called *Hell*, as he believes himself to have discovered that we are 'down there' already."[19] In all probability, this was something that Munch made up on the spur of the moment, for he must have realized that so provocative a remark would be passed on to Strindberg. On the other hand, he would hardly have invented such a thing if he had not in fact been concerned with writing at the time.

Munch grew up in a home where there was a great interest in literature. As a boy, his artistic imagination was captured by such diverse subjects as the Norse sagas and American Indian tales. From the time he was very young, Munch lived in an environment dominated by literary personalities. The so-called Kristiania Bohème of the 1880s, with its unequivocal demand for truth—Thou shalt write thine own life—came to be of fundamental importance for Munch as an artist. Throughout his life, he derived inspiration and ideas from the works of Ibsen.

During his visit to Berlin in 1892-1893, Munch's circle of friends at *Zum Schwarzen Ferkel* consisted chiefly of writers: August Strindberg, Holger Drachmann, Stanislaw Przybyszewski, Ola Hansson, Sigbjörn Obstfelder, Gunnar Heiberg, and more.

In 1891, Munch did a vignette for a collection of poems called *Alruner* by the Danish poet Emanuel Goldstein. A short time later, there was also talk of his doing illustrations for the Danish translation of Maurice Maeterlinck's recently published *Pelléas et Mélisande* and for a planned collection of poems by Sigbjörn Obstfelder.

In Paris, in 1896, Munch worked on illustrations for Charles Baudelaire's *Les Fleurs du mal* and, in the process, did much to develop certain important themes in his own art. This commission also proved to be important to the genesis of "The Mirror."

Paris 1896-1897

The idea for a graphic album on themes from "The Frieze of Life" originated in the course of Munch's stay in Paris in 1896-1897, and it was there that he did most of the "Mirror" prints—in all, seventeen of twenty-five. Impressions formed in Paris may also have contributed to Munch's apparent plan to publish "The Mirror" with his own texts. So before continuing, it is worth having a closer look at the artistic and literary environment and at the people and events that, directly or indirectly, played some part in Munch's work on this project.

When Munch arrived in Paris at the end of February 1896, he had already established himself as an artist/writer in the avant-garde journal *La Revue blanche*. Thadée Natanson, the journal's editor, had been in Norway in the fall of 1895, and in the November issue that year he wrote a piece about a Munch exhibit at the Blomquist Gallery. A month later, Munch's lithograph *The Scream* was reproduced in the magazine with accompanying text by Munch, and Natanson noted for his readers that this was "one of those small poems that Munch is in the habit of attaching to his compositions," adding that it was therefore "a document in support of what we have said about the Norwegian painter's engagement with literature."[20]

Illustrated literary journals like *La Revue blanche* and *Le Mercure de France* played an important role in the artistic circles of the 1890s, and Munch knew a number of people with close connections to both of them. *La Revue blanche* provided a forum in which many of the artists of the day could express their ideas. From 1894, an original print was published in each issue, and at the end of every year these were collected and published as an album: *Album de la Revue blanche*.[21] Presumably Munch was familiar with this practice. A group of artists called "Les Nabis" that included Maurice Denis, Pierre Bonnard, Edouard Vuillard, and Paul Serusier were especially closely associated with this journal, while eminent artists, important particularly in the graphic field, such as Toulouse-Lautrec, Félix Vallotton, and Odilon Redon also contributed works.

Even before he came to Paris in 1896 Munch was undoubtedly familiar with Vallotton's work. Vallotton's well-known 1895 woodcut of Dostoevski—a possible inspiration for Munch's lithograph *Self-Portrait with Skeleton Arm* (cat. no. 120), done the same year—had, for example, been published in the German journal *Pan*, to which Munch had close ties. Vallotton's black-and-white woodcuts of celebrated people were often reproduced in *La Revue blanche*, and Vallotton was the principal contributor of graphics to the magazine. His characteristic device of including the name of his subject in a white space at the lower edge of the print was used effectively by Munch as well, for example, in his lithographic self-portrait of 1895 and in his portraits of August Strindberg and Stéphane Mallarmé of 1896. He uses a similar device in the lithograph *Ashes* (Sch. 69, and part of "The Mirror"), in which the print's title is contained in its lower border.

In the summer of 1896, Munch had a letter from Przybyszewski asking him to get "a portfolio of Félix Vallotton's drawings," so that Przybyszewski could make himself a little money by writing an article on Vallotton. "Perhaps you know him yourself," Przybyszewski wrote. "If so, go to him, tell him who I am, etc., and ask him for his woodcuts."[22] We do not know whether Munch and Vallotton were personally acquainted, but through their mutual friend Meier-Graefe the possibility certainly existed. When, in Paris, in 1898, the first book on Vallotton appeared, the book's author, Julius Meier-Graefe, spent several pages comparing the woodcuts of Vallotton with those of Munch.

Munch undoubtedly had numerous sources of inspiration with regard to the publication of graphic works in portfolio form. In addition to the "Meier-Graefe Portfolio" of 1895, Munch later published two other graphic portfolios. In 1902, on commission from Dr. Max Linde in Lübeck, Munch published a portfolio of sixteen etchings and lithographs called "Aus dem Hause Max Linde" (From the House of Max Linde). A lithographic portfolio called "Alpha and Omega," which included a text by Munch, appeared in 1909. This text, which closely accompanies the exaggerated, satirical prints, was published in French as well as in Norwegian. The sources of this album probably go back as far as 1896, when a sketch for one of its works, *Omega's Death* (OKK T1359) appears to have originated.[23] In April 1896, probably in response to a suggestion of his own, Munch was commissioned by a Norwegian patron of the arts named Axel Heiberg to do a series of portraits—etchings—of Norwegian artists. This project was subsequently abandoned, for reasons that the correspondence between Munch and Heiberg does not make clear, but it may nevertheless have spurred Munch to the creation of the series

of exceptional portraits, primarily lithographs, that he produced in the course of 1896 of, among others, Strindberg, Hans Jæger, Sigbjørn Obstfelder, Stéphane Mallarmé, Gunnar Heiberg, and Knut Hamsun. Another source of inspiration may have been Toulouse-Lautrec's album "Treize Lithographies," published in 1895, with its portraits of well-known actors and actresses.

But of all the things that encouraged Munch to investigate the possibilities of the graphic portfolio, the most important may well have been Toulouse-Lautrec's lithographic album "Elles," from 1896. This series of ten color lithographs plus a cover was exhibited in the "Salon des Cents" beginning April 22, 1896. Printed in an edition of one hundred, the series did not sell well, but it did arouse great interest in artistic circles. That Munch would not have seen this series—either in 1896 or else at the Vollard Gallery where it was exhibited in 1897—is virtually unthinkable. "Elles" was also exhibited at La Libre Esthétique in Brussels in the spring of the following year, where Munch too had works on display and where he himself was present. At the time of Munch's death, in 1944, he owned a copy of the "Elles" portfolio.

Another important event for Munch took place in the spring of 1896, when he was asked by the art dealer Ambroise Vollard to contribute a graphic work to the first album in the series "Peintres Graveurs." Vollard's request resulted in the lithograph *Anxiety* (Sch. 61), printed in black and red. It is tempting to believe that Munch chose this subject, closely associated as it was to *The Scream* (published earlier in *La Revue blanche*), in hopes of creating the expectation of a distinctive Munchian style. The lithograph, published under the French title *Soir* (Evening), was taken by many to be a woodcut.[24] (*Anxiety* was included in "The Mirror" as a woodcut in black with hand coloring in red. Interestingly enough, "The Mirror" also includes two versions of the woodcut *Melancholy* presented under the title *Evening*.) In his memoirs, *Souvenirs d'un marchand de tableaux*, Vollard wrote that the first two albums of "Peintres Graveurs" were far from commercial successes, but that the painters who took part grew more and more interested in this new mode of self-expression. "Several of them," he wrote, "eventually did entire albums for me."[25]

As a result of this assignment for Vollard, Munch was suddenly presented as a graphic artist along with the most well-known avant-garde artists of the day. It is not unlikely that Munch met Vollard through Meier-Graefe, his good friend from Berlin, who was at that time employed at Bing's Salon de l'Art Nouveau. Vollard's gallery on the Rue Lafitte was very near Bing's. (Moreover, Vollard's closest neighbor on the Rue Lafitte was the editorial office of *La Revue blanche*.) For the sake of his contacts, Meier-Graefe must have been very important to Munch in Paris. Being the editor of the German journal *Pan*, Meier-Graefe was also responsible for the French edition of this magazine. Meier-Graefe himself had plans to publish several portfolios in the late nineties, and, along with other well-known artists, Munch was to be represented. It seems that Munch in the years 1897-1900 had an especially hard time living up to promises of this kind. Nevertheless the correspondence between the two men indicates their mutual interest in the creative possibilities inherent in the woodcut. It was a real stroke of luck that Meier-Graefe was employed at Bing's when Munch arrived in Paris in 1896, for it gave Munch a first class opportunity to study Bing's collection of Japanese art and crafts, especially the woodcuts.

The spring of 1896 was an intense, creative period for Munch. Rich in stimuli on many levels, this creative time also included several important exhibitions. In April and May, Munch had ten paintings in an exhibit at the Salon des Indépendants, but his one-man exhibit at Bing's in May and June was probably more important in making a name for Munch among French artists. Here again we see an example of Meier-Graefe's importance, for of course the Bing exhibit came about primarily through his efforts. There was no catalogue, but the exhibit is believed to have included about twenty-five paintings and fifty graphic works.[26]

The now famous account of Munch's work that August Strindberg published in the *Revue blanche* of June 1, 1896, was based on this exhibit at Bing's. Strindberg's poetic and highly personal interpretations of Munch's pictures may very well have been a source of inspiration for Munch's own growing ambitions as a writer. Munch and Strindberg were often together at this time, but their relations grew more discordant and strained as Strindberg's paranoia intensified. His *Inferno* crisis reached a climax in the middle of July, and, shortly afterward, he left Paris. "Strindberg has gone home to Sweden," Munch wrote his aunt in late summer 1896. "I think he's being treated for mental illness—he had so many odd ideas—he made gold, and discovered that the earth was flat and that the stars were holes in the dome of the sky. He had a persecution complex and at one time believed that I was trying to poison him with gas."

But as long as the companionship with Strindberg lasted, it undoubtedly provided Munch with another important gateway to the world of the arts in the French capital. In 1894-1895, Strindberg had reached the height of his fame in France. His play *The Father* was produced at the Théâtre de l'Oeuvre in December 1894. At about the same time, Strindberg became acquainted with Gauguin, and in February 1895, he wrote the foreword—actually a letter—to the auction catalogue of Gauguin's works at the Hôtel Drouot. In January of that year, Strindberg's celebrated and controversial novel *Le Plaidoyer d'un Fou* was published in French. It must have been in the course of his friendship with Strindberg in 1896 that Munch came into possession of the original French manuscript of this revealing autobiographical account of Strindberg's first marriage—a manuscript that did not come to light until 1973.[27]

The importance that Strindberg placed on his often exquisitely decorated original manuscripts cannot have escaped Munch's attention. In fact during the planning stages of *Inferno* in the late summer of 1896 (*Inferno* appeared in the fall of 1897), Strindberg toyed with the idea of publishing it as an illustrated manuscript.[28] As Strindberg's interest in art and artistic theory grew, there was plenty of opportunity for the two men to exchange ideas—though as Strindberg tells it, the influence was more one-sided. *Inferno*, which is based largely on autobiographical notes, contains a passage in which Strindberg tells of "the Danish painter" (Munch) who had been under his influence for a time in Paris but who had tried to free himself. Yet in another passage, Strindberg proposes a kind of collaboration between himself and Munch: a report has just reached them in Paris that Przybyszewski has been arrested in Berlin, charged with murder, and Strindberg suggests to Munch that they rescue "our friend's literary reputation." His idea is that he will write a piece about Przybyszewski's contribution to literature, while Munch will "draw a portrait that will show him to advantage and we will try to get the thing published in Revue Blanche."[29]

This passage also shows how close they were to *La Revue blanche*. It is very likely that Munch met Stéphane Mallarmé either through his association with this journal—the editor, Natanson, was Mallarmé's neighbor during the summers in Valvin—or else through *Le Mercure de France*, described by Jens Thiis as "the organ of the young and most intelligent artistic circle." Mallarmé was the great poetic name of the day. After Paul Verlaine's death in January 1896, Mallarmé took over the role of *prince des poètes*. The acquaintance between Munch and Mallarmé resulted in two portraits—an etching (W. 48) and a lithograph (Sch. 79). Their correspondence suggests a relationship marked by mutual respect and deference, and some of the letters seem to indicate that Munch used a photograph—probably Nadar's well-known one—of Mallarmé in doing the portraits.

But Mallarmé was only the best known of Munch's friends in Paris at this time. In his sketchbooks Munch often wrote down the names and addresses of acquaintances, plus the times of appointments, etc., and it seems clear from these notes that Munch's daily, intimate, and, in the long run, probably most significant contacts during his Paris sojourn were with people whose names are little known today but were, in Parisian literary-artistic circles of the 1890s, quite familiar. Such names as Henry D. Davry, Yvanhoé Rambosson, Julien Leclercq, and Marcel Réja occur repeatedly in Munch's letters and sketchbooks—all of them people who helped to create the peculiar intellectual milieu surrounding *Le Mercure de France*.[30]

The name of Marcel Réja has been mentioned earlier in connection with his poem "La Plante," which he dedicated to Munch. His real name was Paul Meunier, and in daily life he was a doctor, a psychiatrist. Munch's private library contains several collections of Réja's poetry. Strindberg, when he first met Réja in the fall of 1897, expressed great admiration for Réja's recently published *Ballets et variations,* and, subsequently, Réja undertook to edit the original French manuscript of Strindberg's *Inferno,* which appeared in 1898 with a foreword by Réja. André Salmon makes an interesting observation about Réja's art in his book *Souvenirs sans fin.* Having asked the question of whether Réja has talent, he replies, "Yes, a second-class talent, but a talent of the kind that is so often more representative of a school than the chief works of the school's leading master." The point Salmon makes is an essential one. And it is important to note that in the Paris of 1896-1897 Munch established contact with various levels of creative activity within the artistic and literary avant-garde, and that he moved in circles that very well represented the artistic expression of the day.

In the previously mentioned letter that William Molard wrote to Munch in March 1898, Molard states that he is aware that, in Christiania, Munch has "met friends from our circle—Leclercq and Delius." Here is another example of the breadth of Munch's acquaintance. Julien Leclercq, a journalist and author who is virtually unknown today, had close ties to both Gauguin and Strindberg—to the latter particularly during 1895. As a poet, moreover, he must have been a striking example of what Salmon calls a "second-class talent." From the fall of 1896, he was briefly associated with Bing's gallery.

The composer Frederick Delius, rather more well-known, probably met Munch during a visit to Norway in 1889. In the mid-nineties, Delius lived in Paris' Latin Quarter and was one of the first people Munch looked up when he arrived in 1896. Delius was interested in art and was close to other pictorial artists, including Gauguin; in 1898 he bought Gauguin's famous painting *Nevermore*.[31]

Both Leclercq and Delius were members of the group that regularly gathered at the home of the Molard family. Munch's close friendship with William Molard was of the greatest importance to his stay in Paris, and he was also in touch with Molard until late in his life.[32]

William Molard and his Family

The Molard family and their artist friends are the objects of a detailed description in Göran Söderström's *Strindberg and Pictorial Art.* Lionel Carley devotes an entire chapter to "The Molard Circle" in his book *Delius—The Paris Years.* The Molard family was also important to Munch. Through Molard and the circle around him, Munch was exposed to a variety of significant stimuli, many of which had their eventual effect on "The Mirror."

Who was he, this William François Molard who, in very readable Norwegian, wrote friendly, sensitive letters to Munch on the stationery of the French Ministry of Agriculture? Roughly contemporary with Munch—he was born in Mantes on March 9, 1862, and died in Paris in 1936—he grew up in a home where there was a great interest in Norwegian art and literature. His mother, Rachel Hamilton, had been born in Norway, while his father, Victor Molard, a Frenchman, was actively interested in making Norwegian art and culture better known in France. Victor Molard was a professional organist, the whole family loved music, and for young William music became the great passion. At the age of twenty-one he went to work for the Ministry of Agriculture, to the distress of his father, who was afraid that William would remain in this *"trou ministeriel."* His father was right, William did remain in his "bureaucratic hole," but it gave him a small but regular income that allowed him to devote his free time completely to music. According to his friends his compositions were unplayable, and none is known to exist today.

Munch probably got to know William Molard through their mutual friend the Norwegian journalist, editor, and publisher Karl Vilhelm Hammer. As a young man, Hammer had stayed for long periods with the Molard family in France. From the early nineties on, Hammer had close contacts with important newspapers and magazines all across Europe, including *La Revue blanche* and its editor Thadée Natanson. While living in Paris in 1896, Munch wrote a number of letters to Hammer and his wife, Valborg.

In 1891, William Molard married the Swedish sculptress Ida Louise Wilhelmina Ericson, born in Stockholm in 1853 and thus nine years his senior. She had come to Paris in the early 1880s and was to stay there until her death in 1927. She worked in a traditional, academic style and was represented in the Swedish pavilion at the World Exposition of 1900. Along with Judith, Ida's young daughter by an earlier relationship, the Molards took up residence in Montparnasse, at number 6 Rue Vercingétorix. This two-story wooden building, constructed of cheap materials purchased after the Universal Exposition of 1889, is said to have had such exceedingly thin walls that the artists' families who lived there were forced to become good neighbors. For a number of years the Molard home was a gathering place for French and Scandinavian artists, writers, and musicians—a varied and colorful congregation. Edvard Grieg was the guest of honor on one occasion. Henri Rousseau often turned up with his violin. Jens Thiis writes that painters like Vuillard, Bonnard, and Marquet were among the regular guests. Such dissimilar personalities as the playwright Alfred Jarry (who wrote *Ubu Roi*), the composer Frederick Delius, the painter Daniel de Monfried, and the poet Paul Roinard visited frequently. The young intellectuals from the circles around *Le Mercure de France* were habitués.[33]

Through friends of Molard's Swedish-born wife, Strindberg came into contact with the family in the fall of 1894. The Molards are described several times in *Inferno,* and the artists who met there are given a piece of Strindberg's mind: "An entire coterie of anarchistic artists gathers there, and I feel doomed to endure seeing and hearing everything I would rather avoid—shameless behavior, loose morals, deliberate godlessness. There is gathered there much talent, infinite wit; one of them is really a natural genius and has acquired quite a name for himself."[34] The natural genius was of course Paul Gauguin. Toward the end of 1893 or the beginning of 1894, after his first visit to Tahiti, Gauguin moved into a studio one floor above the Molards on the Rue Vercingétorix. A close friendship grew up between them, and Molard later became an important go-between for Gauguin after he had returned to Tahiti for good.

Gauguin and Munch

By the time he arrived in Paris in 1896, Munch had known Gauguin's name for many years. As early as 1884, Gauguin had had three paintings in the Fall Exhibit in Christiania, to which Munch had contributed one.

Munch did not often mention the names of other painters in his letters and notes, but in a letter from Berlin in connection with the great exhibition in Copenhagen in the spring of 1893, where both Munch and Gauguin were represented, Munch asked Johan Rohde to write him "a little about Gauguin and the other pictures [sic] exhibited recently."[35] There is a possibility that the two men met during a short visit Munch made to Paris in June 1895. Molard, whom Munch must have known by that time, was in close touch with Gauguin right up to the day he left for Tahiti. Alternatively, Munch may have met Gauguin through Strindberg. Söderström believes that in the spring of 1895 Strindberg and Gauguin saw each other almost daily until they both left Paris, Strindberg in the middle of June and Gauguin at the end of the month.

There are several reasons for mentioning Gauguin in connection with "The Mirror." Both Munch and Gauguin took a creative and experimental approach to woodcut. Five of Munch's most important color woodcuts are included in "The Mirror," and, as mentioned earlier, he probably meant to include more. Four of these five woodcuts were done in Paris, where Munch associated daily with people intimately familiar with Gauguin's art.

The year 1896 was of critical importance to Munch as a graphic artist. His production that year was impressive. Schiefler has catalogued forty-five graphic works from 1896—seventeen etchings, twenty-three lithographs, and five woodcuts. In Munch's own notes and letters from 1896 he often mentions that he is working with lithography and etching, though oddly enough he makes no reference to woodcut. Munch's first woodcut, *Anxiety* (Sch. 62), which is included in "The Mirror," must have been done in Paris in the spring/summer of 1896. This woodcut, printed from a wooden block worked with a gouge, exists in several variants: black on white, dark red on white, and black and red on white. The copy in "The Mirror" is black with red hand coloring. Even in his earliest woodcuts Munch made use of a technique that he pioneered. By cutting one wooden block into several parts, inking the parts separately, then putting them back together like the pieces of a puzzle, he could print several colors at the same time. In fact Munch's color woodcuts were usually too complex to be done with a single block, but the puzzle technique was always his point of departure. *Man's Head in Woman's Hair*, one of his earliest color woodcuts, was printed from two wooden blocks, of which the one for color was divided into three parts.[36]

Gauguin's first woodcuts appear to have been done in France in 1893-1895, in the period between his first and his final visits to Tahiti, and were intended primarily as illustrations to *Noa Noa*.[37] Whether Gauguin's woodcuts were ever publicly exhibited in the 1890s is not known, and Maurice Malingue, in his book *Gauguin*, writes that the woodcuts were little known for the first quarter of this century. But Malingue also states that while Gauguin's woodcuts have had little influence in France, their influence has been all the greater in Scandinavia, through Edvard Munch.[38]

Munch had plenty of opportunities to see Gauguin's woodcuts during his stay in Paris. A number of different sources (among them Malingue and Marcel Guérin) indicate that before leaving for Tahiti for the last time, Gauguin gave a large number of woodcuts to his good neighbors the Molards.[39] Molard's grandson, Gilles Gérard-Arlberg, says something similar in his article "Nr. 6, rue Vercingétorix." Gauguin was almost like a member of the Molard family, Gérard-Arlberg writes, adding that after a time Gauguin ran out of space in his atelier and so "installed himself in my grandparents' apartment in order to make woodcuts."

In December 1894, Gauguin arranged an exhibit of his woodcuts and monotypes in his atelier at 6 Rue Vercingétorix, and Julien Leclercq wrote it up in *Le Mercure de France*. According to Richard S. Field, there is reason to believe that several of these prints were pasted onto gray cardboard.[40]

We know that Munch must have discussed his own graphic work with Molard, and it is clear from their correspondence that Molard assisted Munch with the practical details of getting his works printed. After Munch had returned to Norway, for example, he acted as intermediary between Munch and his printer, Lemercier. It would be remarkable if in the course of his many visits to the Molards Munch had never seen any of Gauguin's woodcuts. At the Molard's, too, he could have heard a first-hand account of the *way* Gauguin worked in wood.

In *L'Oeuvre gravé de Gauguin*, Marcel Guérin writes that among the woodcuts Gauguin left with the Molards were several important prints for *Noa Noa* that Gauguin had rejected in their first stage. The "Molard package" also appears to have contained woodcuts from blocks that Gauguin had done additional work on with his gouge after mak-ing a black-and-white print. He then made a number of proofs, using a second wooden block to which he added by hand various tones of oil paint.

It was to become one of Munch's main characteristics that he also worked his wooden blocks with a gouge. Another, as mentioned earlier, was that he printed many of his color woodcuts from two blocks—one for the drawing, and a second for the color.

Libuse Sýkorova has pointed out how little difference there often is between Gauguin's sculptural reliefs and his woodcut blocks, and gives examples of reliefs that he made by reworking woodcuts, among others, *Manao Tupupau*.[41] Several of Munch's wooden blocks, too, could easily stand as independent reliefs. In 1898, for the painting *Metabolism*, Munch made two reliefs in wood, one to be placed as an upper frame to the painting and one below. In addition to the fact that they suggest enlarged woodcut printing blocks, these two reliefs are closely related to works in "The Mirror." The relief at the lower edge of the painting has direct affinities to the lithograph *Metabolism*, while the other relief, *The Golden City*, is very similar to the lithograph *In the Land of Crystal*.

It is quite possible that Gauguin's text accompanying the prints in *Noa Noa* might have suggested to Munch the idea of using a similar approach in a publication of "The Mirror."

The history of *Noa Noa* is complicated and still uncertain, and the book has been published in several different versions. The first draft was done in the fall of 1893, its illustrations limited to a couple of loose sketches plus a woodcut as a cover design. The second existing manuscript—now in the Louvre—was copied by Gauguin before he left France in 1895 from a manuscript that he and the author, Charles Morice, had worked on together. In October and November 1897, *Noa Noa* was published by Morice in *La Revue blanche*, and in 1901 it appeared as a book, with both Gauguin's and Morice's names on the cover. When Gauguin copied the manuscript in 1895 he left several pages blank for poems that Morice was to fill in later. Obviously disappointed and displeased with Morice's publication of *Noa Noa* in *Revue blanche*, Gauguin began to fill these blank pages with poems of his own, as well as with woodcuts, drawings, and watercolors.[42]

Munch had returned to Norway by the time *Noa Noa* was published in *Revue blanche*—at about the same time, coincidentally, that "The Mirror" was on exhibit in Christiania, and while Delius and Leclercq were visiting Norway. But through William Molard, Munch must have been familiar with the plans for *Noa Noa* even earlier. It appears from a letter Gauguin wrote to Charles Morice in May 1896, that Gauguin had given Molard complete authority to represent his interests in connection with any publication of *Noa Noa*.[43]

Perhaps, too, Munch knew of Gauguin's further work on *Noa Noa* after its publication in *La Revue blanche*. In *Mutual Aid in the Arts*, Teddy Brunius writes that *Noa Noa* "as a poetic symbolistic effort stands as an important achievement, and when read in Gauguin's calligraphic manuscript it shows a synthesis of text and illustration."[44] This description would also fit Munch's "Tree of Knowledge," which includes a number of works from "The Mirror," several of them accompanied by Munch's own texts. Many of these texts must have been written in the nineties. Not only the literary content but also the visual form of the texts is interesting. Using capital letters, Munch often made use of different colors to emphasize the meaning of the words, in the same way that Strindberg, too, sometimes used different colors for different words on the same page. A good example from "The Tree of Knowledge" is the text to *Kiss:* THE KISS—TWO BURNING LIPS AGAINST MINE (written in red) HEAVEN AND (in blue) EARTH VANISH (in green) AND TWO (in brown) BLACK EYES LOOKED INTO MINE (in black).

Music—Words—Pictures

While in Paris, Munch must also have heard that *Noa Noa* was to be used as the basis for several other projects. Brunius writes that "Molard intended to use Noa Noa as a musical play." Lionel Carley mentions in his book on Delius that Charles Morice was planning to use Gauguin's narrative not only for the poems of *Noa Noa* but also as the basis for "a sort of lyric pantomime or ballet doré," and that Morice thought Molard the obvious composer for such a work.

The concept of a combination of pictures, words, and music also crops up in a letter from Munch to Delius in the summer of 1899. Munch asks Delius, then living in Paris, to give his regards to Molard, then goes on: "Why don't we work out our plans for that idea with engravings and music—and J. P. Jakobsen?" The letter indicates that Delius and Munch had discussed the possibility of such a collaboration earlier—perhaps during Delius's visit to Christiania in October 1897, just when "The Mirror" was on exhibit in the Diorama Hall.

Both Munch and Delius had long been interested in the works of the Danish writer Jens Peter Jacobsen. Delius put music to a number of Jacobsen's poems—several in 1897—and in 1908-1910 he wrote the opera *Fennimore and Gerda*, based on Jacobsen's best-known novel, *Niels Lyhne*. This novel, published in 1880, was widely read and admired by Munch's contemporaries, and we know that Munch was absorbed by it. The similarities between Jacobsen's writing and Munch's have been discussed in several articles.[45]

It is not unthinkable that the Gauguin/Molard/Morice project based on *Noa Noa* served as something of a model for the plan involving Munch's prints, Delius's music, and the words of J. P. Jacobsen. Nor is it unlikely that Munch's work on "The Mirror" provided an additional impulse toward a collaboration with Delius.

In the circles Munch moved in during the 1890s, an interest in literature went hand in hand with an interest in music. In Berlin, in 1892-1893, his closest friends were passionately devoted to music. Przybyszewski's piano interpretations of Chopin and Schumann were legendary. Przybyszewski's wife, the Norwegian-born Dagny Juell, had originally come to Berlin to study voice. Sigbjörn Obstfelder played the violin, and in the course of his short life was in evident doubt as to whether he should pursue music or poetry. Strindberg's "errand boy" at this time, the Swedo-Finnish writer Adolf Paul, was a close friend of Sibelius and studied music with Busoni during his stay in Berlin. Music plays an essential part in Strindberg's *Inferno*, where the writer feels he is being pursued by the music of Schumann's *Aufschwung*, played by "Popoffsky" (Przybyszewski), who he believes has come to Paris to murder him.

In Paris, in the circle that gathered at the Molards', music was the great common interest. Both Strindberg and Gauguin took part in the musical evenings; Strindberg played the guitar, Gauguin, who had a piano in his atelier, played the mandolin. We know little about Molard's own compositions, but in a letter to Munch in March 1898, he mentioned his own work. "I have written music to a play by Roinard called 'Les Miroirs' . . . I have looked upon it as an exercise in composing simply, on the theory that the music is to function as scenery, a sort of backdrop, before which the characteristic emotions of the play are to be portrayed."[46]

There is a fascinating resemblance between Molard's description of the way he wants the music to *Les Miroirs* (The Mirrors) to function and the effect Munch obtained in "The Mirror" by mounting his prints on neutral cardboard. The cardboard can be seen as a kind of backdrop, to use Molard's word, for the various emotions and moods the prints portray. For it is clear that Munch was often concerned with presenting his works against a common background that would help to bind together their different subject matter. A set of pho-

fig. 2 *Funeral March,* pencil, 1897, OKK T 392,
Munch-Museet, Oslo

tographs of an exhibit in Leipzig in 1903 shows how Munch hung "The Frieze of Life" on three walls of one room against a neutral background that extended as a unifying band from the first painting in the series to the last (see fig. 8 of Heller's article).

An interesting footnote to Molard's music for *Les Miroirs:* the young Maurice Ravel was one of the regular guests at the Molards' receptions and often joined in the entertainment by playing the piano. One of Ravel's important early piano compositions, from 1905, is called "Miroirs." Years later, composer Florent Schmidt is said to have told Molard's grandson, Gilles Gérard-Arlberg, that both Schmidt and Ravel were much influenced by Molard's musical theories.

Munch's pictures have often been described in musical terms. Strindberg begins his article in *La Revue blanche* by noting that someone has said it would be necessary to create music to Munch's pictures in order to explain them properly, but that while waiting for the composer he, Strindberg, would like to offer some comments of his own.[47]

Later in his life Munch likened his "Frieze of

Life"—made up of paintings in differing formats but with continuity of subject matter—to a symphony. As early as 1891 he wrote in a sketchbook note, "These pictures will, they must, be able to take hold more powerfully—first a few, then more, then all. Like many violins in a room, when one plays the tone to which the others are tuned, they all sound together."[48] Using music as an illustration, Munch was trying to describe the effect he felt when several of his works with related ideas were grouped together. By looking at one picture, one could grasp the basic tone that went through all.

Among the prints in "The Mirror" is a lithograph entitled *Funeral March.* It shows a pillarlike mass of people striving upward toward the sky. But the reward for their effort is death, for the top of their human pillar is crowned with a cadaver in a coffin. A pencil drawing (OKK T 392, fig. 2), a sketch for this lithograph, makes the picture's title explicit. In the foreground are a number of caricatured, bloated, masklike faces blowing on various musical instruments under the direction of a conductor whose deathly thin face bears Munch's own features.

Another central "musical" work from this period is *Self-Portrait with Lyre* (cat. no. 5) probably from 1896-1897, a work obviously related to several of the prints in "The Mirror," particularly those dealing with the transmutation of the flesh. This self-portrait may have been created as a result of the work Munch did on illustrations for Baudelaire's *Les Fleurs du mal* in the spring of 1896, as it has several important elements in common with a pencil sketch done for that project.

Illustrations *for* Les Fleurs du mal

In Paris during 1896-1897, where most of Munch's creative energy was devoted to graphics, he must quickly have discovered that graphic art was a medium well suited to a more literary and symbolic form of expression. Most of the subjects in "The Mirror" had been treated earlier as paintings. But "The Mirror" contains several new subjects as well. Graphic works such as *Man's Head in Woman's Hair, Lovers in Waves, The Urn, The Flower of Love, In the Land of Crystal, Funeral March,* and *Metabolism* are motifs that had not previously been treated as paintings. An important source for several of these motifs is to be found in Munch's work on the illustrations for Baudelaire's *Les Fleurs du mal.*

Charles Baudelaire was a great idol to the symbolists of the 1890s and was worshipped by the artists of the day especially for his doctrine of "correspondences." Munch must certainly have known Baudelaire's writing before he came to Paris in

1896. Baudelaire's poetry, with its constantly recurring themes of love and death and its fundamental emphasis on the cohesion between man and the universe, between the material and the spiritual, must, for Munch, have been a very nearly ideal source of inspiration. His work on the Baudelaire illustrations took place at the time when the friendship between Munch and Strindberg was at its height, and the occult, mystical, and sometimes demonic quality of Baudelaire's verse was undoubtedly the subject of discussion between them.

It was in April 1896, that Munch was commissioned by La Société des Cents Bibliophiles to do several illustrations for a planned collector's edition of *Les Fleurs du mal*. Not long after it was decided which poems Munch was to illustrate, namely, "Une Charogne" and "Le Mort Joyeux," the president of Les Cents Bibliophiles, Monsieur Piat, died, and the project was canceled.[49] Nevertheless, Munch did a number of preliminary sketches for these poems. Of particular significance is a little sketchbook in the Munch Museum (OKK T 130) which also contains notes on the project and on the death of Monsieur Piat, which made a deep impression on Munch. The sketchbook contains, for example, an account of an imaginary conversation with M. Piat in which Munch asks him what he thought when the doctor told him he was going to die. "There was a rustling before my eyes," the dying man answers. "I saw pale faces around me." Just so had Munch experienced the approach of death in bouts of fever delirium when he was young, and just so had he given it pictorial expression in any number of drawings and studies.

It is quite likely that M. Piat's death contributed to the fact that Munch now again took up important death motifs in his work, as in the lithographs *Death in the Sickroom* and *By the Deathbed*, both of them included in "The Mirror."

The poems "Une Charogne" and "Le Mort Joyeux" possess ideas and a mood that must have appealed strongly to Munch's pictorial imagination. To judge from Munch's own notes in sketchbook T 130, he himself had a hand in the choice of these two poems. Both deal with death, and "Une Charogne" in particular includes thoughts that Munch must have found consistent with his own ideas about life, death, and what occurs after death. But, as Gösta Svenaeus has pointed out, this poem can also be viewed as a love poem.[50] At the same time, it is also a poem about art and the special relationship of the artist to other human beings. The poem begins with a description of a cadaver lying by the side of a road in a state of advanced decay, and the recumbent position of the corpse is likened to the recumbent

fig. 3 Sketchbook page, OKK T 130, Munch-Museet, Oslo

posture of a lascivious woman. In this same way, says the poet to his beloved, she too, despite all her present youth and beauty, will one day be reduced to bone and rotting flesh. But he, the poet, has the consolation of knowing that when they are both reduced to dust his art will survive. And thus the poet, through his work, has immortalized the divine essence of his beloved in a manner that neither death nor decay can assail.

It is astonishing to see how literally Munch has followed Baudelaire's text in some cases. Svenaeus makes the same point and notes that Munch incorporated certain pictorial elements from the Charogne sketches into his lithographs *The Urn* and *The Flower of Love*.

The Urn is pasted into "The Tree of Knowledge" on page 49, to which Munch has added a covering text with the explanatory title, "THE URN–REBIRTH." The theme of rebirth is central to "Une Charogne," especially to stanza three. In a close paraphrase of this stanza, Munch wrote of "Une Charogne" in sketchbook T 130, "Man fertilizes the earth—as he decays—and thereby gives nourishment to new life—." Here Munch returns to a train of thought which had occupied him for years and which he had expressed in several notes from an earlier visit to Paris in 1891-1892.

The lithograph *The Flower of Love,* which is also a treatment of nature's capacity for renewal, has clear antecedents in one of the sketches for "Une Charogne" (OKK T 403). The top of the sketch shows the upper half of a naked couple, embracing, surrounded by blossoming plants, while the lower part of the picture depicts the head and torso of a dead body.

Sketchbook T 130 includes another sketch for "Une Charogne" that is particularly interesting for the pictorial elements it contains of another important motif for Munch—the artist who creates in passion and in pain (fig. 3). Like the other sketches for "Une Charogne," it is divided into two strata: the upper represents life—including resurrected life—while the lower is a picture of death and decay. The poem was meant to be incorporated into the drawings—space has been set aside for several stanzas in the lower right-hand corner of each sketch. In the drawing in question, the lower field—the "underworld"—shows an old man grasping a stringed instrument. A clothed feminine figure stands over him, her upper body above the earth, while her urn-shaped lower body is in the lower stratum, below the earth. To the left of the woman's head is a picture frame without a picture, i.e., *la toile oubliée*—the forgotten canvas, as it is called in "Une Charogne." Stanza seven of the poem is about "the strange music" that is heard from the underworld, while stanza eight describes how forms are slowly obliterated only to rise again on "the forgotten canvas," drawn from the artist's memory.

It seems clear that these two stanzas had special significance for Munch. Only when the dead body in the underworld, in Munch's drawing represented by the old man holding the instrument, has decomposed utterly can the picture on the canvas slowly begin to emerge. The untouched canvas in Munch's sketch is a picture of a future work of art and becomes, in this context, a symbol of rebirth.

The old man with the stringed instrument—Munch's memory of Monsieur Piat?—immediately suggests the Orpheus theme. This sketch must be considered an important forerunner to *Self-Portrait with Lyre,* which treats this same subject—the artist

fig. 4 *Garden Sculpture,* OKK T 383, Munch-Museet, Oslo

who creates in pain, sacrificing his own life to create new life.

The illustration commission from Les Cents Bibliophiles also gave Munch an excellent opportunity to become better acquainted with Baudelaire's poetry. In his personal copy of *Les Fleurs du mal*—an 1894 edition—Munch has marked a cross or written the word "avec" by several of the poems, including, for example, "La Fontaine du Sang" and "Femmes Damnées." This indicates that these poems were included in the discussion of which poems Munch was to illustrate. The last two stanzas of "Femmes Damnées" are without question directly related to Munch's lithograph *The Urn.* The urn in the first state of this lithograph is decorated with what Schiefler describes as a "demonic frieze." "O vierges, ô demons, ô monstres, ô martyres" reads the next to last stanza, and some of the female figures in *The Urn* appear to be monsters, others to be martyrs. The female head that looms above the urn is another reminder of the rebirth motif. Or, as Munch noted after the title of this lithograph in "The Tree of Knowledge," "Up from the filth rose a face full of sadness and beauty."

In "La Fontaine du Sang," the poet likens his own blood, racing wildly through his veins, to the rhythmical sobbing of a fountain. In vain he runs his hands over his body to find the place where he is wounded. This "Fountain of Blood" may have given Munch material for a number of drawings on the general subject of "the artist who creates in pain," among them *The Flower of Pain,* which is a central work. Some of these drawings (e.g., OKK T 383, 384) depict a garden statue, the distorted, suffering torso of a man. In OKK T 383 (fig. 4) the man's hands are behind his back, as if bound, while a woman leans over his naked body with one arm tightly around his neck. This drawing also has affinities to *Salome Paraphrase* (cat. no. 7), to *Vampire*, and to *Man's Head in Woman's Hair*.

Apparently Munch drew inspiration and ideas from Baudelaire's poetry for other works in "The Mirror" as well. The poem "La Mort des Pauvres" (Death of the Paupers) contains pictorial descriptions that agree surprisingly well with Munch's picture of the "crystal land" in the lithograph of that name. *In the Land of Crystal* can be seen as a synthesis of the lithographs *Funeral March* and *Metabolism* (the latter of course a direct result of Munch's work on "Une Charogne"), for this lithograph contains a coffin lifted upward by human bodies—a direct association to *Funeral March*—as well as cadavers in the earth—a variation of the transmutation theme.

Several of the new graphic works in "The Mirror"—*In the Land of Crystal, Funeral March, Metabolism*, all from 1897, and *The Urn* and *The Flower of Love*, from 1896—contain important ideas that cropped up again in 1898 in the large painting *Metabolism* (OKK M 419, cat. no. 46), at least in the form in which that painting was originally exhibited, with carved wood reliefs at its upper and lower edges and, in the center of the painting, in the trunk of a tree, Munch had painted a fetus in a plant. (He later reworked it and removed the fetus and the wood reliefs.) Here also we find the seed of a new motif in Munch's art—the fertility theme. This motif began to take shape about 1898 (see, for instance, the woodcut *Fertility*, Sch. 110) and is a logical consequence of Munch's reflections on death and rebirth.

In 1918, when Munch published his small volume *The Frieze of Life*, he said of the painting *Metabolism:*

> The Frieze was planned as a poem on life, on love and death. The theme of the largest picture, of the two people, the man and woman in the forest, is perhaps somewhat unrelated to the ideas expressed in the other paintings, but it is as necessary to the Frieze as a whole as the buckle is to the belt. It is the picture of life drawing sustenance from the dead, and of the city growing up behind the crowns of the trees. It is the picture of life's power to endure.

The encounter with Baudelaire's poetry stimulated Munch's own attempts to discover a meaning to life and an answer to the question of what comes after death. At the same time that the *Fleurs du mal* sketches obeyed known harmonies in Munch's art, the Cents Bibliophiles commission also suggested a number of new graphic themes that came to be of the greatest importance to the formation of "The Mirror" as it was exhibited in the fall of 1897.

"The Mirror" must be regarded first of all as a highly personal document, a private frieze of life with relevance primarily to Munch's own situation as a human being and an artist. He emphasizes this by beginning the series with works on transmutation and death. His own early confrontations with sickness and death—as well as with a "symbolic death" in the sense of renouncing a normal family life—were for Munch the necessary preconditions for artistic creativity. Through his art, Munch meant to create new life.

In "The Mirror" Munch was trying to explain to himself "life and its meaning," for only after having found some clarification of his own life could he go on and "help others to elucidate theirs." This was precisely what he meant to do in "The Frieze of Life" as it later was presented in painting. "The Frieze of Life" includes all the principal themes of "The Mirror," but in a different order, an order that placed the pictures in a less private and more universal context.

Judith

There are a number of unsolved problems still associated with "The Mirror." It is not known to whom it belonged prior to its acquisition by Dr. Stinnes. When the late Norwegian collector who bought these prints in the 1930s showed them to Munch, he was told that the prints belong to "The Mirror," that they had been exhibited once long ago, and that he, Munch, had given them to a mistress in Normandy.[51]

From the evidence presented thus far, one can assume it most likely that the KB prints were part of the original "Mirror" as presented in the Diorama Hall in 1897. And there is no good reason to dismiss Munch's statement that he gave the prints to a mistress in Normandy, even if we do know that he was fond of saying things merely to shock his listeners.

If we are to look for clues to "The Mirror's" early history it seems natural to begin the search in Paris, where most of the series was done. By the same token, it seems natural to look a little more closely at the title print, *The Mirror* (that is, *Man's Head in Woman's Hair*), one of the first woodcuts Munch executed in Paris in 1896.

The soft profile of a young woman leaning over a man's head seen full face, together against a deep red background, is clearly a Salome motif. The man's head, surrounded by the woman's long red-blond hair, has many similarities to the man's head in *Self-Portrait with Skeleton Arm* (cat. no. 120) of 1895 and to the crayon drawing of Przybyszewski (OKK M 618), done in 1893-1894, in which a masklike head seems to float above two crossed skeletal arms.

fig. 5 *Salome*, 1903, OKK G/1 256-5, Munch-Museet, Oslo

fig. 6 *Salome II*, 1905, OKK G/r 107-20, Munch-Museet, Oslo

In *Inferno* Strindberg refers to this portrait of Przybyszewski as the picture with the "severed head," and he asks Munch where he got the idea for "that decapitation."[52] There is an ink drawing (OKK T 369) of a mournful male face with a mustache. Above it, a woman bends over the man, her face hidden by her hair, which falls beside the man's head. The woman's hands are clasped tightly around the man's throat. The entire background of this ink drawing is painted a deep red, very close to the background red in the title print of "The Mirror." This drawing has clear affinities with both *Man's Head in Woman's Hair* and the 1898 woodcut *Salome Paraphrase* (Sch. 109), which helps to clarify *Man's Head in Woman's Hair* as a Salome motif.

Over the years, Munch did several works on the Salome theme, based on various personal experiences. The 1903 lithograph *Salome* (fig. 5, Sch. 213) is a portrait of Eva Mudocci and Edvard Munch, his pale face framed by her dark hair, and was done during a period of continual contact and close friendship between them. The etching *Salome II* (fig. 6, Sch. 223) as well as another variation of the Salome theme, the etching *Ghosts* (fig. 7, Sch. 224),

fig. 7 *Ghosts*, 1905, OKK G/r 108-4, Munch-Museet, Oslo

were executed in 1905 and are both caricature depictions of Tulla Larsen and a suffering Edvard Munch, whose relationship had ended several years before.

What earlier sources are there for the title print of "The Mirror," *Man's Head in Woman's Hair*, executed during Munch's Paris sojourn of 1896-1897? One name stands out: Ida Molard's daughter, and William Molard's stepdaughter, Judith. The very name has associations to the biblical story of Judith and Holofernes. There is no doubt that Munch knew this "pretty Judith"—as her girlhood friend Gerda Kjellberg later called her—who was always present at the Molards' weekly receptions.

Judith's mother, Ida Ericson Molard, had had an affair as a young woman with the Swedish opera singer Fritz Arlberg. The result was Judith, born in Stockholm February 17, 1881. She matured quickly, both physically an intellectually, and when still very young had an "unusually well-developed taste for literature, music, and painting," according to a letter of her mother's to Ellen Key, the Swedish writer and feminist.[53] She had artistic talent, and in the nineties she studied with Eugene Carrière, among others. In the first years of this century her paintings were often included in the Salon d'Automne.

Judith's real father, whom she had not seen since she was a little girl, always remained a shining ideal for her, which complicated her relations with her kind-hearted stepfather, William Molard. Gerda Kjellberg, who returned to Sweden and became a doctor, got to know Judith in Paris in the 1890s when they were both still girls. In the chapter about the Molard family in her book *Hänt och sant* (Events), she tells how Judith, to compensate for the parental love she believed she had missed, first transferred her need for love to her teacher, a certain Monsieur Floquet. Then, after his death, Paul Gauguin came into her life. A remarkable, erotically charged relationship developed between the middle-aged painter and the very young Judith. Judith herself has written about it in an autobiographical sketch, "La petite fille et le tupapau," which was published in part in Gerda Kjellberg's book.[54] Judith's account also contains some interesting thoughts on Gauguin's art, as well as colorful descriptions of artists she met both at home and at Gauguin's. The evening before Gauguin left for Tahiti for the last time, he took Judith to the theater; the next morning, Judith, along with her family, went with him to the railway station. She describes the immense sorrow and despair she felt when Gauguin had gone. A year and a half later, probably around the New Year 1897, she became engaged, and in December 1902, she married Edouard Gérard, *secrétaire général* by profession, born in Paris in 1872.

Who was Edouard Gérard? A person by this name signed the foreword to the catalogue for Munch's 1897 exhibit in the Diorama Hall. Originally, however, this article had been written in connection with Munch's participation in the Salon des Indépendants in the spring of 1897 and was published in *La Press* in May that year. Munch must have set great store by the article, for he had it printed again on other occasions later in his life.

The Edouard Gérard who wrote it was probably not a professional art critic; his name is not to be found in the indices to French art journals for the late 1890s. In discussing Munch's work, Gérard at one point mentions his own "dilettante's eye," and in another place he writes that one must "know him oneself in order to understand fully how deeply the dramas he unfolds are felt." William Molard concludes his letter to Munch in March 1898, with greetings from Ida and Judith, who "hopes that you will soon come down to visit us," and adds, "Gérard has left us, he has been hired by the Prefect in Toulouse." In a letter to Ellen Key in 1903, Ida Molard describes Judith's husband as "a great art-lover." In light of all this evidence, it seems reasonable to assume that the Edouard Gérard who wrote the article was the same Edouard Gérard whom Judith married in 1902.

By all indications, Munch was an eager visitor at the Molards' from the moment he arrived in Paris in February 1896. So he got to know Judith before she became engaged to Edouard Gérard and at a time when the memory of Gauguin was still fresh but the loss no longer intense. As far as we know, the name Judith occurs only once in Munch's copious notes. On the other hand, this single mention does occur under dramatic circumstances, in a letter written immediately before his admission to the nerve clinic in Copenhagen in the fall of 1908. "I sit here burning out my nerves with whisky," he begins the letter from Gothenburg to his good friend the lawyer Harald Nörregaard, "postponing this ghastly half suicide of committing myself to the sanatorium in Hornbaek—which I feel is my duty—since I must either do so or burn my nerves entirely—out—." He goes on to relate how a few days earlier he ran into the sculptor Stockenström and the two of them went to a restaurant together in Gothenburg. (Albert Stockenström was also in Paris in the 1890s, where he often attended the gatherings at the Molards'. Strindberg was a great admirer of his work—he appears in *Inferno* as the sculptor who sees visions.) The letter, which is unfinished and was never sent, ends with an account of how Munch left the restaurant without Stockenström, whereupon, he writes, "[I stand outside] looking delirious and miserable and say Judith—Judith her fault—she was Molard's daughter—whom you know—And then there was the Göta Canal—and finally—But in actual fact I was thrown out—."

But what was Judith's fault? Can the meeting with Stockenström have awakened special memories of Paris, and hence of Judith? Why do we find the name Judith only once among Munch's numerous notes, considering that that one occurrence suggests an experience of no ordinary kind? Can Munch have written about her or referred to her in his notes by some other name?

The White Cat

There is a distinct possibility that Judith is concealed behind the appelation "the white cat," a pet name Munch evidently used in describing a woman he knew in Paris.

Late in 1903 or early in 1904 Munch wrote to Delius that he was planning to come to Paris in the near future. He mentions Delius's recent marriage to Jelka Rosen, and adds that he himself remains "a free man," that he is enjoying "perpetual springtime with the enemy—woman," and that he is seeing a great deal of Eva Mudocci and fears that he is on the verge of falling in love. But after his affair with "T" (Tulla Larsen), he says, he has become insanely apprehensive. He then asks Delius to write, but not anything about "the white cat, say nothing on that subject." Since the white cat is mentioned in the same breath with Tulla Larsen and Eva Mudocci, it seems natural to suppose that she was a woman to whom Munch had been very close, a woman from the Paris milieu where Munch and Delius had friends in common.

Letters from Munch to his family indicate that he had a white cat at his Paris studio at 32 Rue de la Santé, where he lived from about the beginning of March until the end of December, 1896. Munch also wrote a couple of longer autobiographical notes— one called "The Cat," the other, "The White Cat"— about his efforts to tame this animal, which a friend had given him. At one point he writes, "It had anxious, questioning eyes—the eyes of a human being—and I was almost afraid of its gaze." At another point, he writes, "One day I was working with a female model—a little Parisienne, very lithe and supple—when suddenly I see the cat steal up to her white body, purring and affectionate—They were like two people, or two cats."[55]

In another autobiographical note Munch writes of being with a woman and remembers "the white cat that gazed at us—as it were, straight into our souls." He compares the eyes of the woman with those of the cat, and he continues, "I have seen many

fig. 8 *The Cat,* 1897, OKK G/r 49-15, Munch-Museet, Oslo

women with thousands of changing expressions— like a crystal. But never have I met another who so clearly had just three—though forceful. . . . And this is entirely my picture of the three women. You remember what Dr. R said about my study of one of them. . . ." The Dr. R Munch refers to here can hardly be anyone but the poet and physician Marcel Réja, who was very much a member of the Molard circle and must have been one of Munch's close friends during his time in Paris. But the woman Munch likens to the white cat, the woman with the three facial expressions, can this woman be Judith? In a letter to Ellen Key from May 1897, Judith's mother mentions that she has earlier sent a few photographs of her daughter, and writes that "now you have a third . . . so you can put together an impression of what the child looks like." The photograph shows an attractive young blond woman with a vague likeness to Tulla Larsen but with a slightly

heavier expression, softer in the eyes and rounder in the face.

Munch did a number of works in Paris using a rather young girl as his model. Can Judith have been the model, or the inspiration, for these works, which include the title print for "The Mirror?" In 1897 Munch did an etching entitled *The Cat* (fig. 8, Sch. 89), which is clearly a Salome motif: a young, naked woman lies in a strange, twisted position holding in her outstretched hands the head of a man with a mustache. At the lower edge is the silhouette of a cat. But in 1896 in particular Munch seems to have made frequent use of a young girl as his model. *Girl with Heart* (Sch. 48) was done that year as an etching. There is a sketch (fig. 9, OKK T 371) that suggests that both *Girl with Heart* and *The Urn* sprang in part from the same train of thought. There are two drawings on the same piece of paper. One shows a young nude woman standing beside and looking down into an urn from which smoke is rising. On the foot of the urn is the face of a suffering man. The other drawing on the sheet shows a girl—the same type as in *The Urn*—sitting in a field of flowers holding in her hands a heart from which blood is dripping to the ground. In *Self-Portrait with Lyre,* which must have been done at about the same time, the artist's instrument is blood red and surrounds him on three sides, ending in an arrowlike projection right before his heart. This self-portrait,

too, has a red frame around three sides—reminiscent of several versions of the lithograph *Madonna,* the woman who creates new life through pain. At the upper and lower edges of the self-portrait is a zig-zag border much like the frame to Munch's lithograph of Strindberg, which was done before July 1, 1896.

Somewhat earlier we mentioned the Orpheus myth in connection with *Self-Portrait with Lyre.* In the fall of 1896, in a letter to a friend, Strindberg made an interesting response to a newspaper report that he had been driven from Paris by women—the paper had compared the episode to Orpheus being torn to pieces by the maenads. The women's hatred for him, Strindberg said, had been caused by his own article in *La Revue blanche*—"the article dealt with Munch's women pictures, and Orpheus and the maenads were mentioned."[56] Neither Orpheus nor the maenads were mentioned by Strindberg in this article, which was about Munch's exhibit at the Bing gallery, so Strindberg's statement in the letter is erroneous. But Strindberg was working on this article at about the same time that Munch was working on the Baudelaire illustrations.[57] Munch's Baudelaire commission was undoubtedly a source of discussion between Munch and Strindberg, and it would have been natural to talk about the Orpheus myth. As a parallel to Strindberg's remark in his letter about Munch's "women pictures" and Orpheus being torn to pieces by the maenads, there is a note of Munch's from September 1896: "I have never really loved—I have only felt the passion that moves mountains and alters people—the love that tears coils from the heart and drinks blood."[58]

In 1896 or 1897, Munch did a drawing in the form of a triptych (OKK T 337) that has a separation motif as its central element, while the left field is a variant of *Girl with Heart* and the right is a Salome motif—*Salome Paraphrase*—in which the man's head, full front, is surrounded by a woman's hair and trapped by her hands. From this work and from other drawings, it seems clear that *Man's Head in Woman's Hair* must be closely related to *Girl with Heart* and *Separation,* to *Salome Paraphrase* and to the vampire theme. An autobiographical note from the nineties contains elements of all these themes:

A deep purple darkness descended over all the earth—I sat beneath a tree—whose leaves were beginning to yellow and wither—She had sat down beside me—she had bent her head over me—her blood-red hair had entangled me—had twined itself about me like blood-red serpents—its finest threads had worked itself into my heart—then she rose—I do not know why—and moved slowly away toward the sea—farther and farther away—then came a strange feeling—as if there were invisible threads between us—I felt as if invisible threads of her hair were still twisted around me—and so when she had disappeared completely across the sea—I still felt the pain where my heart bled—because the threads would not break.[59]

Man's Head in Woman's Hair is also closely related to *Jealousy.* The same pale, staring, triangular male face with its mustache appears in both works. *Jealousy* is also closely related to the anxiety theme. The title "The Mirror," consequently, is a logical one for *Man's Head in Woman's Hair,* for this print, perhaps more than any other, *reflects* a number of themes from "The Frieze of Life." There is a text from "The Tree of Knowledge" that underlines the numerous interpretations this one work is open to.

A mysterious look of jealousy
in these two piercing eyes
are concentrated as
in a crystal many reflected
images. The look is
curious searching
hateful and love
filled—an essence
of her who they
all have in common.

Over this whole note Munch has drawn faint, triangular, masklike faces with dark, "piercing" eyes.

Although we cannot say for certain, there is a possibility that Munch presented at least twelve of the prints from "The Mirror"—the KB series—to Judith Molard Gérard. When this presentation might have taken place is difficult to say. France,

and Paris in particular, was a frequent goal for Munch during his hectic traveling activity in the years following 1897.

Numerous attempts to make contact with her family have been unsuccessful. Nevertheless we do know that she was in possession of a large collection of art works from the circle around the Molards, including several works by Gauguin (among them a portrait of her stepfather, William Molard, painted on the back of Gauguin's *Self-Portrait with Hat*). She herself was not only a capable painter but also a graphic artist. We also know that later in her life Judith Molard Gérard lived "among the yokels," as Gerda Kjellberg put it, more particularly, in Ballancourt, Seine-et-Oise, which shares borders with Normandy.[60] The Norwegian Munch, perhaps without an exact knowledge of the geography of France, might have been likely, in a later account, to place Ballancourt in the more well-known Normandy. Judith Molard Gérard died in the 1950s.

There is also the possibility that Judith might have been the model for the young woman in "The Mirror." There is, however, little doubt that Munch considered the "Mirror" series to be one of the principal parts of the 1897 exhibit in the Diorama Hall. The posters Munch had made for this exhibit consisted of a lithographic variant of *Man's Head in Woman's Hair* (not registered by Schiefler), printed in red, green, black, and gold and to a great degree consistent with the title print of "The Mirror," where the background is also red and where Munch painted the woman's hair with red and gold.

It seems appropriate to conclude these thoughts on "The Mirror" by quoting the last few lines of Edouard Gérard's remarks on Munch as they appeared in foreword to the 1897 catalogue.

Munch is one of ours, and this explains the powerful impression his art produces in everyone who once allows himself to feel its effect. The passion that vibrates through his works like a fever reveals the vast compassion Munch feels for the pain of life. One of his works is called *Anxiety.* But this particular title is not really necessary and indeed commends itself not alone to this one print. For fear is everywhere in Munch, in everything that comes from his hand, fear of what we know and fear of what awaits us, the universal dread that has never been stronger and more animate than at the present moment. It is this fear that we find in all of Munch's works, in the uncertain, questioning eyes that are raised to us in anticipation of an answer. Few pictures seem more terrible to me than this pale man's face with its staring eyes gone rigid in their hollows out of dread for the unknown. Here is a symbolic portrayal of Jealousy, pictured in all its horror, ruled by the desire we all nourish to have what we cannot have and what thus enslaves us, a desire that is only intensified by our feeling powerless to win its object—be it a beloved creature or a chimera.

Translated from the Norwegian by Thomas Teal

NOTES

1. The quote is from sketchbook OKK T 186.

2. This letter is reproduced in facsimile in its entirety in Ingrid Langaard, *Edvard Munch Modningsår* (Oslo, 1960), 192-193.

3. The so-called Meier-Graefe Portfolio was published in an edition of sixty-five copies in Berlin, June 1895, with explanatory text by Julius Meier-Graefe. The portfolio contained eight etchings: Sch. 5, 7, 10, 12, 13, 15, 20, and 27.

4. Undated letter from Munch to Mrs. Valborg Hammer. The letter was written from "rue de la Sante 32" and must be from September 1896.

5. Catalogue: *Edvard Munch Maleriudstilling i Dioramalokalet, Karl Johans Gd. 41*, n.d.

6. Reinhold Heller, "Edvard Munch and the Clarification of Life," *Allen Memorial Art Museum Bulletin*, 29, no. 3 (Spring, 1972): 124. (The catalogue of The Epstein Collection.)

7. In exh. cat. *Edvard Munch and Czech Art*, Munch-museet, February 27-April 30, 1971, pp. 9-12 is a discussion of the fact that Munch's exhibition catalogues are often incomplete.

8. Frits Lugt, *Les Marques de collections de dessins & d'estampes, supplément* (Hague, 1956), 193.

9. Olav Krohn's drawing from *Tyrihans*, 1895, is reproduced in Christian Gierløff, *Edvard Munch selv* (Oslo, 1953), 99.

10. In this letter, which begins "Lieber Freund," Munch writes that he has sold the portrait of Hans Jæger to the National Gallery. On the 18th of November, 1897, Munch offered the National Gallery in Oslo four portraits for a total price of 2,200 Norwegian crowns. Only the portrait of Jæger was purchased, for 1,000 crowns.

11. The Munch Museum has a copy of the color woodcut *Girl with Heart* (Sch. 134, OKK G/t 602-2) and of the color woodcut *Meeting in Space* (Sch. 135, OKK G/t 603-1), both of which have been mounted in much the same way as the KB series. The prints have been cut and pasted onto somewhat larger pieces of dark brown cardboard, with the signature "Edvard Munch" on the cardboard in pencil. Both the color and the dimensions of these cardboards are, however, clearly distinct from the cardboards on which the KB prints are mounted.
Cardboard dimensions, *Girl with Heart*: 69.5 x 60.8
Cardboard dimensions, *Meeting in Space*: 69.4 x 63.8
Size of portfolio cover OKK G/t 569-11: 71.7 x 62.5

12. In exh. cat. *Farge på Trykk* (Color in Print), Munch-museet catalogue no. 5, 1968: 26.

13. See Alf Hellevik, *Kongsspegelen*, 5th ed. (Oslo, 1965), Introduction, and the article "Kongespeilet" in *Ashehougs konversasjonsleksikon*, *11*, 1973: 484.

14. OKK N 45.

15. This undated letter to his aunt is not included in *Edvard Munchs Brev. Familien* (Oslo, 1949). He also writes in this letter, "I have moved and live now in a hotel in the Rue de Seine." He must have moved from 32 Rue de la Santé to 60 Rue de Seine after the 20th of December, 1896, because in a letter to the Libre Esthétique in Brussels dated December 20, 1896, he gives his address as 32 Rue de la Santé.

16. Gustav Schiefler, *Meine Graphik-Sammlung* (Hamburg, 1927), 34. New enlarged edition by Gerhard Schack, Hamburg, 1974.

17. It is also interesting to note that later in his life, when Munch was referring (to Dr. Hoppe) to his own texts for his pictures as "poems in prose," he also characterized some of Strindberg's descriptions of Munch's work, in the famous article

in *La Revue blanche*, June 1, 1896, as "poems in prose." See Göran Söderström, *Strindberg och bildkonsten* (Strindberg and the visual arts) (Uddevalla, 1972), 400. Söderström cites a letter from Munch to Ragnar Hoppe of May 5, 1929, in which Munch wrote that Strindberg's article on his work contains "poems in prose to the pictures The Scream, Vampire, The Kiss, Loving Woman, and Jealousy. . . ."

18. In an undated letter from the spring of 1898, Munch refers to Dauthendey's book *Die Schwarze Sonne* (The Black Sun), which was published in the same volume with *Phallus* in 1897. A well-used copy in Munch's library bears the dedication "Freundliche Grüsse von M. D'Authendey, Mexico 1. Dez. 1897" (Friendly Greetings from M. etc.). Of *Die Schwarze Sonne*, Munch writes, "Many of the moods are remarkably similar to my dreams—and death pictures—and I understand it very well—." Together with Gustaf Uddgren, Max Dauthendey (1867-1918) published a little book called *Verdensaltet, Det nye sublime i kunsten* (The Universe, The New Sublimity in Art), Copenhagen, 1893, where (p. 33) the authors describe what they call "the intimate art," a new art form that sought the application of all the senses: "Tone—Farve—Lugt—Smags—og Følesansen" (the senses of hearing, sight, smell, taste, and touch). See also H. G. Wendt, *Max Dauthendey, Poet-Philosopher* (New York: Columbia University Press, 1936).

19. Torsten Eklund, ed., *August Strindbergs brev* (August Strindberg's letters) (Stockholm, 1948-1972), *12*: no. 3620. The letter is undated, but the editor supposes it to have been written about August 19, 1897.

20. Natanson's article on Munch appeared in *La Revue blanche*, no. 59, Nov. 1895. In *La Revue blanche*, no. 60, Dec. 1895, in which *The Scream* is reproduced, Natanson writes that Munch's text to the print "est un de ces petits poèmes que M. Munch a l'habitude de joindre à ses compositions. Il constitue donc un document à l'appui de ce que nous disions des préoccupations littéraires du peintre norvégien" (p. 528). Beneath the reproduction of *The Scream* stands the following text by Munch: "M'arrêtant, je m'appuyai à la balustrade, presque mort de fatigue. Au-dessus du fjord bleu noir pendaient des nuages, rouges comme du sang et comme des langues de feu. Mes amis s'éloignaient, et, seul, tremblant d'angoisse, je pris conscience du grand cri infini de la nature.—E. M."

21. Fritz Hermann, "Die Revue Blanche und die Nabis" (Munich, 1959), 83 (doctoral dissertation).

22. *Edvard Munchs brev. Familien*, no. 154.

23. See Stockholm, Nationalmuseum: exh. cat., *Höjdpunkter i norsk konst* (High Points in Norwegian Art), Sept. 19-Dec. 8, 1968, no. 250, and The University of Houston, the Sarah Campbell Blaffer Gallery: exh. cat., *Edvard Munch*, April 9-May 23, 1976, no. 32.

24. In the catalogue for *La Quatrième Exposition à Bruxelles*, at La Libre Esthétique, Brussels, Feb. 25-Apr. 1, 1897, Vollard's album *Les Peintres-Graveurs* is listed as catalogue numbers 516-37, "Album de 22 estampes originales tirés à 100 exemplaires numerotées et signées." The lithograph *Anxiety* is listed as "Le Soir (bois en deux couleurs)."

25. Ambroise Vollard, *Souvenirs d'un marchand de tableux* (Paris, 1959), 278.

26. In an undated draft of a letter written in the late nineties to the Danish art dealer Kleis, Munch proposes an exhibit of "the paintings of the last 4 years." This will involve "some 25 larger pictures plus about 50 graphic works," and he mentions that they have previously been exhibited at, among others, "Bing, L'Art Nouveau" in Paris. The exhibit at Bing's opened on the 19th or 20th of May, 1896. The reviewer for the newspaper *Soir*

concludes his notice of May 20 as follows: "If Mr. Munch desires to be an artist, then he must refrain from painting frames in garish colors like the one he has done for his 'Madonna,' it would be less pretentious and we would not have to be embarrassed to go look at it."

27. The manuscript, of 362 pages, was found at the Anatomical Institute in Oslo, August 1973. Page 74 was missing. On the find and its background, see Sverre Flugsrud, "En dåres försvarstal. Et Strindberg-manuskript på vandring," *Nordisk Tidsskrift, 3* (1974): 125-137. In the fall of 1974, page 74 of this manuscript was found among Munch's unidentified papers at the Munch Museum.

28. In a letter to Torsten Hedlund, Sept. 1896, Strindberg mentions the possibility of sticking to *Inferno* as an illustrated manuscript, "the ideal form for an occult publication." (*August Strindbergs brev, 11,* no. 3374.) The catalogue *Berömda Strindbergsmanuskript* (Famous Strindberg Manuscripts), an exhibit at the Strindberg Museum, Stockholm, 1974, describes an uncompleted draft of a manuscript for *Inferno I* (catalogue number 6a) as painstakingly done in calligraphic script, with initials in colored pencil, one red, one blue, one green. The title page has different words alternating in red, blue, and green. Compare Munch's use of color in the texts in "The Tree of Knowledge."

29. August Strindberg, *Inferno* (Strindberg i Aldus, Lund, 1962), 53-54.

30. *Henry D. Davray* was on the staff of *Le Mercure de France* and was especially occupied with translations into French. In a letter to Munch dated Aug. 14, 1897, and written on the stationery of *Le Mercure de France,* Davray writes that they all hope to see Munch in their midst again soon and sends special greetings from Rambosson and Réja (Meunier).

Yvanhoé Rambosson (born 1872), French symbolist poet and art critic. Published poetry collections *Le Verger doré* (1895), *La Forêt magique* (1898), *Actes* (1900), among others. (See also Ernest Raynaud, *La Mêlée symboliste 1890-1900, 2,* Paris, 1920.) In an article in *La Plume,* May 15, 1897, he wrote about Munch's paintings in Le Salon des Indépendants that spring and characterized them as the most interesting works in The Salon.

Marcel Réja, pseudonym of Paul Meunier (see Henry Coston, *Dictionnaire des pseudonymes, 2,* Paris, 1969), French doctor and poet. Associated with the circle around *Le Mercure de France,* which published his books of collected poems. In 1896/1897 he wrote the poem "La Plante," dedicated to Edvard Munch, the subject of which is Munch's lithograph *The Flower of Love* (Sch. 70, 1896). The poem has never been published as far as is known and exists in two handwritten copies in the Munch Museum archive. Munch did a black-and-white woodcut of Marcel Réja probably in 1897 (OKK G/t 691, reproduced in Eli Greve, *Edvard Munchs liv i lys av tresnittene,* Oslo, 1963, 97). Munch's own library contains four books by Marcel Réja (all with the author's dedication): *La Vie héroique* (Paris, 1897), *Ballets et variations* (Paris, 1898), *Un après-midi chez Ninon ou Le Chevalier de Villiers* (Paris, 1910), and *Au Pays des miracles* (Paris, 1930). André Salmon, in *Souvenirs sans fin* (5th ed., Paris, 1956, *1:* 257-58) notes that Réja wrote on the subject of art and mental illness. As a psychiatrist, Réja had worked at La Salpêtrière, which, in addition to being a hospital for older women, also treated the mentally ill. It is quite possible that Munch's subject matter for his lithograph *At the Women's Clinic* (Sch. 56, 1896) came from his close association with Réja. The same might also be the case with his lithograph *At the Clinic* (Sch. 55, 1896), in which the principal figure is a caricature of August Strindberg, who was hospitalized with a skin disease in Paris in the winter of 1895. Strindberg, who had great admiration for Réja's poetry as

well as for his knowledge of the occult, got to know Réja in November 1897 through their mutual friend the painter Paul Herrmann, who in Paris took the name Henri Héran. (See Munch's painting the double portrait of Paul Herrmann and Paul Contard, 1897, Kunsthistorisches Museum, Vienna.) Strindberg and Réja conducted a lively correspondence, particularly in the summer of 1898, in connection with the French edition of *Inferno,* published by *Le Mercure de France.* Strindberg's *Legendes* (Legends) contains several episodes dealing with the relationship between Réja and Herrmann.

Julien Leclercq, journalist and author, one of the founders of *Le Mercure de France,* died Nov. 1901. Published a collection of poetry, *Strophes d'amants.* Was particularly interested in phrenology and graphology, and in the nineties he published *La physiognomie, d'après les principes d'Eugène Ledos* and *Le caractère et la main, histoire et documents,* a book about famous personalities and their handwriting as a mirror of their character, in which Strindberg was included. He was close to both Gauguin and Strindberg and performed a number of practical services for both of them. Göran Söderström (*Strindberg och bildkonsten,* 277) writes that Leclercq became for Strindberg in Paris something of what Adolf Paul had been in Berlin—a collaborator and contact man with the outside world. Made several trips to Scandinavia, especially in connection with an exhibit of French art in the fall of 1897, about which he gave a number of lectures. Married a Finnish woman. In a letter to Ellen Key of Mar., 1897, Ida Molard describes Leclercq as "one of our best friends and the one who is perhaps closest to our hearts." With William Molard, he translated Strindberg's *Den romantiske klockaren på Rånö* (The Romantic Parish Clerk on Rånö) into French. Wrote a perceptive article about Strindberg's *Le Plaidoyer d'un fou* in *Revue Encyclopédique,* Feb. 15, 1895, and may have had something to do with the fact that Munch came into possession of the original manuscript of this novel.

31. Gauguin comments on the sale of *Nevermore* to Delius in a letter dated Papeete, Jan. 12, 1899, to the painter Daniel de Monfreid, who had arranged the sale. Gauguin writes that he is very pleased that Delius has bought the painting, because it was the purchase of an art lover rather than a speculator. He adds that he hopes the chances of selling his works will be increased by the fact that this painting will now be seen—and discussed— by visitors to Delius. *Lettres de Paul Gauguin à Georges-Daniel de Monfreid* (Paris, 1930), 114-115. On Delius and Munch see John Boulton Smith, "Portrait of a Friendship: Edvard Munch and Frederick Delius," *Apollo* (Jan. 1966): 38-47, and Lionel Carley, *Delius—The Paris Years* (London, 1975).

32. In a letter dated Paris, Nov. 4, 1926, Munch writes to Jappe Nilssen: "I have been to see Molard, who is very old and has a couple of old friends." See Erna Holmboe Bang, *Edvard Munchs kriseår. Belyst i brever* (Olso, 1963), 105.

33. Some biographical data about the Molard family was obtained from the Prefecture in Paris, Mairie du XIV Arrondisement. In the K. V. Hammer letter collection at the University Library in Oslo, no. 466, is a series of letters from both William Molard and his father, Victor. Otherwise, the information about the Molard family and their circle is to be found principally in the following sources:

Lionel Carley, *Delius—The Paris Years* (London, 1975).

Bengt Danielsson, *Gauguins söderhavsår* (Stockholm, 1954).

Frederick Delius, "Recollections of Strindberg," *The Sackbut, 1* (Dec. 8, 1920): 353-354.

Gilles Gérard-Arlberg, "No 6, rue Vercingétorix," *Konstrevy,* no. 2 (1958): 65-68.

Gerda Kjellberg, *Hänt och sant* (Stockholm, 1951).

André Salmon, *Souvenirs san fin,* vol. I, 5th ed. (Paris, 1956).

André Söderström, *Strindberg och bildkonsten* (Uddevalla, 1972).

34. Strindberg, *Inferno*, 17.

35. From the same letter mentioned in footnote 1.

36. The woodblock for the color, as it exists today, is in four parts: one for the woman's head, one for the man's head, and two parts for the background. Originally, however, the background must have been in only one part. During the course of time (Munch printed new editions from these 1896 blocks in 1901-1902), a crack must have appeared in the block. One small part is missing from the background block today.

37. Richard S. Field, "Gauguin's Noa Noa Suite," *The Burlington Magazine, 110*, no. 786 (Sept. 1968): 500.

38. Maurice Malingue, *Gauguin* (Paris: Hachette ed., 1961), chapter V ("L'homme qui a réinventé la peinture"), 108-138.

39. Maurice Malingue in a note to letter CLVIII from Gauguin to his wife, Mette, in *Lettres de Gauguin à sa femme et à ses amis* (Paris, 1946), 268. Foreword by M. Malingue, in Marcel Guérin, *L'oeuvre gravé de Gauguin* (Paris, 1927), xviii.

40. Field, "Gauguin's Noa Noa Suite," 511.

41. Libuse Sýkorova, *Gauguin Woodcuts* (London, 1973), 7, 19.

42. Philadelphia, Museum of Art: exh. cat., Richard S. Field, *Paul Gauguin, Monotypes* (March 23-May 13, 1973).

43. *Lettres de Gauguin à sa femme et à ses amis*, no. CLXII, 274.

44. Teddy Brunius, *Mutual Aid in the Arts*, Figura 9, Acta Universalisis Uppsaliensis (Uppsala, 1972), 192.

45. Among others: Roy A. Boe, "Edvard Munch og J. P. Jacobsens 'Niels Lyhne,'" *Oslo kommunes kunstsamlinger, Årbok* 1952-1959 (Oslo, 1960): 9-12.

46. *Paul-Napoleon Roinard*, French symbolist poet, born 1856, died 1934. Well-known in his day but did not retain the same recognition later. Among other things, he wrote a series of theater pieces and was for a time connected to Paul Fort's Théâtre d'Art, where, in the early 1890s, he staged a play called *Cantique des Cantiques* and caused a sensation by having perfume sprayed into the hall to heighten the effect. Staff member on a number of journals, among them the anarchist *L'En dehors*. The symbolist drama *Les Miroirs* was written in Brussels, where he lived in exile during the so-called Procès des Trente in 1894. However, the play was not published until 1909. In the catalogue of the great symbolist exhibit at the Bibliothèque Nationale in 1936, he is described as one of the last representatives of the literary bohemians.

47. "Quelqu'un a dit qu'il fallait faire de la musique sur les toiles du Munch pour les bien expliquer. Cela se peut, mais en attendant le compositeur je ferai le boniment sur ces quelques tableaux. . . ." August Strindberg, "L'exposition d'Edvard Munch," *Le Revue blanche, 10*, no. 72 (June 1, 1896). Facsimiles can be found in Ingrid Langaard, *Edvard Munchs Modningsår* (Oslo, 1960), 366, and in Söderström, *Strindberg och bildkonsten*, 304-305.

48. Sketchbook OKK T 2760, the "Violet Diary." The passage quoted occurs under the date "2/1-91-Nizza."

49. In a letter dated May 12, 1896, Monsieur Piat, the president of Les Cents Bibliophiles, asks Munch to come in two days so that they can discuss the sketches Munch has submitted. A letter from Les Cents Bibliophiles of June 24, 1896, requests Munch to confirm which works he carried out for the recently deceased M. Piat.

50. Gösta Svenaeus, "Munch och Strindberg i Inferno," *Kunst og Kultur, 50*, 1: 1-28.

51. Mentioned in conversation with Kaare Berntsen senior and junior by the Norwegian collector who bought the KB series from an art dealer in Berlin in the 1930s.

52. Strindberg, *Inferno*, 54.

53. Letter dated Mar. 1897. Several letters from Ida Molard to various people in Sweden, among them Ellen Key, are in the Royal Library, Stockholm. In the letters to Ellen Key, she often writes about Judith, for example, about her daughter's impending marriage and about her future husband.

54. Judith Gérard, "La petite fille et le tupapau—Den lilla flickan och gengångaren" (The Little Girl and the Spectre), in Gerda Kjellberg, *Hänt och sant* (Stockholm, 1951), 53-74.

55. "Katten," autobiographical note, OKK T 2782, p. 144. "Den hvide Kat," autobiographical note, OKK T 2782, pp. 145-150.

56. Strindberg in a letter to Torsten Hedlund, October 30, 1896. *Strindbergs brev, 11*: no. 3413.

57. It appears from a letter to Les Cents Bibliophiles written on Munch's behalf by Meier-Graefe that Monsieur Piat had approached Munch on the matter of the Baudelaire commission by coming to Bing's L'Art Nouveau in person. The letter is undated but must have been written toward the end of June 1896.

58. OKK T 2782, p. 139. The quote is from a note written on the same paper as a draft for a letter to Mrs. Valborg Hammer, written in Paris probably in the middle of September 1896.

59. OKK T 2782-1, between pages 72 and 73.

60. Note to letter CLI, from Gauguin to William Molard, June, 1894, in *Lettres de Gauguin à sa femme et à ses amis*, 259.

The Mirror

Catalogue by Bente Torjusen

225-3

THE TITLES OF THE PRINTS THAT APPEARED in the original 1897 "Mirror" are set in bold face, capital letters. The prints that form a part of the reconstructed section of "The Mirror" are marked (R) following the title.

Following "Cat. 1897" is information about catalogue number, title, and possibly technique as was given in the catalogue for the exhibition in the Diorama Hall on September 15-October 17, 1897. The sequence here is the same as in the 1897 catalogue.

Two of the prints were lent by the Munch Museum, The City of Oslo Art Collections, and their numbers are entered beside the OKK registration numbers. The other prints, except cat. nos. 227 and 228, were lent by a private Norwegian collection.

The twelve prints from the original "Mirror" were cropped and mounted on brown cardboard. These sheets, as well as the cardboard pages, often have very uneven edges. The dimensions of the leaves from the

In the Land of Crystal (R)   lithograph, 1897
(cat. no. 209)
Lithographic india ink and chalk
Sch. 93, OKK G/1 225-1
36.6 x 47.8
Cat. 1897: "94. *Beyond*"
Munch-Museet, Oslo

The lithograph exists in very few copies; one of them was pasted into "The Tree of Knowledge" on p. 75 and was cropped. On a loose strip of paper inserted at this page, Munch wrote "The Land of the Crystals." On loose page A 31 in "The Tree of Knowledge" Munch wrote *inter alia:* "Death is the beginning of life—a new crystallization."

See the text on loose page A 5 in "The Tree of Knowledge" that is relevant to this motif, to *Funeral March,* as well as to *Metabolism*—the first three catalogue numbers in "The Mirror."

1897 "Mirror" are, therefore, stated in the following manner: height left side/height right side x width at top/width at bottom. All dimensions are given in centimeters.

In choosing prints for the reconstructed part of "The Mirror," we tried to find early prints of a quality that harmonizes with the pages from the original "Mirror." Similarly, we have selected prints with early hand coloring (for instance *Madonna,* cat. no. 216 and *Vampire,* cat. no. 220). Some of the prints in the reconstructed part, like the prints from the 1897 "Mirror," were previously in the collection of Heinrich Stinnes and carry the initials H.S. These initials are noted, together with signatures and anything else written on the prints. None of the prints in the reconstructed part is cropped, but they are all mounted on pieces of brown cardboard, which is very similar to the kind of cardboard that Munch used in 1897.

Any references to the fact that Munch planned to print motifs included in "The Mirror" in great numbers around 1897-1898 are cited. Cases where a motif from "The Mirror" is included in the portfolio "The Tree of Knowledge of Good and Evil" (T 2547) are mentioned, and references are given to the texts in "The Tree of Knowledge" that are relevant to "Mirror" motifs. In a few instances citations from sketchbooks OKK T 130 and OKK T 2601 are given, since the notes in these sketchbooks originated in Paris in 1896-1897, at the same time that the major portion of the motifs in "The Mirror" was created.

Funeral March (R)   lithograph, 1897 (cat. no. 210)
Lithographic india ink and spatula, print from lithographically prepared zinc plate
Sch. 94, OKK G/1 226
Pasted on yellowish paper and signed on the right-hand side below the print: *E. Munch*
The initials *HS* appear below on the left
55.2 x 37.2
Cat. 1897: "95. *Funeral March*"
Private Collection

A copy of *Funeral March* is included in "The Tree of Knowledge," p. 73.

Metabolism (R)   lithograph, 1897 (cat. no. 211)
Lithographic india ink, spatula
Sch. 95, OKK G/1 227-1
36.5 x 25
Cat. 1897: "96. *Metabolism*"
Munch-Museet, Oslo

This lithograph exists in very few copies and is not in-
cluded in "The Tree of Knowledge." Called by Schiefler
"Leben und Tod," this lithograph may be traced back to
Munch's work with illustrations for Baudelaire's *Les
Fleurs du mal* in April-May 1896. The motif is directly
connected to many of Munch's sketches for the poem
"Une Charogne," about which he wrote in sketchbook
OKK T 130, from 1896:

> . . . contrast between life and death is Charogne—The
> substance that is born while it is consumed—The sub-
> stance that is born while it is brought forth—Man who
> fertilizes the earth while he is consumed and then gives
> nourishment to new life—

By the Deathbed (R)   lithograph, 1896 (cat. no. 212)
Lithographic india ink, needle
Sch. 72, OKK G/1 214
The print is numbered on the bottom right: *No. 22/30*
39.7 x 50
Cat. 1897: "97. *Death Agony*"
Private Collection

The motif is not included in "The Tree of Knowledge."

Death in the Sickroom (R)   lithograph, 1896
(cat. no. 213)
Lithographic india ink and chalk, needle
Sch. 73, OKK G/1 215
Signed lower right: *Edv. Munch*
and numbered *No. 22/30*
40 x 54
Cat. 1897: "98. *Death*"
Private Collection

A signed and numbered copy of the lithograph *Death in the Sickroom* is reproduced on p. 8 in the catalogue for the 1897 exhibit in the Diorama Hall. The motif is not included in "The Tree of Knowledge."

Hands (Lust for Woman) (R)   lithograph, 1895
(cat. no. 214)
Lithographic chalk and india ink
Sch. 35, OKK G/1 196
Signed lower right: *E. Munch*
48 x 29
Cat. 1897: "99. *Hands*"
Private Collection

The motif is not included in "The Tree of Knowledge."

Lovers in Waves (R)   lithograph, 1896 (cat. no. 215)
Lithographic india ink and chalk, needle
Sch. 71, OKK G/1 213
30.7 x 41.9
Cat. 1897: "100. *Waves*"
Private Collection

In a letter from Munch to Auguste Clot in the summer of

1897, Munch gave his address as "Aasgaardstrand, pr. Christiania, Norvège," he wrote:

> Monsieur! Vuilles s.v.p. tirer pour commencer les deux pierres, 50 epreuves chaque unes: 1) Deux tetes 2) Une tete de femme sur des vagues. Apres le tirage vuilles m'envoyer les epreuves avec le conte.
>
> *Avec toutes mes sentiments*
>
> Edvard Munch

Next to the two titles in the letter, Munch drew small sketches which leave no doubt that *Deux Têtes* is *Attraction I* (Sch. 65) or *Stars* according to the 1897 catalogue, and that *Une tête de femme sur des vagues* is *Lovers in the Waves.* In a letter to Johan Rohde of March 1898, Munch wrote that the lithograph *The Wave* belongs in a portfolio he hoped to publish soon, and that the lithographs would be printed in no more than 200 copies.

In the Munch Museum there is a copy of this lithograph with the following inscription: *Edv. Munch, Print ca. 1898* (OKK G/1 213-1). A drawing of the motif *Lovers in Waves* is included in "The Tree of Knowledge," together with a text on the loose page inserted between p. 64 and p. 65.

Madonna (R)   lithograph, 1895 (cat. no. 216)
Lithographic india ink and chalk, needle, and spatula
Sch. 33 A a I, OKK G/1 194
Printed on grayish cardboard. Hand colored with watercolor in red, yellow, and blue
Signed lower right: *E. Munch 1896 Paris*
The initials *HS* appear on the bottom left
60 x 44
Cat. 1897: "101. *Loving Woman,* hand colored"
Private Collection

See cat. no. 222 regarding information about the lithograph *Madonna* in the context of a portfolio and about the text in "The Tree of Knowledge."

ATTRACTION II   lithograph, 1896 (cat. no. 217)
Lithographic chalk, hand colored
Sch. 66, OKK G/1 208
The lithograph is hand colored with watercolor in shades of blue, faint yellow, and brown
It has been cropped rather unevenly and mounted on brown cardboard
Signed with pencil on the cardboard on the right below the print: *E. Munch 1897*
The initials *HS* appear in red on the lower left of the cardboard
Print: 37.8/37 x 60.9/60.6
Cardboard: 67/66.7 x 68
Cat. 1897: "102. *Two Heads,* hand colored"
Private Collection

In the Munch Museum there is a probably unique copy of this motif, printed in brown, yellow, and blue. See the catalogue *Farge på trykk* (Color in Print), Catalogue No. 5 of the Munch Museum, 1968, No. 3. Regarding "The Tree of Knowledge," see cat. no. 218.

ATTRACTION I   lithograph, 1896 (cat. no. 218)
Lithographic chalk and india ink, needle, hand colored
Sch. 65, OKK G/1 207
The print was hand colored with blue-green watercolor over the white areas. It was cropped, above along the arc of the sky and pasted on brown cardboard

Signed with pencil on the cardboard on the right below the print: *Edv. Munch 1897*
The initials *HS* appear in red on the lower left of the print
Print: 40.7/41.3 x 34.6/34.4
Cardboard: 69/68.4 x 67.5/67.2
Cat. 1897: "103. *Stars,* hand colored"
Private Collection

This print may have been a predecessor of the copies of *Attraction I* that were printed on gray-green or bluish paper. A copy of *Attraction I,* in black-and-white, is included in "The Tree of Knowledge," p. 15. See text on p. A 45 of the portfolio. In a letter from Munch to Clot, in the late summer of 1897, Munch asked Clot to print fifty copies of this lithograph "as a beginning." See commentaries to cat. no. 215, *Lovers in Waves.*

JEALOUSY   lithograph, 1896 (cat. no. 219)
Lithographic india ink, needle
Sch. 58, OKK G/1 202
The lithograph, printed on paper that has since yellowed, was cropped and pasted onto brown cardboard.
Signed in pencil on the cardboard on the right below the print: *Edvard Munch 1897*
The initials *HS* appear on the cardboard below the left-hand corner of the print
Print: 46.4/46 x 56.3/55.9
Cardboard: 67/66.3 x 67.7/68
Cat. 1897: "104. *Jealousy*"
Private Collection

Another lithographic variant of *Jealousy,* Sch. 57, also from 1896, is included in "The Tree of Knowledge." See text in "The Tree of Knowledge," p. A 43.

Vampire (R)   lithograph, 1895 (cat. no. 220)
Lithographic india ink and chalk, hand-colored
Sch. 34 a II, OKK G/t 567
Printed on gray-green paper, hand colored with watercolors in red shades, in a way that harmonizes with the hand-colored prints from the original "Mirror."
Signed in blue watercolor on the right: *E. Munch 95*
38.2 x 55
Cat. 1897: "105. *Vampire,* hand colored"
Private Collection

A black-and-white copy of the lithograph *Vampire,* cropped, is included in "The Tree of Knowledge," p. 37. See cat. no. 231.

THE URN   lithograph, 1896 (cat. no. 221)
Lithographic india ink and chalk, needle and spatula
Sch. 63 II, OKK G/1 205
Printed on grayish paper, cropped, and pasted on brown cardboard
Signed with pencil on the cardboard on the right below the print: *Edv. Munch 1897*
The initials *HS* appear on the cardboard on the lower left
Print: 45.6 x 26.4/26.1
Cardboard: 68/68.3 x 68.1
Cat. 1897: "106. *The Urn*".
Private Collection

A copy of the lithograph *The Urn* is included in "The Tree of Knowledge" on p. 49. See text in "The Tree of Knowledge," p. A 39.

MADONNA   lithograph, 1895 (cat. no. 222)
Lithographic india ink and chalk, needle and spatula
Sch. 33 AaI, OKK G/1 194
Printed on faintly green paper, cropped and mounted on brown cardboard
Signed with pencil on the cardboard on the right below the print: *Edv. Munch 1897*
The initials *HS* appear in red on the cardboard below the left-hand corner of the print
Print: 59.2/58.6 x 44.1/43.7
Cardboard: 70.7/70.6 x 69.2/69.4
Cat. 1897: "107. *Loving Woman*"
Private Collection

In the letter to Johan Rohde from March 1898, referred to under cat. no. 215, Munch said that the lithograph *Loving Woman* also belongs in the portfolio he soon hopes to issue. On the cover of the catalogue for the 1897 exhibition, *Madonna,* Sch. 33 B, is pictured, but cropped below the breast. A copy of *Madonna,* cropped below the breast, Sch. 33 B, is included in "The Tree of Knowledge," on p. 25. See texts in the "The Tree of Knowledge," pp. 24 and A 35.

SEPARATION II   lithograph, 1896 (cat. no. 223)
Lithographic chalk
Sch. 68, OKK G/1 210
Printed on grayish paper, unevenly cropped, and mounted on brown cardboard
Signed with a pencil on the cardboard at the right below the print: *Edv. Munch 1897*
The initials *HS* appear in red on the cardboard in the lower left-hand corner
Print: 39.4/39 x 60.3/59.3
Cardboard: 65.9/64.5 x 67.5/67.8
Cat. 1897: "108. *The Separation*"
Private Collection

A copy of the lithograph *Separation II*, cropped, is included in "The Tree of Knowledge," p. 29. See text on p. A 37.

The Alley, Carmen (R)   lithograph, 1895 (cat. no. 224)
Lithographic india ink and chalk, needle
Sch 36/a, OKK G/1 197
Signed in the lower right-hand corner: *E. Munch 1895*
42.3 x 26.4
Cat. 1897: "113. *A Street*"
Private Collection

The motif was reprinted in 1897; there is, for example, a lithograph of *Carmen* with the inscription *Print 1897*. A cropped copy of *Carmen* is included in "The Tree of Knowledge," p. 47.

THE FLOWER OF LOVE lithograph, 1896
(cat. no. 225)
Lithographic chalk and india ink
Sch 70, OKK G/1 212
The lithograph was cropped and pasted onto brown
cardboard. Signed in pencil on the cardboard on the
right below the print: *Edv. Munch 1897*
The initials *HS* appear in red on the cardboard on the left
below the print
Print: 58.1/58.3 x 27.5/27.6
Cardboard: 71.1 x 67.3
Cat. 1897: "114. *A Plant*"
Private Collection

The motif was not included in "The Tree of Knowledge."
Marcel Réja's poem "La Plante," dedicated to E. Munch
with the words: "D'un album sur l'amour," deals with the
lithograph *The Flower of Love*. The poem, in the archives
of the Munch Museum in two handwritten copies, in the
poet's own hand, has never before been published. The
poem was probably written in 1896 or 1897.

D'un album sur l'amour

pour E. Munch

"La plante"
Tous vains flambeaux se sont éteints
et tous doutes se sont évaporés
devant la voix imperieuse de l'instinct
qui parle au nom de la vieille loi immanente
. . . et de deux sexes conjurés
est née la plante véhemente.

La plante vivace et vorace
qui s'alimente au coeur des races
germe soudain, s'accroit, s'élance
et, par dessus tous les orgueils et les fracas,
épand, avec des soins graves et délicats
ses rameaux d'ombre et de silence.

Désormais l'étreinte farouche
qui scelle la bouche à la bouche
est le seul rêve et le seul but,
magnifique, de deux passions éperdues.

Tous orgueils et toutes folies
désormais seront abolis;
. . . et chacun d'eux, sentant quel lourd destin les lie
sans savoir par quel noeuds et sans chercher pourquoi
demeure coi.

Les deux êtres sont confondus
au réseau des feuilles tordues;
l'enthousiasme végétal
en son essor anonyme et brutal
propage le mystère et l'extase et la brume
de son feuillage taciturne.

Marcel Réja

The Scream (R) lithograph, 1895 (cat. no. 226)
Lithographic india ink
Sch. 32, OKK G/1 193
Signed lower right "E. Munch 95"
35.2 x 25
Cat. 1897: "116 *Scream*"
Private Collection

Below the motif is printed *Geschrei*. There are other copies of the lithograph *The Scream* with the following inscription printed on them:
    Geschrei
  Ich fühlte das grosse Geschrei
  durch die Natur.
A copy of the lithograph *The Scream*, without inscription, is reproduced on p. 11 in the catalogue for the 1897 exhibition. A faint impression indicates that the motif previously was in "The Tree of Knowledge." See text in "The Tree of Knowledge," p. 53.

Geschrei

Melancholy (R) woodcut, 1896 (cat. no. 227)
Sch. 82, OKK G/t 571
38 x 45.4
Cat. 1897: "118. *Evening,* hand-colored, Woodcut"
Munch-Museet, Oslo

A color woodcut of *Melancholy* is included in "The Tree of Knowledge," p. 45.

Melancholy (R) woodcut, 1896 (cat. no. 228)
Sch. 82, OKK G/t 571
38 x 45.4
Cat. 1897: "119. *Evening,* Woodcut"
Munch-Museet, Oslo

MAN'S HEAD IN WOMAN'S HAIR
(THE MIRROR)   woodcut, 1896 (cat. no. 229)
Black print from a wooden plate worked with a graver, hand colored
Detail of Sch. 80 a, OKK G/t 569

Munch cut out the main motif—the man's head in the woman's hair—from a trial print in black on yellowed paper and pasted it on brown cardboard. He then painted the woman's hair in red and gold. The cardboard is painted with red watercolor in different shades up to 6–7 centimeters from its edge on all sides. At the top of the cardboard, across the whole width of the red area, Munch wrote in large letters in transparent black watercolor:
"THE MIRROR. PART TWO. 1897"
Entire cardboard: 70.3/70.6 x 67.4/67.2
Painted cardboard: 61.8/62.7 x 60.1/61
Private Collection
In the Munch Museum there is a portfolio dust jacket in thick, brown cardboard (71.7 x 62.5) with the woodcut *Man's Head in Woman's Hair* printed on its front (Sch. 80b OKK G/t 569-11). On the back of the jacket Munch wrote in pencil: "*Woodcuts. Kiss. Meteor. The girl with the heart. And others.*"

Also in the Munch Museum is another woodcut with the motif *Man's Head in Woman's Hair* (Sch. 80b, OKK G/t 569-33), printed in red and green on brown cardboard, where the placement of the motif to the left indicates that he planned to place a text above and to the right of the print. On the top right, Munch wrote in pencil: "Eine Mappe. 19 Blatter. Liebe."

Munch used an inverted lithographic variant of *Man's Head in Woman's Hair* as a poster for the 1897 exhibit. The lithograph, printed in red, green, gold, and black, is not listed in Schiefler. A copy of the woodcut *Man's Head in Woman's Hair*, Sch. 80 b, is included in "The Tree of Knowledge," p. 41. See text on p. A 43 of the portfolio.

Munch drew triangular faces above the entire inscription; hardened masks with "piercing" eyes. In sketchbook OKK T 2601, begun during his stay in Paris, 1896-1897, there are two texts that are variants of the one in "The Tree of Knowledge."

ANXIETY   woodcut, 1896 (cat. no. 230)
Printed in black on yellowed paper from a wooden plate worked with a gouge, hand colored
Sch. 62, OKK G/t 568
The page is hand colored with deep red watercolor in a broad field across the sky. The woodcut was cropped and pasted on brown cardboard.
Signed in pencil on the cardboard on the right below the print: *Edv. Munch 1897*
The initials *HS* appear in red in the lower left-hand corner of the cardboard
Print: 45.5/45.4 x 35.8/35.7
Cardboard: 70/69.6 x 69.2/69.4
Cat. 1897: "124. *Anxiety,* hand colored. Woodcut."
Private Collection

A copy of the lithograph, *Anxiety* printed in black and red, Sch. 61, was included by Vollard in the 1896 portfolio *Peintres-Graveurs*. This portfolio was issued in one hundred numbered and signed copies, of which Munch's *Anxiety,* called *Le Soir,* was no. 14. A faint impression shows that the woodcut *Anxiety* was formerly included in "The Tree of Knowledge," on p. 61. See text on loose sheet, A 41, in the portfolio.

In sketchbook OKK T 2601, from 1896-1897, Munch wrote the following on a page facing some loose sketches connected with *Anxiety:*

"People flowed past him like pale ghosts."

VAMPIRE   lithograph, 1895 (cat. no. 231)
Lithographic india ink and chalk
Sch. 34 a II, OKK G/t 567

The black-and-white lithograph was cropped and pasted on brown cardboard. The print is not centered on the cardboard, but has been placed a little to the left. Signed in pencil on the cardboard on the right below the print: *Edvard Munch 1897*
The initials *HS* appear in red on the cardboard on the left below the print.
Print: 37.7/37.5 x 54.1/54.4
Cardboard: 65.5/66 x 67.3/67.5
Not in the 1897 catalogue.
Private Collection

A black-and-white copy of *Vampire,* cropped, (Sch. 34 a II), is included in "The Tree of Knowledge," p. 37.

ASHES   lithograph, 1896 (cat. no. 232)
Lithographic chalk and india ink, hand colored
Section of Sch. 69, OKK G/1 211

The lithograph, printed in black on yellowed paper, is hand colored with red watercolor on the woman's dress. Below on the left is the inscription "ASKE"; the letters SKE intrude into the upper part of the man's body. Munch painted over these letters with black watercolor in such a way that the man's torso appears dark and compact, and only the "A" is visible.
The lithograph was cropped and pasted on brown cardboard.
The hand coloring was done after the print was pasted onto the cardboard; a bit of the black from the print spread onto the cardboard.
Signed in pencil on the cardboard on the right below the print: *Edv. Munch 1897*
The initials *HS* appear in red on the cardboard below on the left.
Print: 29.7/29.9 x 41.4/41.8
Cardboard: 64.3/64.4 x 68/68.2
Not in the 1897 catalogue.
Private Collection

The lithograph was originally in two parts, with the *Ashes* motif making up the lower part. The upper part shows a woman's head, which Munch in this case cut away. See description by Schiefler, 69.

Another lithographic variant of *Ashes*, Sch. 120, OKK G/1 236 from 1899 is included in "The Tree of Knowledge," p. 39. See text on loose sheet, A 51, in the portfolio.

THE KISS   woodcut, 1897 (cat. no. 233)
Black print from a wooden plate worked with a gouge.
Hand colored with watercolor in the blue on the man's body, arm, and head, in faintly blue-violet on the faces and the hands.
Sch. 102 B I, OKK G/t 577
The print was cropped and pasted on brown cardboard.
Signed in pencil on the right below the print: *Edv. Munch 1897*
The initials *HS* appear in red on the cardboard below on the left.
A wide, dark field on the cardboard around the print may be extra paste that had been smeared on before the print was pasted in.
Print: 44.4 x 37.3/37.4
Cardboard: 69.3/69.4 x 66
Not in the 1897 catalogue.
Private Collection

Another variant of *Kiss*, Sch. 102 D, from 1902, is included in "The Tree of Knowledge," p. 21. See text on loose sheet, A 1, in the portfolio.

Poster. Man's Head in Woman's Hair   lithograph, 1897 (cat. no. 234)
The poster for Munch's exhibition in the Diorama Hall September 15-October 17, 1897, printed in red, green, black, and gold.
Not registered by Schiefler.
The lithograph is a mirror-image variant of the title picture *The Mirror*.
63.5 x 47
Private Collection

The poster has the following inscription:
Edvard Munch
Exhibition of Paintings
The Diorama
Carl Johan Street 41
11 A.M. to 10 P.M.
Admission: 50 øre.

Translated from the Norwegian by Erik J. Friis

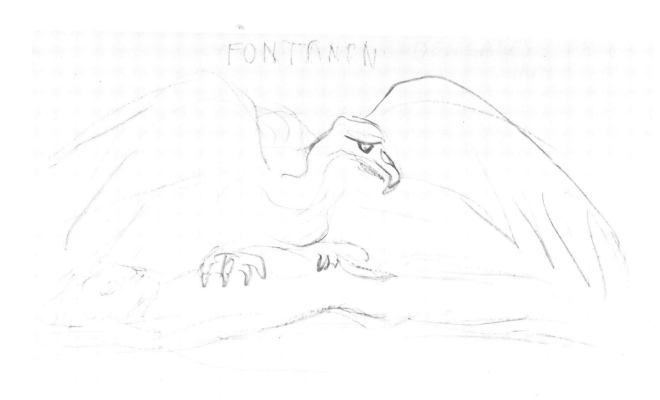

FONTANEN

EN RØD FUGL HAR SAT SIG
FAST I MIT INDRE. DENS KLØR —
HAR HUGGET SIG FAST I MIT
HJÆRTE DETS NÆB HAR.
BORET SIG IND I MIT BRYST
OG DENS VINGESLAG
HAR FORMØRKET MIN
FORSTAND

Notes of a Madman, OKK T 2547-a21, Munch-Museet, Oslo (cat. no. 239)

The Tree of Knowledge of Good and Evil

Gerd Woll

When Edvard Munch died in 1944, he left his works of art to the City of Oslo. His will, which was written in 1940, also contained a paragraph indicating what should be done with his letters, notes, and diaries:

> I leave all my letters to my sister Inger Munch. . . . The drafts for my literary works are to go to the City of Oslo, which in accord with the judgment of experts will decide whether and to what degree they are to be published.

On the cover of the most important of Munch's so-called literary diaries is a similar inscription. An earlier notation to the effect that they are to be burned has been crossed out, and a signed and dated note from September 1932 saying that they "are to be read through by unprejudiced and understanding men after my death" has taken its place.

In a will dated 1930 Munch made the professors Fredrik Stang and Kristian Schreiner his executors, and Schreiner was charged with the final reading of the literary sketches. In an article published in 1946 Schreiner reminisced:

> The fact that Munch gradually told me much about his life was due to his being greatly absorbed in his old notes and the letters he had received in the course of the years, especially during his last years, when few people visited him. When I came in to see him he would always repeat: "It is as if I am living my life over again when I read these old notes." And one day he said: "I have decided that you, after my death, are to go through all this. I believe that some of what I have written may be of literary interest and can throw light on my art.

Schreiner made no attempts at editing the material, as far as is known, and the responsibility for a possible publication of Munch's writings rests today with the City of Oslo Art Collections (Oslo Kommunes Kunstsamlinger). The letters were given to Inger Munch in the will, and she probably removed certain letters or sections that placed Munch in an unfavorable light before she passed them on to the City of Oslo.

Besides the collection of letters and the so-called diaries, the document collection at the Munch Museum includes a mass of loose notes, memoranda, drafts for letters, and much more. A great deal of work still has to be done before the papers are satisfactorily catalogued. As might be expected, only a minor part of this material was dated by Munch himself, and the dating therefore poses sizable problems.

The contents of the notes and memos mentioning actual events will of course give many hints about dates, unlike the freer, more literary writings. Even though these too are concerned with actual events, it may often be exceedingly difficult to determine when they were written. Events and experiences from his early life were important to all facets of Munch's art, including his literary attempts. The same passages have thus been written down on several different occasions—once in a while word for word, at other times with variations. The diaries are in many ways attempts to edit and summarize the loose notes, which may have been written many years previously.

Even though the biographical material in the diaries is fairly obvious, Munch emphasized repeatedly that they were meant to be literary compositions and not diaries in the usual sense of the word. In many of the entries, for example, he talks about himself in the third person, often referring to himself as "Nansen" or "Brand." Other persons appearing in the texts have also been given slightly veiled aliases.

It is not surprising that Munch had ambitions to be a writer. Reading aloud of Norwegian and foreign classics in addition to folk tales, adventure stories, and Westerns was an important part of the Munch family's evening activities. Edvard's uncle, P. A. Munch, was one of Norway's greatest historians, and his literary output was both voluminous and varied. His *History of Norway* and especially his famous *History of the Norwegian People* were enjoyed by a wide circle of readers. Another relative was the poet Andreas Munch—one of the great names in the romantic movement in Norway. It is equally significant, of course, that since his youth, Munch was in close contact with literary men. A number of well-known authors, from Scandinavia as well as the rest of Europe, were among his closest friends. (See the article "The Mirror" by Bente Torjusen.)

Munch's art has been accused of being literary, a notion which is often construed as a distinctly negative characteristic of pictorial art. This is probably due primarily to the emphasis on "l'art pour l'art" formalism throughout most of our century, which has made it impossible to approach problems of content in modern art without a feeling of inferiority. But since pictorial artists once again have been allowed to operate with a clear and meaningful content in their works, the views of earlier art have also markedly changed. It is once again acceptable to concern oneself with the literary content in Munch's art without having to offer a formalistic excuse for doing so.

Munch himself must have felt a need to repudiate the contention that his art was "literary" and "German." In the draft of a 1933 letter to Jens Thiis he wrote:

> In my portfolio I'm keeping the first draft for Kiss and Vampire. They are from the years 1885-86—(Vampire is really that which makes the picture literary. It is in reality only a woman who kisses a man on the neck—
>
> You don't have to go so far in order to explain the making of the Life Frieze.—Its explanation lies in the Bohemian time itself—The thing was to paint living life and one's own life—
>
> Besides, I had also had the entire Life Frieze ready a long time in a literary form, so it was all prepared many years before I went to Berlin—

The demand of the Bohème period—that one must paint or write one's own life—was most clearly formulated by the leading ideologue of the Kristiania Bohème, the author and anarchist Hans Jæger (fig. 1). Like Christian Krohg and other radical Norwegian artists of the 1880s, he was deeply influenced by French naturalism, as represented by the works of Emile Zola. Jæger's program must have been the topic of conversations in the cafés and the apartments in the capital. He has given us a fairly useful summary of his theories in his article "Our Literature," which appeared in *Impressionisten*, a periodical published irregularly from 1886 to 1890:

> Youth is modern when it through its own life has *lived* to obtain the experience that the conditions under which it has grown up have arrested or crippled its development and made it, humanly speaking, into a youth inferior to what it otherwise would have been. A youth who through

fig. 1 *Hans Jæger*, 1896, OKK G/1 218-1, Munch-Museet, Oslo

its own life has *lived* to obtain this experience, and who therefore desires a change in conditions, who can liberate the coming generations from suffering the same fate—*that* youth is "modern". . . .

But if this will is to become reality, then it must also become the will of the public, the great public. And how can that happen? Yes, the great public must be forced to *live* to obtain the same experience that modern youth has lived to obtain—and thus be infused with the same will. And the public can be forced this way through a living, realistic literature, which is *compelling* with the force of living life. . . .

And this Naturalistic literature, it must thus contain their own, this modern youth's own real life, lived in the milieu in which it has been really lived. That which this literature has to do is: to publicize the private life of this youth. But how many, even among modern youth, do you think there are, who will agree to thus undressing themselves and standing before the public completely naked? Few, very few—even among modern youth: be sure of that!

One of the exceedingly few who dared to lay bare his life in this way was, of course, Edvard Munch, even though it was primarily through pictures that he chose to present his experience. By the end of the 1880s he had probably begun to write down experiences that he thought especially important and did additional work on them with a view to making them stories. Both the content and the formulation of these written pieces indicates a close knowledge of the writings of Hans Jæger. Jæger's stories, which created general alarm among the bourgeoisie because of their candid erotic passages and clearly revolutionary tendencies, must also have had an irritating effect because of their unusual verbal orthography. True enough, Munch's modesty—or lack of sexual experience—prevented him from going as far as Jæger in his erotic portrayals, but the underlying idea is much the same as in Jæger's stories. Munch also used a similar characteristic spelling, according to which the words were written as they are pronounced. This must have looked much more unusual one hundred years ago, since the official written language in Norway at that time was Danish, which to some extent was unlike the spoken language. But even today, with the rapprochement of the spoken and written languages which has been fundamental to the development of Norwegian, the orthography used by Jæger and Munch in the 1880s appears extreme.

Jæger's main literary work, *From the Kristiania Bohème*, was published in December 1885 and was immediately confiscated. But thanks to their farsightedness and good planning, the publisher and author succeeded in hiding a number of copies, which were diligently read during the following months. In Jæger's case, the year 1886 was to be remembered for its many lawsuits, and it culminated with his imprisonment. When his case was argued before the Supreme Court, Jæger made a long and fiery speech in which he explained the background and motivation behind naturalistic literature:

> It is written with steaming human blood; the characters who come to meet you in their works are alive; alive with the life of reality. Touch them and feel it! they are alive underneath your fingers, they are made of living human flesh; it is the red blood of reality that flows in their veins, put your hand on them anywhere you wish, and feel; the pulse beats of life, vibrates in every muscular fibre underneath the skin; —listen! and you will hear their hearts beat. It is living human beings, the very urge of life that, most honorable Sirs, assails you from these works that live underneath your hands; and every time you have finished one of them, you have lived one human life more than when you began—you have in a few short hours absorbed all the wisdom of life that another person has paid for with his life. And such a literature is not to be read!—Insanity, most honorable Sirs, it will be read like no literature in the world before it—it has been written in steaming human blood.

Three or four years later Munch made an attempt to formulate a kind of aesthetic program, and in this well-known "St. Cloud Manifesto" he also asserted the importance of real life as a source for the arts:

> There ought no longer to be painted interiors, people who read and women knitting.—They ought to be living human beings who breathe and feel, suffer and love.

In other pronouncements about his art Munch voiced points of view close to the program that Jæger had outlined for naturalistic literature:

> I don't believe in the kind of art which has not forced its way forward through man's need to open his heart. All art, literature as well as music, must be created with one's heart blood. (OKK N 29)
> We want something other than mere photography of nature. Nor is it in order to paint pretty pictures to be hung on the parlor wall. We want to try if we can, whether we might not succeed in such a way that we lay the groundwork for an art devoted to man. An art that seizes and takes hold of one. Art that is created with one's heart blood. (OKK N 39)

Munch's closest—at times only—friend in Paris in 1889-1890 was the Danish poet Emanuel Goldstein, who was also well acquainted with Hans Jæger's writings and views on literature. Both evidently collected notes, perhaps with a half-hearted plan to publish them jointly. Munch wrote to Goldstein about this from Nice in 1892:

> And all those splendid realistic sketches we both made that time in Paris—all the phonographic renderings— that were so ably thought out—will they ever be used— You, too, probably have quite a big batch?

An event that more than anything else was to influence Munch's writing as well as his art during his early stay in Paris was the news that his father had died. Munch learned of it in early December 1889, and it, of course, caused much brooding about life and death in general, about his family, and about his own fate in particular. His father's death also brought back memories of his mother and sister. The fact that it was now too late to reestablish a close relationship with his father also seems to have worried him. Edvard had been quite unable to share his father's religious views, and this, combined with the young artist's associating with the infamous bohemians, must undoubtedly have troubled the old doctor. In a note about his father's death, Munch wrote:

> And then it was Jæger—possibly the greatest sorrow—I almost felt hatred for Jæger—
> For it was my conviction that he was right—but still—
> I was up at Goldstein's
> Now it is you—
> Yes, it always hurts when one has not been in agreement—
> But you see we were fond of each other he was so soft you see as wax—

Is your father still living
Yes
I envied him that
That Jæger—he was a hard one—do you know what he said
Kill him—
My father—he with the heart—I couldn't understand Jæger. I could love him—but also hate him—
That was the worst of it—for my father that thing with Jæger—(OKK N 12)

While Munch's earliest writings were mostly realistic descriptions of a predominantly autobiographical nature, written in a style obviously influenced by Hans Jæger, a change in his style seems to have occurred around 1890. Biographical reasons, such as his father's death and the close contact with Goldstein, may have caused such a change in his style, but it is also surprising to note that this change coincided with a similar change of style in Norwegian literature in 1890. At that time one's attention turned inward, into the depth of the soul. The well-known Norwegian writer Knut Hamsun in 1890 gave a lecture which he called "From the Life of the Unconscious." Many other artists now tackled the exploration of the deeper layers of consciousness, and at the same time certain physicians and philosophers paid greater attention in their work to the subconscious and to the life of the soul.

To Munch such an expansion of the domain of empirical investigation meant greater stress on, rather than an abandonment of, the bohemians' demand that one should write about one's own life. Basing his work on personally experienced events from his childhood and youth, during the 1890s he created the pictures that have been regarded as his chief work—the so-called Life Frieze pictures.

While he gathered his most important paintings into this series, he probably also busied himself with editing the written material that described the same experiences. We can detect how the originally realistic descriptions were somehow condensed, and this corresponds completely to the concentration in Munch's pictures from this time. All unnecessary details were weeded out, and pictures as well as texts were given an exceedingly concentrated and precise formulation. The realistic starting point is generally still present, but it is necessary to have a pretty good knowledge of the biographical background to recognize it.

Munch wrote short commentaries to the majority of the motifs in the "Life Frieze." They are condensed prose poems, and he probably had plans to publish them together with the corresponding picture motifs, as, for instance, in the planned portfolio entitled "The Mirror." (See the article by Bente Torjusen.)

Munch created his first sustained literary work in 1904. Entitled *From the City of Free Love*, it was written in the style of a comic operetta. It was based on his long relationship with a rich Christiania lady, Tulla Larsen, which came to a sudden and dramatic end in 1902, when during a quarrel Munch was shot in his hand and maimed one of his fingers. As a result, Munch harbored a nearly pathological hatred of Tulla Larsen and all their former mutual friends.

Even though the comedy ostensibly is light and gay, Munch probably wrote it in a spirit of revenge. The fact that he had not planned to let this piece of writing rot in a desk drawer is clearly indicated in a letter to his cousin Ludvig Ravensberg in which he asks him to place an advertisement in one of the newspapers in the capital, announcing that the painter Edvard Munch had completed a comedy entitled *The City of Free Love*.

Aside from this comedy, the break with Tulla Larsen and the emotional excitement it caused led to a great deal of other writing. Page after page in diaries and on loose leaves were filled with his attempts to write down all the events that had led to the break and the unfortunate consequences the relationship had for his ability to work. While he in this way was trying to justify himself, his former mistress was changed into a kind of female monster. There are also reflections on Munch's lack of ability to live a normal family life. Inherited sickliness and bad nerves are a constantly recurring theme. In this period of his life the bad nerves, aided by an ever increasing consumption of alcohol, gradually got the upper hand completely, and he said himself that at that time he was on the brink of madness. His friend Goldstein, with whom he was still in close contact, urged him strongly to enter Dr. Jacobson's Clinic in Copenhagen, and in the fall of 1908 Munch did so. During the stay at the clinic he completed a series of lithographs about the first human beings, "Alpha and Omega" (fig. 2), which was issued in a separate portfolio with a long descriptive text written by Munch. It is probable that the dissension-filled relationship with Tulla Larsen influenced the depiction of Alpha and Omega.

During his stay at the clinic Munch was probably forced to reflect upon his life, and one may suppose that it was more through conversations with Dr. Jacobson than through the various treatments that he arrived at a new understanding of himself. The idea of man as a divided being seems to have occupied his mind a great deal at that time, and the many notes about the cleavage of the mind probably originated during his stay at the clinic.

When he was discharged from the clinic in the

fig. 2 *Alpha and Omega*, title page, 1908/1909, OKK G/1 301-60, Munch-Museet, Oslo

spring of 1909, Munch went back to Norway and settled on a large farm near the city of Kragerø. Some years later he also rented a manor house, Grimsrød, in the vicinity of Moss, a city on the other side of the Oslo Fjord. During the years 1909 to 1915, he reviewed all his previous writings and tried to organize them. In the Munch Museum are two huge ledgerlike books with a label showing that they had been bought at a bookstore in Kragerø, and one of them contains a packing list dated March 1910.

One of these ledgers (OKK T 2734) contains a long, thorough account of the work done on the notes in 1929, when he once again had a spell of putting his earlier notes and memoranda in order, and also some very brief, aphoristic statements about his bohemian friends. The other ledger (OKK T 2787) contains an account of how Munch regarded his mental state. It was undoubtedly written right after his stay at the clinic.

> The influence of alcohol carried the split in the mind or the soul to its outermost limits—until the two states like two wild birds tied together pulled in different directions and threatened to dissolve or tear apart the chain—With the violent split of these two mental states there was created a powerful inner tension—an intense inner struggle—A horrible fight in the soul's cage—The value to the artist or the philosopher of this condition depends upon the things in a way being seen by two persons—in two mental states—the things were seen from two sides. The periphery—The thoughts moved toward the periphery of the soul—and were threatened to be flung outside the effective range of the centrifugal force—out into space or darkness—or insanity—
>
> Then at the same time these touched—the finest and most remarkable only dimly perceived life truths and life forces—I imagine the two mental states as the desire for peace and rest—and the other desire for that which drives one to motion and action—
>
> Normally, these two work together, in one's life work, like a negative and positive force in the cylinder of a locomotive. Abnormally, as split and divided states, they have a destructive effect on the machinery—(OKK T 2787)

A third ledger (OKK T 2782) is approximately the same size as the two from Kragerø; it has a label from a bookstore in Moss, and inside are a few notations dated 1915. The contents of this ledger are much more comprehensive and interesting than the other two. True, Munch did not write much in the book itself, but he fastened to the pages a great number of loose slips of paper and notes with clips or pins. Headings at the top of some of the pages indicate that he planned to organize the many notes into definite groups, even though the system has hardly been adhered to. The planned classification, according to the headings, was:

> Childhood — Art — Philosophy — Mental State — Moods—Youthful Reminiscences—Love—Passion—Death

We notice attempts at a similar subject classification of his notes in many of his earlier diaries.

Munch was also busy with the classification of his graphic works when he tried to arrange his notes. This was probably because the galleries and the art dealers needed to obtain a price list of the Munch prints which were for sale. The first systematic listing was made following the exhibition of Munch's graphics in Salong Joël in Stockholm in 1913, which was recorded in photographs. The prints were hanging very close together, and each had been supplied with a tag, on which the catalogue number had been written. These photographs were later printed in a brochure, and, together with another brochure supplying the catalogue numbers and the prices, it made a fairly useful overview of Munch's graphics. The list of numbers was continued in a later catalogue, and there also exists a series of albums with photographs of some of the graphic works with their numbers. The printed brochures constitute what Gustav Schiefler called "Nordic Catalogue" in volume 2 of his catalogue of Munch's art. The first volume of the catalogue had been issued in 1906, and since Munch, of course, did not stop making graphics, it is understandable that the German cataloguer was eager to continue this work. Even before the outbreak of the First World War he had plans to issue a second volume and had obtained the "Nordic Catalogue" to base his work on. The war, however, made contacts between Germany and Norway difficult, and Schiefler had to wait until the late 1920s before starting seriously on volume 2. Munch himself was undoubtedly fully aware of the problems during the intervening years, and there is much to indicate that he wished to get a better perspective of his graphic work.

In addition to the many albums of photographs, in the Munch Museum there is also an enormous volume into which Munch pasted many of his most important graphic motifs and some drawings. The covers measure 655 by 489 millimeters, and the book is about 70 millimeters thick. It contains a total of 99 heavy cardboard pages that have been sewn together in batches of two and four pages. In some places it is quite evident that sheets were removed, and the volume originally consisted of more pages. Whether this book was the result of a mania for getting his work in order or whether it was an attempt to realize Munch's old plan of collecting his most important motifs with the intention of publishing them is hard to say. The fact that the book also contains a few drawings may indicate that the motifs rather than the graphic work were the starting point. This supposition is buttressed by the fact that the pasted-in graphics are quite ordinary. The unwieldiness of the book makes it indeed hard to believe that it was meant for anything but the artist's own use.

This book contains neither labels nor inscriptions that might give us a hint as to when it was put together. Many of the works of art pasted in, especially the drawings, must have been made before 1900, but many of them were executed much later. A number of lithographs made in 1916 constitute an almost separate section, but most of them have been inserted loosely among the pages of the book. The pasted-in impression of the woodcut *The Kiss* is a reprint from 1916, and it is probable that the impression of *The Lonely Ones* may also have been printed at that time. At any rate, a good deal of the work on the book must have been done in 1916.

In January of that year Munch purchased a house with surrounding property known as Ekely outside Christiania and moved there that April. It seems reasonable that during the move he was seized by a new desire to put in order his prints and drawings. We also know that at that time he also had new impressions made of several of his earlier lithographs and woodcuts, and among his new works of 1916 there is a lithograph *Childhood Memory* that is similar to earlier drawings of this motif. Even though this is not much more than circumstantial evidence, it makes it probable that the work on the book took place mainly in 1916.

However, in its present appearance the volume includes an addition of more than twenty loose cardboard pages, somewhat larger than the pages in the book itself. Most of them were inserted between the pages in the first part of the book. The entire volume, including fixed and loose pages, was paginated in 1970 in the order in which the pages appeared at that time. Whether this is the same sequence as the one that Munch intended we do not know.

Munch wrote a great number of passages on the loose cardboard pages, most often in multicolored block letters made with colored crayons. Some of the texts are illustrated with drawings that were either pasted in or drawn directly onto the loose cardboard page. A few of the texts relate to the motifs pasted on the pages of the book, but most of the loose text pages seem to make a single unit. It is probable that they were done as a separate project, perhaps without any connection at all with the large volume.

Among the loose text pages is a title page (OKK T 2547-a9) on which the legend "The Tree of Knowledge of Good and Evil" appears in red and green crayon (cat. no. 235). Below the title there is a circular vignette, with the heads of a man and a woman encircled by a serpent with a flickering red tongue, placed near the man's heart. The design reminds one of the title-page vignette that Munch drew in 1905 for the first volume of Gustav Schiefler's catalogue (fig. 3). In the Schiefler vignette, Munch showed himself in the person of Dante and thus alluded to the Inferno crisis that he was then living through. But in the vignette for "The Tree of Knowledge" he alluded to the biblical myth of the expulsion from Paradise and man's eternal banishment. The man's slightly thrown-back head and the serpent's red tongue also indicate a connection with the self-portraits of the artist with the bleeding heart, *The Flower of Pain* (cat. no. 6), and others.

While on this subject, we might also mention the title page of "Alpha and Omega," Munch's lithographic series about the first human beings, done in 1908. Below the text he placed what looks like the head of a man. The text and vignette are placed in about the same relationship as on the title page of "The Tree of Knowledge," but this is too insignificant for us to conclude that they were made at the same time. Nor does the similarity to the Schiefler

The Tree of Knowledge, Title page, OKK T 2547-a3, Munch-Museet, Oslo (cat. no. 235)

GUSTAV SCHIEFLER

VERZEICHNIS
DES GRAPHISCHEN WERKS
EDVARD MUNCHS
BIS 1906

BERLIN
VERLAG: BRUNO CASSIRER

fig. 3   Vignette for Schiefler's catalogue, 1905

vignette necessarily indicate that they were created at the same time. The publication of Schiefler's volume 2, with a repetition of the title-page vignette, as late as 1927 may have revived Munch's interest in it.

Because of this loose title page the entire book—with its loose as well as permanently fixed pages—has been called "The Tree of Knowledge," even though there is little to indicate that the loose text pages and the large volume were originally planned to make one complete entity.

The date of these loose text pages is as uncertain as the date of the entire volume. Judging by the contents alone, the greater part must have been done after the break with Tulla Larsen in 1902. The way the texts read indicates that they may have been formulated some time in the period 1913-1915.

Christian Gierløff, a good friend of Munch's over many years, was one of the few who knew about "The Tree of Knowledge"; in his 1953 book about Edvard Munch he wrote:

> "He wanted to write *The Notes of a Madman.* Yes, and *The Tree of Knowledge.* And *The Castle of Love. Then* every one would learn what it meant to be insane, an insane young man! In the Grimsrød period, in his fiftieth year, he had a

streak of getting his letters and other writings in order. He had his old "Memoranda" and "Reminiscences"—and I still have a small unfinished notebook in black covers with now his, now my handwriting from that time."

Then follow a number of quotations, which are similar to texts in "The Tree of Knowledge," but, oddly enough, Gierløff does not point to this connection. This shows that the texts must have been fairly clearly formulated about 1913 when Munch was fifty years old, but does not help us as far as the time the actual writing on the big cardboard pages is concerned. His frequent use of colored crayons gives the pages the flavor of the 1920s, at which time Munch often used dry colors in both small and large drawings. A date in the 1920s is also made probable by the fact that Munch at that time was absorbed in his old notes and constantly made new efforts to arrange and edit them. He also gathered together many of his pronouncements on art and the creation of the "Life Frieze" and published them in a few small booklets.

fig. 4 *History,* 1914, OKK G/1, 378-75, Munch-Museet, Oslo

As indicated above, Gierløff mentions that Munch planned to write both "The Notes of a Madman" and "The Tree of Knowledge" besides "The Castle of Love," which is probably identical with the comedy mentioned earlier. "The Notes of a Madman" is a title appearing several times in Munch's notes, and in the 1929 introduction to one of the Kragerø ledgers it seems as if he thought of gathering most of his writings under the title "The Diary of a Mad Poet":

> Notes that I have made or been given by a dear friend— who little by little turned mad—and whom I met at the clinic in Copenhagen in 1908. I add to that some of my own notes, it is chiefly moods and philosophical thoughts —and thoughts about my paintings. All the notes that I have written, and which I have received from my mad friend I am trying to collect—since they sort of comple- ment one another.—There is a whole lot that my friend has written and which he probably fancied as novels or novelettes. (OKK T 2734)

Following this passage is a fairly detailed explana- tion of the contents of the literary sketches, which is also, of course, an account of Munch's life until the gunshot in 1902. He concluded this passage with: "The disfigurement through constant reminders brings him to a state of madness." This introduction, of course, was intended to be read after Munch's death, but the half-hearted attempt to hide his own identity behind the "mad friend" was not very con- vincing. Later in the same memorandum, Munch tried to indicate his intention behind the whole project:

> When I write these notes with drawings—it is not in order to tell about my own life.—To me it is a question of

studying certain hereditary phenomena that determine the life and fate of a human being—Just like phenomena indicating insanity in general. It is a study of the soul, I have since I practically can study myself—used myself as an anatomical soul preparation. But since it in the main is to create a work of art and a study of the soul, I have altered and exaggerated—and have used others for the studies—It is thus wrong to look upon these notes as a confession. I therefore divide—like Søren Kierkegaard —the work in two parts—the painter and his neurotic friend the poet. (OKK T 2734)

Among the loose text pages in "The Tree of Knowledge" are several with the title "The Notes of a Madman." Whether these pages were intended to serve as a section title or as title of a separate work or were to be an alternative title to the whole volume is impossible to determine. The drawings, cardboard pages, and style of writing, however, are so uniform that evidently these text pages all were made at the same time, and we may suppose that "The Notes of a Madman" was intended to constitute an important part of the texts Munch planned to gather in "The Tree of Knowledge."

The title "The Tree of Knowledge of Good and Evil" refers, of course, to the biblical account of Adam and Eve, but the notion of a tree as a carrier of knowledge, wisdom, and vitality is in no way limited to Christian mythology. The tree plays a very prom- inent role in a number of different religions, and the psychologist Carl G. Jung has shown that symbolic pictures of trees appear in dreams and fantasies during critical periods of a person's life.

In a Christian context, the Tree of Knowledge appears often in close connection with the Tree of Life. In Munch's decorations in the Aula in Oslo

University, one may interpret the old oak tree in *History* (fig. 4) as the Tree of Knowledge, and the lush foliage appearing with *Alma Mater* and her progeny on the opposite side as the Tree of Life. The painting *Life* in the Oslo City Hall dates from the same time as the decorations in the Aula. In this picture several generations are grouped at the foot of a big, luxuriant tree. This motif is clearly connected with other similar depictions of fertility in Munch's art, with a man and a woman on each side of a tree. One version of such a motif, from 1908, he even called *Adam and Eve,* but the young man and woman by the apple tree have seemingly little similarity to the more traditional representations of this theme.

Munch grew up in a religious home, and one of the big problems in his relationship with his father was undoubtedly the fact that Edvard couldn't share his faith. But Munch was not completely averse to every form of religion; one might rather say that throughout his life he remained a thoughtful agnostic. In his notes he often discussed such problems as the existence of God, the origin of life, and what happens after death. In one of the diary entries dated Nice, January 8, 1892, he wrote:

> Where that ability is located, of what essence it is, the ability which every living being possesses, the ability it always uses to form itself—develop itself—no one knows that—The Life germ—or if one prefers, the soul or the spirit—It is foolish to deny the presence of the soul—For one cannot deny the existence of the life germ—One must believe in immortality—as far as one can maintain that the life germ—the spirit of life must still exist after the death of the body—This ability—to keep a body together—to bring the substances to development—the life spirit, what happens to it—Nothing perishes—one has no example of that in nature—The body as dead—does not disappear —The substances separate—are converted. But the spirit of life, where does it go? No one can say where—to maintain its nonexistence after death is just as foolish as definitely pointing out of what kind—or *where* this spirit will exist. The fanatical belief in one single religion—for instance, Christianity—brought with it unbelief—brought with it a fanatical belief in a non-god. (OKK T 2760)

Even though Munch was extremely skeptical of Christianity and was completely unable to share the faith of the rest of the family in a personal God, he often used Christian motifs and ideas in his art. Perhaps best known is his *Madonna* (cat. nos. 216 and 222), which does not have much in common with other representations of the Mother of God. In his version, Madonna is the woman in love who, by conception, takes part in the creation of new life and contributes to the continued existence of mankind. The title may refer to the fact that conception is a sacred act, even though it is independent of all religious dogmas and concepts. The act of creation, the resurrection, and continuation of life become some-

The Empty Cross, OKK T 2547-54, Munch-Museet, Oslo (cat. no. 236)

thing that devolves jointly on the man and the woman.

Darwin's theory of the origin of species revolutionized the old ideas of the descent of man and made it impossible for modern artists to depict the myth of Adam and Eve as before. But creation, sin, and suffering were still mysteries that might be dealt with by artists, even if a new iconology was needed. Biblical motifs might continue to be well suited to a secular depiction of such problems, but in that case they were given a wholly or partly new content.

Munch's reworking of a Christian motif is even more evident in *The Empty Cross* than in *Madonna.* In the painting, the empty cross is still adored by a few persons as if nothing had happened; in the drawings (cat. no. 236) the cross stands alone in the background, while a blood-red sun shines across the sea. In a note about his work on the paintings *Inheritance, Dance of Life* and *The Empty Cross,* Munch wrote:

> The other picture—the red sun—Purple red as through a smoky glass the sun shines upon the world. On the heights in the background the cross stands empty and weeping women pray to the empty cross—lovers—whores— drunkards—and criminals fill the terrain below—and to the right in the picture—a steep slope goes down to the sea—the human beings fall down the steep slope—and terror-stricken—they hug the edge of the precipice—In the center of the chaos stands Munch, staring ahead, bewildered and with the frightened eyes of a child at all this—and says why why—It was I here—passion and the vices are raging all over the city—The terror of death lurked behind—a blood-red sun shines down on everything—and the cross is empty. (OKK T 2730)

Munch regarded suffering as a precondition of life as well as of art, and he must have looked upon his task as artist as distinctly parallel to that of the Saviour, although there appears to be no real identification with Jesus. Such a conception in some ways relates to Jæger's program: by exposing his own life, the artist made his life and his experiences available to other people and could thus contribute to their avoiding the same sufferings and experiences. Through the depiction of his sufferings, the artist might make life easier for other people, and in the final analysis this would mean that the artist takes upon himself our sufferings.

The belief that he was "cursed" with undesirable inherited traits created conflicts in his relations with other people. But the key to much of Munch's art is to be found in the reflections he made on his fate. In a note he said:

> A German asked me: but you can get rid of many of your afflictions. Then I answered—they belong to me and my art—they have become one with me and it will ruin my art. I want to keep these sufferings. (OKK T 2784b)

Perhaps his least ambiguous pictures of the suffering artist were the cover illustration for the periodical *Quickborn* in 1898 and the woodcut with the same motif, *The Flower of Pain* (cat. no. 6). A naked male is sitting with his lower body firmly rooted in the earth; the head—with Munch's own features—is thrown back, one hand is held behind his neck, while the other is placed on the man's heart, from which blood is flowing. At the spot where the blood flows into the ground, a beautiful blood-red lily is sprouting. Munch used this motif of the bloodstream from the artist's heart giving rise to a pretty flower in other pictures too.

There is reason to believe that following his stay at Dr. Jacobson's clinic in 1908-1909, Munch—whether he liked it or not—was rid of "many of his afflictions," and many people have maintained that this fact also destroyed his creative ability. Suffering was probably more important as a source for creative activity in his earlier pictures than in his later ones, but it was through reflection that he was able to give artistic expression to his suffering. In his later pictures this power of reflection—as might be expected—played an ever greater role, and one might say that the depiction of the old man in *History* shows that the reflecting artist has taken the place of the suffering artist. Through his tales about places and events in his long, full life, the old fisherman conveys his experiences to the new generation, in the person of the little boy, in the same way that Munch wanted to have other people share his life's experiences through his art.

In such a situation the written notes assumed a great importance, partly as a direct support for his memory and partly by giving Munch a chance to obtain a clearer view of the meaning of the main events in his life. During the various times he reviewed and edited the notes, there was naturally some weeding out, as well as a change in his interests. The purely realistic impressions from the 1880s and the early 1890s receive very modest space in the later drafts of notes and diaries; instead the eternal problems occupy his mind to a much higher degree: life, death, love, etc. The written childhood reminiscences are almost exclusively concerned with sickness and death, and the most important of them are included in subsequent drafts. Accounts of actual amorous relationships and erotic scenes are included only to the extent that they can be given a more general character or connected directly to the motifs of the pictures. As is true of the text pages in "The Tree of Knowledge," the whole is apt to be woven into a pattern in which, for instance, the theme of the transubstantiation of matter remains a central one—dead life provides nourishment for new life, generations follow generations as a result of the love between man and woman. Concurrently, a dualistic view of man often becomes apparent in these notes: man is bound to the earth by his desires and sufferings, but the soul is always yearning for something outside the sphere of man—for something infinite, pure, and beautiful.

The text pages in "The Tree of Knowledge" in many ways sum up Munch's world view much more clearly than any of his other writings. His philosophy was formed by pantheistic ideas with a marked strain of Darwinism. There are only two childhood reminiscences among the loose text pages, and they both appear with almost unchanged wording in several other renderings (see text in "Tree of Knowledge," p. A 28).*

On the first page of the big volume is a pasted-in pencil drawing which clearly illustrates this paragraph. The text and the drawing here give the impression of an idyllic scene, and it is hard to understand why Munch inserted them there. The continuation of the text is missing, however, whether by a conscious omission on the part of Munch or by accident. But it seems indeed a bit strange that Munch should have cut out what must have been the point of the story: death suddenly and horribly enters and spoils the idyll. The continuation appears in one of Munch's earliest diaries as follows:

> There is a white tent, and further away many white tents. Outside the tent sat a man and the woman and the man spoke long together—In the center of the yard was a table of gray stone and chairs of stone all about. There was a big

*A summary of the contents of "The Tree of Knowledge," with a translation of the texts, follows this article. Page numbers given here refer to this translation.

barn on one side of the yard with a high barn bridge, on the other side there were low buildings for the cows and sheep. One of the lambs had broken its leg, and they beat it until it died. It was so small and completely white. It lay flat on the floor and was just about alive. (OKK T 2761)

The next entry in this early diary is a short description of his mother telling her children that she is soon going to die, followed by a memory of a walk with his mother. The description of the walk is included in "The Tree of Knowledge" with about the same wording (see text in "Tree of Knowledge," p. A 9).

There is no illustration of this incident among the loose pages or in the big volume, but the motif did appear among the new lithographs that Munch printed in 1916. Reminiscences from his youth, his first love and his first erotic experiences are included in "The Tree of Knowledge" only in a few of the texts accompanying the pictures.

The earliest written indications of the fact that Munch regarded life eternal to have become actuality through transubstantiation are found in a couple of notes from 1892, which probably refer to an experience in Paris a few years earlier:

> I was walking up on the heights enjoying the soft air and the sun—The sun was warm and only once in a while some cool puffs—as if from a deep cellar. The moist earth was steaming—there was a smell of rotting leaves—and how quiet it was around me—and still I felt how things were in ferment and lived—in this steaming earth with the rotting leaves—in these bare branches that were soon again to sprout and live and the sun was to shine on the green leaves and flowers—and the wind was to bend them.
>
> I felt it to be a rapture to pass into, be united with—become this earth which always, always fermented, always shone upon by the sun—and lived, lived—and there were to grow plants up and out of my rotting body—and trees and flowers and the sun were to warm them and I was to be in them and nothing was to come to an end—that is eternity.

A reference to this theme is found in the text written on a small card placed in the volume (see text in "Tree of Knowledge" between p. 60 and p. A 41).

In the ledger compiled at Moss (OKK T 2782) there are two detailed notes which probably refer to something similar:

> I was standing on a high mountain and I saw the whole world below me—the world after thousands of years— I saw the small and the large planets which, obeying the laws of nature followed their fixed orbits—I saw the small planet Earth—which circled the sun. I saw how the transubstantiation began—how the air corroded the earth— how the desire first arose in the hard mass of the earth to be united with the air—and the transitory forms between the stones and the air were created: the living: men, animals—plants—There was a desire for procreation— for combustion, and the animals, men—the plants mated—Obeying the laws, the male loved the female—I saw men multiply—and were gathered in masses—they

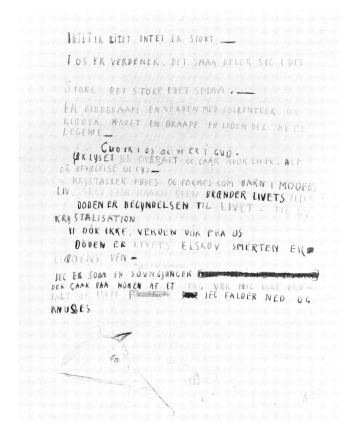

Nothing is small. Nothing is great, OKK T 2547-a31, Munch-Museet, Oslo (cat. no. 237)

spread over the earth and where the mass became lumpy and encountered other masses, they fought in order that the stronger would win—so also did the animals, men, and so also the plants. (OKK T 2782 - bi)

In "The Tree of Knowledge" are several text pages that deal with the beginnings of the earth and of man (see text in "Tree of Knowledge," pp. A 27 and A 7).

A definitely pantheistic view is expressed in other paragraphs (see text in "Tree of Knowledge," p. A 31 and cat. no. 237).

This passage is accompanied by a drawing in which a head is growing out of some boulders on a hill in the foreground. Far below is a wide landscape.

He touched on the lot of man on earth in a text that exists in two practically identical versions in "The Tree of Knowledge," one of them written with ink and colored crayon on a sketchbook page, which was pasted onto the cardboard page, and the other—which appears on the other side of the same page—was drawn with multicolored crayon directly on the cardboard (see text in "Tree of Knowledge," p. A 14).

Vision, OKK T 2547-85, Munch-Museet, Oslo (cat. no. 238)

Notes of a Madman, OKK T 2547-a21, Munch-Museet, Oslo (cat. no. 239)

Even though Munch by and large adopted a conception of man based on natural science, he was not quite willing to let go of the concept of man as a creature belonging to a higher, metaphysical reality. Even though man, through his body, is indissolubly bound to the earth, man's brain may be capable of soaring thoughts and yearning toward something bigger and more pure than itself. There are many examples of such dualism in Munch's art—man who is a prisoner of his passions and lives in vice and in sin, but yearns toward a better and purer existence. The drawings and the notes about *Vision* should probably be looked at in this connection. Among the text pages of "The Tree of Knowledge" there are no notations dealing with this motif, but he did paste a pencil drawing of *Vision* in the big ledger, where there is some space for a text (cat. no. 238). A comparable rough drawing is fixed to the Moss ledger,

and it is there supplied with the following text:

> I lived down in the depths among slime and animals. I forced myself up to the surface, yearning for the light colors—a dazzlingly white swan was gliding over there on the shiny surface—it mirrored its clean lines in the water—which also reflected the light clouds in the sky. I reached my hands out for it—asked it to come—but it couldn't—couldn't reach it across the ring of mud and slime that surrounded me, it dirtied its white breast and glided away. (OKK T 2782 - a7)

"The Tree of Knowledge" contains several sketches of a man, divided into three centers of power with corresponding force lines that show how man is tied to the earth through his legs, while the body (with heart, stomach, and sex organs) links him with other living beings, and the head connects him with the higher spheres. As a heading for one such drawing he wrote "The Notes of a Madman" (cat. no. 239). There are texts on this theme in "The Tree of Knowledge." Remembering his own mental state during the years after 1902, he tried to portray a split personality—or the cleavage of the soul, as he prefers to call it. "The Notes of a Madman" is often accompanied by one or two birds and that is true in "The Tree of Knowledge" (see text p. A 21 below a

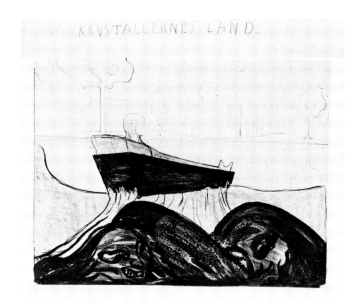

In the Land of Crystal, OKK T 2547-75, Munch-Museet, Oslo (cat. no. 240)

The Urn, OKK T 2547-49, Munch-Museet, Oslo (cat. no. 241)

drawing of a big bird sitting on the chest of a prostrate, naked man).

Here not only is the intellect clouded but the mind is also split. Another drawing shows two big birds flying in different directions; this too has been given the title "The Notes of a Madman," and the text makes it clear what the drawing is supposed to depict (see text in "Tree of Knowledge," p. A 33).

A brief passage written on the same page as "nothing is small, nothing is great" must also presumably be looked at in connection with the circumstances leading to his breakdown (see text in "Tree of Knowledge," p. A 31, "To a woman . . ."). The fact that the warning was not heeded becomes quite evident in a text and drawing on another loose page (see text in "Tree of Knowledge," p. A 23).

As we have seen, Munch considered transubstantiation as a possible solution to the problem of life and death, but this is a rather unsatisfactory solution as far as the single individual is concerned. Munch's idea of an existence after death could also assume concrete forms—in the form of *In the Land of Crystal* where everything was cleansed and radiantly clear. Death became a kind of metamorphosis, during which the body merged into another state—was crystallized. Through crystallization the elements are cleansed of all impurities and are resurrected in a completely pure state. This is indeed a beautiful image, which Munch depicted in the lithograph *In the Land of Crystal*, made in 1896. In "The Tree of Knowledge" ·he included a passage that has a close relationship to this motif (see text on p. A 5).

An impression of *In the Land of Crystal* was pasted

on p. 75 of the big volume (cat. no. 240), and on the preceding page is the lithograph *Funeral March*, in which the theme of transubstantiation is even more obvious.

The text, however, is more closely related to a later lithograph, in which the coffin with the dead person is in the foreground, and a dark-skinned man is ringing a huge bell. We have not arrived at a certain date for this lithograph, but c. 1916 is a reasonable guess.

The lithograph *The Urn* (cat. no. 241) is a beautiful image of rebirth as part of the process of transubstantiation. The print is included in the big volume, with a short text written in multicolored pencil on a piece of thin tissue paper which has been pasted onto the same sheet (see text in "Tree of Knowl-

The Voice, 1894/1895. OKK T 2547-7, Munch-Museet, Oslo (cat. no. 242)

edge," p. A 39).

Besides the rather philosophical texts, "The Tree of Knowledge" also contains several shorter texts that are fairly closely connected with some of Munch's pictures. It may be useful to consider the various pictures in the order they appear in the book and offer comments at the same time.

On p. 1 in the big volume is the drawing of people haying; both this motif and the attached text were explained above.

The next picture is a drawing of *The Voice*, pasted on p. 7 (cat. no. 242). The motif is also found in the small woodcut pasted on p. 13. In a few notes in the ledger from Moss we can clearly see the close connection between this motif and other Munch depictions of the young man's awakening erotic interest:

> How pale you are in the moonlight, and how dark are your eyes—They are so big that they cover half the sky—I can hardly see your features—but I can make out your white teeth when you smile—When you stand this way—and my eyes look into your large eyes—in the pale moonlight—do you know then—delicate hands weave invisible threads—that are bound around my heart—leading from my eyes—through your large dark eyes—through your heart—Your eyes are so large now that you are so close to me—They are like two large dark heavens. (OKK T 2782-a1)

> The summer night shed gold over your face and your hair—Only your eyes—were dark—and sparkled with a mystical glow—A gold pillar stood in the water—and rocked back and forth—it melted because of its own brilliance—and gold flowed on the surface—

> When our eyes met, invisible hands tied fine threads—

that went through your large eyes in through my eyes and bound our hearts together. (OKK T 2782 ah)

The first of the loose pages also has a text that seems to be closely related to this theme, but it evidently refers to *The Kiss* (see text in "Tree of Knowledge," p. A 1). A copy of the woodcut *The Kiss* was pasted into the big volume on p. 21.

A passage in "The Tree of Knowledge" concentrating on the eyes may have been intended for *The Voice*, but it fits *Attraction I* on p. 15 (see text on p. A 45).

Separation is of course closely related to this motif; here the woman is leaving the man, while her hair flutters behind her and maintains the link with the man. In the big volume, the lithograph *Separation II* was pasted on p. 29, and on the preceding page Munch pasted a large sheet of tissue paper, on which he wrote in block letters, using watercolor (see text on p. A 37).

This text is so brief and concise that it is rather difficult to understand unless one knows some of the other notes about the invisible threads that bind the hearts together. In Munch's pictures this theme has been formulated in a concrete manner by having the woman's hair entwine the man's heart. In the list from Moss there is an interesting notation about this, which also seems to refer to the woodcut *Man's Head in Woman's Hair* (p. 41), which is usually interpreted as a Salomé motif:

> Deep violet, darkness fell over the earth—I sat under a tree—whose leaves were beginning to yellow, to wilt—She had been sitting next to me—she had bent her head over

mine—the blood-red hair had entwined itself around me. It had twisted itself around me like blood-red snakes—its finest threads had entangled themselves in my heart— then she had risen—I don't know why—slowly she moved away toward the sea—farther and farther away—then the strange thing had arrived—I felt as if there were invisible threads between us—I felt as if invisible threads of her hair still entwined me—and thus when she disappeared completely across the sea—then I still felt how it hurt where my heart was bleeding—because the threads could not be cut. (OKK T 2782-1)

Some of the mystical summer night mood found in *The Voice* also appears in quite a few other motifs. Among those in the big volume, we might mention the woodcuts *The Stump* (p. 17) and *The Lonely Ones* (p. 9). But in these two woodcuts the melancholy mood is somewhat more pronounced than young love, and they seem to be more closely related to *Melancholy* (p. 45). This is emphasized by a note in the ledger from Moss:

> On the beach. Melancholy.
> I walked along by the sea—the moon was shining through dark clouds—the stones protruded above the water, mystically like sea people some of them were large white heads that grimaced and laughed—some up on the beach others down in the water—the dark blue violet sea rose and fell—sighed among the stones—
> One evening I walked by myself by the water—it sighed and swished among the stones—there were gray long clouds along the horizon—everything was as if extinct— as if in another world—a deathlike landscape—but now there was life over by the pier—it was a man and a woman—and another man came—with oars over his shoulder—and the boat was lying down there—ready to go out (OKK T 2782-bw)
> It was evening. I walked along the ocean—there was moonlight between the clouds. The stones protruded through the water, mystically like sea people, there were large white heads laughing—someone up on the beach, others down in the water—and she who walked by my side looked like a mermaid—with bright eyes, and her flowing hair shines like gold in the light from the horizon. (OKK T 2782-r)

No texts in "The Tree of Knowledge" seem to fit these woodcuts, nor is there any text fitting the woodcut pasted on p. 11—a curiously elongated picture with the heads of a man and a woman on a background that shows some kind of a city.

Pasted on p. 23 is a copy of the lithograph *Jealousy I*, and among the loose pages there is a text relevant to this motif. On a gray-brown cardboard page, of a different kind than the other loose cardboard pages, Munch wrote in multicolored pencil, adding pictures of human eyes (see text in "Tree of Knowledge," p. A 43).

Pasted on the back of the same page is a text on the same kind of paper as the texts for the two childhood reminiscences (see text on p. 24). The same text also appears, written with colored crayon, on a loose tissue paper (see text on p. A 35).

Moonlight glides over your face, OKK T 2547-64, Munch-Museet, Oslo (cat. no. 243)

On the facing page is pasted an impression of the lithograph *Madonna*, printed in black, and this is one of the few places where there is a direct tie-in between picture and text in this volume.

There are many variants of the texts to *Madonna*, the earliest ones probably having been formulated some time between 1890 and 1895. A note which communicates the feeling of a personal experience probably belongs to an early date:

> Your face contains all the tenderness in the world—your eyes dark like the bluish-green sea—suck me to you— your mouth has a painfully tender smile—as if you wanted to ask my forgiveness for something—your lips are sensual—like two blood-red snakes—There is piety in your face under the moonlight lamp—from your pure forehead your hair is brushed back—your profile is that of a Madonna—your lips glide apart as in pain. (OKK T 2782-ar)

There is another drawing with text loosely inserted in the book; it closely resembles *Madonna* but also points to another motif not included in the big volume, namely *Lovers in Waves*. The sketch, drawn with a brush in red and black on top of a faint pencil drawing, depicts a tightly embracing, nude couple, surrounded by wavelike lines, and it has the following text (cat. no. 243, see text on sheet inserted between p. 64 and p. 65).

The woodcut *Meeting in Space* (p. 33) and the lithograph *Decorative Design* (p. 65) depict man and woman like two planets, or different worlds, and a text, written on a heavy piece of cardboard, suits both drawings equally well (see text on p. A 47).

Two people merging and creating a bright flame were depicted by Munch in the lithograph *The Flower of Love*, but this print was not included in the big volume. We may get an idea of the subsequent state in *Ashes,* pasted on p. 39. A brief text on the same theme was pasted on one of the loose cardboard pages (see text on p. A 51).

An autobiographical note in one of his diaries also offers a description that seems to fit this motif rather well:

> She had never before stayed as long as this with him—he implored her not to leave—he was more ardent than ever before—he had to embrace her again feel her kisses again—as soon as the fervor had burned out again when they got up—She stood straight fixing her hair with the posture of a queen. There was something in her expression that made him feel fearful—he didn't know what it was (OKK T 2781-ah)

There doesn't seem to be any text for the woodcut *The Heart* (p. 35), either in "The Tree of Knowledge" or elsewhere. Nor is there any clear and unambiguous text to go with such an important motif as *Vampire* (p. 37) among the loose leaves. In another note Munch described the experience on which the motif may have been based:

> Intermezzo. He sat with his arm around her waist—her head was so close to him—it was so strange to have her eyes, her mouth, her breast so close to him—he saw every hair in her eyelashes—looked at the greenish shades in her eyes—there was the transparency of the ocean—the pupil was large in the semidarkness—he touched her mouth with his finger—her lips' blood flesh yielded at the touch—and her lips were drawn into a smile while he felt her big blue-gray eyes rest on him—he investigated her brooch which gleamed with red lights—he touched it with his trembling fingers And he placed his head on her breast—he felt the blood course through her veins—he listened to her heartbeat—He buried his face in her lap he felt two burning lips on his neck—it made him tremble through his body—a freezing rapture—so that he convulsively pulled her to him. (OKK T 2771)

Man's desire for woman is the motif of the lithograph *The Alley* (p. 47) and probably also of *Man's Head under Woman's Breast* (p. 81). Munch wrote very few texts to pictures of this type; he probably thought that the picture spoke for itself, but on the back of a letter he scribbled with a pencil:

> You are like one who walks down a street of hands that reach for your naked body. (OKK T 2801)

Munch also at times attempted to express his view of woman through the symbolic depiction of three women—or woman in three stages. A copy of the

lithograph was undoubtedly pasted in the big volume at one time, since one of the pages still shows a clear imprint of this lithograph. There is no caption for the picture among the loose pages, but in a booklet about the origin of the "Life Frieze," printed after 1925, Munch provided us with a good "explanation" of the motif. He here related that Henrik Ibsen turned up at his exhibition at Blomqvist in 1895, and, joined by Munch, walked around and looked at every picture displayed:

> He especially took an interest in the woman in three stages. I had to explain it to him.—It is the dreaming woman—the woman with a zest for life—and the woman as nun—she stands there pale behind the trees—....
> Some years later Ibsen wrote *When We Dead Awaken*—....
> The three women—Irene the whiteclad dreaming out toward life—Maja with a zest for life—the naked one. The woman of sorrow—with the staring pale head among the tree trunks—Irene's fate, nurse—
> These three women appear in Ibsen's drama—as in my picture many places.
> —During a light summer's night the darkly dressed one had been seen walking in the garden together with Irene, who was naked or in a kind of bathing suit.
> —The lustful white body against the black colors of sorrow—all in the light summer's night where life and death walk hand in hand.

The fear of death and of life is a thread through most of Munch's art. He worked out some of the fear by giving it artistic expression, but he was never able to rid himself of it completely. He expressed this most powerfully, it seems, in the many versions of *The Scream*. Strangely enough, this motif was not included in the big volume as it appears today. Perhaps this may be explained in a very prosaic way: Munch may have had very few impressions of this lithograph and needed the few he had for exhibitions, etc. However, in "The Tree of Knowledge" there is a text, painted with watercolor on thin tissue paper, relevant to *The Scream* (see text on p. 53).

On the following sheet, p. 55, are marks indicating that a pasted-in sheet of paper has been removed, and according to the size it might very well have been *The Scream*. The text was painted in much the same way as the one pasted in right before the lithograph *Separation*. Both are so different from the other text pages that it is reasonable to suppose that they were made at some other time. Both pages feature a concise text, indicating that they were written at a late point in time. There is not much of the original feeling of terror that must have been the impulse for *The Scream* left in the very condensed version. Munch attempted to describe this experience in a more detailed manner in many other places. The following text appears on the back of an impression of the lithograph, printed on violet

The Tree, 1915. OKK T 2547-135, Munch-Museet, Oslo (cat. no. 244)

The Waterfall of Blood, OKK T 2547-109, Munch-Museet, Oslo (cat. no. 245)

cardboard (now in the Landesgalerie in Stuttgart):

> I walked along the road with two friends. The sun went down—The sky was blood red—and I felt a breath of sadness—I stood still tired unto death—over the blue-black fjord and city lay blood and tongues of fire My friends continued on—I remained—trembling from fear—I felt the great scream—Nature.

The text was repeated below, with the last part formulated in a different way:

> —over the blue-black fjord and the city lay the clouds like blood and tongues of fire. My friends continued on and I remained trembling from fear. I felt the great infinite scream through nature.

The woodcut *Anxiety* was also originally included in the big volume but was later removed. It is infused with a similar mood, although the motif was worked out somewhat differently. A suitable text for this picture also appears on a sheet pasted onto one of the loose cardboard pages (see text on p. A 41).

Even though Munch primarily gave expression to the fear and despair of the individual in pictures like *The Scream* and *Anxiety*, there is also a clear indication of the more universal character of such fear in these pictures. Based on Munch's personal fears, the pictures also express the rootlessness and fear of people in a society in dissolution. This universal aspect became more marked when Munch reverted to the theme of fear in a number of graphics made in 1915 and 1916. The world community was at that time not only about to dissolve, it was facing a complete collapse. The outbreak of the First World War in the autumn of 1914 was no doubt a shock to most people in Europe, and as the reports of the horrors of war poured in, many must have thought that the extinction of man was about to become a reality.

During the first six months of the war Munch made seven small lithographs that he exhibited under the title *Ragnarok* (in Norse mythology, the end of the world). People with taut expressions, staring straight ahead, walk in groups toward an unknown fate, at times at the bottom of a deep chasm or on the rim of a precipice. Others cling in despair to the mountainside. A somewhat larger lithograph was also made at about that time, as was a woodcut in which the panic-stricken horde walks straight ahead. He also depicted the horrors of war in a series of magnificent woodcuts from 1916-1917, based on Henrik Ibsen's play *The Pretenders*. He dealt with mass death in a more direct manner in other graphics, such as the three lithographs of *The Tree* from 1915 and 1916. A copy of the 1915 version was loosely inserted in the big volume. There is a pile of dead human bodies at the foot of the tree, while the landscape reveals an almost endless, steaming battlefield. But the sun is shining in the sky, and its rays penetrate the tree's foliage and illuminate the macabre collection of corpses (cat. no. 244).

The belief in transubstantiation brings with it a measure of hope in all the misery. In 1916 Munch reverted to this motif in a lithograph of a nude, pregnant woman, leaning against a tree, while the sun sheds its light over the entire scene. But on the ground, next to the woman and the tree, are the rotting plants and bodies that are the nourishment of new growth.

In other depictions of battlefields it is more difficult to detect this faith in the continuity of life; their most marked characteristic seems to be hopelessness in the face of interminable slaughter. This is most strongly evident in *Waterfall of Blood*, of which he made several versions. There is both a drawing in colored crayon and a hand-colored lithograph of

The Land of Neutralia, 1915. OKK G/l 395-59, Munch-Museet, Oslo (cat. no. 246)

United States of Europe, OKK T 2547-137, Munch-Museet, Oslo (cat. no. 247)

this motif in the big volume, both loosely inserted (cat. no. 245). The blood is pouring down the mountainside in an unending stream; the picture makes a powerful statement on the war's meaningless sacrifice of human lives.

While Europe was ravaged by war, there were many who profited greatly from it in those countries that remained nonbelligerent. Munch also made an apt commentary on the situation of the neutral countries in the lithograph *The Land of Neutralia,* which originally was made as a poster for an exhibition of Scandinavian art in Copenhagen in 1915 (cat. no. 246). In this picture he depicted the neutral countries (Norway and Denmark) as two young, beautiful girls picking apples, completely unaffected by the ship sinking in the sea beyond.

According to a notation made by Mr. Nielsen, a printer, the lithograph *Waterfall of Blood* was printed on April 29, 1916, and on the same day he also printed a number of other lithographs for Munch.

One of them was *Battlefield,* which also has been loosely inserted in the big volume. Another is the previously mentioned *Childhood Memory,* with the mother and the two oldest children. A third motif is another repetition of an old idea: the woman ascending out of an urn. In three new lithographs he applied this theme to the battlefield and the situation in Europe (cat. no. 247). One version was supplied with a text both above and below the picture. Above the picture is: "Can't I come soon? Les etats Europa . . . Est ce que je peut venit?" and below the picture is "Est ce que je peut venir? Latats Reuni Europa." Rebirth was given a political aspect: on the battlefields of Europe, where brother fought against brother for many years, a united Europe will arise and create a new future. Munch developed his ideas about a united Europe in a few notes:

The flame of culture dies and lives again. A spark that is ignited, burns and goes out in order to ignite again in another place—live—die—A flickering igniting spark. The flame was lit and died out in the kingdoms of the east, burned on in Palestine, Egypt—Greece and Rome—and in Europe—Greece Rome—Europe America—Greece gave her spirit to Rome after having bled to death in civil

fig. 5 *Workers Digging,* 1920, OKK G/1 418-40, Munch-Museet, Oslo

wars—That will probably happen to Europe too. Bled to death it will give its flame to America where it will once again live and die—and live again in the lands of the Orient? When will it happen? The United States of Europe seem to be the only thing that can keep the flame alive. (OKK N 67)

As we know, the last years of the First World War saw the outbreak and the victory of the Russian Revolution. The revolution immediately spread to Finland, which at that time was a Russian grand duchy. This country, which had not taken an active part in the war, now became the scene of a bloody civil war. Both the "Reds" and the "Whites" committed atrocities until the Finnish bourgeoisie, with the aid of German troops, was able to vanquish the opposition. This was followed by a systematic persecution and slaughter of the defeated side, creating a feeling of horror at home and abroad. In 1918 Munch offered his view of the execution of the Finnish Communists in several drawings and a lithograph. The pictures show great similarity to Manet's and Goya's stirring pictures of similar occurrences.

But the war finally came to an end, and life continued for the lonely artist at Ekely. Even though the hermit refused to receive annoying journalists and others who would waste his time, he was very much concerned with what happened around town. The razing of old buildings and the construction of new ones, discussions about the colors of the buildings facing Karl Johan Street, and plans for a new city hall were all matters that interested him greatly. When a big fire occurred in the center of the city in 1919 he was on the spot and shortly after did a painting with a motif from the fire. He was busy with

a new frieze—dedicated to the life and work of the laboring classes—throughout most of the 1920s (fig. 5). As was the case with so many of his big plans, this one too remained unfinished. But the plans bear witness to an artist who was not only a vital force but also retained his ability to think in the grand manner.

His many attempts to bring order to his diaries and notes gradually assumed great dimensions, even though the work always came to nothing. "The Tree of Knowledge" and "The Notes of a Madman" may also belong among these great projects that were never finished. It was probably a project that was primarily intended to gather together—and eventually have published—texts of somewhat restricted character. It is first and foremost descriptions of Munch's state of mind during the years 1902-1908 that belong in "The Notes of a Madman," while "The Tree of Knowledge" probably was an attempt to create a comprehensive theory of perception and to express his thoughts on creation, life, death, and the development of man. It is typical that none of the texts in "The Tree of Knowledge" deals with Munch's view of art, but this may be explained by the fact that he had published his ideas on art in a separate booklet.

The texts that belong to certain pictures were most often pasted in, either on the loose cardboard pages or in the volume itself. They may therefore have been written for some other reason than were the big cardboards. Perhaps they were made at the time the cardboards were mixed in with the book's pages, and Munch then saw a chance to link everything into one whole.

It is hoped that future research will provide further clarification regarding the background of "The Tree of Knowledge" and the dating of the texts, as well as information about the volume itself. There is still so much that we simply do not know—especially regarding the later part of Munch's life. Not until this material has been carefully gone through and everything is seen in its proper context will there be hope of having all the pieces fall into place.

Translated from the Norwegian by Erik J. Friis

The Tree of Knowledge, Title page, OKK T 2547-a3, Munch-Museet, Oslo (cat. no. 235)

Tree of Knowledge: Catalogue and Translation

THE FOLLOWING IS A DESCRIPTION OF THE CONTENTS of "The Tree of Knowledge." The pages are listed in the order they currently appear. Numbers A1, A3, and so on, designate loosely inserted sheets, and numbers 1, 3, and so on, are pages bound in the volume.

The text was translated by Alf Bøe, with the advice of James Edmondston, British Council Representative in Norway.

A1 Text written in multicolored crayon
64.7 x 50
The kiss
two burning lips against mine
heaven and earth passed away
and two black eyes looked into
mine—

A3 Title page
Text and drawing in red and green crayon
65.7 x 50
The Tree of Knowledge
of
good and evil

A5 Text written in multicolored crayon
64.7 x 50
Below the text are marks from a mounted sheet of
paper
The soil of the earth longed for the air
air became water and earth and earth became air
   I dreamt in the night:
A coffin stood on a hill. In it was a corpse. Beside it
a moor stood and rang a great bell
The moor sang go thou into the land of crystals
a file of men and women was passing below
repeating go thou into the land of crystals
heaven split asunder and threw down its light—a
great
realm of crystals was seen playing in all
the colors of the rainbow against diamond clear
crystals great and small. Some took
the form of palaces others of trees

A7 Text written in blue crayon
64.7 x 50
Above the text is a mounted drawing of a naked
woman and trees in a rainstorm
Black and brown crayon on paper measuring
41 x 25
   The air gnawed at the earth
The earth sweated slime which became
people animals and plants
the water evaporated into clouds
the clouds fell down as rain
People and animals and trees are
flames which rise up from the earth

1 Mounted on the page:
Mowers at Work (Mowing the Grass)
Pencil, charcoal, and green crayon
32.7 x 25.6
OKK T 2547-1

3 Marks from a mounted sheet of paper,
about 50 x 35

A9 Text written in pencil, green crayon, and red
watercolor on a mounted sheet of paper measuring
29 x 22.2
It was dark and gray
all the way down the stairs the boy who
held her by the hand could
not get down fast enough
   why do you walk so slowly? he asked
she paused at every
step to draw her breath
   Outside in the entrance daylight
blinded him
   She wore a bleached lilac
colored hat long ribbons fluttered with every breath of wind
   The air was so strangely warm and close yet with cool
drafts
the grass shot up between
the cobblestones–light green grass
It was spring

A10 (Reverse of A9)
Marks from a mounted sheet of paper, about 50 x 25

A11 Text written in red crayon
64.7 x 50
The earth was aflame

A13 Text and drawing of the sun with rays in multi-colored crayon
64.7 x 50
The earth struck flames toward the peripheries of the universe
the flames burnt down to ashes again
eyes I saw–blue and shining
dark with glow-filled flashes
asking
seeking
yearning
willing it
they sought their way out toward the periphery
freed from the earth–children of man
to fall back
to blend their ashes with maternal earth
why? for what?
out of will, out of compulsion they rose and fell
sparks and glow in the darkness of night
God is in all
All is in us (God)
Brothers in the mighty play of life!
The play is willed dared and done
For once again to will and dare and die

A14 (Reverse of A13)
Text written in pen and crayon on mounted paper measuring 25.2 x 19
The earth struck flames toward
the peripheries of the universe–the flames
burnt down to ashes again–
eyes I saw blue and shining, dark
with glow-filled flashes—asking
seeking, yearning, willing it they sought
their way out toward the periphery–freed from
the earth–child of man–to
fall back–to blend their ashes
with maternal earth–
Why?–For what?–out of will
out of compulsion they rose and fell
sparks and glow in the darkness
of night
Sparks from the earth!
God is in all all is in us–
–Brothers in the mighty play of life–
–The play is ended willed dared and done
–in order once more to will and live and die

A15 Mounted on the page:
The Iguano
Black crayon
41.5 x 31.5

A17 Text written in black crayon
64.7 x 50

We die not
The world dies from us

A19 Text written in black crayon
64.7 x 50
Nothing is small. Nothing is great

A20 (Reverse of A19)
Text written in brown crayon
64.7 x 50
Joy is sorrow's friend
spring autumn's messenger
Death is life's birth

A21 Drawing in green crayon of a bird of prey sitting on the chest of a naked man and text written in multicolored crayon
64.7 x 50
The fountain
Notes of a mad-
man
A bird of prey has taken
hold within me. Its claws
have gripped my
heart. Its beak has
buried itself in my breast
and the beatings of its wings
have darkened my
reason

A23 Text written in multicolored crayon
64.7 x 50
Below the text is a drawing of a naked man lying on the ground, holding up a bleeding hand
The blood seethed inside him. A hellish
brew fermented from the plant's blood the wine–blended with the poison of the woman-vampire–it was a boiling hot
brew in the machinery of the brain
    The cellular tissue of the brain was expanded, on the boiled and blown tissue was written as
in a phonograph a devilish script
    The cellular tissue which was swollen like a balloon blown near to bursting–deflated like a crumpled leaf again to be boiled and swollen
and to scream as in a choir of devils–a pyre of cadavers of the plant–the tobacco sent
its stunning and pestilential ashes into the crevices and labyrinths of the cranium
    He saw a mass of faces staring
toward himself
    He lay crushed in the street
he raised a blood-red arm

A25 Text written in crayon
64.7 x 50
Drawing in brown crayon on mounted paper measuring 40.8 x 25, of a man inscribed in three power-circles.
Notes of a madman–
    Man and the circles of man
Above the periphery reaches

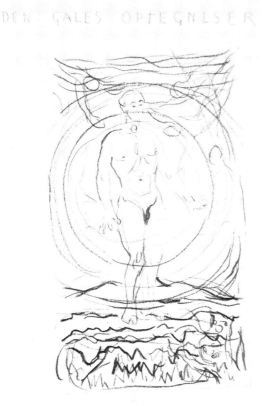

DEN GALES OPTEGNLSER

MENNESKET OG DEIS CIRKLER
OVENTIL CAAR PEREFERIEN
OP I ÆTHER SVINCNINGER –
OG NEDENTIL I JORDSVINCNINGER

Man and the Circles of Man, OKK T 2547-a25, Munch-Museet,
Oslo

Up into the vibrations of the ether–
and below into the vibrations of the earth

7 Mounted on the page:
The Voice 1894 or 1895
Pencil and india ink
32.5 x 50
On the reverse is a sketch for *The Kiss*

8 (Reverse of 7)
Marks from a mounted paper about 23 x 45

9 Mounted on the page:
The Lonely Ones 1899
Woodcut printed in black and gray
47 x 63.7
OKK G/t 601–47, Sch. 133

11 Mounted on the page:
Man and Woman 1899 (?)

Woodcut
17.8 x 51.5
OKK G/t 676–3

13 Mounted on the page:
The Voice 1898
Woodcut
38.3 x 16.7
OKK G/t 585–9, Sch. 113

14 (Reverse of 13)
Marks from a mounted paper, about 23 x 45

15 Mounted on the page:
Attraction I 1896
Lithograph
51.2 x 39
Signed in pencil: "Edv. Munch"
OKK G/1 207–44, Sch. 65

16 (Reverse of 15)
Imprint from the woodcut *The Stump*
mounted on page 17

A27 Text written in multicolored crayon on mounted
paper measuring 39.7 x 24.2
Earth loved the air–the air
fretted it away and the earth became
air and the air became earth
the trees stretched their branches
toward heaven devouring air
the trees uprooted themselves from
the earth and mankind was
born
all is life and movement
Even inside the earth are
found the sparks of life
    Thousands of years passed
a pain was born some hope
some smile and the hope disappeared the smile died away
and generation trampled
on generation

A28 (Reverse of A27)
Text, written in green and blue crayon and red
watercolor on mounted paper measuring 29 x 22
It was a high hill with
green grass and far up at the top
against the sky was the forest–
cows and sheep were
grazing and the tinkling of bells
was heard
    The sky above was blue
with white clouds
the grass in the valley was so
green
    There, down in the valley people were making
hay

A29 Text and drawing of power-circles in charcoal and
multicolored crayon
64.7 x 50

Mankind and its three centers of power–
Ethereal waves
The brain
The heart
The passions
Earth waves

A31 Text and drawing of a head in the rock, and a landscape far below in multicolored crayon
64.7 x 50

Nothing is small nothing is great–
Inside us are worlds. What is small divides itself into
what is great the great into the small.–
A drop of blood a world with its solar center and planets. The ocean a drop a small part of a body—
　　God is in us and we are in God.
　　Primeval light is everywhere and goes where life is–everything is movement and light–
　　Crystals are born and shaped like children in the womb. Even in the hard stone burns the fire of life
　　Death is the beginning of life–of a new crystallization
　　We do not die, the world dies away from us
Death is the love-act of life pain is
the friend of joy
　　To a woman
I am like a sleepwalker
who walks on the ridge of a roof Do not wake me brutally or I shall fall down and
be crushed

A33 Text and drawing of two birds of prey in multicolored crayon
64.7 x 50

Notes of a madman
My soul is as two
wild birds which pull
each its separate way

17 Mounted on the page:
The Stump, Mystery of the Shore 1899
Woodcut printed in black and green from two blocks
41 x 64.3
OKK G/t 593, Sch. 125

19 Marks from a mounted paper, about 28 x 42

21 Mounted on the page:
The Kiss 1902
Woodcut printed in black and gray from two blocks on thin japan paper
60 x 49
The print has been mounted with the reverse up, which gives it a special blurred quality
On the front is an inscription by the printer, dated 28/10. 1916
OKK G/t 580–32, Sch. 102 D

23 Mounted on the page:
Jealousy 1896

Lithograph
36.5 x 50.5
OKK G/1 201–21, Sch. 57

24 (Reverse of 23)
Mounted on the page:
Text written in red watercolor on paper measuring 29 x 22.2

The pause when all the world stayed
its course
your face holds all the beauty of this
earth
your lips carmine as
the ripening fruit move
apart as in pain
the smile of a corpse
now life gives its hand to death
the chain is completed which binds
the thousand generations that are
dead to the thousand generations that are to come

A35 Text written in multicolored crayon on a loose, thin sheet of paper measuring 29.3 x 39.2

The same text as on page 24, written on a loose, thin sheet of paper, and with different line lengths.

A37 Text written in multicolored watercolors on a thin sheet of paper measuring about 63 x 47
The sheet is glued to page 27 along the inner edge

When You left me over
the ocean it was as if
fine threads still united us tearing as
in a wound.

29 Mounted on the page:
Separation II 1896
Lithograph
41 x 62.5
On the page are marks of glue, which indicate that a bigger sheet of paper had been mounted there before
OKK G/1 210–22, Sch. 68

31 Marks of glue from mounted paper

33 Mounted on the page:
Meeting in Space 1899
Woodcut printed in black, red, and green
30 x 37
OKK G/t 603–46, Sch. 135

35 Mounted on the page:
The Hearth 1899
Woodcut printed in black, red, and green
34.2 x 29.6
OKK G/t 602–48, Sch. 134

37 Mounted on the page:
Vampire 1895
Lithograph
38.6 x 55.2
OKK G/t 567–83, Sch. 34

39 Mounted on the page:
Ashes 1899
Lithograph printed in black on green paper
44.5 x 61.6
OKK G/1 236–37, Sch. 120

41 Mounted on the page:
Man's Head in Woman's Hair 1896
Woodcut printed in gray, red, and blue
63.3 x 47
Signed in pencil: "Edv. Munch"
OKK G/t 569–41, Sch. 80

42 (Reverse of 41)
Imprint from the lithograph
The Woman 1899
Sch. 122

43 Marks from a mounted paper, about 46 x 63, probably the lithograph *The Woman* of which there is an imprint on the opposite page

45 Mounted on the page:
Melancholy III
Woodcut printed in black, yellow, and green
43 x 48
OKK G/1 571–27, Sch. 81

47 Mounted on the page:
The Alley 1895
Lithograph
43 x 26.8
OKK G/1 197–83, Sch. 36

A39 Text written in multicolored crayon on thin paper measuring 63 x 49.2, glued to page 49
The Urn.
Rebirth–
Out of the impure substance rose a face
full of sorrow and beauty

49 Mounted on the page:
The Urn 1896
Lithograph
50 x 30.5
OKK G/1 205–40, Sch. 63

51 Mounted on the page:
Salome-Paraphrase 1898
Woodcut
54.5 x 33.7
OKK G/t 581–15, Sch. 109

53 Mounted on the page:
Text written in multicolored watercolor on thin paper measuring 45.5 x 46.5
I walked along the road
with two friends then
the sun went down the
sky suddenly turned into
blood and I felt
the great scream in
nature

55 Marks from a mounted paper, about 46 x 40

A Mysterious Stare, OKK T 2547-a43, Munch-Museet, Oslo

57 Mounted on the page:
The Empty Cross 1896/1897
India ink and gouache
46 x 50
OKK T 2547–54
Drawn on the back of a sea chart for northern Norway

56- Lying loose between the pages a bit of paper
57 9.5 x 14.5, with text written in brown crayon.
The empty cross.

58- Lying loose between the two pages:
59 *Battlefield/The Killed Ones* 1916
Lithograph
35.5 x 55.6
Inscription by the printer: "Forsøkstryk 10.
29/4-1916 Nielsen"
OKK G/1 511–15

60- A loose bit of paper, 9.5 x 14.5, inserted between
A41 p. 60 and p. A41, with text written in brown crayon
From my festering
body flowers
shall rise–
and I shall be in
them–eternity.

A41 Mounted on a paper 64.7 x 50:

Text written in red crayon on a sheet of paper
measuring 19 x 25.2
I see all men
behind their masks
smiling, composed faces
pale corpses who without
rest hurry on along a
twisted road at
the end of which
is the grave

A43 Text written in multicolored crayon on brownish
paper measuring 65.3 x 47.5
A mysterious stare this stare of the jealous
In these two madly stabbing eyes
(are) concentrated as
in a crystal many re-
flections.–The glance is
searching interested
hateful and amor-
ous an essence
of her whom they
all have in common

A45 Text written in multicolored crayon on paper
measuring 65 x 47.6
When we stood fronting each
other and your eyes
looked into my
eyes then I felt
as if invisible
threads led from
your eyes into
my eyes and
tied our hearts
together

A47 Text written in multicolored crayon on thick paper
measuring 64.6 x 48.5
Human destinies
are like heavenly bodies
they meet in
space only to
disappear once
again. Few merge one into the
other in glowing flame

A49 Text written in multicolored crayon and drawing
of a head in the rock
64.7 x 50
Notes of a madman
Even the hard mass of the rock lives–

A51 Mounted on paper 64.7 x 50
Text written in red crayon on a sheet of paper
measuring 19 x 25.2
I felt our love
lying on
the ground like a
heap of ashes

61 Marks from a mounted sheet of paper–imprint by

the woodcut
Anxiety 1896 Sch. 62

63 Mounted on the page:
Flower of Pain 1898
Woodcut
58 x 48
OKK G/t 586–17, Sch. 114

64 (Reverse of 63)
Imprint from
Decorative Design Sch. 92

64- Lying loose between the pages:
65 *Lovers in Waves* 1894 or 1895
Pencil, india ink, watercolor, and gouache
62 x 47
Above the drawing is a text written in pencil and
watercolor
Moonlight glides across your face
which is full of all the world's beauty and pain.
Your lips are like two snakes
and filled with blood as is the crimson fruit
–they move apart as in pain
the smile of a corpse–For
now the chain is bound which ties generation
to generation–
Like one body we slide out upon
a vast sea–on long billows which change in color
from deep violet to blood red

65 Mounted on the page:
Decorative Design 1897
Lithograph printed in black and pink
29.5 x 38
OKK G/1 224–9, Sch. 92

71 Mark from a mounted sheet of paper about 52 x 33

73 Mounted on the page:
Funeral March 1897
Lithograph
59.5 x 41.5 OKK G/1 226–26, Sch. 94
Lying loose between page 74 and 75, a bit of thin
paper
7.5 x 55, with the text:
The land of crystal

75 Mounted on the page:
The Land of Crystal 1897
Lithograph printed on papier collé
44.7 x 63.2
OKK G/1 225–4, Sch. 93

81 Mounted on the page:
Man's Head under Woman's Breasts 1908/1909
Woodcut
52 x 27.3
OKK G/t 619–13, Sch. 338

83 Mounted on the page:
Toward the Light c. 1916
Lithograph
62 x 48
OKK G/1 487–4

Decorative Design, 1897. OKK T 2547-65, Munch-Museet, Oslo

85 Mounted on the page:
Vision 1891
Pencil and india ink
50.3 x 31
OKK T 2547–85

91 Marks from a mounted sheet of paper

Woman in Three Stages, 1893. Munch-Museet, Oslo (cat. no. 98)

CHECKLIST OF THE EXHIBITION

Items without catalogue numbers are not discussed or illustrated in the essays. Dimensions in this list are given in inches, height preceding width. The abbreviation *Sch.* refers to the catalogues of Edvard Munch's graphic works by Gustav Schiefler, *Verzeichnis des graphischen Werks Edvard Munchs bis 1906* (Berlin: Bruno Cassirer, 1907); *Edvard Munch, das graphische Werk 1906-1926* (Berlin: Euphorion Verlag, 1927).

Self-Portrait with Cigarette
Oil on canvas, 1894-1895
$43\frac{1}{2}$ x $33\frac{5}{8}$
Nasjonalgalleriet, Oslo
cat. no. 4

TWO MAJOR SERIES OF THE 1890s

I. Love: Exhibited Berlin 1895

Death in the Sickroom
Oil on canvas, 1893-1895
$59\frac{1}{16}$ x $65\frac{15}{16}$
Nasjonalgalleriet, Oslo
cat. no. 41

Starry Night
Oil on canvas, c. 1893
$53\frac{1}{8}$ x $55\frac{1}{8}$
Private Collection
cat. no. 32

Eye in Eye
Oil on canvas, c. 1894
(retouched later)
OKK M 502 $53\frac{9}{16}$ x $43\frac{5}{16}$
Munch-Museet, Oslo
cat. no. 35

The Voice
Oil on canvas, 1893
$34\frac{1}{2}$ x $42\frac{1}{2}$
Museum of Fine Arts, Boston,
Ernest Wadsworth Longfellow Fund
cat. no. 31

The Kiss
Oil on canvas, c. 1892/1893
OKK M 59 $37\frac{3}{8}$ x $31\frac{7}{8}$
Munch-Museet, Oslo
cat. no. 43

Ashes
Oil on canvas, 1894
$47\frac{7}{16}$ x $55\frac{1}{2}$
Nasjonalgalleriet, Oslo
cat. no. 47

Vampire
Oil on canvas, c. 1894
$39\frac{3}{8}$ x $43\frac{1}{4}$
Private Collection
cat. no. 33

The Maiden and Death
Tempera (?) on canvas, c. 1893
OKK M 49 $50\frac{7}{16}$ x $33\frac{7}{8}$
Munch-Museet, Oslo
cat. no. 79

Madonna
Oil on canvas, c. 1893/1895
OKK M 68 $35\frac{7}{16}$ x 27
Munch-Museet, Oslo
cat. no. 37

Woman in Three Stages (Study)
Oil and tempera on cardboard
1893 (retouched later)
OKK M 57 $28\frac{9}{16}$ x $39\frac{3}{8}$
Munch-Museet, Oslo
cat. no. 98

Separation
Oil on canvas, c. 1894
OKK M 24 $38\frac{3}{16}$ x $50\frac{9}{16}$
Munch-Museet, Oslo

Hands
Oil and tempera on cardboard,
c. 1893/1894
OKK M 646 $35\frac{1}{16}$ x $30\frac{5}{16}$
Munch-Museet, Oslo

Melancholy (The Yellow Boat)
Oil on canvas, 1891-1892?
$25\frac{13}{16}$ x $37\frac{13}{16}$
Nasjonalgalleriet, Oslo
Gift of Charlotte and
Christian Mustad
cat. no. 27

Evening on Karl Johan Street
Oil on canvas, 1892
$33\frac{1}{4}$ x $47\frac{5}{8}$
Rasmus Meyers Samlinger
cat. no. 28

Anxiety
Oil on canvas, 1894
OKK M 515 37 x $28\frac{3}{4}$
Munch-Museet, Oslo
cat. no. 34

The Scream
Pastel, tempera, oil on cardboard, 1893
$35\frac{7}{8}$ x 29
Nasjonalgalleriet, Oslo
cat. no. 29

Metabolism
Oil on canvas, 1898
(c. 1894/1895?),
reworked c. 1918
OKK M 419 $67\frac{3}{4}$ x $56\frac{5}{16}$
Munch-Museet, Oslo
cat. no. 46

II. The Mirror: Exhibited Paris 1897

In the Land of Crystal
Lithograph, 1897
OKK G/l 225-3, Sch. 93
$14\frac{7}{32}$ x $18\frac{13}{16}$
Munch-Museet, Oslo
cat. no. 209

Funeral March
Lithograph, 1897
OKK G/l 226, Sch. 94 $21\frac{3}{4}$ x $14\frac{5}{8}$
Private Collection
cat. no. 210

Metabolism
Lithograph, 1897
OKK G/l 227-1, Sch. 95   14 3/8 x 9 13/16
Munch-Museet, Oslo
cat. no. 211

By the Deathbed
Lithograph, 1896
OKK G/l 214, Sch. 72   15 5/8 x 19 11/16
Private Collection
cat. no. 212

Death in the Sickroom
Lithograph, 1896
OKK G/l 215, Sch. 73   15 3/4 x 21 1/4
Private Collection
cat. no. 213

Hands (Lust For Woman)
Lithograph, 1895
OKK G/l 196, Sch. 35   18 7/8 x 11 3/8
Private Collection
cat. no. 214

Lovers in Waves
Lithograph, 1896
OKK G/l 213, Sch. 71   12 1/16 x 16 1/2
Private Collection
cat. no. 215

Madonna
Lithograph, hand colored, 1895
OKK G/l 194, Sch. 33   23 5/8 x 17 5/16
Private Collection
cat. no. 216

Attraction II
Lithograph, hand colored, 1896
OKK G/l 208, Sch. 66   14 7/8 x 24
Private Collection
cat. no. 217

Attraction I
Lithograph, hand colored, 1896
OKK G/l 207, Sch. 65   16 x 13 5/8
Private Collection
cat. no. 218

Jealousy
Lithograph, 1896
OKK G/l 202, Sch. 58   18 1/4 x 22 1/8
Private Collection
cat. no. 219

Vampire
Lithograph, hand colored, 1895
OKK G/t 567, Sch. 34   15 1/16 x 21 5/8
Private Collection
cat. no. 220

The Urn
Lithograph, 1896
OKK G/l 205, Sch. 63   17 15/16 x 10 3/8
Private Collection
cat. no. 221

Madonna
Lithograph, 1895
OKK G/l 194, Sch. 33   23 5/16 x 17 3/8
Private Collection
cat. no. 222

Separation II
Lithograph, 1896
OKK G/l 210, Sch. 68   15 1/2 x 23 3/4
Private Collection
cat. no. 223

The Alley, Carmen
Lithograph, 1895
OKK G/l 197, Sch. 36   16 5/8 x 10 3/8
Private Collection
cat. no. 224

The Flower of Love
Lithograph, 1896
OKK G/l 212, Sch. 70   22 15/16 x 10 7/8
Private Collection
cat. no. 225

The Scream
Lithograph, 1895
OKK G/l 193, Sch. 32   13 7/8 x 9 7/8
Private Collection
cat. no. 226

Melancholy
Woodcut, 1896
OKK G/t 571, Sch. 82   14 15/16 x 17 7/8
Mr. and Mrs. Alan Press
cat. no. 227

Melancholy
Woodcut, 1896
OKK G/t 571-25, Sch. 82   14 15/16 x 17 7/8
Munch-Museet, Oslo
cat. no. 228

Man's Head in Woman's Hair (The Mirror)
Woodcut, hand colored, 1896
OKK G/t 569, Sch. 80   24 1/4 x 23 5/8
Private Collection
cat. no. 229

Anxiety
Woodcut, hand colored, 1896
OKK G/t 568, Sch. 62   17 15/16 x 14 1/8
Private Collection
cat. no. 230

Vampire
Lithograph, 1895
OKK G/t 567, Sch. 34   14 7/8 x 21 7/16
Private Collection
cat. no. 231

Ashes
Lithograph, hand colored, 1896
OKK G/l 211, Sch. 69   11 3/4 x 16 7/16
Private Collection
cat. no. 232

The Kiss
Woodcut, hand colored, 1897
OKK G/t 578, Sch. 102b
17 1/2 x 14 3/4
Private Collection
cat. no. 233

Poster, Man's Head in Woman's Hair
Color lithograph, 1897
OKK G/t 569, Sch. 80   25 x 17 1/2
Private Collection
cat. no. 234

PAINTINGS AND DRAWINGS 1881-1943

The Church of Gamle Aker
Oil on cardboard, 1881
OKK M 1043   8 1/4 x 6 5/16
Munch-Museet, Oslo
cat. no. 190

Self-Portrait
Oil on paper, 1881/1882
OKK M 1049   11 1/4 x 7 1/4
Munch-Museet, Oslo
cat. no. 1

The Infirmary at Helgelandsmoen
Oil on wood panel, c. 1882
OKK M 185   26 x 22 11/16
Munch-Museet, Oslo
cat. no. 197

Self-Portrait
Oil on cardboard, c. 1882/1883
10 1/16 x 7 1/4
City Museum of Oslo
cat. no. 2

Morning, Girl at the Bedside
Oil on canvas, 1884
38 x 40 3/4
Rasmus Meyers Samlinger
cat. no. 24

The Artist's Aunt in a Rocking Chair
Oil on canvas, 1884
OKK M 1108   18 1/2 x 16 3/16
Munch-Museet, Oslo
cat. no. 196

The Artist's Father and Sister Inger
Oil on canvas, c. 1885
OKK M 627   17 15/16 x 30 1/2
Munch-Museet, Oslo
cat. no. 199

The Artist's Father With His Pipe
Oil on canvas, c. 1885/1886
OKK M1056   14 3/4 x 11 1/16
Munch-Museet, Oslo
cat. no. 195

By the Deathbed
India ink, c. 1885/1889
OKK T 287 $6\frac{5}{16}$ x $8\frac{5}{16}$
Munch-Museet, Oslo
cat. no. 201

Self-Portrait
Oil on canvas, 1886
13 x $9\frac{5}{8}$
Nasjonalgalleriet, Oslo
cat. no. 3

Inger on the Beach
Oil on canvas, 1889
$49\frac{3}{4}$ x $63\frac{5}{8}$
Rasmus Meyers Samlinger
cat. no. 25

Portrait of Colonel Georg Stang
Oil on canvas, 1889
$35\frac{1}{2}$ x $23\frac{1}{2}$
Private Collection

The Military Band on Karl Johan Street
Oil on canvas, 1889
(reworked c. 1893?)
$42\frac{1}{2}$ x 59
Kunsthaus, Zürich

Man and Woman in Bed
India ink, c. 1890
OKK T 365 $11\frac{7}{8}$ x $11\frac{1}{4}$
Munch-Museet, Oslo
cat. no. 110

Bridge at St. Cloud
Oil on canvas, 1890
$18\frac{3}{4}$ x $23\frac{3}{4}$
Private Collection

Night in St. Cloud
Oil on canvas, 1890
$25\frac{1}{4}$ x $21\frac{1}{4}$
Nasjonalgalleriet, Oslo
cat. no. 26

View from a Window, St. Cloud
Oil on canvas, 1890
24 x $19\frac{5}{8}$
Vassar College Art Gallery
Gift of Mrs. Morris Hadley
(Katherine Blodgett, '20)

Rue de Rivoli
Oil on canvas, 1891
$32\frac{1}{2}$ x $26\frac{1}{4}$
Fogg Art Museum,
Harvard University
Gift of Rudolf Serkin

Death in the Avenue
India ink, c. 1891/1892
OKK T 290A $15\frac{1}{8}$ x $11\frac{3}{8}$
Munch-Museet, Oslo
cat. no. 147

Self-Portrait Under Mask of a Woman
Oil on canvas, c. 1892
OKK M 229 $27\frac{3}{16}$ x $17\frac{1}{8}$
Munch-Museet, Oslo
cat. no. 8

Evening on Karl Johan Street
Pencil, charcoal, 1892
OKK T 2390 $14\frac{5}{8}$ x $18\frac{1}{2}$
Munch-Museet, Oslo
cat. no. 125

The Storm
Oil on canvas, 1893
$36\frac{1}{8}$ x $51\frac{1}{2}$
The Museum of Modern Art,
New York
Gift of Mr. and Mrs. Irgens Larsen
and Purchase, 1974
cat. no. 30

Red and White
Oil on canvas, 1894
OKK M 460
$36\frac{5}{8}$ x $50\frac{15}{16}$
Munch-Museet, Oslo
cat. no. 36

Puberty
Oil on canvas, 1894/1895
$59\frac{5}{8}$ x $43\frac{3}{8}$
Nasjonalgalleriet, Oslo
cat. no. 38

Jealousy
Oil on canvas, 1895
$26\frac{3}{8}$ x $39\frac{3}{8}$
Rasmus Meyers Samlinger
cat. no. 39

Inheritance
Oil on canvas, 1897/1899
OKK M 11 $55\frac{9}{16}$ x $47\frac{1}{4}$
Munch-Museet, Oslo
cat. no. 44

Self-Portrait with Lyre
Pencil, india ink, watercolor
and gouache, c. 1897/1898
OKK T 2460 27 x $20\frac{13}{16}$
Munch-Museet, Oslo
cat. no. 5

The Empty Cross
India ink and watercolor, c.1897/1899
OKK T 2452 17 x $24\frac{11}{16}$
Munch-Museet, Oslo

The Red Vine
Oil on canvas, 1898
OKK M 503 $47\frac{1}{16}$ x $47\frac{11}{16}$
Munch-Museet, Oslo
cat. no. 50

Melancholy (Laura in Room)
Oil on canvas, 1898
OKK M 12 $43\frac{5}{16}$ x $49\frac{5}{8}$
Munch-Museet, Oslo
cat. no. 45

Self-Portrait/Salome Paraphrase
Watercolor, india ink, and pencil,
c. 1898
OKK T 369 $18\frac{1}{8}$ x $12\frac{7}{8}$
Munch-Museet, Oslo
cat. no. 7

Train Smoke
Oil on canvas, 1900
OKK M 1092 $33\frac{1}{16}$ x $42\frac{15}{16}$
Munch-Museet, Oslo
cat. no. 48

Winter Night
Oil on canvas, 1901
$57\frac{1}{16}$ x $69\frac{11}{16}$
Nasjonalgalleriet, Oslo
cat. no. 51

Girls on the Pier
Oil on canvas, 1902
$53\frac{3}{8}$ x $49\frac{3}{8}$
Nasjonalgalleriet, Oslo
cat. no. 49

Summer Night in Åsgårdstrand
Oil on canvas, c. 1904
39 x $41\frac{3}{4}$
Private Collection
cat. no. 52

Self-Portrait with Brushes
Oil on canvas, 1904/1905
OKK M 751 $77\frac{5}{8}$ x 36
Munch-Museet, Oslo
cat. no. 10

Self-Portrait/Inferno
Oil on canvas, 1904/1905
OKK M 591 $32\frac{1}{8}$ x $25\frac{13}{16}$
Munch-Museet, Oslo
cat. no. 9

The Death of Marat
Oil on canvas, c. 1905/1907
(reworked later)
OKK M 351 $59\frac{1}{16}$ x $78\frac{5}{8}$
Munch-Museet, Oslo
cat. no. 53

Self-Portrait in Weimar
Oil on canvas, 1906
OKK M 543 $43\frac{1}{2}$ x $47\frac{7}{16}$
Munch-Museet, Oslo
cat. no. 11

Amor and Psyche
Oil on canvas, 1907
OKK M 48 $47\frac{1}{16}$ x $39\frac{3}{8}$

Munch-Museet, Oslo
cat. no. 55

Men Bathing
Oil on canvas, 1907/1908
81¹⁄₁₆ x 89⅜
The Art Museum of the Ateneumin,
Coll. Antell., Helsinki
cat. no. 54

Springtime Work in the Skerries
Oil on canvas, 1910/1911
OKK M 411   36⅝ x 46⅛
Munch-Museet, Oslo
cat. no. 56

Galloping Horse
Oil on canvas, 1910/1912
OKK M 541   58⁵⁄₁₆ x 47¼
Munch-Museet, Oslo
cat. no. 57

Self-Portrait
Woodcut, 1911
OKK G/t 627-16, Sch. 352
21⁵⁄₁₆ x 13¹³⁄₁₆
Munch-Museet, Oslo
cat. no. 13

Self-Portrait with Cast Shadow
Color woodcut, 1911
28⅝ x 16¼
The Art Institute of Chicago,
The Clarence Buckingham Collection
cat. no. 17

Yellow Log
Oil on canvas, 1912
OKK M 393   51³⁄₁₆ x 62⅝
Munch-Museet, Oslo
cat. no. 58

Winter Landscape
Oil on canvas, 1915
57¹⁄₁₆ x 69¹¹⁄₁₆
Mrs. Heddy Astrup
cat. no. 59

Self-Portrait in Bergen
Oil on canvas, 1916
OKK M 263   35¼ x 23⅝
Munch-Museet, Oslo
cat. no. 15

Self-Portrait/Inner Turmoil
(With Open Coat)
Oil on canvas, c. 1919
OKK M 76   59½ x 51³⁄₁₆
Munch-Museet, Oslo
cat. no. 16

Model by a Wicker Chair
Oil on canvas, 1919/1921
OKK M 499   48⁵⁄₁₆ x 39⅜
Munch-Museet, Oslo

cat. no. 60

Self-Portrait/Night Wanderer
Oil on canvas, 1920/1930
OKK M 490   35¼ x 26⅝
Munch-Museet, Oslo
cat. no. 18

Starry Night
Oil on canvas, 1922/1924
OKK M 32   47½ x 39⅜
Munch-Museet, Oslo
cat. no. 62

Self-Portrait/By the Window
Oil on canvas, 1940
OKK M 446   33¹⁄₁₆ x 42⅜
Munch-Museet, Oslo
cat. no. 20

Self-Portrait Between the Clock
and the Bed
Oil on canvas, 1940/1942
OKK M 23   58⅞ x 47⁷⁄₁₆
Munch-Museet, Oslo
cat. no. 22

Self-Portrait with Pastel Crayon
Pastel, 1943
OKK M 749   31 x 23⅝
Munch-Museet, Oslo
cat. no. 23

Watercolors

Seated Model
Pencil, crayon, and watercolor, 1897
OKK T 2459   24⅜ x 18¹³⁄₁₆
Munch-Museet, Oslo

Nude Near a Window
Charcoal, watercolor, and gouache,
1907/1909
OKK T 2457   24 x 19⁷⁄₁₆
Munch-Museet, Oslo

Women and Children
Charcoal and watercolor, 1907/1909
OKK T 2268   19⁷⁄₁₆ x 14⁹⁄₁₆
Munch-Museet, Oslo

Two Nudes
Watercolor, 1917
44⅛ x 33½
Mrs. Heddy Astrup

Girls at the Shore
Watercolor and pencil, c. 1920
OKK T 310   9⅜ x 11¹³⁄₁₆
Munch-Museet, Oslo

Standing Blue Nude
Watercolor, after 1920
OKK T 1072   19⅞ x 13⅜

Munch-Museet, Oslo

Kneeling Nude
Watercolor, 1921
RES B 124   13¹⁵⁄₁₆ x 20⅛
The Gift of Rolf Stenersen
to the City of Oslo

Model Undressing
Watercolor and crayon, c. 1925
OKK T 2464   13¹⁵⁄₁₆ x 10⅛
Munch-Museet, Oslo

From the Tree of Knowledge

The Tree of Knowledge of Good and Evil
Title page
Sheet A3, crayon
25½ x 19¹¹⁄₁₆
Munch-Museet, Oslo
cat. no. 235

A Bird of Prey Sitting
on the Chest of a Naked Man
Sheet A21, crayon
25½ x 19¹¹⁄₁₆
Munch-Museet, Oslo
cat. no. 239

A Man Inscribed in Three Power-Circles
Sheet A25, crayon
25½ x 19¹¹⁄₁₆
Munch-Museet, Oslo

A Mysterious Stare
This Stare of the Jealous
Sheet A43, crayon
25¹¹⁄₁₆ x 18¹¹⁄₁₆
Munch-Museet, Oslo

Lovers in Waves
Sheet between 64-65, pencil, india ink,
watercolor, and gouache, 1894/1895
24⅜ x 18½
Munch-Museet, Oslo
cat. no. 243

Decorative Design
Sheet 65, color lithograph, 1897
OKK G/l 224-9, Sch. 92   11⅝ x 14¹⁵⁄₁₆
Munch-Museet, Oslo

MAJOR THEMES

I.   The Voice

The Voice
Oil on canvas, c. 1893
OKK M 44   35⅞ x 46¹⁄₁₆
Munch-Museet, Oslo
cat. no. 63

The Voice/Eyes
Charcoal, 1896
OKK T 2373   19¹¹⁄₁₆ x 25½
Munch-Museet, Oslo

cat. no. 64

The Voice/Eyes
Crayon and pencil, 1896
OKK T 329   16⅜ x 19¹¹⁄₁₆
Munch-Museet, Oslo
cat. no. 65

The Voice/Summer Night
Drypoint and aquatint, 1895
Sch. 19   9¹³⁄₁₆ x 12⅞
Nasjonalgalleriet, Oslo

The Voice/Summer Night
Color woodcut, 1896
OKK G/t 572-4, Sch. 83   15 x 22³⁄₁₆
Munch-Museet, Oslo
cat. no. 67

The Voice/Summer Night
Woodcut, 1898
OKK G/t 585-4, Sch. 113   9⅞ x 3⅝
Munch-Museet, Oslo
cat. no. 68

Sphinx
Lithograph, 1896
OKK G/l 206-1, Sch. 64   12⅝ x 22¹⁄₁₆
Munch-Museet, Oslo
cat. no. 69

II.   Kiss

The Kiss
Oil on canvas, 1892
28½ x 35¾
Nasjonalgalleriet, Oslo
Gift of Charlotte and Christian Mustad
cat. no. 71

The Kiss/Goodbye
Pencil, 1890
OKK T 2356 10⅝ x 8¹⁄₁₆
Munch-Museet, Oslo
cat. no. 70

The Kiss
Pencil, c. 1894
OKK T 362   7⁷⁄₁₆ x 11⅜
Munch-Museet, Oslo
cat. no. 72

The Kiss
Pencil, 1894/1895
OKK T 419A   15¹⁵⁄₁₆ x 24⁷⁄₁₆
Munch-Museet, Oslo
cat. no. 73

The Kiss
Charcoal on cardboard, 1894/1895
OKK T 421   23¹³⁄₁₆ x 15⁵⁄₁₆
Munch-Museet, Oslo
cat. no. 74

The Kiss
Etching, drypoint, and aquatint, 1895

Sch. 22   13⅝ x 10⅞
Private Collection

The Kiss
Woodcut, 1897/1898
OKK G/t 577-9, Sch. 102A
23⁵⁄₁₆ x 18
Munch-Museet, Oslo

The Kiss
Woodcut, 1897/1898
OKK G/t 577-2   23⁵⁄₁₆ x 18
Munch-Museet, Oslo

The Kiss
Woodcut, 1897/1898
OKK G/t 577-4, Sch. 102A
23⁵⁄₁₆ x 18
Munch-Museet, Oslo
cat. no. 81

The Kiss
Color woodcut, 1898
Sch. 102C   16⅛ x 18⅜
Private Collection

The Kiss
Color woodcut, 1902
OKK G/t 580-3, Sch. 102D
17⅝ x 17⅝
Munch-Museet, Oslo
cat. no. 84

The Kiss
Color woodcut, 1902
Sch. 102D   18½ x 18¹¹⁄₁₆
Private Collection

The Kiss
Color woodcut, 1902
18½ x 18¹¹⁄₁₆
Private Collection

III.   Madonna

*Sketch of a Model Posing
(Study for Madonna)*
Pastel, 1893
30⅛ x 20⅞
The Solomon R. Guggenheim
Museum, New York
cat. no. 90

Study for Madonna
Charcoal and pencil, 1893
OKK T 2430   29⁷⁄₁₆ x 23⁹⁄₁₆
Munch-Museet, Oslo
cat. no. 91

Study for Madonna
Charcoal and crayon, 1893/1894
OKK T 2449   24¼ x 18½
Munch-Museet, Oslo
cat. no. 89

Madonna
Drypoint, 1895
OKK G/r 15-3, Sch. 16   14³⁄₁₆ x 10⁷⁄₁₆
Munch-Museet, Oslo
cat. no. 92

Madonna
Color lithograph, 1902
Sch. 33 A-B   23⅝ x 17⅜
Private Collection

Madonna
Lithograph, hand colored, 1895-1898?
Sch. 33   23¹³⁄₁₆ x 17⁵⁄₁₆
The Art Institute of Chicago,
Print and Drawing Fund Purchase

Lovers in the Waves
Mezzotint, 1896
OKK Gr/r 32-10, Sch. 43   8¼ x 11½
Munch-Museet, Oslo
cat. no. 96

IV.   Melancholy

Evening/Melancholy (The Yellow Boat)
Oil on canvas, 1891
OKK M 58   28¾ x 39⅝
Munch-Museet, Oslo
cat. no. 114

Evening/Melancholy
India ink, 1891
OKK T 2355   5⁵⁄₁₆ x 8¼
Munch-Museet, Oslo
cat. no. 115

By the Fireplace
India ink and pencil, 1892/1893
OKK T 291   13¾ x 10⅜
Munch-Museet, Oslo
cat. no. 111

The Path of Death
India ink, 1889
OKK T 250A   8¹³⁄₁₆ x 7
Munch-Museet, Oslo
cat. no. 109

Melancholy/Salome
Pencil, 1895/1896
OKK T 305   11⁷⁄₁₆ x 7⅛
Munch-Museet, Oslo
cat. no. 132

*Separation/Salome Paraphrase
Wash, 1894*
OKK T 337   10⁷⁄₁₆ x 25⅝
Munch-Museet, Oslo
cat. no. 116

Despair
Charcoal and oil, 1892
OKK T 2367   14⅝ x 16⅝
Munch-Museet, Oslo
cat. no. 113

Melancholy
Woodcut, 1896
OKK G/t 571-23, Sch. 82   16 x 17 7/8
Munch-Museet, Oslo
cat. no. 136

Evening/Melancholy
Color woodcut, 1901
Sch. 144   14 13/16 x 18 9/16
Private Collection

Evening/Melancholy
Color woodcut, 1896
Sch. 82   16 1/4 x 18
The Museum of Modern Art,
New York
Abbey Aldrich Rockefeller Fund

V. The Sick Child

The Sick Child
Oil on canvas, 1896
47 13/16 x 46 5/8
Göteborgs Konstmuseum, Sweden
cat. no. 42

The Sick Child
Drypoint and roulette, 1894
Sch. 7 V/c   14 1/8 x 10 5/8
Private Collection

The Sick Child
Etching and drypoint, hand colored, 1896
OKK G/r 43-6, Sch. 60   5 1/16 x 6 5/8
Munch-Museet, Oslo
cat. no. 152

The Sick Child
Lithograph, 1896
Sch. 59   16 5/16 x 22 7/16
Nasjonalgalleriet, Oslo

The Sick Child
Lithograph, hand colored, 1896
OKK G/l 203-17, Sch. 59 16 5/8 x 22 1/4
Munch-Museet, Oslo
cat. no. 155

The Sick Child
Color lithograph, 1896
OKK G/l 203-2   16 3/16 x 22 1/4
Munch-Museet, Oslo
cat. no. 156

The Sick Child
Color lithograph, 1896
OKK G/l 203-10, Sch. 59 16 3/16 x 22 1/4
Munch-Museet, Oslo
cat. no. 157

The Sick Child
Color lithograph, 1896
Sch. 59   16 1/2 x 22 1/4
Private Collection

The Sick Child
Color lithograph, 1896
Sch. 59   16 1/2 x 22 1/4
Mr. and Mrs. Philip A. Straus

The Sick Child
Pastel, c. 1896
16 15/16 x 15 3/4
Klaus-Bernt Hegewisch, Hamburg

The Sick Child
Lithograph, hand colored, 1896
OKK G/l 203-5, Sch. 59   16 3/16 x 22 1/4
Munch-Museet, Oslo
cat. no. 161

The Sick Child
Lithograph, hand colored with oil, 1896
Sch. 59   16 1/2 x 22 1/4
Private Collection

VI. Fever/By The Deathbed

By the Deathbed
Pastel, 1893
OKK M 121   23 5/8 x 31 9/16
Munch-Museet, Oslo
cat. no. 181

By the Deathbed
India ink and crayon, 1892/1893
OKK T 286   4 1/2 x 7 1/16
Munch-Museet, Oslo
cat. no. 169

By the Deathbed
Pencil, 1892/1893
OKK T 2366   9 x 12 1/2
Munch-Museet, Oslo
cat. no. 173

By the Deathbed
India ink, 1896
OKK T 289A   13 1/2 x 11 5/8
Munch-Museet, Oslo
cat. no. 170

By the Deathbed
India ink, 1896
OKK T 296   12 x 19
Munch-Museet, Oslo
cat. no. 172

By the Deathbed
India ink and pencil, 1896
OKK T 295   12 1/4 x 18 7/8
Munch-Museet, Oslo
cat. no. 171

By the Deathbed
Lithograph, 1896
OKK G/l 214-12, Sch. 72
15 1/2 x 19 15/16
Munch-Museet, Oslo
cat. no. 176

By the Deathbed
Lithograph, 1896
OKK G/l 214-19, Sch. 72
15 1/2 x 19 15/16
Munch-Museet, Oslo
cat. no. 179

By the Deathbed
Lithograph, 1896
OKK G/l 214-11, Sch. 72
15 1/2 x 19 15/16
Munch-Museet, Oslo
cat. no. 175

By the Deathbed
Lithograph, 1896
OKK G/l 214-16, Sch. 72
15 1/2 x 19 15/16
Munch-Museet, Oslo
cat. no. 177

By the Deathbed
Lithograph, 1896
OKK G/l 214-18, Sch. 72
15 1/2 x 19 15/16
Munch-Museet, Oslo
cat. no. 178

By the Deathbed (Fever)
Oil on canvas, 1895
35 7/16 x 47 7/16
Rasmus Meyers Samlinger
cat. no. 40

Fever/Death Struggle
Lithograph, hand colored, 1896
OKK G/l 214-7, Sch. 72
15 1/2 x 19 15/16
Munch-Museet, Oslo
cat. no. 174

Study for the Sickroom
Ink and blue crayon, 1896
19 3/4 x 25 1/4
Private Collection

VII. Death in The Sickroom

Death in the Sickroom
Pastel, 1893
OKK M 214   35 1/8 x 42 15/16
Munch-Museet, Oslo
cat. no. 167

Death in the Sickroom
Pencil and crayon, 1893/1896
OKK T 297   14 15/16 x 19 1/16
Munch-Museet, Oslo
cat. no. 162

Death in the Sickroom
Charcoal and oil, 1892
OKK T 294   18 7/8 x 12 5/8

Munch-Museet, Oslo
cat. no. 163

Death in the Sickroom
Charcoal, 1893/1894
OKK T 2380 13 13/16 x 18 1/8
Munch-Museet, Oslo
cat. no. 164

Death in the Sickroom
Lithograph, hand colored, 1896
OKK G/l 215-8, Sch. 73 15 3/4 x 21 1/4
Munch-Museet, Oslo
cat. no. 165

The Dead Mother and Child
Tempera on canvas, 1893/1894
OKK M 420 41 3/16 x 70 11/16
Munch-Museet, Oslo
cat. no. 204

The Dead Mother
Pencil and charcoal, 1896
OKK T 301 19 x 25 5/8
Munch-Museet, Oslo
cat. no. 200

The Dead Mother and Child
Etching, aquatint, and drypoint, 1901
12 1/4 x 19
Private Collection

The Odor of Death
Tempera (?) on canvas, 1893
OKK M 34 39 3/8 x 43 5/16
Munch-Museet, Oslo
cat. no. 206

VIII. *Metabolism*

Vision
Oil and pencil on canvas, 1892
OKK M 114 28 1/2 x 21 13/16
Munch-Museet, Oslo
cat. no. 122

Vision
India ink, 1892
OKK T 2347 7 1/8 x 4 5/8
Munch-Museet, Oslo
cat. no. 123

Harpy
Pencil, 1893/1894
OKK T 2291 11 1/4 x 12 13/16
Munch-Museet, Oslo
cat. no. 121

Harpy
Drypoint, 1894
OKK G/r 4-36, Sch. 4 11 1/6 x 8 5/8
Munch-Museet, Oslo
cat. no. 127

Family Tree
Watercolor and gold paint, 1894/1895
OKK T 391 25 x 18 1/2
Munch-Museet, Oslo

The Flower of Pain
(Cover for *Quickborn*)
Watercolor, pen and ink, 1898
OKK T 2451 19 11/16 x 16 15/16
Munch-Museet, Oslo

Art
India ink, sepia, and pencil, 1894/1895
OKK T 407 9 11/16 x 11 15/16
Munch-Museet, Oslo
cat. no. 118

Self-Portrait with Skeleton Arm
Lithograph, 1895
18 1/8 x 25 5/8
The Museum of Modern Art,
New York,
Gift of James L. Goodwin
in memory of Philip L. Goodwin
cat. no. 120

The Girl and Death
Drypoint, 1894
Sch. 3-II 11 9/16 x 8 1/8
Private Collection

Metabolism
India ink, 1894
OKK T 405 9 1/16 x 12 3/4
Munch-Museet, Oslo
cat. no. 117

The Dead Mother
Oil on canvas, 1893
OKK M 516 28 3/4 x 37 1/4
Munch-Museet, Oslo
cat. no. 207

Metabolism
India ink, 1896
OKK T 411 18 15/16 x 14 3/8
Munch-Museet, Oslo
cat. no. 202

Madonna in the Churchyard
India ink, wash, watercolor, and crayon 1896
OKK T 2364 19 11/16 x 17 11/16
Munch-Museet, Oslo
cat. no. 146

The Kiss (Illustration for Charles Baudelaire *Les Fleurs du mal*)
Pencil, india ink, pen, and wash, 1896
OKK T 404 11 3/8 x 8 1/16
Munch-Museet, Oslo
cat. no. 76

"Une Charogne" (Illustration for Charles Baudelaire *Les Fleurs du mal*)
Pencil, india ink, pen, and wash, 1896
OKK T 403 11 3/8 x 8 1/16
Munch-Museet, Oslo
cat. no. 77

"Le Mort Joyeux" (Illustration for Charles Baudelaire *Les Fleurs du mal*)
Pencil, india ink, pen, and wash, 1896
OKK T 402 11 1/8 x 8 1/16
Munch-Museet, Oslo
cat. no. 78

Symbolic Study
Gouache, 1893
OKK M 1033 21 7/8 x 27 1/16
Munch-Museet, Oslo
cat. no. 124

The World, Time, Marriage
India ink, black and violet wash, 1894
OKK T 1380 8 1/2 x 11 13/16
Munch-Museet, Oslo
cat. no. 126

Metabolism
India ink, charcoal, and gouache
1896/1898
OKK T 2447 25 1/2 x 19 9/16
Munch-Museet, Oslo
cat. no. 203

Woodblocks

Moonlight
Woodblock, 1896
OKK 570A
Munch-Museet, Oslo

Into the Woods
Woodblock, 1897
OKK 575
Munch-Museet, Oslo

Into the Woods
Woodblock, 1897
OKK 644
Munch-Museet, Oslo

Two Women on the Shore
Woodblock, 1898
OKK PT 589
Munch-Museet, Oslo

The Kiss
Woodblock, 1898-1902
OKK 577-580
Munch-Museet, Oslo

Head by Head
Woodblock, 1902
OKK GP 612
Munch-Museet, Oslo

Master Prints

The Solitary One
Mezzotint, hand colored, 1896-1897?
OKK G/r 816-1, Sch. 42 11 5/16 x 8 9/16

Munch-Museet, Oslo

The Solitary One
Mezzotint, hand colored, 1896-1897?
Sch. 42 $11\frac{5}{16}$ x $8\frac{9}{16}$
Mr. and Mrs. Alan Press

The Solitary One
Mezzotint, hand colored, 1896-1897?
Sch. 42 $11\frac{5}{16}$ x $8\frac{9}{16}$
The Art Institute of Chicago,
The Clarence Buckingham Collection

The Solitary One
Mezzotint, hand colored, 1896-1897?
Sch. 42 $11\frac{9}{32}$ x $8\frac{1}{2}$
Private Collection

The Scream
Lithograph, 1895
OK 193/3, Sch. 32 $13\frac{15}{16}$ x $9\frac{15}{16}$
Munch-Museet, Oslo
cat. no. 129

Desire
Lithograph, 1895
OKK G/l 234-31, Sch. 108
$11\frac{13}{16}$ x $16\frac{15}{16}$
Munch-Museet, Oslo

Vampire
Color lithograph and woodcut,
1895-1902
Sch. 34 $15\frac{3}{16}$ x $21\frac{3}{4}$
Nasjonalgalleriet, Oslo

Separation I
Lithograph, hand colored, 1896
OKK G/l 209, Sch. 67 $17\frac{13}{16}$ x $22\frac{1}{8}$
Rasmus Meyers Samlinger
cat. no. 130

Karl Johan Street
Lithograph, hand colored, 1896-1898?
$16\frac{3}{4}$ x $24\frac{3}{32}$
Private Collection

Nude (Sin)
Lithograph, 1901-1902
Sch. 142 $27\frac{3}{8}$ x $15\frac{3}{4}$
Private Collection

Nude (Sin)
Color lithograph, 1901-1902
Sch. 142 $19\frac{1}{2}$ x $15\frac{3}{4}$
The Museum of Modern Art,
New York, Gift of James Thrall Soby

Madonna (Woman with Brooch)
Eva Mudocci
Lithograph, 1903-1904
Sch. 212 $23\frac{5}{8}$ x $18\frac{1}{8}$
The Museum of Modern Art,
New York, Purchase

Veiled Naked Girl/Moonlight
Lithograph, 1908
OKK G/l 446-5 $16\frac{5}{16}$ x $11\frac{5}{8}$
Munch-Museet, Oslo

Moonlight
Woodcut, 1896
OKK G/t, 570-1, Sch. 81 $15\frac{3}{8}$ x $18\frac{1}{2}$
Munch-Museet, Oslo

Moonlight
Color woodcut, 1896
Sch. 81 16 x $18\frac{1}{2}$
Mr. and Mrs. Philip A. Straus

Moonlight
Color woodcut, 1896
Sch. 81 16 x $18\frac{1}{2}$
Private Collection

Moonlight
Color woodcut, 1896
Sch. 81 16 x $18\frac{1}{2}$
Private Collection

Anxiety/Red Sky
Color woodcut, 1896
Sch. 62 $18\frac{7}{16}$ x $14\frac{13}{16}$
Private Collection

Into the Woods
Color woodcut, 1897
Sch. 100B $19\frac{11}{16}$ x $25\frac{5}{16}$
Private Collection

Into the Woods
Color woodcut, 1897 and later
Sch. 444 $19\frac{7}{8}$ x $25\frac{5}{16}$
Private Collection

Red and Black
Color woodcut, 1898
OKK G/t 587-5, Sch. 115 $10\frac{1}{16}$ x $7\frac{1}{2}$
Munch-Museet, Oslo

Nude (AKT)
Color woodcut, 1898
OKK G/t 583-1, Sch. 111
$17\frac{1}{16}$ x $12\frac{9}{16}$
Munch-Museet, Oslo

Melancholy/Red Dress
Color woodcut, 1898
Sch. 116 $13\frac{1}{4}$ x $16\frac{1}{2}$
Private Collection

Two Women on the Shore
Color woodcut, 1898
Sch. 117 $17\frac{7}{8}$ x $20\frac{1}{8}$
Private Collection

Two Women on the Shore
Color woodcut, hand colored,
1898 and later
B 30464 15 x $20\frac{1}{8}$
National Gallery of Art
Rosenwald Collection and
Ailsa Mellon Bruce Fund, 1978

Two Women on the Shore
Color woodcut and linoleum block,
1898 and later
B 30466 $15\frac{3}{4}$ x $20\frac{1}{2}$
National Gallery of Art
Rosenwald Collection and
Ailsa Mellon Bruce Fund, 1978

Two Women on the Shore
Color woodcut and linoleum block,
1898 and later
B 30465 16 x $20\frac{1}{4}$
National Gallery of Art
Rosenwald Collection and
Ailsa Mellon Bruce Fund, 1978

Two Women on the Shore
Color woodcut, 1898 and later
B 30467 18 x 20
National Gallery of Art
Rosenwald Collection and
Ailsa Mellon Bruce Fund, 1978

Two Women on the Shore
Color woodcut and paper overlay,
1898 and later
B 30468 18 x $19\frac{7}{8}$
National Gallery of Art
Rosenwald Collection and
Ailsa Mellon Bruce Fund, 1978

Girl's Head Against the Shore
Color woodcut, 1899
OKK G/t 597-9, Sch. 129 18 x $15\frac{13}{16}$
Munch-Museet, Oslo

Girl's Head Against the Shore
Color woodcut, 1899
Sch. 129 $18\frac{1}{8}$ x $16\frac{1}{4}$
Private Collection

Man and Woman Kissing Each Other
Color woodcut, 1905
Sch. 230 $15\frac{1}{2}$ x $21\frac{1}{4}$
Private Collection

Into the Woods
Color woodcut, 1915
OKK 644-6, Sch. 444 $19\frac{7}{8}$ x $25\frac{9}{16}$
Munch-Museet, Oslo

Into the Woods
Color woodcut, 1915
Sch. 444 20 x $25\frac{7}{16}$
Private Collection

Winter Landscape in Moonlight
Woodcut, 1916/1917
OKK G/t 677-1 $14\frac{9}{16}$ x $15\frac{3}{4}$
Munch-Museet, Oslo

Gothic Girl
Woodcut, hand colored, c. 1931?
$21\frac{7}{8}$ x $12\frac{5}{8}$
Private Collection